PAUPER CAPITAL

To Hilary Guite

With love and affection

Pauper Capital
London and the Poor Law, 1790–1870

DAVID R. GREEN
King's College London, UK

ASHGATE

Published by
Ashgate Publishing Limited
Wey Court East
Union Road
Farnham
Surrey, GU9 7PT
England

Ashgate Publishing Company
Suite 420
101 Cherry Street
Burlington
VT 05401-4405
USA

www.ashgate.com

British Library Cataloguing in Publication Data
Green, David R., 1954–
Pauper capital : London and the Poor Law, 1790–1870.
1. Poor laws–Great Britain–History–19th century. 2. Poor–Services for–England–London–History–19th century.
I. Title
362.5'8'09421'09034–dc22

Library of Congress Cataloging-in-Publication Data
Green, David R., 1954–
Pauper capital : London and the Poor Law, 1790-1870 / David R. Green.
p. cm.
Includes bibliographical references and index.
ISBN 978-0-7546-3008-1 (hardcover : alk. paper)
1. Poor laws–England–History–19th century. 2. Poor laws–England–London–History–19th century. 3. Poor–England–London–History–19th century. I. Title.

KD3310.G74 2009
344.4203'25–dc22

2009030050

ISBN 9780754630081 (hbk)
ISBN 9780754699033 (ebk)

Mixed Sources
Product group from well-managed forests and other controlled sources
www.fsc.org Cert no. SA-COC-1565
© 1996 Forest Stewardship Council
FSC

Printed and bound in Great Britain by
MPG Books Group, UK

Contents

List of Figures

Appendix

List of Tables

Preface

> It is not what London fails to do that strikes the observer, but the general fact that she does everything in excess. Excess is her highest reproach, and it is her incurable misfortune that there really is too much of her. She overwhelms you by quantity and number.[1]
>
> Henry James, (London, 1888)

Research into the English poor law has a long and illustrious history with one glaring omission – no study has yet appeared that explores how it operated in London between the late eighteenth and late nineteenth century – a period during which the poor law and the city both underwent immense change.[2] Had London not been of such importance in the working of the poor law, this omission could be overlooked. However, in relation to the number of paupers, the cost of pauperism and poor law policy itself that was not the case. In an earlier book, *From Artisans to Paupers*, I examined the processes and impacts of economic and social change in London during this period. *Pauper Capital* extends that analysis to explore how the poor law coped with those changes in the decades both before and after the Poor Law Amendment Act of 1834.

Start and end points of research can sometimes be arbitrary products of the historian's imagination but in this instance there are good grounds for framing the study in the years between about 1790 to 1870 – a period that witnessed a growing interest in the reform of poor relief. The harsher economic climate of the late eighteenth century ushered in a period of intense debate about how to accommodate the needs of the poor, whether it be by charity or poor relief. Changing ideologies of economic justice, which involved a shift from a moral economy, based around the concept of a just price for labour and goods, to a political economy in which the market ruled, had a profound effect on attitudes towards the poor and policies relating to relief. This debate culminated in the reforms that ushered in the new poor law in 1834 and the subsequent decades witnessed how that new ideology was put into practice in relation to the provision of relief. The end point of this work is marked by the financial panic and economic downturn that struck London in the late 1860s which focused attention on how to deal with the mounting pressures of metropolitan pauperism. How those tensions were resolved marks the point at which this study ends.

---

1 Henry James, *London*, first published in 1888 and reprinted in *London Stories and Other Writings* (Padstow, 1989), p. 269.

2 The term English poor law is used throughout to include both England and Wales.

This book is less about pauperism *per se* than it is about the relationships between place and policy and the actions and intentions of those individuals involved in the operation of the poor law – as overseers and guardians, as paupers and paid officials. In spanning both the old and the new poor law, it questions assumptions about the significance of the transition from one to the other. It is also an attempt to understand how relief practices operated on the ground. It locates this analysis in the context of transformations in London's economic and social geography as well as in the political and ideological contexts within which the poor law operated.

The significance of scale and density, and the effects of proximity – important elements in what constitutes a city – have influenced the research. The fluidity of urban life, particularly in relation to the poor, always ran up against the permanence of boundaries that determined the limits of parochial financial responsibility and the tensions this generated were apparent in several ways. The spatial proximity of poor law authorities in the city meant that relief policies adopted in any given district were always likely to have an impact in the surrounding areas. Such proximity also meant that those in need of assistance could try their luck in several places, sometimes in short succession. Therefore, in order to understand how the poor law functioned in any one district, we need to move beyond the individual parish or union and take account of the broader geographical context in which the system operated. We need, as Steven King has recently suggested, to be aware of the way that the spatial dynamics of poor relief structured the experiences of welfare.[3] To do so this book argues that we need to focus on the city as a whole since it is only at that scale that individual experiences of poor relief in specific localities can be fully understood.

The dilemma in studying the poor law at this scale is how to convey a sense of complexity without losing sight of the human dimension. Individual actions play a central role in understanding the relationships involved in the provision of welfare, both in terms of those who ran the system and those who were the recipients of relief. Abstract policy decisions made by the central Poor Law Commissioners had to be translated into practical applications on the ground, and here the voice of the poor and their power to negotiate relief were crucial components in influencing outcomes. It is an important and salutary fact that even behind the workhouse walls paupers were not without power to influence relief.

Historical parallels are both inviting and dangerous in equal measure. The period covered by this book spans several significant financial crises in London, notably in the mid 1820s and again in the late 1860s. In both cases, welfare systems adapted to the changing economic conditions but not without a good deal of hardship for those dependent on relief. At the time of completing this book, governments were also struggling to cope with the effects of uncertainty in the

[3] Steven King, '"It is Impossible for our Vestry to Judge his Case into Perfection from Here": Managing the Distance Dimensions of Poor Relief, 1800–40', *Rural History*, 16 (2005), p. 163.

world financial markets. The scale of the problem may be different but the impact on the provision of welfare is likely to be profound. There is, therefore, an uncanny contemporary resonance to the issues raised in this book. The poor law has long since disappeared but questions about how best to provide collective forms of welfare remain.

David R. Green
Greenwich, 19 December 2008

Acknowledgements

The research on which this book is based has a long history. It commenced many years ago when I was funded to complete a doctorate by the then Social Science Research Council. In the end, the thesis took a different direction and the poor law was relegated to a relatively minor part in the work. A long term interest in the history of poverty and welfare ensured that I eventually returned to the subject and this book represents the fruits of that research. Many people have helped in ways they knew and in ways they did not. Tom Gray and Anne Keirby from Ashgate Publishing have shown incredible patience and I am grateful for their faith in the project long after they had reason to doubt if it would ever see the light of day. My thanks are also due to Anthea Lockley for the help she provided in preparing this book for publication. Leonard Schwarz very kindly read an early draft and offered his usual insightful and helpful comments. Various aspects of this research have been presented at the University of Leicester, the Institute of Historical Research at the University of London, and at the Robert Bosch Stiftung in Dusseldforf and I am grateful for the comments made by participants at those seminars. Some parts of Chapter 5 first appeared in 'Pauper protests: power and resistance in early nineteenth-century London workhouses' published in *Social History*, 31 (2006) and I am grateful to the editors for their permission to reproduce this material. I am indebted to the Senate House Library, University of London for permission to reproduce Figures 4.2, 4.13, 4.14 and 6.10; to the City of London, London Metropolitan Archives for permission to reproduce Figures 4.3 and 4.4; to the trustees of the London Journal for permission to reproduce Figure 2.6; to Peter Higginbotham for permission to reproduce Figure 4.5 and to Royal Holloway University of London for permission to reproduce Figure 5.1.

Over the years I have benefited enormously from the assistance and expertise of librarians and archivists at the British Library, the National Archives, the London Metropolitan Archives, the Guildhall Library, the City of Westminster Archive Centre, London Borough of Southwark Archives, London Borough of Greenwich Local History Centre and those at the London Borough of Camden Archives, especially Richard Knight. The staff at the Goldsmith's Library and at the Special Collections in the University of London Library have also been extremely helpful over the years. When London and the poor law threatened to overwhelm me by quantity and number, family, friends and colleagues provided the encouragement to continue. Particular thanks in this respect go to Craig Bailey, Tim Butler, Alastair Owens and Janette Rutterford. Lester Jones translated the idiosyncrasies of poor law statistics into patterns on the page and I am very grateful to him for the maps that appear throughout this book. Roma Beaumont expertly recreated the illustration of Greenwich Union workhouse which appears in Chapter 4.

Two people in particular have helped make this book possible. For perhaps longer than he realises, Ted Yates has always been a great source of support, both as a former colleague in the Geography Department at King's College London and as a friend. His commitment to primary research and the clarity with which he has always sought to identify the important questions that lurk behind the historical record has been a source of inspiration. Long may he continue to delve in the archives of his beloved Selborne. Finally, Hilary Guite has lived with this book for almost as long as I have – and probably for longer than she would have wished. She has constantly reminded me that many of the questions raised by this research have contemporary resonance. Though the centuries in which we work are very different, the issues are in some ways very similar. We share common beliefs about the importance of the collective provision of welfare for the well being of society and whilst I study that in the past, she practises it in the present. Books can makes strangers of partners, but not once has she complained about my disappearance into the world of the poor law. To her I owe a profound debt of gratitude.

List of Abbreviations

BL	British Library
COS	Charity Organisation Society
CLHC	Camden Local History Centre
CLRO	Corporation of London Record Office
CWAC	City of Westminster Archives Centre
GL	Guildhall Library
LMA	London Metropolitan Archives
MCPF	Metropolitan Common Poor Fund
PP	Parliamentary Paper, House of Commons
SLSC	Southwark Local Studies Centre
TNA	The National Archives

Introduction
The Context of Poor Law Reform

The English poor law

Writing about care for the poor on a visit to London in 1766, Benjamin Franklin noted

> There is no country in the world where so many provisions are established for them, so many hospitals to receive them when they are sick or lame, founded and maintained by voluntary charities; so many almshouses for the aged of both sexes, together with a solemn general law made by the rich to subject their estates to a heavy tax for the support of the poor.[1]

This 'solemn general law', the English poor law, touched the lives of countless numbers of individuals – most obviously as recipients of relief, but also as ratepayers, as overseers charged with managing the system and as justices of the peace, who were involved in all aspects of the poor law from removals through to adjudicating disputes between aggrieved paupers and over-zealous officials. The poor law also provided employment to a small army of officers who administered relief at the parish level and was a profitable source of income for suppliers of goods and services to the poor. As a source of patronage and power it generated its own set of vested interests and, as Paul Slack has noted, was 'a focus of attention at every point at which people participated in public life'.[2] The poor laws meant that children were born, clothed, educated and apprenticed at the parish expense; the sick, mentally ill and infirm were cared for inside and outside the workhouse, however badly; adults were provided with food and shelter, and when they died a pauper they were often buried by the parish. From cradle to grave, as pauper or ratepayer, the poor law therefore touched the lives of almost everyone in the country.

Immersed in the particularities of the system, it is easy to forget how distinctive – and how remarkable – the English poor law was compared to the rest of Europe.[3]

---

[1] Quoted in Sidney Webb and Beatrice Webb, *English Local Government: English Poor Law History, Part 2: The Last Hundred Years* (London, 1929), p. 11.

[2] Paul Slack, *The English Poor Law 1531–1782* (London, 1990), p. 56.

[3] Comparative studies of poor relief are rare. Two exceptions are Frances Gouda, *Poverty and Political Culture: The Rhetoric of Social Welfare in the Netherlands and France, 1815–1854* (Lanham, 1995) and Peter Hennock, *The Origin of the Welfare State in England and Germany, 1850–1914: Social Policies Compared* (Cambridge, 2007).

In terms of content and context it differed in several important ways. First, despite local variations, it was available throughout England and Wales in a fairly uniform and comprehensive manner. Indeed, the fact that the right to assistance was governed by legislation that stretched back to the sixteenth century, albeit filtered through the prism of local acts governing the provision of relief, meant that national coverage was never in doubt. In Ireland, no poor law existed until 1837 and in Scotland, where poor relief was administered through the churches, the system was reformed in 1845, not because relief had been too generous but rather that it had been too little.[4] From that date, therefore, the poor law existed in one form or another throughout the United Kingdom.

Despite the fact that it was to a greater or lesser extent a national system, prior to 1834 central government was reluctant to interfere in local affairs and as a result parochial control over poor relief was paramount. Until then responsibility for administering relief and collecting the rates lay with more than 15,500 parishes and townships. As far as the poor law was concerned, England therefore comprised 'a confederation of localities'.[5] However, by creating a central authority, the Poor Law Commissioners, and amalgamating separate parishes into about 600 unions, the so called 'new poor law' established after 1834 created an entirely new administrative grid across the country. That grid, however, rested uneasily on jealously guarded local autonomy, as well as on a series of customary rights and obligations buttressed by the law. As a result, the administrative reforms ushered in by the new poor law were implemented with varying levels of intensity over several decades.[6]

The extent to which changes were implemented after 1834 depended on local circumstances and here both politics and economics had a part to play. In the early years of the new poor law, the Commissioners struggled to impose their authority over individual parishes and boards of guardians. The initial legislation had limited the life of the Poor Law Commission to five years and with the expiration of that term it had to rely for its existence on annual votes in Parliament. The Whig majority after 1834, however, was never strong and came to an end in 1841 and thereafter the Commissioners had to tread carefully for fear of alienating both Tory and Radical opponents.[7] This politicised landscape added a further layer of complexity to an already intricate mosaic of relief practices. Similarly, the anti-poor law movement, though never national in scope, was sufficiently powerful in

4 E. Young, 'Paupers, Property and Place: A Geographical Analysis of the English, Irish and Scottish Poor Laws in the mid-19th Century', *Environment and Planning D*, 12 (1994): 325–40.

5 J. R. Poynter, *Society and Pauperism: English Ideas on Poor Relief 1795–1834* (London, 1969), p. xx.

6 Further discussion of the geography of implementation can be found in Felix Driver, *Power and Pauperism: The Workhouse System 1834–1884* (Cambridge, 1993).

7 Nassau Senior, 'Annual Reports of the Poor Law Commissioners for the years 1835, 1836, 1837, 1838, 1839, 1840 and 1841', *Edinburgh Review* vol. 74 no. 149 (1841): 35–7.

some areas to hinder progress. Where local opposition existed, especially where this involved guardians with clear political links to the poor law's parliamentary detractors, the Commissioners only hesitatingly sought to impose their authority. As a result, the early rules and regulations were riddled with exceptions to accommodate local conditions and placate hostile elites.[8]

Local autonomy was further enhanced as a result of the settlement laws, introduced in 1662, which conferred a legal entitlement to individuals seeking relief from their parish.[9] These laws limited parochial responsibilities to the settled poor, although the grounds by which a settlement could be achieved were exceptionally complex. Those who did not possess a settlement could be removed, although given the range of conditions by which a settlement could be achieved, the cost and effort of establishing entitlement and enforcing removals were sometimes not worth the time and trouble. As a result certain categories of paupers who did not have a settlement but who were likely to have been a short term drain on local ratepayers, notably able bodied men, were sometimes relieved rather than removed. Meanwhile others, especially widows or single mothers with children, who might have become long term and therefore costly paupers, were more likely to have been passed back to their place of settlement. This situation persisted until the middle of the nineteenth century when the right to receive relief was extended to the poor who resided in parishes in which they did not necessarily have a legal settlement. Until that time, as George Coode noted in 1851 'By one act of legislation, 15,535 parishes were made the gaols of their own poor people, and fortresses against all others.'[10] Given this situation, it was little wonder that local autonomy continued to be a significant element of the poor law even after the 1834 reforms.

The second way in which the English poor law differed from its European counterparts was its apparent generosity, especially prior to 1834, and the way in which it was financed. In the 1770s poor law expenditure in England and Wales accounted for 1.6 per cent of the national income and between 1795 and 1834,

---

[8] Anthony Brundage, *England's 'Prussian Minister': Edwin Chadwick and the Politics of Government Growth 1832–1854* (London, 1988), pp. 44–5.

[9] There is a considerable literature on the evolution and implementation of the settlement laws. For overviews see David Feldman, 'Migrants, Immigrants and Welfare from the Old Poor Law to the Welfare State', *Transactions of the Royal Historical Society*, 13 (2003): 79–104; Norma Landau, 'The Laws of Settlement and the Surveillance of Immigration in Eighteenth-Century Kent', *Continuity and Change*, 3 (1988): 391–420; Norma Landau, 'The Eighteenth Century Context of the Law of Settlement', *Continuity and Change*, 6 (1991): 417–39; Keith Snell, 'Pauper Settlement and Poor Relief', *Continuity and Change*, 6 (1991): 375–415; James Taylor, 'The Impact of Pauper Settlement 1691–1834', *Past and Present*, 73 (1976): 42–73; James Taylor, *Poverty, Migration and Settlement in the Industrial Revolution* (Palo Alto, 1989).

[10] PP 1851 XXVI Report of George Coode to the Poor Law Board, on the law of settlement and removal of the poor, p. 257.

according to Peter Lindert, this figure always remained over two per cent of the national product, compared to 1.5 per cent for the Netherlands, Belgium and France.[11] After 1834, the relative cost of relief in England and Wales fell significantly and the levels of poor relief between countries converged. However, even after this date the per capita amount provided in relief still remained higher in England and Wales compared to other European countries. To some extent this reflected the fact that informal assistance and charity were more important in Europe where the 'mixed economy of welfare' was spread more evenly between different forms of provision.[12] Religious charities in particular were far more important sources of assistance on the continent than in relatively secular Britain. Rather than having to rely on charitable donations, the English poor law was funded instead by taxation on property gathered by each parish and this in turn put it on a more secure financial footing. Even in times of economic crisis, the compulsory nature of taxation meant that it was generally possible to ensure sufficient funds to cover the costs of relief. Only in very exceptional circumstances in specific localities, notably the Lancashire cotton famine in the early 1860s and in some eastern districts in London later in the decade, did the system fail to cope.

Relative generosity, however, did not necessarily translate into large handouts to paupers and in this final respect the English poor law also differed from its continental counterparts. European countries more reliant on charities than the state tended to provide a greater proportion of domiciliary help to the poor. This in turn was administered mainly through voluntary agencies and visitors. Compared to such countries, however, England lacked a network of voluntary visitors and inspectors of relief. Indeed, the enormous difficulties many parishes experienced

---

[11] See Paul Slack, *The English Poor Law 1531–1782* (London, 1990), p. 30; Peter Lindert, *Growing Public: Social Spending and Economic Growth since the Eighteenth Century* (Cambridge, 2004), p. 48. See also Sara Horrell, Jane Humphries and Hans-Joachim Vorth, 'Destined for Deprivation: Human Capital Formation and Intergenerational Poverty in Nineteenth-Century England', *Explorations in Economic History*, 38 (2001): 354–62.

[12] On this topic see Andreas Gestrich, Steven King and Lutz Raphael (eds), *Being Poor In Modern Europe: Historical Perspectives 1800–1940* (Bern, 2006); Marco van Leeuwen, 'Logic of Charity: Poor Relief in Preindustrial Europe', *Journal of Interdisciplinary History*, 24 (1994): 589–613. For examples of how this operated in urban European contexts see Marco van Leeuwen, 'Surviving With a Little Help: The Importance of Charity to the Poor of Amsterdam 1800–50 in a Comparative Perspective', *Social History*, 18 (1993): 319–38; Marco van Leeuwen, *The Logic of Charity: Amsterdam 1800–1850*, (Houndmills, 2000). For England see Joanna Innes, 'The "Mixed Economy of Welfare" in Early Modern England: Assessments of the Options from Hale to Malthus (c. 1683–1803)', in Martin Daunton (ed.),*Charity, Self Interest and Welfare in the English Past* (London, 1996), pp. 139–80; Alan Kidd, 'Civil Society or the State? Recent Approaches to the History of Voluntary Welfare', *Journal of Historical Sociology*, 15 (2002): 328–42; Steven King and Alannah Tomkins (eds), *The Poor in England 1700–1850: An Economy of Makeshifts* (Manchester, 2003).

in persuading ratepayers to serve civic office was one of the reasons why vestries turned to paid relieving officers even before 1834. As Peter Hennock has argued, without the network of voluntary visitors and inspectors on which domiciliary help was based, those responsible for providing relief turned to the workhouse as the only feasible way of preventing imposture whilst at the same time avoiding the need to employ large numbers of professional staff.[13] As a result, the reliance on providing indoor relief, especially after 1834, though in some places before that date, meant that a significant part of the money raised for supporting the poor went to constructing and maintaining workhouses rather than on individual assistance. For that reason the apparent generosity of poor relief hinted at by the overall figures on expenditure did not necessarily translate into larger handouts for the poor.

Shifting ideologies and poor law reform

From the mid-eighteenth century, debates about poverty and the merits or otherwise of the poor law occupied a great deal of attention and parliamentary time.[14] No less than 44 parliamentary enquiries took place on the poor and the poor law between 1750 and 1834 and enough books and pamphlets were published to fill a small library.[15] Such debate took place against a background of growing political divisions and changes associated with the transition from an agrarian to a commercial and increasingly industrialised economy.[16] Such changes fostered a willingness to question assumptions about the nature of traditional social, political and economic relations. Debates about the poor law and calls for its abolition were lent urgency at the end of the eighteenth and start of the nineteenth century by sharply rising costs and apparent increases in the numbers of paupers. Such calls marked a distinct shift in contemporary understanding of poverty characterised by harsher views about the poor and the problems they posed as a drain on the national finances.[17] By the early nineteenth century, as Lynn Lees has argued, and long before the new poor law had been introduced, the poor had lost the legitimacy

13 See Hennock, *The Origin of the Welfare State in England and Germany*, pp. 56–62.

14 For discussion of the debates in the earlier part of the eighteenth century see A. W. Coats, 'Economic Thought and Poor Law Policy in the Eighteenth Century', *Economic History Review*, 13 (1960): 39–51 and the more recent account in Paul Fideler, *Social Welfare in Pre-industrial England* (Houndmills, 2006), pp. 166–71.

15 For a list of parliamentary enquiries see Frederick Purdy, 'The Statistics of the English Poor Rate Before and Since the Passing of the Poor Law Amendment Act', *Journal of the Statistical Society*, 23 (1860): 287–9. The most complete discussion of the debate remains Poynter, *Society and Pauperism*.

16 For a summary see Fideler, *Social Welfare in Pre-Industrial England*, pp. 166–90.

17 For summaries of these debates see Raymond Cowherd, *Political Economists and the English Poor Laws* (Athens, 1977); David Eastwood, *Governing Rural England Tradition and Transformation in Local Government 1780–1840* (Oxford, 1994), pp. 101–32;

they once might have enjoyed and work, confinement and discipline became the central motifs for the evolving political economy of welfare.[18]

The break seemed to come around the 1780s or early 1790s. According to Karl Polanyi, the transformation in ideas took place sometime between the publication of Adam Smith's *Wealth of Nations* in 1776 and Joseph Townsend's *Dissertation on the Poor Laws*, published ten years later.[19] Between the two, he argues, an ideological chasm opened up in which Smith's optimistic view of gain as the motor for progress gave way to a more pessimistic belief in poverty as the spur to improvement. Though we might question the precise chronology of this ideological shift, as does Gertrude Himmelfarb in suggesting that the key change was Adam Smith's concept of the 'invisible hand' of the market, which marked the transformation from moral philosophy to political economy, the direction of change is less in doubt.[20] What is clear is that by the end of the eighteenth century traditional discourses concerning the poor were in disarray and new, more pessimistic views about poverty prevailed.[21] The question is to what extent such ideological changes helped to define the parameters of debate in which reform of the poor law took place.[22]

Townsend's argument centred on the belief that hunger alone was the 'spur and goad on to labour'.[23] Anything which acted to reduce the effect of hunger, notably the poor laws, was therefore anathema to progress. His dislike of the poor laws and call for their abolition was echoed in the following decade by other authors. Thomas Ruggles in *The History of the Poor; Their Rights, Duties, and the Laws Respecting Them*, published in 1793, reserved his main criticism for the settlement laws which hindered the free movement of labour. Attitudes hardened further as prices rose and the war against France turned into a national struggle

---

Gareth Stedman Jones, *An End to Poverty?* (London, 2004), pp. 64–109; Poynter, *Society and Pauperism*, pp. 45–185.

[18] See Lynn Lees, *The Solidarities of Strangers: The English Poor Laws and the People, 1700–1948* (Cambridge, 1998), p. 83.

[19] Karl Polanyi, *The Great Transformation* (Boston, 1957), pp. 111–29.

[20] Gertrude Himmelfarb, *The Idea of Poverty: England in the Early Industrial Age* (London, 1984), pp. 42–63.

[21] In addition to the classic account of attitudes contained in Poynter, *Society and Pauperism*, see Mitchell Dean, *The Constitution of Poverty: Towards a Genealogy of Liberal Governance* (London, 1991), pp. 137–47; Mitchell Dean, 'A Genealogy of the Government of Poverty', *Economy and Society*, 21 (1992): 227–39, and Sandra Sherman, *Imagining Poverty: Quantification and the Decline of Paternalism* (Columbus, 2001).

[22] These changes also affected attitudes towards charity. See Donna Andrew, *Philanthropy and Police: London Charity in the Eighteenth Century* (New Jersey, 1989).

[23] Joseph Townsend, *Dissertation on the Poor Laws by a Well-Wisher to Mankind* (1786) cited in George Boyer, *An Economic History of the English Poor Law 1750–1850* (Cambridge, 1990), p. 52.

with the threat of the Jacobin crowd looming larger.[24] In this context the drain on the nation's finances appeared more serious and the poor more menacing. Only the fear of change in uncertain times held back demands for root and branch reform of poor relief.

The subsistence crises of 1795 and 1800 and the food rioting that accompanied them gave rise to three other important studies of poverty: David Davies, *The Case of the Labourers in Husbandry* (1795), Frederick Eden's *The State of the Poor* (1797) and, perhaps most significantly, Thomas Malthus' *Essay on the Principle of Population* (1798). However, Eden and Malthus on the one hand, and Davies on the other, came to quite different conclusions as to the causes of poverty. Davies blamed changes in the rural economy, notably the decline of cottage industry, loss of commons through enclosure and the rise in prices as the main reasons for higher levels of pauperism. In contrast, Eden and Malthus, the latter mainly in subsequent editions of the *Essay*, blamed the existing system of poor relief as the 'parent of idleness' and the cause of pauperism.

Malthus, who was by far the most influential of the critics, touched on the poor law briefly in the first edition of the *Essay* but significantly expanded his scope in subsequent volumes. In the 1798 edition, he seriously underestimated the size of the British population, which he supposed to have been about seven million when in fact the first census of 1801 showed it to have been much larger at 10.9 million. Although writers in previous decades had valued population growth as a sign of national vigour, for Malthus and others writing in the context of steeply rising prices and wartime stringency, the increase was more alarming for the fact that it was accompanied by rising levels of pauperism and poor law expenditure. The situation was blamed on sliding scales of relief, the best known of which was that introduced by the magistrates at Speenhamland in Berkshire in 1795, which linked the amount of assistance to the size of the family. This, Malthus argued, merely encouraged labourers to have larger families and destroyed the incentive to save. In the long run he concluded it was the poor laws that therefore created the poor.

Political economists agreed. Those, like Malthus, who adhered to the wage fund theory, by which 'whoever ... is maintained by the law as a labouring pauper, is maintained instead of some other individual who would otherwise have earned by his own industry', argued that because all forms of poor relief reduced the amount of money available as wages to labourers, they inevitably caused wage rates to fall in both the long and the short term.[25] By taxing ratepayers who provided employment, poor relief merely diminished the stock of money from which wages

---

24 See Jones, *An End to Poverty?*, pp. 79–109. The average price of a quartern loaf in London, for example, rose from 7d in 1794 to 1s 5d in 1812 and never fell below 10d until 1821. See B. R. Mitchell and Phyllis Deane, *Abstract of British Historical Statistics* (Cambridge, 1962), p. 498.

25 See PP 1817 VI Select committee to consider the poor laws, p. 17; Webb and Webb, *English Local Government*, p. 43. See also Andrew, *Philanthropy and Police*, pp. 143–4.

were paid. As such, poor relief was doomed to create the very problem it was supposed to solve and, far from diminishing poverty, it merely increased it. Under these circumstances, Malthus and fellow political economists, including Nassau Senior, concluded that the poor law should either be abolished or significantly reformed to remedy the ills it was apparently responsible for creating.[26]

Poor law reforms

The profusion of literature on poverty and the poor laws contrasted sharply with legislative inaction and the absence of reform. When it came to promoting change political expediency prevailed over ideological conviction. 'Faulty and defective as our Poor System may be', warned Sir Frederick Eden, 'he must be a bold and rash political projector who should propose to level it to the ground.'[27] During the Napoleonic war concerns about the revolutionary mob and the unsettled state of the country meant that reforms were only hesitatingly proposed. Large scale rural unrest in various parts of the country in the immediate post-war years, notably in East Anglia, focused attention on the difficulties of maintaining order in the absence of a rural police force. Similarly, the increasing number of protest meetings organised by radicals, including those which resulted in the Spa Fields riot in London in 1816 and the Peterloo massacre in 1819, also demonstrated the strength of urban working-class opposition to the government.[28] Popular constitutionalism and Painite radicalism in these years drew upon a similar language of traditional rights and those who threatened to subvert such liberties were roundly condemned by supporters of both sets of ideas.[29] Therefore, despite rapidly escalating costs of relief and the rising number of paupers, Tory governments, which were in power for most of the period from 1784 until 1830, were reluctant to interfere with the poor law or revoke what was traditionally seen as the right to receive relief. Pragmatism

---

[26] Senior was one of the members of the Royal commission appointed to enquire into the operation of the poor laws and generally credited with framing the Poor Law Amendment Act of 1834. For a discussion of the influence of classical economics on the poor law see Cowherd, *Political Economists and the English Poor Laws*.

[27] Frederick M. Eden, *The State of the Poor, or an History of the Labouring Classes in England*, (London, 1797), vol. 2, p. 470.

[28] For an overview of these social protests see John Stevenson, *Popular Disturbances in England 1700–1832* (Harlow, 1992); Edward P. Thompson, *The Making of the English Working Class* (Harmondsworth, 1968), pp. 249, 515–659.

[29] John Belchem, 'Republicanism, Popular Constitutionalism and the Radical Platform in Early Nineteenth-Century England', *Social History*, 6 (1981): 1–32; John Belchem, *Orator Hunt: Henry Hunt and English Working-class Radicalism* (Oxford, 1985). See also James Epstein, 'The Constitutional Idiom: Radical Reasoning, Rhetoric and Action in Early Nineteenth Century England', *Journal of Social History*, 23 (1990): 553–74.

took precedence over rhetoric and political expediency over intellectual debate. Little was proposed and even less was done to reform the poor laws.

However, following Eden's extensive investigation and in the light of Malthus' ongoing polemic against the poor law, it became difficult to defend the *status quo*, particularly as poor rates rose. Recognition of the necessity of reform meant that some efforts were made to amend the poor laws both through parliamentary intervention as well as local initiatives. In 1796, William Pitt's bill to reform the poor laws which included measures to legitimate the allowance system along similar lines to that adopted in Speenhamland and elsewhere, failed to gain sufficient support. A similar fate awaited a measure proposed by Samuel Whitbread in 1807 which would have shifted the balance of power within vestries away from smaller ratepayers to those who contributed most to parish rates. Although passing the committee stages, this measure too failed to find parliamentary support and was dropped.[30]

When the state of the poor laws was next considered in 1817 against a backdrop of economic downturn, rural unrest and rapidly rising rates, the parliamentary select committee presented a powerful defence of the abolitionist case but failed to recommend any substantial changes. Members blamed the increase in pauperism on the improper administration of poor relief, and accepted the Malthusian idea of the wage fund.[31] Nevertheless, the committee stopped short of any fundamental changes, recommending only the appointment of paid overseers, the formation of select vestries comprising the major ratepayers to manage relief and the amendment of the settlement laws so as to reduce the costs of litigation.[32] The only measure to emerge at this time was the Poor Employment Act of 1817 which provided public money from the Exchequer for the employment of the poor on public works.[33] Nor did much change in the following decade: select committees on rural distress, agricultural wages, emigration and able bodied relief each failed to suggest mechanisms whereby the poor laws could be reformed.

One institutional response that did not arouse much opposition but which ultimately proved important was the move to amalgamate parishes thought too

---

30 Webb and Webb, *English Local Government*, pp. 34–9. See also Eastwood, *Governing Rural England*, pp. 125–7; Poynter, *Society and Pauperism*, pp. 207–22.

31 See PP 1817 VI Select committee to consider the poor laws; Webb and Webb, *English Local Government*, p. 43.

32 See PP 1817 VI Select committee to consider the poor laws, p. 27. See also Eastwood, *Governing Rural England*, pp. 128–9. Eastwood makes the point that these administrative measures were more appropriate to large urban parishes than smaller, rural communities.

33 Act to Authorize the Issue of Exchequer Bills, and the Advance of Money out of the Consolidated Fund, to a Limited Amount, for the Carrying on of Public Works and Fisheries in the United Kingdom, and Employment of the Poor in Great Britain, in Manner Therein Mentioned (Poor Employment Act), 58 Geo III c. 34. See Michael Flinn, 'The Poor Employment Act of 1817', *Economic History Review*, 14 (1961): 82–92.

small to deal with the problem of pauperism.[34] As the administrative unit of poor relief, the parish provided a check against any expenditure that might have been imposed by an unelected centralised authority. However, the difficulties that parishes experienced in coping with rising levels of pauperism were exacerbated where parliamentary enclosure and the decline of rural industries had been most marked.[35] Many of these places were already those in which high rates of population growth contributed to mounting levels of poverty resulting in the scattering of small pockets of structural poverty throughout rural areas. Furthermore, high rates of rural-urban migration and the importance of young, single adults in this movement left some parishes with disproportionate numbers of the very young and old, thereby exacerbating the problem of dependency on the poor law. All these changes raised questions as to the extent to which the parish could function effectively as the body responsible for administering relief.

One response was the amalgamation of parishes for the administration of poor relief and this took place in two distinct but related ways. Incorporation of individual parishes and townships under local acts took place sporadically in the first half of the eighteenth century, primarily in towns, including London, but gathered pace after mid-century, especially in East Anglia.[36] The process of incorporation, however, was both complex and costly, requiring separate parliamentary acts on each occasion. Recognition of the advantages of amalgamating small parishes for the purpose of building a workhouse for the impotent poor underlay Gilbert's Act of 1782.[37] This general act regularised the union of such parishes, which proved cheaper than pursuing individual incorporations. It also demonstrated the growing belief in parliamentary legislation as a means of influencing and reforming poor relief itself.[38] Taking both forms of amalgamation into account, between 1674 and 1833 there were approximately 125 incorporations of parishes under local acts, covering about 10 per cent of the population of England and Wales, with a further 71 unions involving nearly 1,000 parishes formed under Gilbert's Act.[39]

---

34 Peter Solar, 'Poor Relief and English Economic Development Before the Industrial Revolution', *Economic History Review*, 48 (1995): 17–18.

35 For further discussion see Keith Snell, *Annals of the Labouring Poor: Social Changes and Agrarian England 1660–1900* (Cambridge, 1985).

36 Anthony Brundage, *The Making of the New Poor Law: The Politics of Inquiry, Enactment and Implementation 1832–39* (London, 1978), p. 6.

37 Act for the Better Relief and Employment of the Poor (Gilbert's Act), 22 Geo. III c. 83.

38 Eastwood, *Governing Rural England*, pp. 106–7.

39 See PP 1844 X Select committee on poor relief (Gilbert Unions), evidence of G. Cornewall Lewis q. 47–8; see also Driver, *Power and Pauperism*, pp. 42–3. Other sources estimate the number of parishes under Gilbert's Act as 924 in 67 unions. See E. W. Martin, 'From Parish to Union: Poor Law Administration 1601–1865', in E. W. Martin (ed.) *Comparative Development in Social Welfare* (London, 1972), p. 33; Peter Dunkley,

The other main set of reforms that took place reflected the harsher attitudes towards the poor outlined above. Restraint and submission rather than an assumption to the rights to relief were the key elements of this approach and more carceral policies with a new emphasis on deterrence its most concrete form of expression.[40] The most famous, though by no means the only, illustration of this approach was Bentham's plan for the construction of panopticons, outlined in his *Management of the Poor*, published in 1796, which lumped together penitentiaries, prisons, houses of industry, workhouses, poor houses, manufactories, mad houses and hospitals.[41] However, experiments in workhouse construction that reflected these new concerns took place throughout the country, together with the introduction of harsher kinds of regimes, including replacing useful forms of work with demeaning and economically worthless tasks, strict control over dietaries and separation of the sexes.[42] The new workhouse at Southwell, Nottinghamshire built in 1824, for example, which played such an important role in influencing the Royal Commission established in 1832 to enquire into the operation of the poor laws, was but one of several attempts to implement this new regime. The Reverend John Becher's description of the workhouse in *The Antipauper System* highlighted the paramount importance of strict discipline in reducing the number of able bodied paupers seeking relief, noting that '... subjected to a System of secluded restraint and salutary discipline ... they soon apply for their discharge'.[43] Southwell was an iconic but by no means an isolated example of this new approach.[44] Although such reforms remained piecemeal in scope, it is clear that with the exception of a centralised bureaucracy, many of the elements of the new poor law which emerged after 1834, including the formation of unions of parishes, paid officers, the principle of deterrence and the emphasis on indoor relief and workhouse discipline, were

The Crisis of the Old Poor Law in England 1795–1834 (London, 1982), pp. 114–15. No London parishes adopted Gilbert's Act.

[40] See John Marriott and Masaie Matsumura (eds), *The Metropolitan Poor: Semi-Factual Accounts* (London, 1999), vol. 1, pp. xv–xxii ; M. J. Roberts, 'Public and Private in Early Nineteenth-Century London: The Vagrant Act of 1822 and its Enforcement', *Social History*, 13 (1988): 273–94; M. J. Roberts, 'Reshaping the Gift Relationship: The London Mendicity Society and the Suppression of Begging in England', *International Review of Social History*, 36 (1991): 201–31; Nicholas Rogers, 'Policing the Poor in Eighteenth-Century London: The Vagrancy Laws and their Administration', *Histoire Sociale-Social History*, 24 (1991): 127–41.

[41] Jeremy Bentham, *Management of the Poor* (Dublin, 1796).

[42] See, for example, W. M. Clarkson, *An Inquiry into the Cause of the Increase of Pauperism and the Poor Rate* (London, 1816); James Bosworth, *The Practical Means of Reducing the Poor's Rate and Encouraging Virtue* (London, 1824). See also Mandler, 'The Making of the New Poor Law *Redivivus*', *Past and Present*, 117 (1987): 141–2; Martin, 'From Parish to Union', p. 39.

[43] See John Thomas Becher, *The Antipauper System* (London, 1828), p. 15.

[44] See, for example, Thomas Pemberton, *An Attempt to Estimate the Increase of the Number of Poor During the Interval of 1785 and 1803* (London, 1811).

already in circulation. It was, according to Peter Mandler, only the lack of political will prior to this date that hindered their implementation at a national level.[45]

From the old to the new poor law: the new administrative framework

The appointment of a royal commission to enquire into the poor laws in 1832, and the subsequent scale of enquiry into relief practices, was a very significant undertaking. The published minutes of evidence, rural and town questionnaire returns and reports themselves ran to several large volumes and provided a substantive body of evidence for reform, the scale of which had not previously been seen.[46] The extent of the reforms ushered in by the Poor Law Amendment Act of 1834 which emerged from the commission's recommendations is still the topic of debate.[47] How 'new' the 'new poor law' actually was, however, partly depends on what is being examined and where.[48] Certainly the principle of uniting parishes for the construction of workhouses, the employment of paid assistant overseers,

---

45 Peter Mandler, 'The Making of the Poor Law *Redivivus*', pp. 147–8.

46 The report of the Royal commission into the operation of the poor laws has been explored in Bryan S. Green, *Knowing the Poor: A Case Study in Textual Reality Construction* (London, 1983). See also Gertrude Himmelfarb, *The Idea of Poverty*, pp. 147–68.

47 The literature on continuity between the old and new poor law at a local level is voluminous. Recent work has focused on the diversity in experience at a local level before and after 1834. See, for example, W. Apfel and P. Dunkley, 'English Rural Society and the New Poor Law: Bedfordshire 1834–1863', *Social History*, 10 (1985): 37–68; Peter Dunkley, 'The "Hungry Forties" and the New Poor Law: A Case Study', *Historical Journal*, 17 (1974): 329–46; Elizabeth Hurren and Steven King, '"Begging for Burial": Form, Function and Conflict in Nineteenth-Century Pauper Burial', *Social History*, 30 (2005): 321–41; Steven King, 'Poor Relief and English Economic Development Reappraised', *Economic History Review*, 50 (1997): 360–68; Peter Mandler, 'The Making of the Poor Law *Redivivus*', pp. 131–57; Peter Mandler, 'Tories and Paupers: Christian Political Economy and the Making of the New Poor Law', *Historical Journal*, 33 (1990): 81–103; Paul Searby, 'The Relief of the Poor in Coventry 1830–1863', *Historical Journal*, 20 (1977): 345–61.

48 The historiography of the old and new poor law is enormous. Major recent studies include Anthony Brundage. *The Making of the New Poor Law* (London, 1978); Anthony Brundage, *The English Poor Laws 1799–1930* (Houndmills, 2002); David Englander, *Poverty and Poor Law Reform in Nineteenth-Century Britain 1834–1914* (Harlow, 1998); Bernard Harris, *The Origins of the British Welfare State: Social Welfare in England and Wales, 1800–1945* (Houndmills, 2004), pp. 40–58; Elizabeth T. Hurren, *Protesting About Pauperism: Poverty, Politics and Poor Relief in Late-Victorian England, 1870–1900* (Woodbridge, 2007); Alan Kidd, *State, Society and the Poor in Nineteenth-Century England* (Houndmills, 1999); Steven King, *Poverty and Welfare in England, 1700–1850: A Regional Perspective* (Manchester, 2000); Lynn H. Lees, *The Solidarities of Strangers: The English Poor Laws and the People, 1700–1948* (Cambridge, 1998); Keith Snell, *Annals of the Labouring Poor: Social Change and Agrarian England 1660–1900* (Cambridge, 1985); Pat Thane (ed.), *The Foundations of the Welfare State* (London, 1996);

the streamlining of administration and the implementation of deterrence in various forms were already the subject of legislative experiment and local initiatives. The impotence of piecemeal and local reforms, however, was brought home in 1830 by the widespread rural unrest associated with the Swing riots and this, coupled with the new Whig administration, proved to be the catalyst for a more thorough attempt to reform the poor law. The fall of the Tory government in 1830 marked the end of serious resistance to reform and both liberal Tories as well as Whigs supported change in the way that poor relief was administered.[49] The appointment of a royal commission to investigate the poor law and subsequent report resulted in the Poor Law Amendment Act of 1834 which ushered in the new poor law.

According to Nassau Senior, the main author of the report, the legislation showed an 'anxious desire to avoid unnecessary innovation and direct interference' and left untouched the fundamental right to receive relief.[50] What was different, though, was the creation of a central Poor Law Commission with powers to survey and direct the course of relief. This new framework, according to Senior, was the most original and important element of the Act and 'the part to which it owes its whole efficiency.'[51]

The structure depended on creating an entirely new administrative grid comprising unions of parishes. Edwin Chadwick's intense dislike of vestries and his desire to prise poor relief from their control underpinned the arrangements and the first responsibility for the new assistant poor law commissioners appointed by the central authorities was to form parishes into unions. By 1840 the 15,500 or so parishes and townships in England and Wales had been grouped into 531 poor law unions, rising to more than 600 by the 1850s. Where unions were formed, decisions relating to relief passed from overseers of the poor appointed by the vestry to separately elected boards of guardians.

The formation of new poor law unions had other implications. First and foremost, it provided a much enlarged financial unit. Edwin Chadwick had insisted on the need for unions in order to provide the fiscal basis to pay for the new workhouses that formed the backbone of the new deterrent policy. Without expanding the capacity to raise funds, such construction would have been impossible. Parishes, therefore, were required to contribute to a common fund with which to construct the union workhouses that were to be a visible reminder of the permanence of the new system.

Karel Williams, *From Pauperism to Poverty* (London, 1981). The classic account remains that of the Webbs. See Sidney Webb and Beatrice Webb, *English Local Government*.

49 Mandler, 'Tories and Paupers', pp. 81–103.

50 Senior, 'Annual Reports of the Poor Law Commissioners', p. 28.

51 Ibid., 26. This opinion is echoed more recently by Phillip Harling, 'The Power of Persuasion: Central Authority, Local Bureaucracy and the New Poor Law', *English Historical Review*, 108 (1992): 30–53.

However, expanding the boundaries of the local poor law beyond the parish also meant abandoning the communal context in which relief was usually dispensed.[52] The inevitable increase in the number of applicants to the poor law meant that it became increasingly unlikely that paupers would have been personally known to those dispensing relief, either as neighbours, acquaintances, relatives, tenants or employees. To cope with this situation, unpaid local overseers were to be replaced by professional staff appointed by boards of guardians. Such officials were able, indeed required, to ignore traditions of mutuality and paternalism that might have operated when both paupers and overseers were known to each other personally.[53] Dispensing relief therefore became less a question of personal discretion as to whether an applicant showed deference or was considered a deserving case. Instead, paupers were to be relieved according to the category into which they fitted, the most crucial of which was whether they were young, old, able bodied, sick or infirm. As the Poor Law Commissioner, George Cornewall Lewis, noted in 1837 during his meeting with Hammersmith parishioners, who were concerned that their inclusion in a union with some 110,000 people would have made it impossible to enquire about the merits of individual applications, 'The only merits into which they had to enquire was, did the parties want relief or not. They had nothing to do with the character of the parties.'[54]

Determining relief according to standard criteria was also important in two further ways. First, it helped the central authorities to communicate policy decisions in a more systematic way, and the various orders and regulations issued by the Poor Law Commissioners is evidence of that fact. Second, it helped to keep administrative costs low, even after 1834 when it became compulsory to employ professional staff. From that date parishes were required to employ relieving officers and workhouse masters and matrons and in this situation the costs of providing relief would have been prohibitive unless the system could operate with relatively small numbers of paid officials. To do so meant streamlining how decisions about relief were made and in this respect the rules and regulations issued by the Commissioners were crucial, although the extent to which they were applied in specific places still depended on local conditions and the willingness of officials to follow appropriate procedures. So, too, was the workhouse test, which was envisaged as a quick and convenient way of distinguishing the deserving from the non-deserving poor.[55] Classifying paupers according to standard criteria, and

---

52 Peter Dunkley, 'Whigs and Paupers: The Reform of the English Poor Laws 1830–1834', *Journal of British Studies*, 20 (1981): 124–49.

53 This point is made by K. Snell and J. Millar, 'Lone Parent Families and the Welfare State: Past and Present', *Continuity and Change*, 2 (1987): 413.

54 *The Times*, 4 February 1837.

55 See Timothy Besley, Stephen Coate and Timothy W. Guinnane, 'Incentives, Information and Welfare: England's New Poor Law and the Workhouse Test', in William Sundstrom, Timothy W. Guinnane and Warren C. Whatley (eds), *History Matters: Essays on Economic Growth, Technology and Demographic Change* (Stanford, 2003), pp. 245–70.

determining the type and amount of relief that were appropriate for each category, allowed officers to make relatively rapid and seemingly objective decisions that in turn helped reduce the costs of administration.[56] It also had the virtue of allowing the central authorities to monitor more closely the decisions made by local officials appointed under the new poor law.[57]

The extent to which these changes were implemented by individual unions, however, was always open to negotiation and local practice often differed from national policy. Ambiguity in the way that paupers were classified, particularly those defined as able bodied, allowed guardians discretionary powers to dispense relief in ways contrary to the wishes of the central Commissioners. Outdoor relief, for example, continued to be used in northern, industrial unions as a way of dealing with the problems of cyclical unemployment, whilst medical relief was often used in a similar way to disguise what was also, in effect, outdoor relief to the able bodied.[58] Efforts were made to remedy this through various outdoor relief orders that defined the conditions under which assistance could be provided – the Outdoor Labour Test of 1842, the Outdoor Relief Prohibitory order of 1844 and finally the 1852 Outdoor Relief Regulation Order – but variations persisted.[59] Political insecurity also ensured that in the early years of the new poor law, the Commissioners had to tread carefully. Unlike their successors at the Poor Law Board, they appointed assistant commissioners rather than inspectors, with more limited powers to advise and cajole reluctant guardians into following their instructions. The outcome of these circumstances meant that despite the creation of a centralised authority, considerable local variations existed in the way that the new system was implemented.

Although the Commissioners' power to dictate relief policy was contested, their surveillance of pauperism by and large was not. Prior to 1834 the collection

---

56 This point is central to recent discussions of different welfare systems. See Hennock, *The Origin of the Welfare State in England and Germany, 1850–1914*.

57 Harling, 'The Power of Persuasion: Central Authority, Local Bureaucracy and the New Poor Law.' Harling points out that the Commissioners sought to have former non-commissioned officers appointed as workhouse masters and relieving officers, as much for their adherence to discipline as to their appreciation of the importance of hierarchical systems of authority.

58 See George Boyer, *An Economic History of the English Poor Law 1750–1850* (Cambridge, 1990), pp. 233–64; George Boyer, 'The Evolution of Unemployment Relief in Great Britain', *Journal of Interdisciplinary History*, 34 (2004): 393–433; Anne Digby, 'The Labour Market and the Continuity of Social Policy after 1834: The Case of the Eastern Counties', *Economic History Review*, 28 (1975): 69–83; Anne Digby, 'The Rural Poor Law', in Derek Fraser (ed.), *The New Poor Law in the Nineteenth Century* (London, 1976), pp. 149–70; Michael Rose, 'The Allowance System Under the New Poor Law', *Economic History Review*, 19 (1966): 607–20.

59 The orders and the unions in which they applied are noted in William C. Glen, *The General Orders of the Poor Law Commissioners, the Poor Law Board, and the Local Government Board Relating to the Poor Law* (London, 1898).

of statistics on poor relief had been haphazard. Although figures on the cost of poor relief had been provided at various times, no systematic evidence existed before 1803 when the MP George Rose proposed the publication of an abstract of returns.[60] Sporadic publication of figures on expenditure, numbers and types of paupers appeared but it was not until after 1834 that evidence on pauperism, albeit focused primarily on expenditure, was published on a regular and systematic basis.[61] From that time on, detailed evidence on the extent of pauperism and amount of expenditure appeared in the Commissioners' annual reports. Quantifying this arithmetic of woe, as Sandra Sherman has perceptively noted, was a way of developing a new and more impersonal rhetoric of poverty based on numerical abstraction.[62] In so doing, the poor were seen less as individuals deserving of support than as impersonal objects to be managed and governed. Although the legitimacy about who was to determine policy remained, the need to govern pauperism was never in question.

London and the poor law

The growing number of local studies of the poor law has made it possible to explore the regional dimensions of poor relief in more detail than was previously the case. Recent work by Steven King and others has argued convincingly for an emerging distinction in relief and welfare practices between places in the north and west of England compared to those in the south and east. The line that separated them, running roughly between the East Riding of Yorkshire to Devon, distinguished those regions to the north in which industrialisation was beginning to take hold, and those places in the south characterised by declining rural industry and falling agricultural wages. Harsher attitudes towards assisting the poor and lower levels of provision characterised the former whilst the latter districts witnessed rising expenditure and increased reliance on poor relief.

In this historiography, however, London is conspicuous by its absence. Claims that London was different to elsewhere and deserved separate consideration had been made by Charles Booth in the 1890s.[63] More recently, Mary MacKinnon

---

60 See George Rose, *Observations on the Poor Laws and the Management of the Poor in Great Britain Arising from a Consideration of the Returns Now Before Parliament* (London, 1805).

61 In 1837 the new Registrar General's registration districts for the collection of vital statistics were based on these poor law unions and in 1851 they were also used for taking the census. This new grid, therefore, provided the basis not just for the analysis of pauperism but for the collection of other vital information on the state of the nation.

62 See Sandra Sherman, *Imagining Poverty: Quantification and the Decline of Paternalism* (Columbus, 2001).

63 Booth's claims for London exceptionalism were made in relation to elderly paupers. See Charles Booth, *The Aged Poor* (1894), p. 23 cited in George Boyer and

has also suggested that distinctions in the operation of the poor law between London and the rest of the country were particularly marked in the latter part of the century.[64] But we know little about the situation in earlier decades. Despite a growing number of studies of the poor law, we know relatively little about how it operated in London nor about how the city fitted into the broader regional geography of relief. It remains, as Steven King has recently remarked, 'something of an oddity' and this book is an attempt to fill that gap.[65]

To some extent the problems of the providing for the urban poor and managing poor relief were common to London and other large towns and cities.[66] At the same time, however, the range of private acts and institutions responsible for managing and providing poor relief, a highly complex administrative structure, the existence of a relatively comprehensive network of welfare institutions and fluidity of the pauper population helped to generate a very different and diverse set of experiences that distinguished London from other urban centres. Such differences were accentuated by the city's size, its population density and political fragmentation, all of which made the implementation of poor relief exceptionally complex. For these reasons, studies of the metropolitan poor law have either tended to concentrate on one or a handful of parishes rather than the city as a whole, or have focused on a specific aspect of relief.[67] However, it is only at the city wide scale that the operation of the poor law in any given district can fully be understood and only at that scale that we can place London in its broader regional context.

Timothy P. Schmidle, 'Poverty Amongst the Elderly in Victorian England', *Economic History Review*, 61 (2008): 15.

[64] Mary MacKinnon, 'The Use and Misuse of Poor Law Statistics, 1857 to 1912', *Historical Methods*, 21 (1988): 14.

[65] King, *Poverty and Welfare in England*, p. 13.

[66] For general discussion of the urban poor law and urban poverty see David Ashforth, 'The Urban Poor Law', in Derek Fraser (ed.), *The New Poor Law in the Nineteenth Century* (London, 1976), pp. 128–48; John Treble, *Urban Poverty in Britain 1830–1914* (London, 1979).

[67] See Elaine Murphy, 'The Metropolitan Poor Farms, 1722–1834', *London Journal*, 27 (2002): 1–18; Elaine Murphy, 'The New Poor Law Guardians and the Administration of Insanity in East London, 1834–44', *Bulletin of the History of Medicine*, 77 (2003): 45–74; Pat Ryan, 'Politics and Relief: East London Unions in the Late Nineteenth and Early Twentieth Centuries', in Michael Rose (ed.) *The Poor and the City: The English Poor Law in its Urban Context* (Leicester, 1985), pp. 133–72; Andrea Tanner, 'The City of London Poor Law Union 1837–1869', (unpublished Ph.D. thesis, University of London, 1995); Andrea Tanner, 'The Casual Poor and the City of London Poor Law Union, 1837–1869', *Historical Journal*, 42 (1999): 183–206. A notable exception is Lynn Lees, 'The Survival of the Unfit: Welfare Policies and Family Maintenance in Nineteenth-Century London', in Peter Mandler (ed), *The Uses of Charity* (Philadelphia, 1990), pp. 68–91. See also Lees, *The Solidarities of Strangers*.

At the start of the nineteenth century London was a sprawling city of some one million people, growing to more than four million by the end. Size alone meant that it contained the largest concentration of paupers and this in turn provided opportunities for developing the collective provision of services that was not feasible elsewhere in the country. Statistics on pauperism hint at London's national significance. Between 1803 and 1870 it accounted for between 8 and 18 per cent of total relief expenditure in England and Wales, gaining in relative importance as the period progressed. Early in the century it accounted for a disproportionately large number of paupers – approximately one in six of all indoor paupers and between 10 and 20 per cent of those receiving casual relief. Between a third and a half of paupers removed within England and Wales came from London and by the end of the period, a third of deaths in all workhouses took place in the capital. Failure to appreciate its quantitative importance, therefore, is to leave a significant gap in our understanding of the poor law.

Size, however, had another, more politicised dimension that posed separate challenges in relation to implementing national policies. The fact that several London parishes were as large if not larger than most major industrial towns meant that local politicians could develop important power bases in their own right. This became very evident in relation to the introduction of the new poor law which aroused widespread opposition in the capital, not so much in terms of changes in relief practices, many of which had already been introduced prior to 1834, but in terms of relationships between the vestries and the central state. Ratepayer democracy, which was particularly strong in London, provided the basis on which local politicians could operate as a significant political force at a national level. London supporters of parochial reform were part of a wider network that included some of the most prominent radicals in the country. Faced with such a strong though potentially fragmented power base, the central state had difficulty in imposing its will where it ran counter to the desires of local ratepayers and politicians and this proved to be particularly problematic in the context of the new poor law.

Social geography compounded these problems. Widening geographical disparities of wealth and poverty combined with jealously guarded local political autonomy ensured that, for most of the period, the city's poor law authorities operated more or less independently of each other.[68] Contrasting conditions created a mosaic of different practices with varying degrees of harshness and generosity. In poorer districts, hard pressed ratepayers exercised close vigilance over the provision of relief whilst in wealthier places less stringent conditions applied. These differences, together with the close juxtaposition of poor law authorities, the varied nature of their constitution, and the shifting balance of power between localities and the centre meant that London was a peculiarly complex setting for

---

[68] For a discussion of disparities in wealth see David R. Green, 'A Map For Mayhew's London: The Geography of Poverty in the Mid-Nineteenth Century', *London Journal*, 11 (1986): 115–26; Leonard Schwarz, 'Social Class and Social Geography: The Middle Classes in London at the End of the Eighteenth Century', *Social History*, 7 (1982): 167–85.

the operation of the poor law. In the context of poor relief, this complexity, the variety of conditions and the magnitude of its problems relating to poverty all made London impossible to ignore yet almost as impossible to administer. That serious consideration was given to omitting the city entirely from the Poor Law Amendment Act of 1834 bears witness to this fact.[69] It comprised, as the Poor Law Commissioners and Edwin Chadwick soon came to realise, a legal and administrative quagmire which proved remarkably resistant to change.

The outcome in relation to changes in poor relief was that after 1834 London appeared to lag behind other places. New workhouse construction was slow compared to the rest of the country, despite complaints about the inadequate state of some of the older metropolitan workhouses from the assistant poor law commissioners responsible for overseeing the operation of the new system. In an administrative sense, London also appeared to have been a laggard. Prior to 1834 the poor law was administered by over 170 separate bodies, each operating according to a complex amalgam of practice, precedent and law. In some cities, population growth had prompted the reorganisation of the way that relief was administered, and by the early eighteenth century corporations of the poor had emerged in places such as Bristol, Gloucester and Norwich.[70] In London, with no history of civic unity, what reorganisation had taken place had been at the level of the parish, resulting in specific local acts relating not only to the provision of relief but also the composition of the vestry, the levying of rates and the mode of parochial assessment. These complex arrangements, the size of its constituent parishes and the strength of local vestries meant that from the inception of the new poor law in 1834 the central authorities struggled to exert control over the actions of individual districts, far less over the city as a whole. As a result, for much of the period until 1867, when crisis forced the issue, about a third of London parishes remained outside the terms of the Poor Law Amendment Act.

In other respects, however, London led the way. Whilst the city remained an administrative patchwork of new unions and old parishes for several decades after 1834, relief in practice was more amenable to change. Indeed, many of the recommendations by the Royal Commission on the Poor Laws, such as the workhouse as a test for destitution, labour tasks for the able bodied outdoor poor, paid overseers and more rigid classification of paupers, were already in place in several London parishes before 1834. The changes in relief practices under the new poor law were therefore less traumatic in London than in many other regions and as a result met with relatively little working-class opposition. Although comparatively few new workhouses were built in London in the decades immediately after 1834, this did not necessarily mean that the city ceased to be at the forefront of innovations in relief. Economies of scale provided new opportunities to develop collective responses to the problems of metropolitan pauperism and as a result specialist institutions, such as district schools and poor law infirmaries, paid for

---

69 See Brundage, *The Making of the New Poor Law*, pp. 54–7.

70 King, *Poverty and Welfare in England*, p. 22.

collectively by parishes, appeared earliest in the capital. The changes introduced by the Metropolitan Poor Act of 1867 which allowed the construction of free hospitals for the poor financed by the local state was particularly important in this respect.[71]

* * *

This book is primarily an attempt to understand London's significance in relation to the poor law between the late eighteenth century until its final and full incorporation under the Poor Law Board in 1867. Chapter 1 focuses on the period prior to 1834 and outlines the uniqueness of London in relation to patterns of expenditure. Not surprisingly, perhaps, its share of the total expenditure on poor relief mirrored the size of the city. But compared to the rest of the country, the pattern of expenditure was different in two important respects: the relative importance of indoor relief and the significance of the casual poor. To a large extent, the two aspects were part of the same problem. Rapid urban growth, fuelled by large scale migration from the countryside, had made it increasingly difficult to administer outdoor relief, particularly in the context of the thousands of migrants without a settlement who applied for assistance. Removals from the city were ineffective as a way of dealing with this issue, and local poor law authorities turned increasingly to paid officers and indoor relief as ways of coping with the tide of paupers that at times threatened to overwhelm individual parishes. Such innovations, which were later incorporated as part of the new poor law, suggested that in some ways London led rather than followed the changes that were to take place in the rest of the country after 1834.

Urban change, however, meant that differences emerged between districts in the scale and type of relief provided, and these geographical variations are the focus of the following chapter. Workhouse construction was uneven and many of the smaller City parishes relied on pauper farming as a way of dealing with their indoor poor. By contrast, eastern districts and those places to the west and in the suburbs that were growing most rapidly relied more on indoor relief. The problem with the reliance on the workhouse was that during periods of economic downturn the system proved too inflexible to cope with demand and as a result expenditure on outdoor relief rose. This situation worsened following the deep recession of 1825 and the accompanying rise in poor law expenditure focused attention on the need to reform the system. However, rather than seeking to address the structural inequalities between districts that underpinned the problems of the poor law,

---

71 For further discussion see Gwendoline Ayers, *England's First State Hospitals 1867–1930* (London, 1971); David R. Green, 'Medical Relief and the New Poor Law in London', in Ole P. Grell, Andrew Cunningham and Robert Jütte (eds), *Health Care and Poor Relief in 18th and 19th Century Northern Europe* (Aldershot, 2002), pp. 220–45; Ruth Hodgkinson, *The Origins of the National Health Service: The Medical Services of the New Poor Law 1834–1871* (London, 1967).

attention turned towards a condemnation of select vestries, parochial incompetence and corruption as an explanation of how the problems had arisen.

It was in this highly politicised landscape that the Poor Law Amendment Act of 1834 alighted, and Chapter 3 discusses the struggles to implement the legislation in the context of parochial reform. As Derek Fraser and others have argued, the politics of both the old and the new poor law was a crucial element in understanding how the system of relief was implemented at a local level and this was as true in London as it was elsewhere.[72] The Poor Law Amendment Act itself was permissive rather than mandatory and despite the efforts of the central Poor Law Commissioners, about a third of metropolitan parishes refused to adopt it. As Edwin Chadwick learned to his cost, any attempt to circumvent parochial authority by cutting through the labyrinthine framework of local responsibilities for the poor law was bound to generate opposition from some of the largest vestries in the country. In addition to the advantages derived from patronage, which were not unimportant for local tradesmen and officials, those who opposed the centralised machinery of Somerset House did so for other reasons more closely linked to parochial democracy and popular radicalism. Though centralisers castigated this opposition as little more than that of self-seeking office holders keen to preserve their privileges under the old system, nevertheless more was at stake than just place-holding and self-advancement. The outcome was that no uniform administrative framework existed for providing poor relief until the Metropolitan Poor Act of 1867 came into operation.

The new union workhouses took pride of place as the most iconic feature of the changes ushered in after 1834. However, the workhouse was only one of several poor law institutions that included district schools, pauper farms and county lunatic asylums which collectively provided an entire system of provision for different categories of pauper. In most places, such a panoply of institutions was impractical but in London economies of scale meant that it was feasible to provide relief in collectively funded specialist establishments, which in turn limited the need for individual districts to construct new workhouses. What London lacked by way of new workhouse provision, therefore, was made up by the construction of other specialist institutions that operated alongside the workhouse itself. This system is explored in Chapter 4 and although London districts were often conspicuous by their reluctance to build new workhouses after 1834, nevertheless the city played a pivotal role in experimenting with other forms of institutional provision for the poor.

---

72 Derek Fraser, 'The Poor Law as a Political Institution', in Derek Fraser (ed.), *The New Poor Law in the Nineteenth Century* (London, 1976), p. 111. See also John Foster, *Class Struggle and the Industrial Revolution: Early Capitalism in Three English Towns* (London, 1977); Derek Fraser, *Urban Politics in Victorian England*, (Leicester, 1976), pp. 55–90 and Elizabeth T. Hurren, *Protesting About Pauperism: Poverty, Politics and Poor Relief in Late-Victorian England, 1870–1900* (Woodbridge, 2007). For the political dimensions of the old poor law at a local level see Steve Hindle, 'Power, Poor Relief, and Social Relations in Holland Fen, c. 1600–1800', *Historical Journal*, 41 (1998): 67–96.

However harsh the new poor law appeared to be, it did not absolve officials from their obligation to provide some form of assistance to those who applied for relief. Paupers themselves were often aware of their rights and recent studies of the poor in the eighteenth and nineteenth centuries have emphasised the variety of ways with which they pressed their claims for relief. Histories of the poor 'from below' have elevated the struggles to enforce expectations of help and customary rights to assistance to a central role in determining the outcome of poor relief practices.[73] As Lynn Lees has remarked, 'Understanding the meaning of welfare requires looking beyond abstract pronouncements and lurid exposes to the routine encounters of applicant and overseer, where communal aid was negotiated.'[74]

Chapter 5 is an attempt to develop just such an understanding based on paupers' experiences and in doing so it seeks to provide a more rounded appreciation of the way the poor law operated. This requires delving beyond the instructions, circulars and policies issued by the Poor Law Commissioners and unravelling the actual day-to-day encounters between local officials and paupers. Most of these routine interactions went unrecorded, and only occasionally were the voices of the poor heard or the actions of relieving officers brought to light. The encounters between paupers and officials remind us of one of the central tenets of the poor law, namely that it had a statutory status and as such both those who administered it and those who received relief were linked together in a set of mutual rights and legal obligations.[75] How these customs, rules and regulations were interpreted and used was often the cause for contention, and paupers as well as relieving officers frequently found themselves in court either to seek redress or to answer for their actions. In either case, these daily encounters remind us that although the Commissioners required that relieving officers should ignore character and

---

[73] For discussions about popular opposition to the poor law see Nicholas Edsall, *The Anti-Poor Law Movement 1834–44*, (Manchester, 1971); John Knott, *Popular Opposition to the 1834 Poor Law*, (London, 1986). More day-to-day negotiations by individuals are dealt with in a variety of contexts by David R. Green, 'Pauper Protests: Power and Resistance in Early Nineteenth-Century London Workhouses', *Social History*, 31 (2006): 137–59; Tim Hitchcock, *Down and Out in Eighteenth Century London*, (London, 2007), pp. 125–49; Gary Howells, '"For I was tired of England, Sir": English Pauper Emigrant Strategies 1834–60', *Social History*, 23 (1998): 181–94; Thomas Sokoll, 'Negotiating a Living: Essex Pauper Letters from London 1800–1834', *International Review of Social History*, 45 (2000): 19–46; Thomas Sokoll, *Essex Pauper Letters 1731–1837* (Oxford, 2001); Thomas Sokoll, 'Writing for Relief: Rhetoric in English Pauper Letters', in Andreas Gestrich, Steven King and Lutz Raphael (eds), *Being Poor In Modern Europe: Historical Perspectives 1800–1940* (Bern, 2006), pp. 91–112; James Taylor, 'Voices in the Crowd: The Kirkby Lonsdale Letters 1809–36', in Tim Hitchcock, Peter King and Pamela Sharpe (eds), *Chronicling Poverty – The Voices and Strategies of the English Poor 1640–1840* (Houndmills, 1997), pp. 109–26.

[74] Lees, *The Solidarities of Strangers*, p. 177.

[75] See Pamela Sharpe, '"The Bowels of Compassion": A Labouring Family and the Law c. 1790–1834', in Hitchcock, King and Sharpe (eds), *Chronicling Poverty* (1997), pp. 87–108.

focus only on categorising types of paupers, personal qualities and a willingness to contest authority were important elements in the way that relief was negotiated.

The mounting problems of financing poor law expenditure in London, particularly in eastern districts, are dealt with in the final two chapters. The pattern of indoor and outdoor expenditure is explored in Chapter 6, which highlights the growing imbalance between districts that emerged in the 1850s and 1860s. During these decades London's share of the overall national poor law budget grew sharply, and much of this was accounted for by a relatively small number of metropolitan districts. This situation arose largely as an outcome of social changes that resulted in growing class separation. In some districts this pattern of change undermined the ability of the local poor law to keep pace with demand and as the fiscal crisis in these places deepened so calls for reform mounted. These calls are the focus of the final chapter which explores the different ways that existed to deal with the crisis. Had removals been a viable option, the fiscal crisis of the metropolitan poor law arguably could have been contained. However, this was not the case and different solutions that redistributed funds rather than paupers were required to overcome the structural inequalities in relief that had become such a striking feature of the London poor law. Various forms of redistribution were introduced, culminating in the Metropolitan Poor Act of 1867 which recognised once and for all the collective responsibility of metropolitan districts to provide relief for the poor. Assessing the impact of this act in terms of reducing rating inequalities between districts and in reforming the administrative machinery as well as the institutional provision of relief provides an end point to the study.

Chapter 1
London and the Regions under the Old Poor Law

Introduction

Prior to 1834 the English poor law operated under a bewildering array of legal arrangements that governed the administration of relief in specific localities. Different economic conditions, attitudes towards the poor, customary expectations of relief and individual experiments in poor law policy added further layers of complexity to the system. As a result the number of paupers, types of relief and the amounts of assistance provided could vary significantly between places, reflecting a patchwork of local circumstances and individual policy decisions. Local variations in policy and practice, however, were to some extent overlain by broader social, political and economic factors that structured the way that the poor law operated. These regional differences and variations in policy, concentrating on London's position in the historical geography of the old poor law, are the focus of this chapter.

Paupers and prices: counting the cost of pauperism

Counting the cost of poor relief and the number of paupers was – and to some extent still is – an inexact science. During the eighteenth and early nineteenth centuries, systematic evidence of pauper numbers and poor law expenditure was rare and it proved difficult for contemporaries to draw firm conclusions about trends in pauperism.[1] Concern about the cost of relief prompted counts of expenditure in 1748–50, 1774–76 and 1783–85, though typically such returns were compiled at times of crisis and were neither systematic nor complete. With the publication of Thomas Malthus' *Essay on the Principle of Population* in 1798 and the subsequent republication of the 1803 edition with updated population figures from the first census, the need to collect more accurate figures for both population and the number of paupers became more pressing.[2]

---

1 For an early attempt at comparison see Thomas Pemberton, *An Attempt to Estimate the Increase of the Number of Poor During the Interval of 1785 and 1803* (London, 1811).

2 For a discussion of Malthus and the abolitionist debate see J. R. Poynter, *Society and Pauperism: English Ideas on Poor Relief 1795–1834* (London, 1969), pp. 144–85,

In response to the emerging debate and the appearance of the much enlarged second edition of Malthus' *Essay*, the MP George Rose proposed the publication of an abstract of returns of expenditure and the number of paupers, including children and those aged above 60, together with the types of relief provided, distinguishing permanent relief to indoor and outdoor paupers from those who were relieved only occasionally.[3] Some 14,611 parishes and townships completed the returns, which made this the most comprehensive survey of poor relief at the time. Further concerns about rising costs prompted the publication of figures on expenditure from 1813 to 1815, together with information on the number of persons relieved permanently inside and outside the workhouse, as well as those relieved occasionally.[4] Although the figures are not without their problems, and the basis on which they are compiled differed from previous years, notably by omitting children, nevertheless the two sets of returns are in some respects similar in scope and allow comparisons of expenditure and numbers and types of paupers in the early years of the nineteenth century.[5] Information on expenditure, though not on the number of paupers or types of relief, was published annually from that time on. Except for counts of paupers in 1824 and 1832, the latter included as part of the evidence collected for the Royal Commission on the Poor Laws, both of which were less complete with some 382 and 1,332 districts respectively providing returns, there is little evidence on the numbers of persons in receipt of relief.[6] However, taken together these sets of figures allow us to reconstruct the national trends and regional patterns of poor relief and to examine the broader context in which the London poor law operated.

As ratepayers were only too well aware, the costs of poor relief began to escalate from the 1760s and increased sharply towards the end of the century. Annual costs had risen from an average of £689,971 for the three years ending in 1750 to £1,912,241 for the period 1783 to 1785.[7] The outbreak of war in 1793

225–48; James Huzel, 'Malthus, The Poor Law and Population in Early Nineteenth-Century England', *Economic History Review*, 22 (1969): 430–52.

3 See PP 1803–04 XIII, Abstract of the answers and returns made pursuant to Act 43 Geo 3, relative to the expense and maintenance of the poor in England. See also George Rose, *Observations on the Poor Laws and the Management of the Poor in Great Britain Arising from a Consideration of the Returns Now Before Parliament* (London, 1805). Figures for expenditure by county for 1748, 1749 and 1750 were reprinted in PP 1818 V Select committee to consider the poor laws: Appendix 1.

4 PP 1818 XIX Abstract of the answers and returns made pursuant to an act intituled 'An act for procuring returns relative to the expense and maintenance of the poor in England.'

5 Returns were submitted by 14,640 places, including 10,593 parishes and 4,047 other places including townships, tythings and hamlets making separate returns.

6 Karel Williams, *From Pauperism to Poverty* (London, 1981), pp. 147–55.

7 J. Marshall, *A Digest of All the Accounts Relating to the Population, Production, Revenues, Financial Operations, Manufactures, Shipping, Colonies, Commerce &c &c of the United Kingdom of Great Britain and Ireland* (London, 1833), p. 36.

was followed by severe food shortages and price rises resulted in further steep increases in poor law expenditure to £4,077,891 in 1803.[8] The national trend was mirrored at local levels. In Oxfordshire, for example, the costs of relief rose very steeply after 1796, as they did in Bedfordshire and other southern counties.[9] Nor were northern districts immune from these increases: in Tottington, Lancashire, for example, expenditure on relief in the 1790s was six times higher than it had been in the 1760s.[10] These spiralling increases were matched by a relative rise in the amount of the national income devoted to supporting the poor. As a share of the national product, the proportion consumed by relief had also risen from about 1.5 per cent at the middle of the eighteenth century to over two per cent by the end, fuelling serious concern about the drain that poor relief imposed on the nation's wealth.[11] By 1818 expenditure had nearly doubled to £7.9 million, a sum that was little short of the total cost of all civil government departments combined.[12]

The official statistics, however, are misleading in two respects. First, unless set against the cost of living the true extent of any increase cannot be established. Second, the national figures mask local variation. With outdoor relief accounting for about 75 per cent of the total expenditure, what was of critical importance in determining the real cost of the poor law was the price of bread since it was that which underpinned the amounts provided under the various sliding scales of relief.[13] Figure 1.1 shows nominal and real expenditure on poor relief in England and Wales from 1813 using Feinstein's cost of living index, which weights bread and wheat flour as the two most

---

8 Figures for expenditure were reprinted in PP 1818 V Select committee to consider the poor laws, Appendix 1. See also Rose, *Observations on the Poor Laws and the Management of the Poor in Great Britain*.

9 David Eastwood, *Governing Rural England: Tradition and Transformation in Local Government 1780–1840* (Oxford, 1994), p. 137; Samantha Williams, 'Poor Relief, Labourers' Households and Living Standards in Rural England, c. 1770–1834: A Bedfordshire Case Study', *Economic History Review*, 58 (2005): 492.

10 Margaret Hanley, 'Being Poor in Nineteenth-Century Lancashire', in Andreas Gestrich, Steven King and Lutz Raphael (eds), *Being Poor In Modern Europe: Historical Perspectives 1800–1940* (Bern, 2006), pp. 79–81.

11 Peter Solar, 'Poor Relief and English Economic Development Before the Industrial Revolution', *Economic History Review*, 48 (1995): 7; Peter Lindert, 'Poor Relief Before the Welfare State: Britain Versus the Continent, 1780–1880', *European Review of Economic History*, 2 (1998): 114–15; Peter Lindert, *Growing Public: Social Spending and Economic Growth since the Eighteenth Century* (Cambridge, 2004), pp. 46–8.

12 Peter Dunkley, *The Crisis of the Old Poor Law in England 1795–1834*, (London, 1982), p. 1. Civil expenditure in 1803 was £9,072,087 and in 1818 was £9,566,231. As a proportion of public expenditure on civil government, therefore, the cost of relief had risen dramatically. See A. Aspinall and E. A. Smith (eds), *English Historical Documents*: *Volume XI 1783–1832* (London, 1959), pp. 576–7.

13 In 1803 indoor relief expenditure in England and Wales was £1,016,446 compared to £3,061,447 for outdoor relief. See Marshall, *A Digest of All the Accounts*, p. 32.

important items for this period.[14] What emerges is the divergent paths of the two series. To some extent the cost of relief rose and fell depending on the state of the economy, though this was not the entire story. Once the economic dislocation of the Napoleonic wars had ended, the nominal cost of relief began to fall and continued to do so for the next few years, helped by economic recovery in the early 1820s. This brief respite, however, was halted by the financial crisis that began in late 1825 which heralded the start of several years of rising costs. However, what is most marked is less these short term fluctuations than the divergence between the nominal and real cost of relief. From 1818 onwards, this divergence is marked, particularly after 1825, and it continued to widen throughout the early 1830s. During this period prices seemed to fall quicker than did the cost of relief. Crucially the cost of wheat fell from 126s a quarter in 1812 to 66s in 1831.[15] However, poor law expenditure fell more slowly, if at all, and as a result the real cost of relief actually rose. This pattern suggested that, for whatever reason, when prices fell overseers were reluctant to reduce the amount of money given to the poor. It was this apparent generosity which so angered critics and fuelled calls for abolition of the poor law.

The apparent generosity of relief was also blamed for the increase in the number of individuals that seemed to rely on the poor law to get by. Although official figures are difficult to interpret, most commentators, including Malthus, thought that there had been an increase not just in the number of paupers but also in the proportion of the population dependent on relief. Figures for England and Wales suggest that in the early years of the century, during the Napoleonic wars, between about 10 and 12 per cent of the population were in receipt of some form of poor relief.[16] In 1803 the official returns show there were more than a million persons in receipt of relief which represented over 11 per cent of the population. Two thirds of this number were able-bodied adults on permanent outdoor relief. Even allowing for the crisis years during which the count had taken place, these figures confirmed the extent to which the poor law had departed from the ideal of support only for the old and infirm. Further counts took place between 1813 and 1815 at which point over 895,000 persons were in receipt of relief, comprising about eight per cent of the population.

---

14 Charles H. Feinstein, 'Pessimism Perpetuated: Real Wages and the Standard of Living in Britain During and After the Industrial Revolution', *Journal of Economic History*, 58 (1998): 635, 652–3.

15 B. R. Mitchell and Phyllis Deane, *Abstract of British Historical Statistics* (Cambridge, 1962), p. 488.

16 David Eastwood, *Governing Rural England: Tradition and Transformation in Local Government 1780–1840*, p. 103. The figure varies depending on the precise method of defining who was in receipt of relief. See Steven King, *Poverty and Welfare in England 1700–1850: A Regional Perspective* (Manchester, 2000), pp. 141–2, 181–2.

However, this figure did not include children, who had accounted for about a third of the numbers relieved in 1803, and adding this proportion to the total meant that the final number of paupers was very similar in both sets of years.[17]

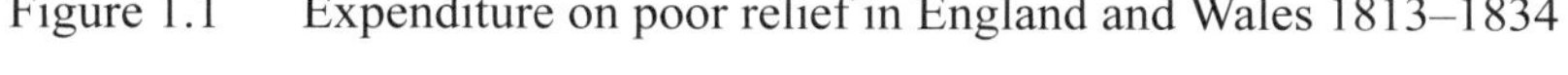

Figure 1.1 Expenditure on poor relief in England and Wales 1813–1834

Note: Nominal prices have been deflated using Feinstein's (1998) cost of living index, based on 1813 price levels.

Source: J. Marshall, *A Digest of All the Accounts* (London, 1833), pp. 36–7; PP 1839 XLIV (1) A return of the amount expended for the relief of the poor in each county of England and Wales during the year ended 25th March.

The national figures, however, also mask regional and local differences in the number of paupers, the rate of pauperism and the costs of relief. Although conditions varied, contemporaries were well aware of the pauperised state of many rural parishes in southern and eastern England. The crisis years of the Napoleonic

17 The figures are taken from PP 1803–04 XIII Abstract of the answers and returns made pursuant to Act 43 Geo 3, relative to the expense and maintenance of the poor in England, p. 715; PP 1818 XIX Abstract of the answers and returns made pursuant to an act intituled 'An act for procuring returns relative to the expense and maintenance of the poor in England', p. 648. In St Marylebone from 1769 to 1781, children aged below 16 comprised nearly 30 per cent of workhouse admissions. See Alysa Levene, 'Children, Childhood and the Workhouse: St Marylebone, 1769–1781', *London Journal*, 33 (2008): 44.

wars had highlighted structural changes in the rural economy in southern counties that had resulted in higher rates of seasonal unemployment and levels of poverty. The decline of annual hiring, a process encouraged by parliamentary enclosure, was important in this respect. So, too, was the decline of rural cottage industries, which traditionally had helped to supplement agricultural labourers' household incomes.[18] At the same time other sources of help appeared to be spread more thinly, forcing those who would otherwise have turned to charitable handouts to seek poor relief. The outcome was that the poor law in such places began to support a wider range of individuals, many of whom were relatively young and able-bodied.[19]

Based on the counts of paupers in 1803 and between 1813 and 1815, Table 1.1 shows that places in southern and eastern England – typically those agricultural counties reliant on cereal growing in which outdoor allowances were most important – had much higher rates of pauperism than did northern counties. These local differences are highlighted in Figures 1.2 and 1.3 which show the proportion of the population in receipt of poor relief by county in 1803 and between 1813 and 1815. Even allowing for the fact that the figures are somewhat crude, they nevertheless provide a broad indication of the regional variations in pauperism. In southern counties such as Berkshire, Suffolk and Sussex the rate of pauperism was more than double that in most northern counties. However, there were some important variations and changes, notably regarding the much higher rates of pauperism in London and West Midland counties that prevailed from 1813 onwards. There the impact of the return to peace and the demobilisation of large numbers of soldiers caused major economic dislocation with consequent pressure on poor relief and a significant rise in the numbers of casual poor. In London, for example, the number of casual paupers increased from 24,765 in 1803 to an average of 80,582 from 1813 to 1815 and although such paupers might not have been a permanent drain on parish finances, nevertheless by sheer weight of numbers they posed a significant problem for the poor law authorities.

---

18 For discussions of these processes see Mark Blaug, 'The Myth of the Old Poor Law and the Making of the New', *Journal of Economic History*, 23 (1963): 167–72; Mark Blaug, 'The Poor Law Report Re-examined', *Journal of Economic History*, 24 (1964): 241–2; George Boyer, 'The Old Poor Law and the Agricultural Labour Market in Southern England: An Empirical Analysis', *Journal of Economic History*, 46 (1986): 113–35; Keith Snell, *Annals of the Labouring Poor: Social Change and Agrarian England 1660–1900* (Cambridge, 1985).

19 John Broad, 'Parish Economies of Welfare, 1650–1834', *Historical Journal*, 42 (1999): 1003–5.

Table 1.1 Rate of pauperism 1803–1815 (per cent of population in receipt of poor relief)

	North I	**North II**	**West Midlands**	**East Midlands**	**South West**	**South**	**East**	**London**
1803	6.2	5.5	7.9	7.7	8.6	11.2	10.5	6.2
1813	6.8	6.8	10.3	9.8	9.4	10.5	11.4	11.0
1814	6.7	6.1	10.1	9.3	8.9	10.0	10.8	11.8
1815	6.5	5.9	9.7	9.1	8.8	9.6	10.4	11.2

Note: North I: Cumberland, Durham, Northumberland, Westmoreland
North II: Cheshire, Lancashire, Yorkshire (East Riding) Yorkshire (North Riding), Yorkshire (West Riding)
West Midlands Derbyshire, Herefordshire, Shropshire, Warwickshire, Worcestershire
East Midlands: Leicestershire, Northamptonshire, Nottinghamshire
Southwest: Cornwall, Devon, Gloucestershire, Somerset
South: Bedfordshire, Berkshire, Buckinghamshire, Dorset, Hampshire, Hertfordshire, Kent, Oxfordshire, Surrey, Sussex, Wiltshire
East: Cambridgeshire, Essex, Huntingdonshire, Lincolnshire, Norfolk, Rutland, Suffolk
London: Middlesex

Source: PP 1803–04 XIII Abstract of the answers and returns made pursuant to Act 43 Geo 3, relative to the expense and maintenance of the poor in England; PP 1818 XIX Abstract of the answers and returns made pursuant to an act intituled 'An act for procuring returns relative to the expense and maintenance of the poor in England.'

According to more detailed local studies, however, the proportions of persons dependent on relief suggested by the national counts are likely to have been underestimates, particularly during crisis years. In the Essex parish of Ardleigh in 1796, for example, Thomas Sokoll estimated that as much as 41 per cent of households were in receipt of relief, although in the early 1820s, by which time conditions had improved, the total had fallen to just over a quarter.[20] Other studies confirm that in southern and eastern counties in the early nineteenth century between a third and a half of the population were likely to have received some assistance in any given year. In Oxfordshire in 1803 Eastwood estimated that nearly 20 per cent of the population were given relief whilst in some Bedfordshire parishes Williams found that up to a third of residents received assistance, rising higher in the worst years.[21]

---

20 For Essex see Thomas Sokoll, 'The Pauper Household Small and Simple? The Evidence From Listings of Inhabitants and Pauper Lists of Early Modern England Reassessed', *Ethnologia Europaea*, 17 (1987): 25–42; Gregory Clark and Marianne Page, 'Is There a Profit in Reforming the Poor? The English Poor Law 1830–42', unpublished paper, (2000), p. 5.

21 Eastwood, *Governing Rural England*, 143–5; Samantha Williams, 'Poor Relief, Labourers' Households and Living Standards in Rural England', pp. 495–516.

Northern and western parishes typically had lower proportions of paupers but even there by 1810 the poor law probably dealt with between one fifth and a quarter of the population.[22]

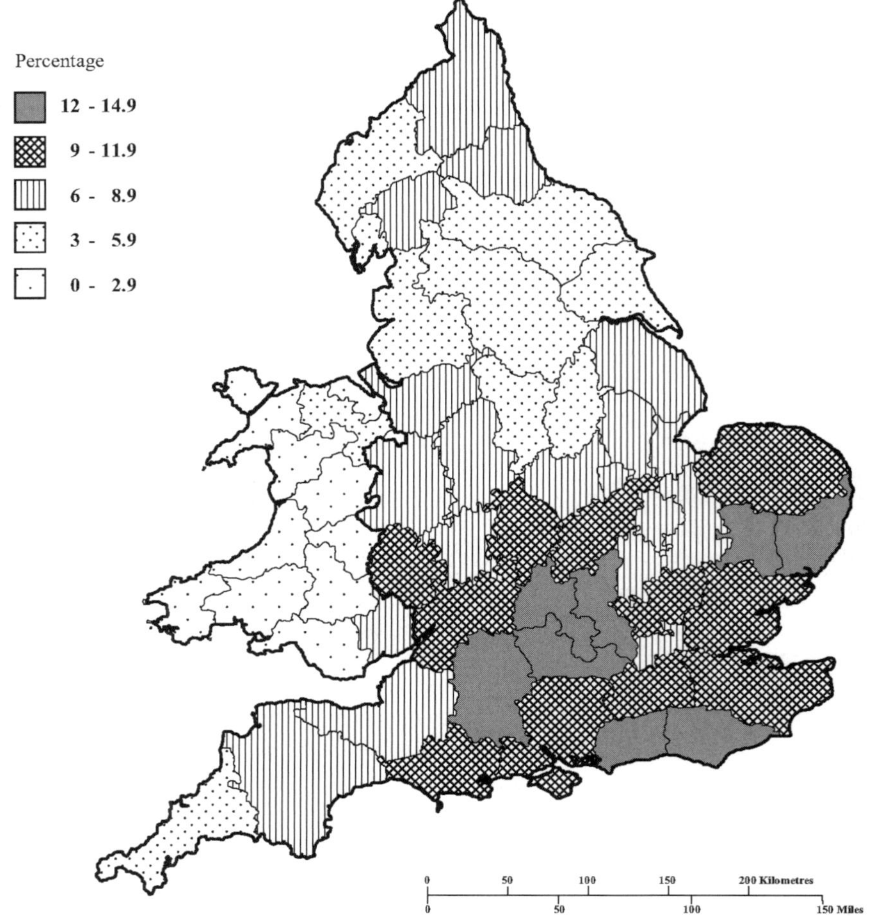

Figure 1.2 Percentage of paupers in England and Wales 1803

Source: 1803–04 XIII Abstract of the answers and returns made pursuant to Act 43 Geo 3, relative to the expense and maintenance of the poor in England.

[22] For an overview of these local studies see King, *Poverty and Welfare in England*, pp. 141, 164, 209.

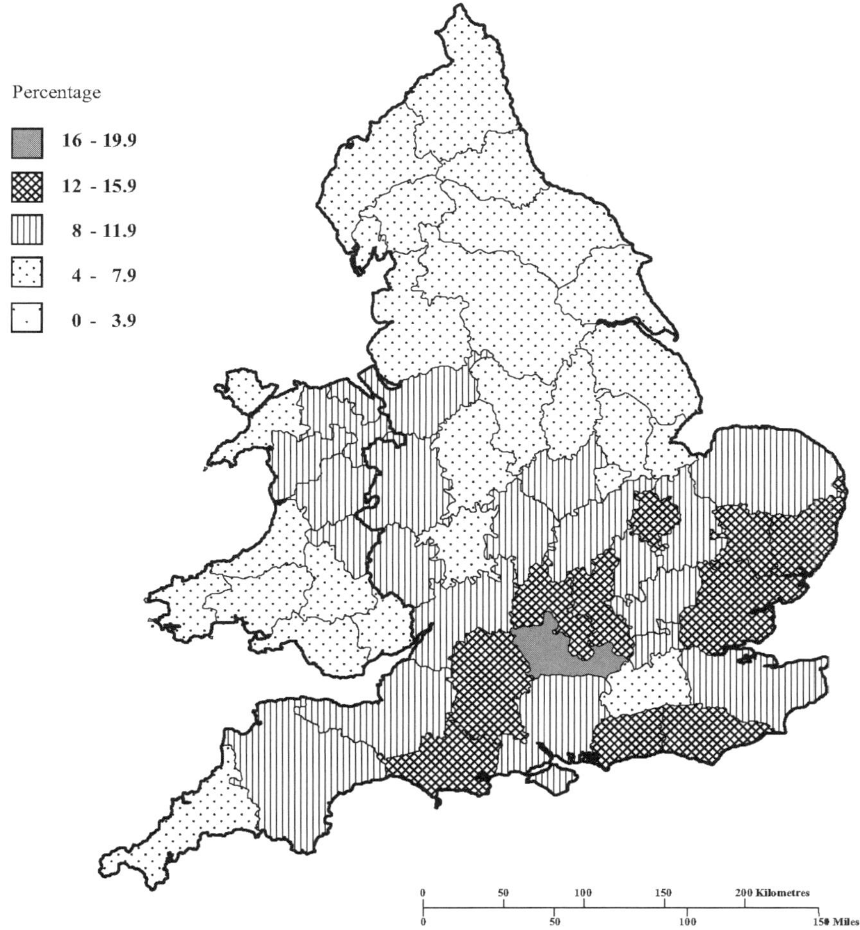

Figure 1.3 Percentage of paupers in England and Wales 1813–1815

Source: 1818 XIX Abstract of the answers and returns made pursuant to an act intituled 'An act for procuring returns relative to the expense and maintenance of the poor in England.'

Regional differences in the rates of pauperism were mirrored by patterns of expenditure. Although variations in relief existed depending on the policies of individual parishes, local studies have shown that the value of poor law pensions in northern and some midland parishes was about half that of those in the south and east.[23] These differences can be traced from 1813 onwards, when expenditure figures for counties first become available on an annual basis. Figure 1.4 shows the real cost of relief per pauper between 1813 and 1831, based on estimates of the numbers of paupers and the amount of relief expenditure. In the absence of numbers of paupers for the period as a whole, the figures are derived by estimating the population for each county extrapolated from the censuses for 1811, 1821 and 1831. The numbers of paupers were estimated by using the rate of pauperism based on the returns for 1803, those being the most comprehensive available for the period. Expenditure per pauper was then calculated using a multiplier based on Feinstein's cost of living index. The results broadly confirm the distinction between counties in the north, west midlands and southwest in which costs per pauper were relatively low, and those high cost counties in the east midlands, south and east, together with London.[24] Indeed, by the end of this period, the relative cost of pauperism in London exceeded that of all other regions.

The peculiarity of London: patterns of relief

That London was becoming relatively more important with regard to poor law expenditure was hardly surprising. The city's population grew rapidly from the start of the century and this in turn fuelled higher expenditure. Between 1811 and 1831, London's population increased by over 45 per cent matched by an increase of nearly 36 per cent in relief expenditure from about £502,000 in 1813 to a peak of over £688,000 in 1832. Taking price changes into account, as illustrated in Figure 1.5, the increase was even greater and in real terms the costs of relief in London more than doubled over the period. As a proportion of total expenditure on poor relief in England, the city's share rose from just over 7.5 per cent in 1813 to more than 10 per cent by the early 1830s.

23 Ibid., pp. 257–8.

24 Figures for expenditure on separate metropolitan parishes were not available on an annual basis until 1825. Between 1825 and 1834 on average Middlesex accounted for 83 per cent of the total expenditure for London, the rest being made up by metropolitan parishes in Surrey and Kent, and therefore the county total can be used as a surrogate measure for the city as a whole.

Figure 1.4 Real cost of poor relief per pauper in England and Wales 1813–1831

Note: Nominal prices have been deflated using Feinstein's (1998) cost of living index, based on 1813 price levels.

Source: J. Marshall, *A Digest of All the Accounts*, pp. 36–7; PP 1839 XLIV A return of the amount expended for the relief of the poor in each county of England and Wales during the year ended 25th March.

Over and above the impact of a growing population, other important transformations were taking place that resulted in higher demands for poor relief. Larger numbers of beggars reflected the economic impact of the end of the Napoleonic wars, and the increase in the proportion of the population in receipt of relief between 1803 and 1813–15, largely a function of the growth in the casual poor, hints at this change. By 1818, however, the worst appeared to have passed and the nominal costs of poor relief began to taper off. In real terms, however, this fall was misleading and the cost of relief continued to rise until the early 1820s, before turning sharply upwards as a result of the disastrous financial crisis in 1825. In that year over 70 provincial banks failed within six weeks, prompting a run on London banks which was only halted with difficulty by the intervention of the Bank of England. Throughout London the impact was immediate and profound: construction work slowed, trade stagnated and unemployment rose.[25]

[25] David R. Green, *From Artisans to Paupers: Economic Change and Poverty in London 1790–1870* (Aldershot, 1995), pp. 43–57.

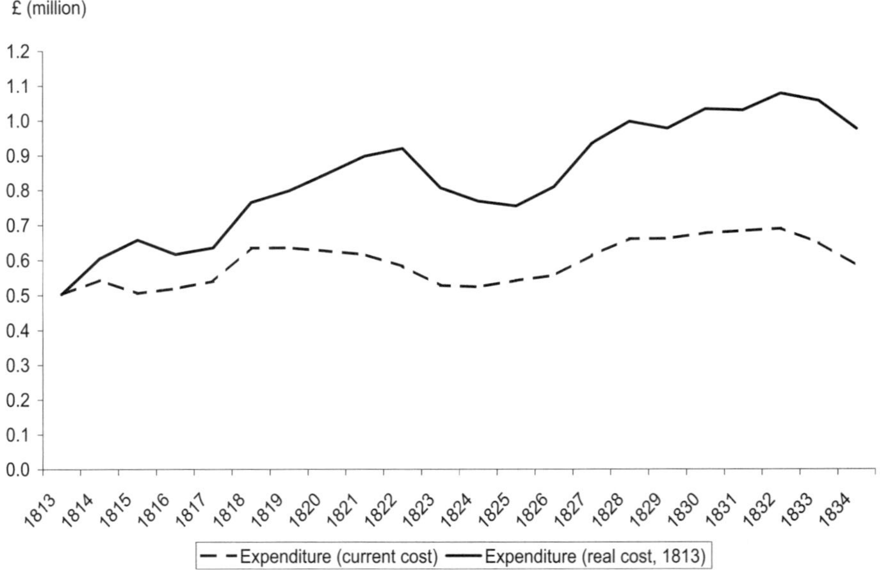

Figure 1.5 Poor Law Expenditure in Middlesex 1813–1834

Note: Nominal prices have been deflated using Feinstein's (1998) cost of living index, based on 1813 price levels.

Source: J. Marshall, *A Digest of All Accounts*, pp. 36–7; PP 1839 XLIV A return of the amount expended for the relief of the poor in each county of England and Wales during the year ended 25th March.

In Spitalfields, where the silk trade was already in structural decline as a result of fierce foreign and provincial competition, distress was acute and by early 1826, 8,600 looms were lying idle, throwing an estimated 30,000 people out of work.[26] Hard pressed ratepayers in Bethnal Green meeting at the workhouse called for a public subscription to supplement an already overstretched relief budget.[27] Elsewhere in the city nearly 1,500 letter press printers were said to have been unemployed and employers everywhere took the opportunity of enforcing wage cuts in a variety of trades.[28] Building activity collapsed and the number of new

[26] *Trades Newspaper and Mechanics Weekly Journal*, 8, 22 January, 5 February, 30 July, 3 September, 8 October 1826. The repeal of the Spitalfields Acts in 1824 removed protection from the London trade and opened it to much higher levels of competition with consequent downward pressure on wages. See Green, *From Artisans to Paupers*, pp. 158–60.

[27] *The Times*, 27 January 1826.

[28] *Trades Newspaper and Mechanics Weekly Journal*, 22 January, 5 February, 30 July, 3 September 1826.

house deeds registered in Middlesex, which had peaked in 1825, started a deep and prolonged decline.[29]

The effects of this downturn were felt throughout the city but particularly in those districts in which large amounts of building were taking place. In St Marylebone, which was the largest parish in London and had the highest annual expenditure on poor relief, the collapse of house building was accompanied by a steep rise in applications for casual relief. There the total number of paupers rose sharply from an average of about 4,000 in the summer of 1825 to over 5,500 by the last quarter of 1826 and over 7,000 in the first quarter of 1827.[30] By the 1830s, the St Marylebone overseers regularly relieved more than 8,000 paupers during the peak winter quarter. The cost of relief in the district also rose accordingly: from just over £37,000 in 1825 to more than £58,000 by 1828. Similar increases were evident in other parishes, including the large eastern districts of Bethnal Green and St George in the East, where expenditure rose by more than 50 per cent between these years.[31]

The rising cost and the relative expense of poor relief focused attention on two related aspects of the city's growth. First, London attracted large numbers of migrants, many of whom would have had settlements elsewhere in the country and as such were not legally entitled to receive permanent relief in the city. Although it was possible to establish new settlements, particularly for women who upon marriage took the settlement of their husband, in practice many of the poor never obtained the legal right to receive permanent relief from a London parish. At the same time, distance from the rest of the country meant that the cost of removing such paupers was relatively high, particularly for groups such as the Irish who in some districts comprised a large proportion of those in need of relief.[32] For that reason, the non-settled poor were often provided with casual relief in the hope that they would either disappear elsewhere or return to their legal places of settlement. At the same time, the close juxtaposition of parishes made it relatively easy for the casual poor to apply for relief to different parishes, sometimes concurrently, and this proved troublesome. Keeping track of casual applicants was a thankless task for hard pressed officials and fraudulent applications for relief appeared to have been relatively common. Partly for that reason, London parishes turned increasingly to indoor relief, which by its very nature tended to be more expensive

[29] Francis Sheppard, Victor Belcher and Philip Cottrell, 'The Middlesex and Yorkshire Deeds Registries and the Study of Building Fluctuations', *London Journal*, 5 (1979): 176–216.

[30] LMA P89/MYR1/517–22 St Marylebone Directors of the Poor, Minutes, 1825–33.

[31] Figures taken from PP 1830–31 XI An account of the money expended for the maintenance and relief of the poor ... for the five years ending 25th March 1825, 1826, 1827, 1828 and 1829.

[32] Until 1819, under the Act to amend the Law for the Relief of the Poor (Select Vestry Act), 59 Geo. III c. 12, Irish could not be removed unless they had committed an act of vagrancy.

than that provided outside the workhouse. London parishes were therefore caught in a dilemma: either pay casual relief and hope that paupers would disappear or turn to the workhouse as a way of detecting imposture.

Indoor relief

Arguably, the most significant difference between London and other regions was the relatively heavy reliance on various forms of indoor relief. Indeed, this was one of the main reasons why the relative costs of the poor law were so high. The proportion of paupers relieved inside the workhouse and the costs of indoor relief for 1803 are shown in Figures 1.6 and 1.7. In that year there were just under 17,000 indoor paupers in Middlesex accounting for over 29 per cent of the total number relieved. This figure represented over one in six indoor paupers in England rising to nearly one in three if the increasingly urbanised counties of neighbouring Surrey and Kent are taken into account.[33] No other county even approached this proportion of indoor paupers. Nor did this pattern alter much in the coming years. Although in relative terms the proportion of the indoor poor in Middlesex fell in 1815 to a little under 47 per cent of the total number relieved, and in Surrey and Kent to 43 and 36 per cent respectively, this was due less to a shift in policy than to the unusually large numbers of casual poor who applied for relief at the end of the Napoleonic wars. In that year there were just over 19,000 indoor poor, excluding children, recorded in London workhouses, which accounted for nearly a quarter of all those relieved in workhouses throughout England and Wales.[34] In this respect, rather than being peripheral to the problems of pauperism under the old poor law, in terms of indoor relief London occupied a central position.[35]

[33] In 1803 Middlesex accounted for 1 in 12 of paupers in receipt of occasional relief and in 1813 1 in 5. Figures for Middlesex refer almost entirely to the county's London parishes.

[34] PP 1818 XIX Abstract of the answers and returns made pursuant to an act intituled 'An act for procuring returns relative to the expense and maintenance of the poor in England.' In 1815 there were 88,186 indoor paupers in England and Wales and 30,525 in Middlesex, Surrey and Kent. See Marshall, *A Digest of All the Accounts*, p. 38.

[35] For a discussion of the workhouse under the old poor law see Timothy Hitchcock, 'The English Workhouse: A Study in Institutional Poor Relief in Selected Counties 1696–1750' (unpublished Ph.D. thesis, University of Oxford, 1985), and James Taylor, 'The Unreformed Workhouse 1776–1834', in E. A. Martin (ed.), *Comparative Development in Social Welfare* (London, 1972), pp. 57–84.

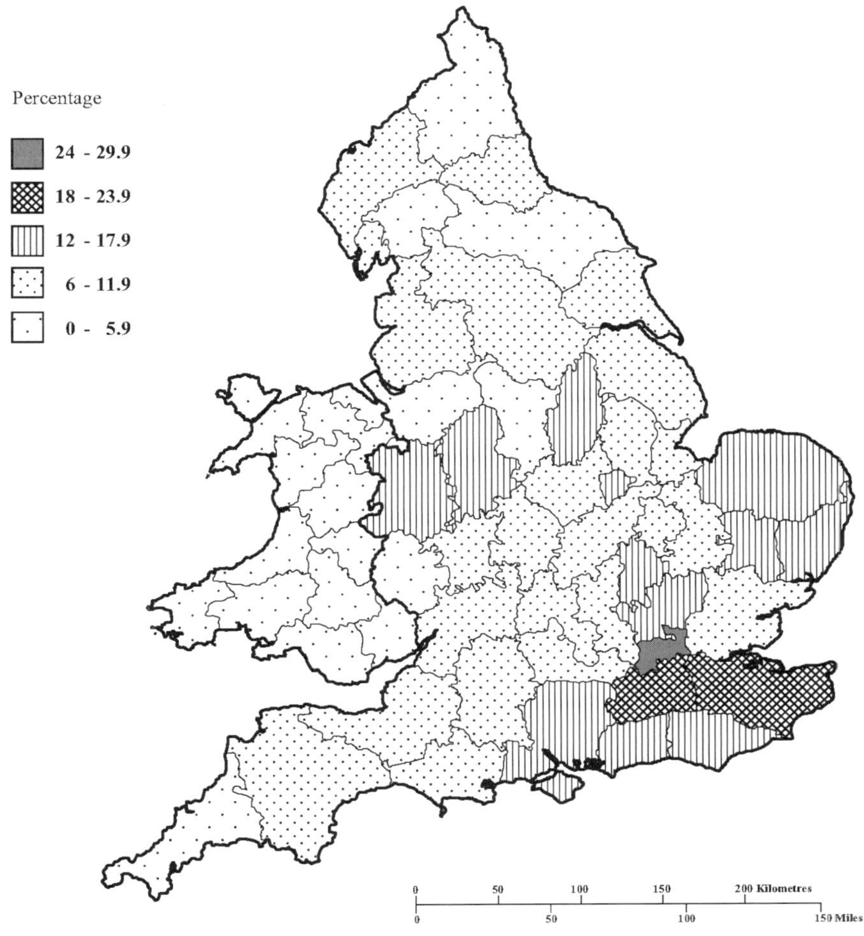

Figure 1.6 Indoor paupers in England and Wales 1803 (% total paupers)

Source: J. Marshall, *A Digest of All the Accounts*, p. 38.

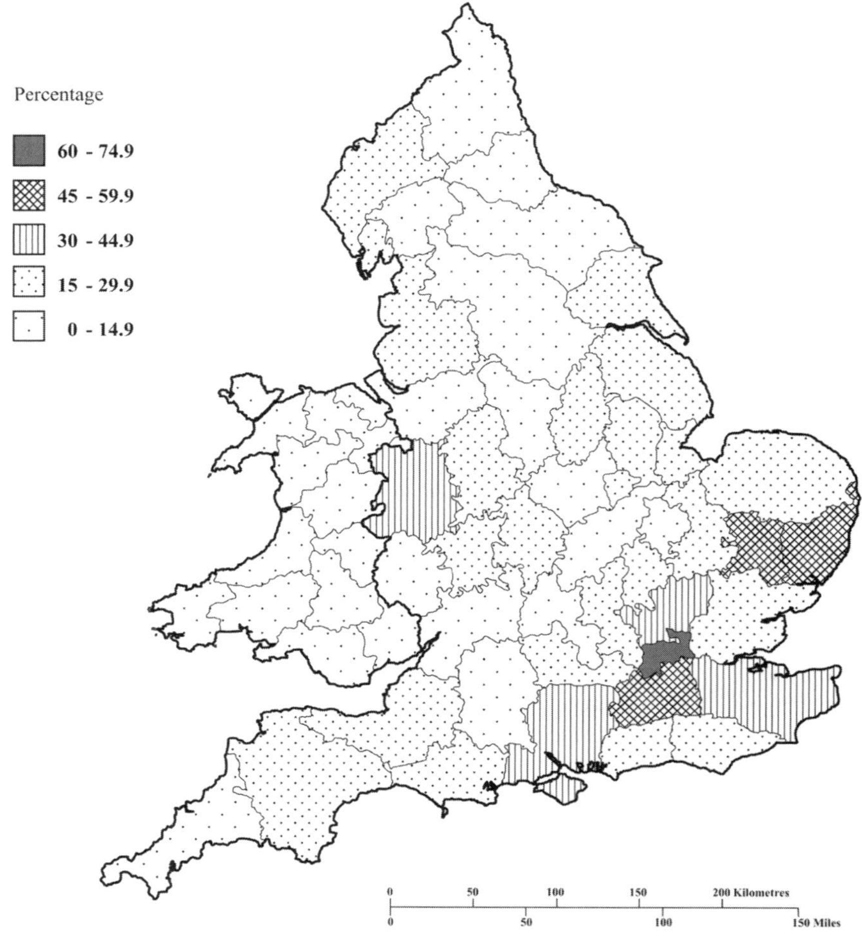

Figure 1.7 Expenditure on indoor relief in England and Wales 1803 (% total relief)

Source: J. Marshall, *A Digest of All the Accounts*, p. 36.

In view of the different costs associated with indoor and outdoor relief, this reliance on institutional provision had clear financial implications. Typically indoor relief was far more costly than providing allowances or occasional relief outside the workhouse: in 1803 annual costs varied from around £12 4s per indoor pauper to £3 4s for the permanent outdoor and occasional poor.[36] Localities relying

[36] These figures reflect the total amount spent on poor relief divided by the numbers relieved inside and outside the workhouse, including the occasional poor. It does not take account of any multiple applications by the occasional poor and is therefore an overestimate

on the workhouse, therefore, were liable to incur much higher costs than those which emphasised outdoor relief. Such was the case in London with metropolitan parishes in Middlesex and Surrey each spending over half their budgets on indoor relief and those in Kent nearly 43 per cent.

Given the fact that indoor relief was so costly the policy in London parishes might have seemed at odds with good economic sense. However, specific sets of circumstances set the city apart. First, London's casual labour market was permanently overstocked and there was no need, therefore, to rely on allowances in aid of wages to maintain a labour force in anticipation of peak seasonal demand, as was the situation in southern agricultural parishes. Furthermore, it would have been foolish for individual parishes to pay outdoor relief to the able-bodied poor since there was no guarantee that paupers supported in one place would necessarily find work in the same locality. Other than casual relief for those in temporary need, therefore, there was little incentive to relieve able-bodied paupers outside the workhouse.

Second, in a large and complex city like London, with high levels of population turnover, it was exceptionally difficult to keep track of those in receipt of outdoor relief and fraudulent claims were not uncommon. Frequent changes of residence coupled with the difficulty and personal discomfort associated with visiting the homes of the poor, made the investigation of paupers' circumstances difficult. The transient habits of the poor were compounded by the temporary nature of the overseers. Those who served as overseers of the poor frequently did so on a voluntary basis and few were keen to carry out the onerous task for longer than a year. One way round this was to employ paid overseers and in the years leading up to 1834 this became more common in London parishes. Another way, however, was to restrict outdoor relief and to use the workhouse as a test for destitution – a course of action that became enshrined in national poor law policy after 1834. Some parishes were evidently using the workhouse in this way at an early stage and as costs began to mount in the 1820s so more places adopted stricter indoor regimes.[37] Given these circumstances, the workhouse appeared to be a pragmatic and efficient way of dealing with some of the specific problems of metropolitan pauperism.

Casual relief and the non-settled poor

One of the major difficulties facing overseers of the poor in London was how to deal with the poor who did not have a legal settlement in the city. The extent of the problem was significant: at the start of the nineteenth century perhaps as much as

---

of the likely total number of persons. The figures refer to England and are taken from J. Marshall, *A Digest of All the Accounts*.

[37] See, for example, John Leslie, *Remarks on the Present State of the Poor Law Question with Illustrations of the Advantages Arising for the Poor by Means of the Workhouse System of Relief* (London, 1834).

a third or more of the city's population was born outside London, a large number of which came from surrounding agricultural counties and many of whom would not have a settlement in the city.[38] The letters written by non-resident paupers in London who had settlements in Essex parishes, testifies to the importance of this group in the capital.[39] Where a pauper had spent the previous night in a parish, the overseers were obliged to provide some casual relief.[40] In the event of repeated applications for relief, parishes could bring a charge of vagrancy and if the pauper was convicted, the costs of removal were then borne by the county.[41]

It was usually cheaper to provide some form of temporary handout for these casual paupers than to order indoor relief or seek their removal, at least until their legal entitlement could be determined. This kind of assistance could amount to little more than a night's lodging in the workhouse or a small amount of food or money, sometimes with a stipulation to move elsewhere. Under these circumstances, officials were forced to tread a cautious line between providing niggardly amounts of assistance on the one hand and using threats and compulsion on the other to encourage paupers to try their luck elsewhere. In Spitalfields, for example, William Hale, treasurer to the governors of the poor, noted how the normal practice was to offer unemployed applicants a small sum for two or three weeks during which time the overseers would make investigations and if necessary would try to provide work inside the workhouse.[42] In some cases bribery was used as well as coercion. William Bodkin, secretary to the Mendicity Society, claimed that London overseers sometimes paid paupers 6d or 1s to move into another parish rather than become chargeable to their own.[43] With so many contiguous parishes in London, this was a relatively simple though questionable strategy for dealing with the poor.

---

[38] Between 1781 and 1831 about 773,000 people migrated from southern counties. See Phyllis Deane and W. A. Cole, *British Economic Growth 1688–1959* (Cambridge, 1969), p. 118. In 1851, migrants comprised 38.3 per cent of London's population. See H. A. Shannon, 'Migration and the Growth of London, 1841–91: A Statistical Note', *Economic History Review*, 5 (1935): 81.

[39] See Thomas Sokoll, *Essex Pauper Letters 1731–1837* (Oxford, 2001).

[40] The casual poor were usually defined as those poor without a settlement who were in need of temporary relief. See Paul F. Aschrott, *The English Poor Law System: Past and Present* (London, 1888, reprinted 2006), p. 250; M. Dorothy George, *London Life in the Eighteenth Century* (Harmondsworth, 1966), p. 220.

[41] See Nicholas Rogers, 'Policing the Poor in Eighteenth-Century London: The Vagrancy Laws and Their Administration', *Histoire Sociale-Social History*, 24 (1991): 138.

[42] PP 1828 IV Select committee on that part of the poor laws relating to the employment or relief of able-bodied persons from the poor rate, p. 169.

[43] Ibid., p. 18.

Estimating the extent of casual pauperism in London is difficult and prior to 1834 figures on the number of non-settled poor need to be interpreted with caution.[44] Counts in 1803 and between 1813 and 1815 allow some comparison, although the former referred to non-parishioners only and the latter to the occasional poor, some of whom may have been settled in the parish. As Figure 1.8 shows, in 1803 nearly half the total number of paupers in Middlesex and Kent, and more than 60 per cent in Surrey, received casual relief. Between 1813 and 1815, as illustrated in Figure 1.9, the proportion was over 70 per cent. To some extent, the discrepancy between the two sets of figures can be accounted for by the different groups to which the evidence refers, although the end of the Napoleonic wars and resulting discharge of large numbers of men in the armed forces had an immediate impact on the numbers of beggars in the London streets and must also have swelled the ranks of non-settled paupers. Both sets of figures, however, point to the significance of the casual poor in London compared to counties elsewhere.

The largest and most conspicuous group of the casual poor was the Irish, who until 1819 could not be removed from the parish in which they applied for relief. The proportion in any one district varied but overall they usually comprised between about a third and a sixth of the total relieved.[45] A survey of the Irish poor in 1815 found that there were 6,876 adults and 7,288 children in London, which, if the figures are correct, would have been about one in six of the total non-settled poor relieved in the city in that year.[46] In some districts, the proportion was considerably higher: the survey noted that 1,210 adult Irish poor, representing over one in five of the total, resided in St Giles and nearly two thirds of expenditure in that district went towards their support.[47] Only the fear of being removed as a vagrant, it was said, helped to keep down the number of Irish applicants, though at the same time it increased the likelihood that they would be forced to beg.[48] Perhaps for that reason, in the immediate post-war years, nearly one third of beggars relieved by the Mendicity Society were Irish.[49]

---

44 Given the ease with which paupers sometimes obtained relief from more than one district, repeated applications by the same individual to different poor law authorities were counted as separate applications and therefore the real number of non-settled poor may have been lower than the number of reported applications.

45 In 1851 the Irish born comprised 4.6 per cent of London's population.

46 The survey comes from PP 1814–15 III Select committee on the state of mendicity in the metropolis, p. 325.

47 Ibid., pp. 284, 325.

48 Ibid., pp. 240, 283.

49 Society for the Suppression of Mendicity, Second Annual Report (London, 1819), p. 3. Of the 4,682 cases registered in that year, 1,561 appeared to be Irish.

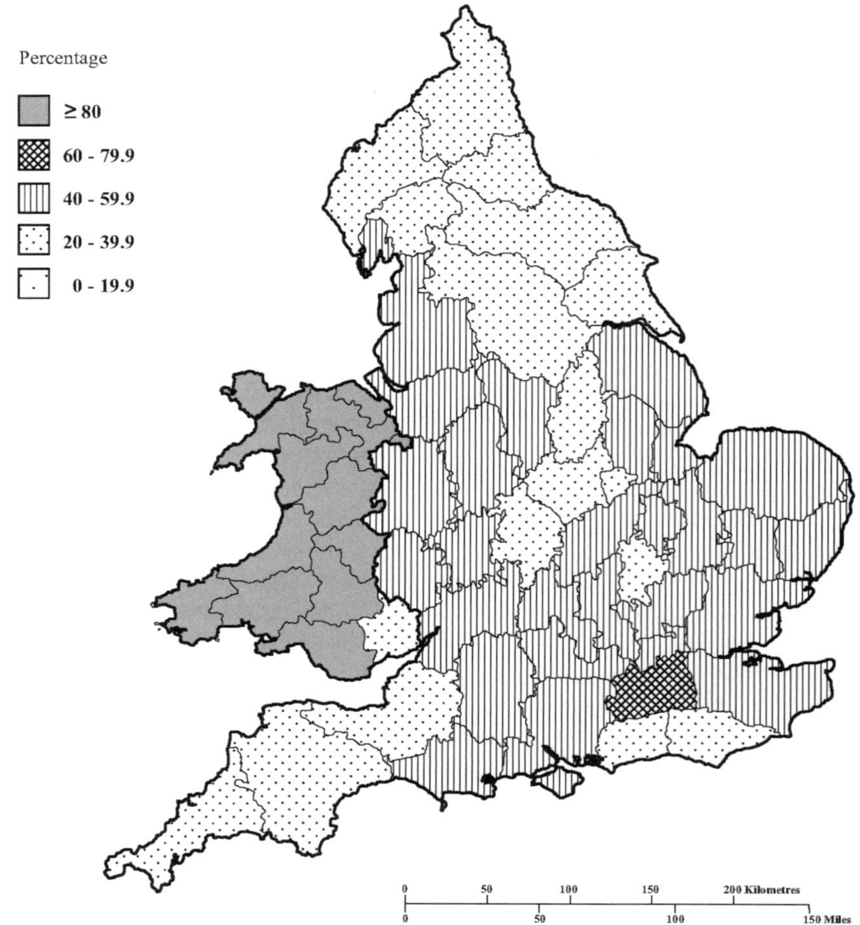

Figure 1.8 Non-parishioners relieved in England and Wales 1803 (% total paupers)

Source: J. Marshall, *A Digest of All the Accounts*, p. 36.

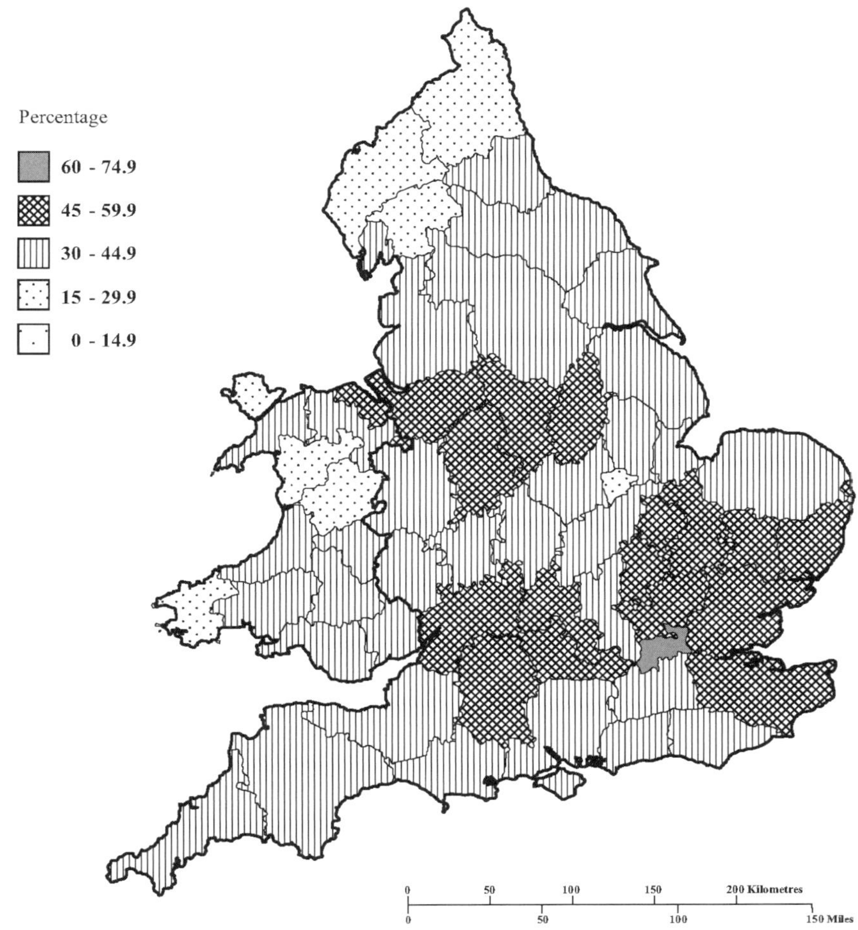

Figure 1.9 Occasional paupers relieved in England and Wales, 1813–1815 (% total paupers)

Source: J. Marshall, *A Digest of All the Accounts*, p. 34.

After 1819, Irish paupers could be returned back to their place of settlement, but when this threat of removal was withdrawn, such as in 1826 when the Irish removal order was temporarily suspended, parishes found themselves inundated with requests for relief. In St Marylebone, for example, in December of that year over 1,100 Irish applied for relief.[50] When the issue again arose during the Royal

[50] LMA P89/MYR1/518 St Marylebone Directors of the Poor, Minutes, 29 December 1826.

Commission's investigations into the poor laws, Edward Church, vestry clerk to Norton Folgate in the City, noted that 'If the Act passes to prevent Irish paupers or labourers from being removed, the system of the poor laws in many parishes cannot last twelve months. Nothing but the fear of removal keeps them in order and the out-parishes from utter ruin.'[51]

If bribery and coercion failed, and harsh treatment did not deter the non-settled poor, removal remained a last resort. However, with the grounds of settlement difficult to prove and commonly disputed, parishes not surprisingly sought other quasi-legal means to rid themselves of the burden. The most common way of doing so was through 'friendly orders' which were agreements between sets of parishes to accept removals without the need to make detailed and often costly enquiries about the pauper's settlement. At the start of the century, for example, Christchurch, Spitalfields operated such friendly orders with the neighbouring parishes of Mile End, Bethnal Green, Shoreditch, Bishopsgate and Whitechapel and similar practices operated elsewhere.[52]

The alternative to these friendly orders was for overseers to apply to a magistrate for an order of removal and although in the early years of the century between 12,000 and 13,000 paupers were passed annually from Middlesex, in general most parishes tried to avoid this course of action unless absolutely necessary.[53] An indication of that reluctance is the fact that typically London parishes spent relatively little on legal and removal expenses compared to the rest of the country. Between 1813 and 1815, for example, Middlesex parishes spent approximately 4.5 per cent of the total maintenance of the poor on legal expenses and removals compared to 7.7 per cent for England and Wales as a whole.[54] The question that arises, therefore, is why London parishes appeared reluctant to use removals as a way of ridding themselves of the relatively large number of non-settled poor.

Three answers to this question arise. The first concerns the relatively high cost of removals from London; the second relates to the extent to which alternative approaches to dealing with the casual poor made removals unnecessary, and the third takes note of the way in which removals themselves were carried out. In terms of the first, removals were costly, time consuming and open to dispute. Even

---

51 PP 1834 XXXV Royal commission on the administration and practical operation of the poor laws, answers to town queries, Norton Folgate, q. 42; St Leonard Shoreditch, q. 42.

52 PP 1817 VI Select committee to consider the poor laws, p. 32. Walking passes were also issued by magistrates which allowed the respectable poor to travel through a parish without being molested by officials keen to move on anyone who threatened to fall on the rates. Ibid., 37–8.

53 PP 1814–15 III Select committee on the state of mendicity in the metropolis, pp. 289–91.

54 PP 1818 XIX Abstract of answers relative to the expense and maintenance of the poor. Question 4 referred to the amount of expenditure 'in suits of law, removals, journeys, and expenses of overseers and other officers'.

if a pauper could remember his or her settlement, the grounds for establishing its legality were often surrounded by confusion and the laws so complicated that, according to Francis Coster, churchwarden of St Mary le Strand, they were 'seldome to be understood by officers'.[55] Whilst it was possible for individuals to gain a settlement other than by birth or marriage, notably by apprenticeship, hiring or rental, the opportunities for acquiring the rights to relief through these routes were increasingly curtailed in London and elsewhere during these years.[56] The decline of apprenticeship, for example, reduced one important route for male settlement, which in turn had an impact on women since on marriage they took the settlement of their husbands.[57] Similarly, annual hiring was of little importance in London where most contracts of employment were for shorter periods. Perhaps the most important route for establishing a settlement in London, other than by birth or parentage, was rental of property to the value of £10 a year. This was of particular significance in eastern and southern districts where working-class housing was more readily available.[58] However, establishing the precise rent and dates of residence were fraught with uncertainty, often relying on the faulty memory of paupers and landlords. Under such arrangements, confusion was the norm and disputes between parishes keen to contest the bill for relief were commonplace.

Geography also counted against metropolitan parishes. London lay at a distance from much of the country and the cost of removals was therefore relatively high. Patrick Colquhoun, who as a magistrate was in a good position to know the problems first hand, noted how removals to the west country and north of the Trent were rare on account of their expense, a view also echoed by John Leigh, clerk to the St George Hanover Square directors of the poor.[59] Nor were the time and expense spent on removal necessarily effective. In Middlesex the process of removing the non-settled poor and vagrants was organised through pass masters who contracted to convey them beyond the county borders. In 1821 the pass master for Middlesex, William Davis, received £350 for his services, from which he was to pay the cost of keeping the paupers for up to three days and all other expenses. Paupers were taken by wagon in the morning to one of the four houses he kept just beyond the county borders, at Cheshunt, Egham, Colnbrook and Ridge.[60] However, once the county border had been crossed those who did not

55 PP 1834 XXXV Royal commission on the administration and practical operation of the poor laws, answers to town queries, St Mary Le Strand, q. 14.

56 See Norma Landau, 'The Regulation of Immigration, Economic Structures and Definitions of the Poor in Eighteenth-Century England', *Historical Journal*, 33 (1990): 566–7.

57 See Green, *From Artisans to Paupers*, pp. 122–5.

58 See PP 1817 VI Select committee to consider the poor laws, p. 35; PP 1818 V Select committee to consider the poor laws, p. 175.

59 PP 1814–15 III Select committee on the state of mendicity in the metropolis, p. 285; PP 1817 VI Select committee to consider the poor laws, p. 64.

60 PP 1821 IV Select committee on existing laws relating to vagrants, pp. 21, 26–7.

wish to continue were apparently free to leave, with the result that many merely returned to the city to resume begging.[61] Davis remarked how he would sometimes pass the same person five or six times a year.[62] It is hardly surprising, given the questionable efficacy and the potentially large costs, that removals were therefore seen as a last resort.

Conclusion

In London at the start of the nineteenth century the problem of casual pauperism and begging came to dominate debates about poor relief. Although some individuals, such as the magistrate Sir Nathanial Conant, cast doubt on whether or not the number of beggars was rising, the general view was that the problem appeared to be growing.[63] Patrick Colquhoun estimated in 1797 that there were at least 3,000 beggars in the city, but this was seen as a gross underestimate by Matthew Martin, whose own survey of begging was based on detailing the life histories of some 2,000 adults with 3,000 dependent children. Martin believed that the correct number of beggars was at least double this number, and that if children were included the true total was over 15,000 beggars on the capital's streets.[64] Difficult economic conditions after the war with France merely exacerbated the situation. The parliamentary select committee appointed in 1814 to enquire into mendicity in London heard evidence about the apparently easy money to be made by beggars. Stories about the innumerable cadges to dupe the public and beggars grown wealthy on misplaced generosity were paraded by witnesses eager to demonstrate the inducements to idleness that existed in the city. Although such claims were ridiculed by those with most knowledge, nevertheless they had some resonance with public opinion. The select committee's report reflected the view that considerable profits were to be made by beggars, 'the success of which affords a direct encouragement to vice, idleness and profligacy'.[65]

Against this background explanations for the apparent increase in begging reflected a new and more condemnatory attitude towards poverty that had been emerging in the context of debates about poor law reform. Images of the poor, as Vic Gatrell has so perceptively noted, shifted in these years away from more sympathetic representations of the congeniality and fraternity of beggars towards

---

61 Ibid., p. 32.

62 Ibid., p. 27.

63 PP 1814–15 III Select committee on the state of mendicity in the metropolis, p. 271.

64 Patrick Colquhoun, *A Treatise on the Police of the Metropolis* (London, 1797), p. xi; Matthew Martin, *Report on Mendicity in London* (1803) British Museum, Pelham Papers, Additional Manuscript MS 33111, folio 5. See Tim Hitchcock, *Down and Out in Eighteenth-Century London* (London, 2007), pp. 3–7.

65 PP 1816 V Select committee on the state of mendicity in the metropolis, p. 393.

a more discipline-minded moralism in which criminality and deception were the key motifs.[66] As pathos, sympathy and charity were replaced by harsher attitudes, so policies to deal with the poor shifted. Just as Malthus and others argued against poor relief and charity as a way of tackling rural pauperism, so urban commentators followed suit. Colquhoun himself in a later edition of the *Treatise on the Police of the Metropolis* argued against any increase in charity or poor relief as a way of dealing with the problem.

> It is not pecuniary aid that will heal this *gangrene*: this *Corruption of Morals*. There must be the application of a correct System of Police calculated to reach the root and origin of the evil. Without *System, Intelligence, Talents, and Industry* united in all that relates to the affairs of the Poor, millions may be wasted as millions have already been wasted, without bettering their condition.[67]

Police, of course, meant more than just patrolling the streets, although this was part of the changes invoked. Stricter attention to a more preventative policy of policing took place in the City of London, where it was claimed officers had been as 'strict in looking after beggars as street thieves'.[68] More importantly, policing meant surveillance and control, and in this respect the foundation of the London Society for the Suppression of Mendicity in 1818 and the subsequent tightening of the various vagrancy acts in the following years, were significant elements in a more carceral and punitive approach to the problems of poverty.[69]

The control and suppression of begging, however, was not the only weapon in the arsenal against idleness. Overseers of the poor turned towards stricter deterrent practices that included a growing emphasis on indoor relief coupled with a tightening of the workhouse regime. Useful forms of work, for example, such as making and repairing clothing, was replaced by task work, such as picking oakum, which was both demeaning and economically worthless.[70] Dietaries were

---

66 Victor Gatrell, *The City of Laughter: Sex and Satire in Eighteenth-Century London* (London, 2006), pp. 559–69.

67 Patrick Colquhoun, *A Treatise on the Police of the Metropolis* (London, 1806, 7th edition), p. 358.

68 PP 1814–15 III Select committee on the state of mendicity in the metropolis, p. 252.

69 John Marriott and Masaie Matsumura (eds), *The Metropolitan Poor: Semi-Factual Accounts* (London, 1999), vol. 1, pp. xv–xxii ; M. J. Roberts, 'Public and Private in Early Nineteenth-Century London: The Vagrant Act of 1822 and its Enforcement', *Social History*, 13 (1988): 273–94; M. J. Roberts, 'Reshaping the Gift Relationship: The London Mendicity Society and the Suppression of Begging in England', *International Review of Social History*, 36 (1991): 201–31; Nicholas Rogers, 'Policing the Poor in Eighteenth-Century London: The Vagrancy Laws and their Administration', *Histoire Sociale-Social History*, 24 (1991): 127–41.

70 Peter Mandler, 'The Making of the New Poor Law *Redivivus*', *Past and Present*, 117 (1987): 141–2.

reduced and discipline tightened. Through such deterrent policies officials sought to control the rising number of paupers that beat a path to their door and in doing so the workhouse assumed greater importance.

Chapter 2
Metropolitan Geographies of Pauperism: The Old Poor Law

The urban poor law

The system of poor relief in eighteenth-century London, as Tim Hitchcock has remarked, was 'extensive, expensive and remarkably comprehensive'.[1] It addition to the workhouse, it comprised a variety of other institutions and sources of help that collectively provided a set of essential resources for the poor. To understand how this system developed and changed, however, requires an awareness of the role played by the quintessentially urban characteristics of proximity, density and difference.

Rapid population growth meant larger numbers of poor and this tested the capacity of parishes to make adequate provision for relief. Urban growth also sucked in large numbers of migrants which in turn generated distinct problems regarding the legality of claims for assistance from the poor law. Meanwhile, changing residential patterns, notably the movement of population from central areas to new suburbs, meant that balancing rate income with the demand for relief was in constant flux. As a result, significant differences in poor law practices existed between parishes that were sometimes in close proximity. This proximity in turn provided opportunities both for overseers keen to shift the burden of support elsewhere and for paupers willing to try their luck in several different places at once. At the same time, the large number of poor and proximity of parishes provided opportunities to develop specialist institutions for particular groups of paupers. This unique set of demographic and social characteristics underpinned a distinctive metropolitan geography of pauperism, which is the focus of the current chapter.

---

1 Tim Hitchcock, *Down and Out in Eighteenth-Century London* (London, 2007), p. 132.

Population growth, social change and the rights to poor relief

In the first half of the century, London experienced massive growth and urban change. The population increased from just under a million in 1801 to 1.9 million by 1841. In that year London was nearly double the size of the next five largest cities in the United Kingdom combined and several of its parishes, including St Pancras and St Marylebone, were as large as places such as Leeds or Bristol. The extent of growth, however, varied significantly between districts. Figure 2.1 and Table 2.1 show that as warehouses and commercial premises squeezed out housing, the City itself began to lose population. Between 1801 and 1841, City parishes within the walls lost over 2,000 houses and their population fell from 75,377 to 54,626.[2] Meanwhile, parishes immediately surrounding the City grew but at a relatively slow pace compared to newer suburban areas, particularly those in the north and east, which experienced the most rapid rates of increase. Such growth meant, on the one hand, that some parishes had little or no incentive to construct or enlarge new workhouses, whilst in others the need was more pressing.

Table 2.1 Share of population growth in London by region 1801–1841

	Population growth 1801–1841	**Percentage share 1801–1841**
West	149,659	15.2
North	251,463	25.5
Central	84,296	8.6
City	-4,116	-0.4
East	213,809	21.7
Inner South	93,976	9.5
Outer South	196,427	19.9

Note: for regional groupings see Figure 2.1

Source: R. Price Williams, 'The Population of London, 1801–1881', *Journal of the Statistical Society*, 48 (1885): 349–432.

2 The figures are taken from the census abstracts for each year.

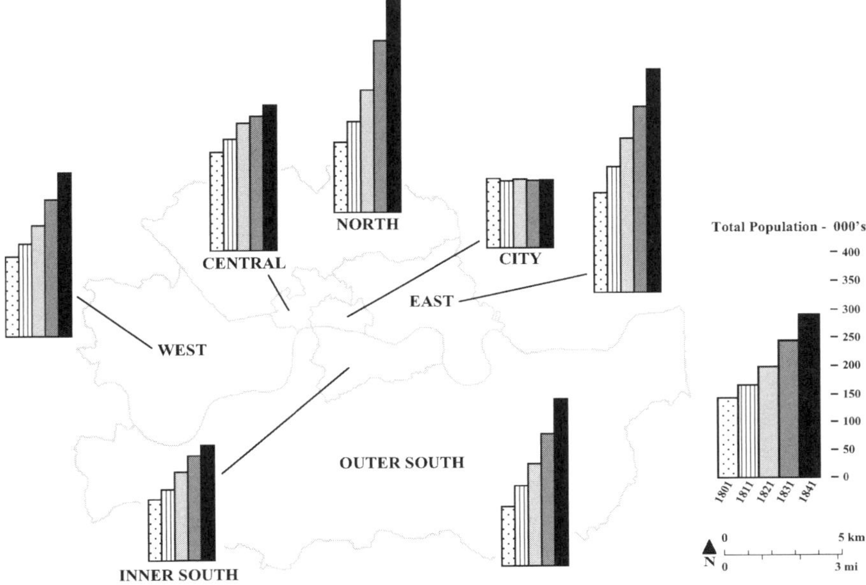

Figure 2.1 Population growth in London regions 1801–1841

Note: The geographical division of London is based on the 36 registration districts contained in the 1851 census. See Appendix 1.
West: Chelsea, Kensington, St George Hanover Square, St James Westminster, St John and St Margaret, St Martin in the Fields.
North: Hackney, Hampstead, Islington, St Marylebone, St Pancras.
Central: Clerkenwell, Holborn, St Giles, St Luke, Strand.
City: City of London, East London, West London.
East: Bethnal Green, Poplar, Shoreditch, Stepney, St George in the East, Whitechapel.
Inner South: Bermondsey, Newington, Rotherhithe, St George Southwark, St Olave Southwark, St Saviour Southwark,
Outer South: Camberwell, Greenwich, Lambeth, Lewisham, Wandsworth.
Source: R. Price Williams, 'The Population of London, 1801–1881', pp. 349–432.

Although demographic growth *per se* necessitated changes in poor law provision, the shift in social composition of districts was if anything more important in directing the way in which policies were forced to adapt. From at least the middle of the eighteenth century wealthy families had begun to move away from the overcrowded and insanitary inner parishes westwards into new aristocratic estates.[3] Even within the City itself, significant social differences had emerged by

[3] See John Summerson, *Georgian London* (London, 1945), p. 146.

the start of the nineteenth century that, according to some, necessitated spreading the cost of relief between richer and poor parishes.[4] Although the City retained a core of high status households, by the early decades of the nineteenth century the balance of wealth had clearly shifted westwards.[5] As D. M. Evans remarked a few years later in 1845, 'A dwelling in the City is a thing not now considered desirable – all move either towards the west, or emigrate to the suburbs – the one for fashion, the other for economy and fresh air.'[6]

In the wake of this middle-class migration, City parishes were left with a scattering of tradesmen together with large numbers of casual labourers, carmen, porters, hawkers, Jewish pedlars and 'people who do not know, when they rise in the morning, by what chance jobs in the streets or the markets they are to get food for the day'.[7] The poor were also squeezed out into the surrounding districts, notably to the east, which absorbed the brunt of this transformation. In Shoreditch, for example, the number of houses more than doubled between 1801 and 1831 and in Bethnal Green it nearly trebled.[8] The exodus of wealth was less marked in these districts compared to the City, there being fewer middle-class families in the first place, but even here suburban flight had commenced by the 1840s, leaving in its wake a mass of the poor that periodically threatened to overwhelm the capacity of both philanthropy and the poor law to provide adequate relief during times of crisis.

In relation to the poor law there were two main issues: first, those moving into eastern districts were themselves relatively poor, and second, the new population would be able to gain a settlement and therefore would become entitled to receive poor relief. The vestry clerk in Bethnal Green, for example, was fully aware of this when he complained to the Royal Commission on the Poor Laws that the parish was encumbered with too many paupers on account of the number of small houses that had been built and inmigration of the poor from surrounding areas.[9]

---

4 See for example George Stonestreet, *Domestic Union; or London as it should be!! Containing Observations on the Present State of the Municipality of London* (London, 1800), pp. 24–5. See also Patrick Colquhoun, *The State of Indigence and the Situation of the Casual Poor in the Metropolis* (London, 1799), p. 30.

5 Leonard Schwarz, 'Social Class and Social Geography: The Middle Classes in London at the end of the Eighteenth Century', *Social History*, 7 (1982): 172.

6 D. M. Evans, *The City, or the Physiology of London Business* (London, 1845), p. 190.

7 Joseph Fletcher, 'The Metropolis: Its Boundaries, Extent and Divisions for Local Government', *Journal of the Statistical Society*, 7 (1844): 70.

8 The number of houses is taken from the 1801 and 1831 census abstracts for Middlesex parishes. In 1801 the number of inhabited houses in Bethnal Green was 3,586 and by 1831 it had risen to 10, 877. In Shoreditch the figures were 5,752 in 1801 and 10,698 by 1831.

9 PP 1834 XXXV Royal commission on the administration and practical operation of the poor laws, answers to town queries, St Matthew Bethnal Green, evidence of R. Brutton, q. 30.

In terms of poor relief, this pattern of movement in itself was not a problem provided that parishes continued to support their non-resident paupers irrespective of where they lived. Such arrangements, which had no legal status but were maintained for mutual convenience, allowed paupers living in another parish to receive relief from their place of settlement. This system was important, not just in northern manufacturing areas where it appeared to be part of a set of arrangements to ensure the availability of an industrial labour force, but also in London.[10] However, where individuals acquired another settlement responsibility was passed to the new parish. The issue was how and where such settlements could be made.

The grounds for establishing a settlement other than by birth and, for women, marriage were complex and frequently rested on half remembered facts that could stretch back over many years.[11] Rental of property and apprenticeship were two important ways of obtaining a settlement and in London such routes were common. Overseers often took this opportunity to apprentice children to cotton mills and manufacturers in northern and midland counties.[12] But restrictions introduced in 1816 prevented apprenticing children more than 40 miles from London and this had the effect of throwing the problem back onto metropolitan parishes. Overseers keen to shift long term responsibility for their own pauper children therefore had to find alternative sources of apprenticeship, and this increasingly involved binding the children to employers in traditional London trades such as clothing, shoemaking and silk weaving. This was particularly prevalent in the cheaper branches of production that were typically found in eastern districts, and overseers in those places were quite rightly suspicious that other parishes were using this route as an opportunity to rid themselves of potential long term drains on their own finances.[13]

---

10 See George Boyer, *An Economic History of the English Poor Law 1750–1850* (Cambridge, 1990), pp. 233–64; James Taylor, 'A Different Kind of Speenhamland: Nonresident Relief in the Industrial Revolution', *Journal of British Studies*, 30 (1991): 183–208.

11 The literature on settlements is voluminous. See, for example, David Feldman, 'Migrants, Immigrants and Welfare from the Old Poor Paw to the Welfare State', *Transactions of the Royal Historical Society*, 13 (2003): 79–104; Keith Snell, 'Pauper Settlement and Poor Relief', *Continuity and Change*, 6 (1991): 375–415; James Taylor, 'The Impact of Pauper Settlement 1691–1834', *Past and Present*, 73 (1976): 42–73; James Taylor, *Poverty, Migration and Settlement in the Industrial Revolution* (Palo Alto, 1989).

12 For an account of this experience see John Brown, *A Memoir of Robert Blincoe, an Orphan Boy; Sent ... to Endure the Horrors of a Cotton-Mill*, (Manchester, 1832, reprinted Firle, 1977).

13 For further discussion see M. Dorothy George, *London Life in the Eighteenth Century* (Harmondsworth, 1966), pp. 213–61. For the geography of production and the growth of cheaper production in eastern districts see David R. Green, *From Artisans to Paupers: Economic Change and Poverty in London 1790–1870* (Aldershot, 1995), pp. 140–80. The Poor Law Commissioners disliked apprenticing pauper children and from 1844 preferred poor law unions to provide industrial training themselves.

The other main route by which to establish a settlement was rental of property and here the geography of house building had an important role to play, particularly in eastern districts. In these parishes the main problem was the large number of poor who were able to gain a settlement by virtue of renting property worth £10 a year for a period of 40 days, equivalent to about four shillings a week.[14] The period of rental was increased in 1819 to a full year and two further acts were passed in 1825 and 1830 to clarify the requirements, although, as George Nicholls remarked, the necessity of passing three acts in the space of 12 years was evidence of 'the difficulties and intricacies with which the question in all its branches is beset'.[15] However, despite these problems, any district with large amounts of cheap housing was always likely to attract poor residents who, through rental for a year, were then eligible to claim relief. In Spitalfields, for example, according to John Heaver, one of the parish overseers, the majority of paupers had gained a settlement in this way.[16]

Figures for the assessed rental value of property in 1830, outlined in Figure 2.2, clearly show the overwhelming significance of such housing in districts bordering the City to the east and south, and therefore the potential for gaining a settlement by this route. In the Tower division, which consisted of all the districts to the east of the City stretching from Shoreditch and Hackney to Poplar, houses valued at between £10 and £20 comprised over 48 per cent of the total number assessed for house duty, compared to 25 per cent in Finsbury and 18 per cent in Holborn to the west. The poorest quality housing in Bethnal Green was described by Hector Gavin in 1848 who noted how many of the properties were wooden shacks 'altogether unadapted to any other purpose than the most temporary protection from the inclemency of the weather' with privies little more than holes dug in the ground.[17] In Southwark cheap housing also predominated with over 43 per cent of the assessed housing stock valued at below £20. The situation was completely different in more affluent western districts such as Marylebone and Westminster, where the majority of housing was valued at above £40. It was far more difficult for the working class to afford to live in these places and as such there were relatively few paupers able to claim a settlement by renting.

In this way, the changing social and economic geography of London was profoundly important in understanding the pattern of poor relief in the early decades of the nineteenth century. In several places social change unhinged the balance between rich and poor making some districts, notably those in the east into which the poor had moved, particularly vulnerable to large increases in the

---

14 Richard Burn, *The Justice of the Peace, and Parish Officer* (London, 1800), p. 642.

15 George Nicholls, *A History of the English Poor Law* (London, 1898), vol. 2, pp. 188–9, 198–9.

16 PP 1817 VI Select committee to consider the poor laws, p. 35.

17 Hector Gavin, *Sanitary Ramblings, Being Sketches and Illustrations of Bethnal Green* (London, 1848), p. 12.

demand for relief. This change, coupled with harsher attitudes towards the poor, focused attention on the workhouse as a test of pauperism. In these parishes the main question was not whether but how large to build a workhouse. To make this decision, the vestry had to judge the current and likely future demand for space based on the size of the population. With little or no accurate information, and with such rapid rates of change, these decisions were always difficult to make. But unless workhouse capacity increased in line with population growth, overseers were at risk of having to rely more on outdoor relief at a time when the balance of opinion was shifting decisively against this kind of assistance. How parishes coped with this situation is the focus of the remainder of the chapter.

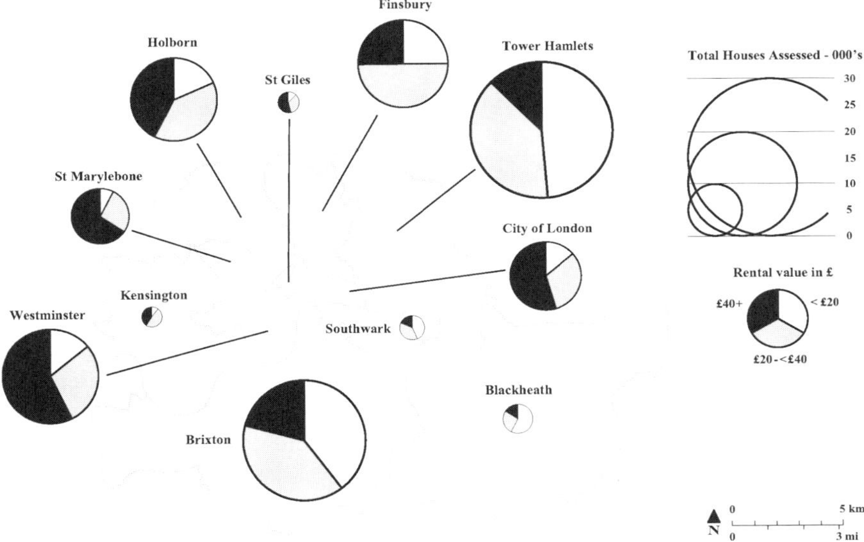

Figure 2.2 House Duty in London 1830

Source: J. Marshall, *A Digest of All the Accounts*, pp. 42–3, Houses assessed to house duty in the year ending 5 April 1830.

Indoor relief: workhouses and pauper farms

The policy of providing indoor relief relied on having sufficient workhouse accommodation and in this respect London was relatively well served compared to the rest of the country. Following Knatchbull's Act of 1723 many parishes across England and Wales were able to combine in order to build a workhouse. Across the country some 300 new parish workhouses had been built by 1732 and another 300 by 1750.[18]

An Account of the Work-houses in Great Britain, first published in 1725 but re-issued in 1732 and again in 1786, provides detailed descriptions of many of these new workhouses, including those built in London. Whilst some workhouses in the city had been converted from existing houses, several others had been enlarged or purpose built. Following the Great Fire of 1666, new building had taken place mainly in those districts which had expanded rapidly, notably surrounding the City. The *Account* made a point of noting that many of these new buildings were made from brick, including the workhouses for St Botolph without Bishopsgate, St Giles Cripplegate, St James Clerkenwell, St James Westminster, St Mary Lambeth and St Andrew Saffron Hill.[19] The new St George Hanover Square workhouse in Mount Street, for example, which was opened in 1726, was a substantial three storey building, about 170 feet long and topped with a graceful cupola.[20] Neighbouring parishes also had large workhouses: in St Giles, the new workhouse built in 1725 regularly contained between 250 and 300 persons, depending on the season. The workhouses in St James Westminster, St Margaret Westminster and St Martin in the Fields were of similar size, each with space for more than 300 inmates. New workhouses were also constructed south of the river. In Lambeth, a 'large new Brickhouse' was opened in 1726 with space for 60 persons, whilst a similar size building was also erected in St George Southwark a few years later.[21] Indeed, by the early 1730s all the Southwark parishes with the exception of St Thomas had built large workhouses. By that time there were at least 48 workhouses and charity schools in London that collectively could accommodate several thousand persons.

Despite construction of these new workhouses, rapid population growth in the second half of the eighteenth century soon outpaced capacity. The St George Hanover Square workhouse, which initially could accommodate 250 paupers, had to be enlarged in 1743 and again in 1772, when as many as 600 inmates were housed. In St Marylebone rapid growth meant that the workhouse which had been built in 1752 soon proved inadequate. By 1772, 220 inmates were occupying accommodation designed for 40 and although additional storeys

---

[18] Act for Amending the Laws Relating to the Settlement, Employment, and Relief of the Poor (Knatchbull's Act), 9 Geo. I c. 7. The Act, also known as Knatchbull's Act after its main promoter, Sir Edward Knatchbull, allowed parishes to purchase or hire workhouses, and stipulated that a person who refused to enter the workhouse was no longer entitled to relief. See Tim Hitchcock, 'The English Workhouse: A Study in Institutional Poor Relief in Selected Counties 1696–1750', (Unpublished Ph.D. thesis, University of Oxford, 1985), p. 218.

[19] Kathryn Morrison, *The Workhouse: A Study of Poor-Law Buildings in England* (Swindon, 1999), p. 15.

[20] Ibid.

[21] [Anon] *An Account of the Work-houses in Great Britain in the Year MDCCXXXII* (London, 1786, 3rd edition). pp. 60, 79–81.

were added, it proved necessary to construct a new building in 1776 which could cater for up to 1,000 paupers.[22]

A survey of workhouses in 1776 showed that were at least 80 in London with space for some 16,000 poor, a significant increase compared to 50 years earlier.[23] As shown in Figure 2.3, most of the large workhouses were located in the rapidly growing north western parishes, such as St George Hanover Square and St Martin in the Fields each of which could accommodate 700 inmates and in St James, St Marylebone and St Giles. Elsewhere, only those workhouses in St George in the East, St Saviour and St George's Southwark were of comparable size. South of the river, workhouses tended to be smaller, although most could hold at least 200 inmates. The Lambeth workhouse, for example, which was a substantial three storey brick building located prominently by Lambeth Butts, could hold 270 inmates, although by the early 1800s it contained well over 400 paupers and by 1815 the number had risen to nearly a thousand.[24] By contrast, most City parishes were generally too small to warrant separate workhouses and rather than maintain or share buildings, they tended to farm out their poor. As Figure 2.4 shows, only nine City parishes within the walls had their own workhouse, most of which were relatively small and concentrated on the eastern margins, although the extra mural parishes which had much larger populations also had workhouses to match.

22 Alan Neate, *St Marylebone Workhouse*, (London, 2003), pp. 7–11.

23 The figures are taken from House of Lords Papers, Abstract of returns made pursuant to an act passed in the 16th year of the reign of his majesty King George the Third by the overseers of the poor within the several parishes, townships and places within England and Wales, 1776. See also [Anon] *An Account of the Work-houses in Great Britain in the Year MDCCXXXII* (London, 1786, 3rd edition); Hitchcock, 'The English Workhouse'.

24 On Horwood's map of 1813 the workhouse is shown occupying a large site fronting Workhouse Lane. For the Lambeth workhouse see PP 1818 XIX Abstract of the answers and returns made pursuant to an act intituled 'An act for procuring returns relative to the expense and maintenance of the poor in England', p. 450.

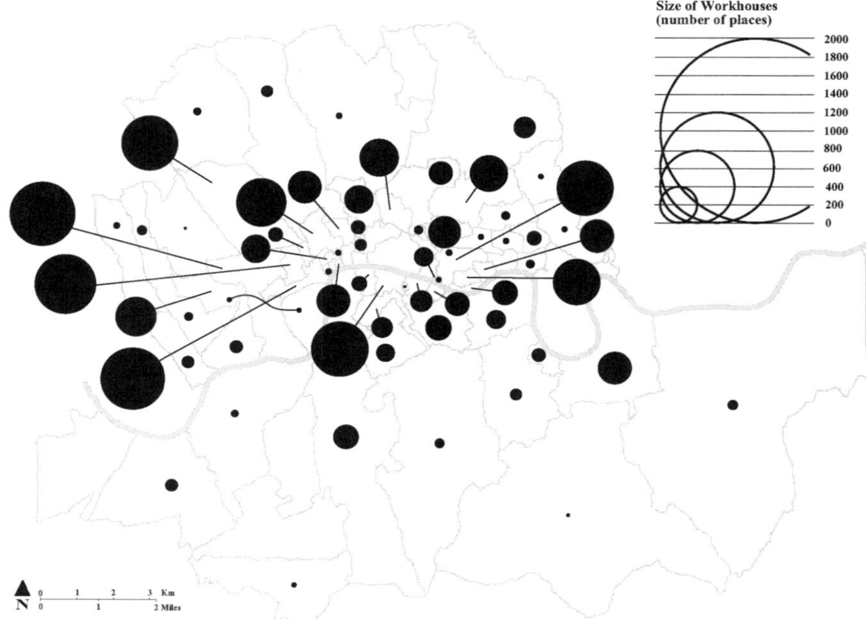

Figure 2.3 Workhouses in London (excluding the City) 1776

Source: House of Lords Papers, Abstract of returns made pursuant to an act passed in the 16th year of the reign of his majesty King George the Third by the overseers of the poor within the several parishes, townships and places within England and Wales, 1776.

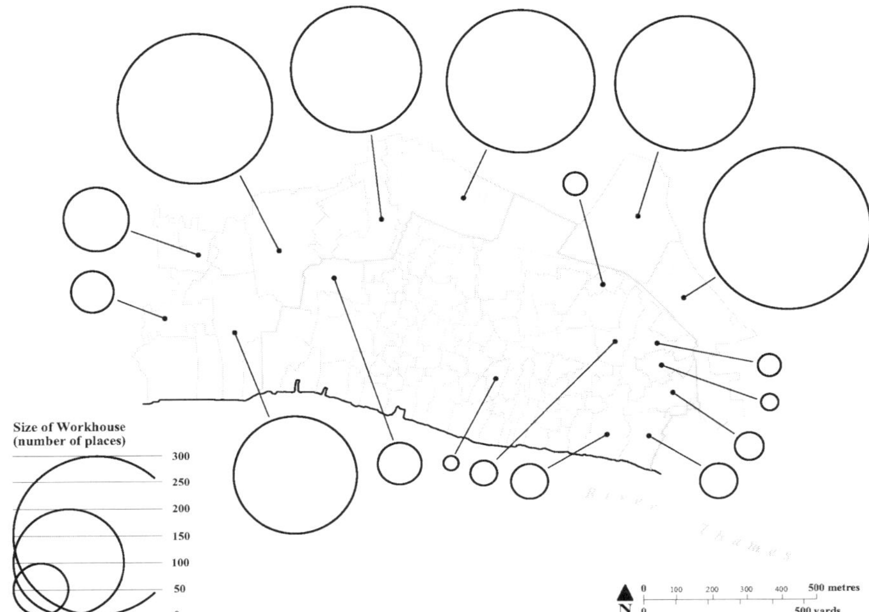

Figure 2.4 Workhouses in the City of London 1776

Source: House of Lords Papers, Abstract of returns made pursuant to an act passed in the 16th year of the reign of his majesty King George the Third by the overseers of the poor within the several parishes, townships and places within England and Wales, 1776.

Pressure on workhouse space continued to mount in most London parishes in the late eighteenth century. In some cases, more paupers were merely crammed into the same space, though this policy clearly had its limits. In the St James Westminster workhouse, for example, which had been built in 1725–27, paupers were said to be sleeping three to a bed in 1814.[25] It was only after the outbreak of fever in 1815 that the vestry sanctioned the construction of additional buildings, which were finally completed in 1821.[26] In neighbouring St Marylebone, where construction struggled to keep pace with exceptionally rapid population growth, the new workhouse built in 1776 soon proved inadequate even with the addition of a large infirmary in 1792. By 1796 there were 1,168 inmates and in the 1820s it proved necessary to enlarge the infirmary and erect a new boys' school.

[25] F. H. W. Sheppard (ed.), *Survey of London, The Parish of St James Westminster Part II North of Piccadilly*, vol. 32 (London, 1963), p. 213.

[26] Peter Higginbotham, *The Workhouse*. [Online]. Available at: http://www.workhouses.org.uk/ [accessed: 2 October 2008].

Nevertheless, by 1834 there were 1,334 paupers in the workhouse, 30 per cent more than the number for which it had originally been built in 1776.[27]

Several other parishes also added new buildings to an existing workhouse. In Islington the workhouse built in 1777 and described then as 'a commodious edifice of brick' had to be enlarged in 1802.[28] Population growth following the construction of docks in Poplar was matched by adding two new buildings to the existing workhouse in 1815–17.[29] But such piecemeal additions did little to improve the classification of paupers, as the vestry clerk from St Giles noted in his response to the Royal Commission on the Poor Laws:

> Many of the London workhouses are old houses enlarged from time to time to meet the exigencies of the occasion. In a concourse of buildings thus muddled together it is impossible to make such arrangements and classifications as are necessary in an establishment which has to serve all the purposes of an hospital, a school, and asylum, and a workhouse.[30]

The most comprehensive way of dealing with the problem was to build an entirely new workhouse and this mainly occurred in rapidly growing districts. New workhouses were started in Lewisham in 1817, St Anne Limehouse in 1827 and St John Southwark in 1831.[31] The largest expansion took place in St Pancras where the old workhouse, built in 1776, could house 120 persons. In 1788 a new workhouse was built but by 1809 this had been replaced by another building which by 1832 could accommodate over 1,000 paupers.[32]

The extent of this expansion is evident from counts of the number of poor relieved inside workhouses for 1776, 1803 and between 1813 and 1815, though the basis on which each set of figures was compiled differed and as such need to be treated with caution.[33] The returns to questionnaires sent out in 1832 as part of the Royal Commission's investigation into the operation of the poor laws contain counts of the poor in specific workhouses and can therefore be used as a way of comparing changes in the scale of provision. These counts are outlined in Table 2.2,

---

27 Ibid.; PP 1834 XXXV Royal commission on the administration and practical operation of the poor laws, answers to town queries, St Marylebone, q. 15.

28 S. Lewis, *The History and Topography of St Mary Islington* (London, 1842), p. 139.

29 F. H. W. Sheppard (ed.), *Survey of London, Poplar, Blackwall and the Isle of Dogs*, vol. 43, (London, 1994), p. 79; Higginbotham, 'The Workhouse.'

30 PP 1834 XXXV Royal commission on the administration and practical operation of the poor laws, answers to town queries, St Giles in the Fields, q. 23.

31 *The Times*, 21 April 1817, 28 April 1827, 12 March 1831.

32 C. R. Ashbee (ed.) *Survey of London, St Pancras*, vol. 19 (London, 1938), p. 52.

33 This report was an attempt to gauge the amount of provision for the poor rather than a count of actual paupers, and was in some ways far less comprehensive than subsequent counts, which were based on the actual numbers relieved.

together with information for the earlier years. In total, 153 London parishes responded to the town questionnaires, of which 54 stated they had their own workhouse.[34] Of this total, 39 parishes had also provided details to the 1776 survey and for this group we therefore have a direct way of comparing the actual and potential numbers that could be accommodated in their workhouses. In 1776 the average size of the workhouse for these districts was 262 but by 1832 the average number of indoor poor reported for the same workhouses was 376. Even allowing for the fact that the size of workhouse did not necessarily correspond to the actual number of paupers it contained, what is clear is that between these two dates the scale of indoor relief expanded significantly.

Table 2.2 Workhouses and indoor poor in London 1776–1832

	Workhouses	**Size of workhouses**	**Number of indoor poor**	**Average number in workhouse**
1776	80	16,100		201
1803			16,888	
1815			19,723	
1832 (a)	54 (n=153)		17,714	328
1832 (b)	39		14,652	376

Note: (a) all London parishes responding to the Royal commission on the poor laws' questionnaires
(b) London parishes represented in both the 1776 survey and the 1834 Royal commission on the poor laws, report.

Source: House of Lords Papers, Abstract of returns made pursuant to an act passed in the 16th year of the reign of his majesty King George the Third by the overseers of the poor within the several parishes, townships and places within England and Wales, 1776; PP 1803–04 XIII Abstract of the answers and returns made pursuant to Act 43 Geo 3, relative to the expense and maintenance of the poor in England; PP 1818 XIX Abstract of the answers and returns made pursuant to an act intituled 'An act for procuring returns relative to the expense and maintenance of the poor in England'; PP 1834 XXXV Royal commission on the administration and practical operation of the poor laws, answers to town queries; PP 1834 XXXVI Royal commission on the administration and practical operation of the poor laws, answers to town queries.

This increase was particularly noticeable in eastern parishes bordering the City which struggled to deal with the growing number of resident poor. One of the only means available to stem this tide of pauperism was to operate stricter relief policies, imposing harsher labour tests for the casual poor, or using the workhouse as a test of destitution. To do so, however, required both the capacity and the will to provide indoor relief. In some eastern districts, the number of indoor poor

[34] Lewisham responded to the rural questionnaires but is included in this total.

rose significantly between 1803 and 1832, as shown in Figure 2.5. In Bethnal Green, the number relieved in the workhouse increased from 332 in 1803 to 900 by 1832, and in St George in the East, despite the importance of casual relief, indoor numbers also rose from 316 to 797. In Shoreditch the number of indoor poor almost doubled. In this context, the vestry clerk, John Ware, noted the use of the workhouse as a deterrent:

> In the present pauperised state of parishes like this, it seems necessary that, in addition to the workhouse being a refuge for those who need it, it should be in some measure a House of Correction, or as its name imports, a Workhouse in reality for the idle and profligate. Some of the regulations adopted in the best managed houses of correction, might, perhaps, be applicable to workhouses, or be exercised by the Master under the control and periodical (as well as uncertain) visitation of a Committee.[35]

However, the high cost of maintaining paupers inside the workhouse meant that such policies came at a price and unless there was a permanent reduction in the numbers relieved, such strategies were difficult to maintain in the long run without building new premises. In Spitalfields, the long serving parish treasurer William Hale, noted how pressure of numbers had resulted in the workhouse regime becoming much laxer between 1815 and 1828.[36] There was certainly little or no extra capacity in the workhouse and no apparent desire to build a new one or enlarge the old. In Bethnal Green, where in 1803 more than 90 per cent of poor law expenditure went on indoor relief, only 20 settled paupers were relieved outside the workhouse. As the silk trade declined, however, so pressures on relief increased and by the 1830s not only had the numbers in the workhouse trebled but parish officials also estimated that between 6,000 and 7,000 were in receipt of outdoor relief, noting ruefully that 'it will be readily perceived that there must shortly be an end of things unless employment and better wages become the order of the day'.[37] Clearly, even in those districts with a workhouse, indoor relief had its limits and once these had been reached, other approaches were required.

---

35 PP 1834 XXXV Royal commission on the administration and practical operation of the poor laws, answers to town queries, St Leonard Shoreditch, q. 23.

36 See William Hales evidence to PP 1814–15 III Select committee on the state of mendicity in the metropolis, p. 307; PP 1828 IV Select committee on that part of the poor laws relating to the employment or relief of able-bodied persons from the poor rate, pp. 168–71.

37 PP 1834 XXXV Royal commission on the administration and practical operation of the poor laws, answers to town queries, Bethnal Green, q. 18. See also *The Times*, 27 January 1826.

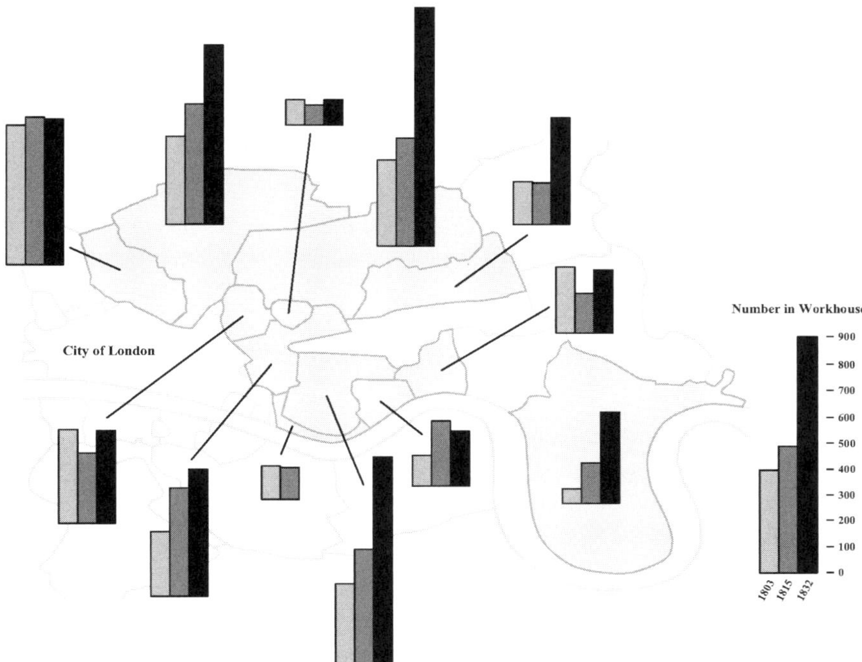

Figure 2.5 Numbers in the workhouse in eastern districts 1803–1832

Note: The district of St Dunston Stepney is divided into Mile End Old Town (shaded) and Stepney. There is no data for Stepney.

Source: J. Marshall, *A Digest of all the Accounts*; PP 1834 XXXV Royal commission on the administration and practical operation of the poor laws, answers to town queries.

Parishes faced with constraints on the capacity of the workhouse could turn to other forms of institutional provision. In London, economies of scale arising from the concentration of relatively large numbers of the poor allowed specialist institutions catering for specific types of paupers and run by private contractors to operate. This mixed provision of relief had been made possible following Knatchbull's Act of 1723 which allowed authorities to contract out relief. These provisions were used extensively in London, both by City parishes too small by themselves to construct a workhouse, and also by other parishes that engaged contractors to run workhouses in their own right. It also encouraged the development of privately operated pauper farms that were used increasingly to deal with excess numbers of the poor as well as the more troublesome paupers. Jonas Hanway's Act of 1767, which required all metropolitan parishes to send their pauper children aged below six at least three miles away in the country, added another layer of provision by allowing the use of nurses and also encouraged the formation of specialist establishments catering for parish infants and children too young to be apprenticed.[38] At the start of the nineteenth century, therefore, London parishes operated a mixed system of institutional relief that encompassed both private and public provision through the use of parish workhouses, private contractors, pauper farmers and children's nurses.

For those districts without a workhouse pauper farms offered an alternative way of providing indoor relief. Several London parishes contracted out their poor in this way and during the eighteenth century these establishments developed into large concerns, some catering for several hundred poor.[39] City parishes in particular relied on pauper farms to deal with their indoor poor. Most were too small to have their own workhouses and although Gilbert's Act of 1782 permitted parishes to combine together for the purposes of building and maintaining a workhouse, few places in the City did so. Of the 84 City parishes that completed the town questionnaires for the 1834 Royal Commission on the Poor Law, only 11 had their own workhouses whilst the rest farmed out their indoor poor to private contractors at rates generally between 4s and 6s a week. For some, the practice had been going on since 'time immemorial' whilst for others the practice was more recent. Whitefriars precinct, for example, had farmed their poor at Stepney for 'a hundred years' whilst St Ethelburgas had farmed theirs for thirty.[40]

Whilst most of the City parishes farmed their indoor poor as a matter of course, other districts which had workhouses tended to use poor farming as a way of disciplining refractory paupers. St Luke's, for example, only sent its worst behaved paupers to be farmed whilst in St Pancras 50 of the most disorderly paupers were farmed out, with benefits for a peaceful workhouse.[41] Few other benefits accrued and in 1814–15 the Parliamentary Select Committee on Mendicity concluded that although the proprietors of pauper farms claimed that inmates carried out various types of work, including sewing for government contracts, many of them were either too old or infirm or too ill disciplined to do any useful work.[42]

With demand for poor farms concentrated in the City, most concerns were located just beyond its borders, mainly in eastern districts within easy reach of the centre, as shown in Figure 2.6. Several of the pauper farms were substantial concerns, comparable to some of the largest workhouses in London. Edward

---

38 Act for the Better Protection of Parish Poor Children (Hanway's Act), 7 Geo. III c. 39.

39 Elaine Murphy, 'The Metropolitan Poor Farms, 1722–1834', *London Journal*, 27 (2002): 1–18.

40 PP 1834 XXXV Royal commission on the administration and practical operation of the poor laws, answers to town queries, q. 21 St Ethelburga, Whitefriars parish. Knatchbull's Act of 1723 had allowed for the use of pauper farmers, and many of the arrangements probably date from that time.

41 Ibid., q. 20, St Luke, St Pancras.

42 PP 1814–15 III Select committee on the state of mendicity in the metropolis, pp. 52, 311.

Deacon, for example, ran two poor houses, one at Mile End with 350 inmates, and another at Old Ford, Bow for 170 paupers. James Robertson farmed 300 paupers in Hoxton drawn from 40 parishes at a cost of between 5s and 6s a week. Thomas Tipple also ran a nearby poor house for up to 300 paupers which in 1821 was described as a 'spacious substantial built dwelling house, now used as the poor house, with brick tenements, outbuildings, and large yard behind; and three good brick-built dwelling houses, with yards adjoining'.[43] The entire establishment had a frontage of nearly 90 feet and at the expiration of its current lease was reckoned to have been worth at least £110 a year.

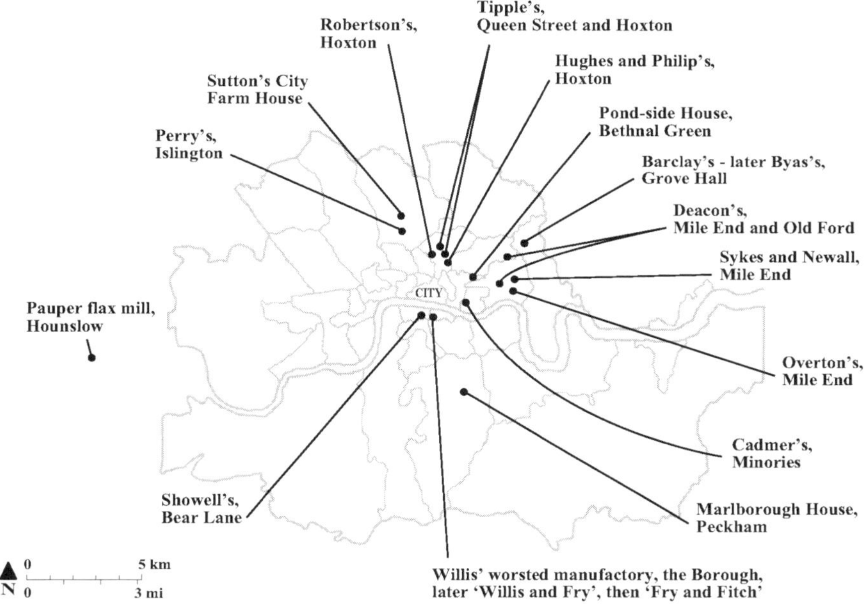

Figure 2.6 Poor farms in London c. 1800

Source: Elaine Murphy, 'The Metropolitan Poor Farms, p. 4. Reproduced with kind permission of the trustees of the *London Journal*.

Compared to the costs of maintaining the poor in a workhouse, pauper farming was relatively expensive and it therefore had to serve a particular purpose. In 1833 the weekly cost of farming the poor was normally between 4s 6d and 5 shillings per pauper, compared to the average cost of about 3s 11 ¾d for maintaining the poor

43 *The Times*, 22 March 1821.

in the workhouse.[44] For those smaller parishes without a workhouse, it remained a viable alternative to constructing a new building. However, in those places with an existing workhouse, it was considered worth the extra cost to farm out the most ill disciplined paupers. Several parishes including St Giles, Islington, Kensington, Paddington, St Pancras, Shoreditch, St George Hanover Square, St Martins and St James Westminster, chose to farm out their more difficult paupers.[45] In St Luke's Middlesex, 12 of the worst paupers were farmed at a weekly cost of 5s 3d per person compared to 3s 2d indoors whilst in St Pancras disorderly paupers were farmed at a cost of 4s 6d per person compared to 3s 10d in the workhouse. In St Pancras as elsewhere the principal benefit was harmony in the workhouse whilst at the same time the discomforts of the farm house apparently persuaded most of those sent there to provide for themselves. Evidently this role was important since in 1832 the Royal Commission's report noted that some of the establishments contained as many as 500 people, most of whom were 'persons whose character is so bad that they are excluded from the society of the thieves and prostitutes in the regular workhouse'.[46] Pauper farming, therefore, provided an additional element of institutional relief to what was already an extensive system of workhouse accommodation.

The importance of indoor relief, hinted at by the scale of London workhouses and pauper farming, is confirmed by expenditure figures. As already noted in the previous chapter, London was characterised by generally higher rates of indoor relief than other parts of the country. Figure 2.6 shows this situation in more detail. In 1803 with few exceptions, London parishes spent at least 60 per cent or more of their annual expenditure on indoor relief. Typically, districts that spent relatively little tended to be those without adequate workhouse accommodation which relied more on pauper farming or outdoor relief. Very few City parishes, for example, maintained a workhouse and of those that did, none were very large. As a result, most spent well over half their total budget on the outdoor poor. As a whole, City parishes accounted for about 20 per cent of the total metropolitan expenditure on outdoor relief compared to under nine per cent of the indoor total. By contrast, high spending parishes tended to be clustered in eastern parts of the city, reflecting the higher pressure that pauperism was already imprinting on the social landscape. In Bethnal Green, Shadwell and Whitechapel, for example, between 85 and 92 per cent of poor law expenditure went on indoor relief compared to 46 per cent in City parishes. The only exceptions to the rule were parishes close to the docks, including St George in the East and St John Wapping, where it was cheaper to

44 Of the 31 parishes outside the City of London which had workhouses and which answered the town queries for the Royal commission on the administration and practical operation of the poor laws, the average weekly cost per head was 3s 11 ¾d.

45 See PP 1834 XXXV Royal commission on the administration and practical operation of the poor laws, answers to town queries, answers to q. 20.

46 PP 1834 XXVIII, Royal commission on the administration and practical operation of the poor laws, Appendix A: assistant commissioners' reports, p. 93.

provide casual relief for dock labourers for one or two days a week than force them into the workhouse.[47]

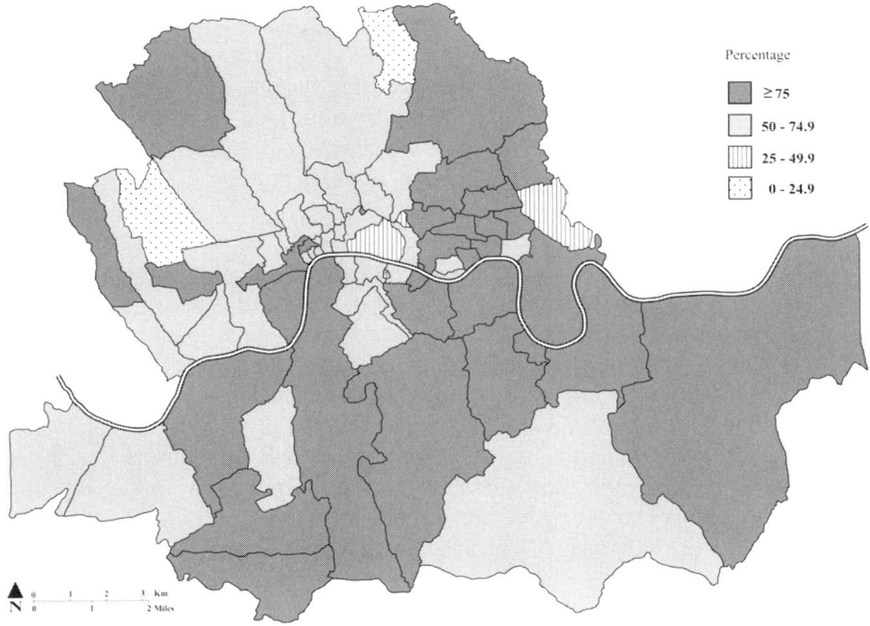

Figure 2.7 Expenditure on indoor relief in London 1803 (% total relief)

Source: PP 1803–04 XIII Abstract of the answers and returns made pursuant to Act 43 Geo 3, relative to the expense and maintenance of the poor in England.

Outdoor relief and the casual poor

In terms of numbers, though not necessarily cost, outdoor paupers far exceeded those receiving relief inside a workhouse or other institution. It was cheaper to relieve paupers outdoors though in so doing parishes were in danger of encouraging speculative applications from the labouring poor. Districts with stricter policies could to some extent protect themselves against a rush of applications by refusing help or making conditions so onerous that the destitute would choose to seek relief elsewhere. However, upon becoming destitute, even the non-settled poor had the right to receive temporary assistance although it may only have been shelter for

47 PP 1834 XXXV Royal commission on the administration and practical operation of the poor laws, answers to town queries, St Ann Limehouse, q. 32, 35.

the night or a small handout. There were limits as to the extent to which officials could withhold assistance, not least because the poor could appeal to justices of the peace against over zealous actions by local overseers keen to protect the parish purse. Faced with this possibility, it may have been better for overseers to provide some assistance than to have to face the time-consuming and potentially uncomfortable task of having to appear before the courts to explain their actions.

The number in receipt of outdoor relief also depended on other factors more to do with local circumstances. The number of paupers, especially those receiving outdoor relief, fluctuated depending more on the season and state of the economy than on the size of the local population. This was most evident with casual paupers who sought temporary help and who often flitted in and out of districts depending on personal circumstances, the availability of work and the opportunity of a handout. The seasonality of the London economy, and the greater difficulties faced by the poor during winter, meant that applications for relief tended to rise and fall in relation to the temperature and the state of the economy. These secular and seasonal fluctuations are well illustrated in Figure 2.7 which show the quarterly totals of paupers relieved in St Marylebone between 1821 and 1833. The figures emphasise the impact of the 1825 economic crisis and the marked rise in the number of paupers towards the end of that year. They also show how the economic downturn accentuated the seasonal peaks and troughs in the numbers relieved. The winter quarter always witnessed sharp increases driven largely by applications for casual relief but these fluctuations were more marked after the crisis of 1825 than they had been before.

Such fluctuation makes it difficult to determine if there was any consistent change in policy regarding outdoor relief in particular districts. Nor is it possible to compare returns for different years since the basis on which they were compiled varied. Counts of paupers in 1803 distinguished the permanent poor with a settlement in a parish from non-parishioners but failed to note the kind of relief offered to the latter. Figures for the years 1813 to 1815 failed even to make this distinction and doubt was cast at the time as to the accuracy of the returns. We are therefore forced to rely on imperfect data with which to gauge the numbers who were in receipt of outdoor relief. Taking these reservations into account, in 1803 in London as a whole the outdoor poor comprised about 60 per cent of all permanent paupers. However, there were some important variations, as shown in Figure 2.8. Suburban parishes such as Chelsea, Lewisham, Poplar and Lambeth, which generally had smaller workhouses, relied much more on relieving the poor outdoors. In their cases at least three quarters of the permanent poor were relieved outdoors. By contrast, in eastern districts the outdoor poor comprised a relatively small number of those relieved. In Bethnal Green, for example, just over 10 per cent of permanent paupers were relieved outside the workhouse and in the neighbouring districts of Mile End and Spitalfields the figure was between 20 and 25 per cent. The relatively low rates reflect the fact that these districts tended to emphasise indoor relief, as the figures for workhouse expenditure discussed earlier demonstrated. Here stricter attention was paid to offering permanent paupers the house rather than a pension and as such their approach predated the emphasis on indoor relief ushered in after the 1834 reforms.

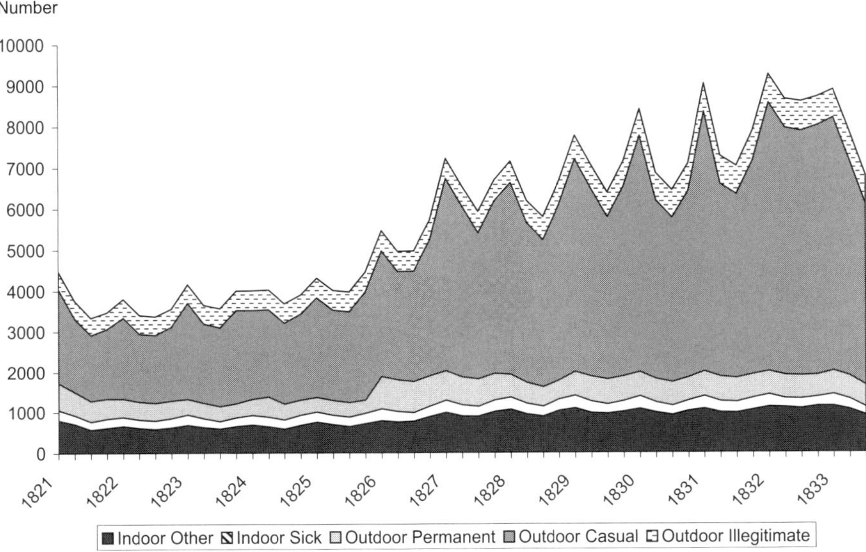

Figure 2.8 Numbers of paupers relieved in St Marylebone 1821–1833 (quarterly average)

Note: The figures reflect the average quarterly total of paupers relieved.

Source: LMA, P89/MYR1/514–21 St Marylebone Directors of the Poor, Annual Reports 1820–33.

The most difficult group of paupers to assess are the casual poor who sought some form of temporary help. In many cases, these paupers did not possess a settlement and in this situation overseers had a choice. They could hold firm and refuse to offer relief, choosing instead to seek an order of removal. New overseers of the poor in St Giles were warned to take this course of action if they wanted to prevent the district becoming 'a common receptacle for vagrants from all quarters'.[48] They were particularly warned against providing any help to pregnant women without a settlement since any illegitimate children would become the responsibility of the parish.[49] They could, on the other hand, provide small amounts of relief, usually for a short while, either in money or in kind, in the hope that this would suffice to tide applicant over the immediate crisis.

[48] [Anon] *Hints and Cautions for the Information of the Churchwardens and Overseers of the Poor of the Parishes of St Giles in the Fields and St George's Bloomsbury in the County of Middlesex* (London, 1781), p. 8.

[49] Ibid., p. 10.

Given the pressures on workhouse space and the difficulties associated with enforcing removals, parishes often resorted to providing temporary handouts or an overnight stay, though repeated applications meant that a pauper was liable to be charged under the vagrancy laws and forcibly removed.

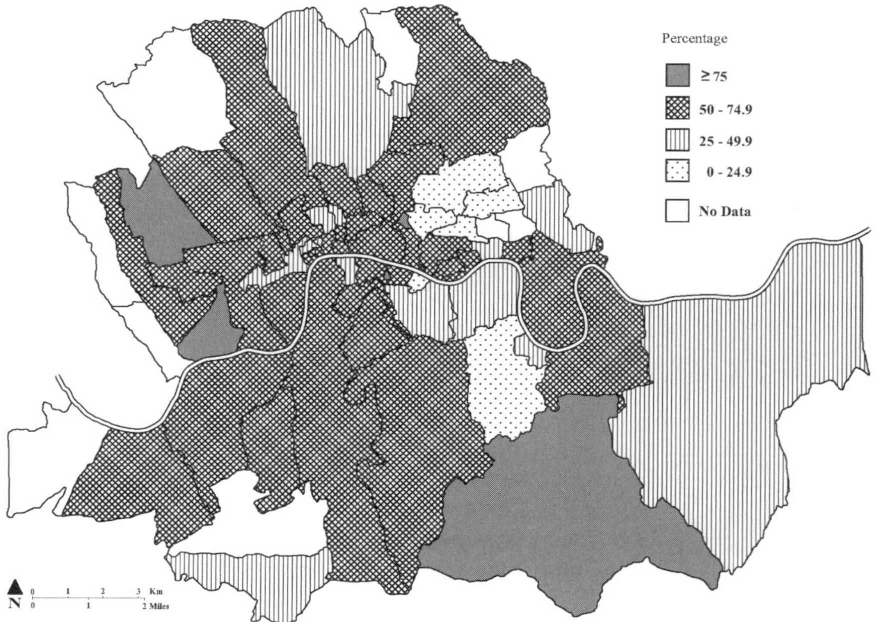

Figure 2.9 Outdoor paupers in London 1803 (% total permanent poor)

Source: 1803–04 XIII Abstract of the answers and returns made pursuant to Act 43 Geo 3, relative to the expense and maintenance of the poor in England.

Estimating the number of casual paupers is especially difficult since the returns are notoriously inaccurate. The figures for 1813 to 1815, for example, only appeared to deal with those who possessed a settlement, although even here the way that vestry clerks reported numbers was by no means consistent. The returns in 1803 made a clearer distinction between different categories of pauper and the relief they received, and provide an idea of how policies differed between places. In that year the non-settled poor in receipt of temporary relief accounted for nearly 47 per cent of the total number of paupers. However, their numbers were particularly sensitive to the state of the economy and any downturn was likely to have been accompanied by sharp increases in the proportion of casual paupers. In St Marylebone, as discussed above, from 1815 the casual poor never formed less than 40 per cent of those relieved, rising to over 50 per cent in the 1820s and over 70 per cent by 1832.

Despite the fact that the casual poor had a right to receive relief in the parish to which they applied, significant differences existed in the way they were treated. In the City, the police actively sought to move on beggars and when apprehended vagrants were frequently sent to the Bridewell for a week to a month.[50] By contrast, unless they were vigilant, poor law officers in surrounding districts could find themselves inundated with requests for assistance from the casual poor, shovelled out from the City to find cheap lodgings elsewhere. William Hale, treasurer of the Directors of the Poor in Spitalfields and a local silk manufacturer, recorded in 1828 how his district had become a 'casual parish':

> A number of people hear that workmen are wanting in London, that there are some alterations in the Bank, or houses building; bricklayers and labourers come and obtain work for a month or two, and come into Spitalfields for cheap lodgings; in a few months they are out of work and some of them will then apply to the parish for relief.[51]

Whether the poor moved to these parishes by choice or were encouraged there by the actions of parish officers elsewhere was a constant bone of contention. Since the right to receive casual relief arose from having spent the previous night in a parish, officials were often keen to ensure that paupers were moved into neighbouring districts at the first opportunity, either by bribing them to shift, arresting them as vagrants or refusing to give any relief whatsoever.[52] Despite complaints from neighbouring parishes, there was relatively little that they could do other than keep an equally vigilant eye over applicants for casual relief and to make their own relief policies as stringent as possible.

Irish paupers were particularly troublesome for local officials. Until 1819 they could not be removed unless they had committed an act of vagrancy and therefore parishes were often obliged to provide some form of relief.[53] This burden could prove onerous, as was the case in St Marylebone. In March 1826, in an attempt to dissuade Irish casuals from applying for relief, work 'of the most laborious kind' was stipulated at wages 'considerably lower than those which the Irish may obtain by their general employment'.[54] However, even stone breaking failed to deter Irish applicants and later in the year the vestry were called upon to petition

---

50 PP 1814–15 III Select committee on the state of mendicity in the metropolis, pp. 244, 251.

51 PP 1828 IV Select committee on that part of the poor laws relating to the employment or relief of able-bodied persons from the poor rate, p. 169.

52 PP 1814–15 III Select committee on the state of mendicity in the metropolis, p. 299.

53 James Taylor, 'A Different Kind of Speenhamland', p. 191.

54 LMA P89/MYR1/518 St Marylebone Directors of the Poor, Minutes, 17 March 1826.

Parliament for the formation of an Irish poor law.[55] In St Giles, which contained a large community of Irish poor, the problems were even more severe.[56] John Smith, the parish beadle, was in little doubt as to the cause of the problem. In his evidence before the 1817 Select Committee on the Poor Laws, he claimed that cheap lodging houses and fellow countrymen attracted the Irish poor to the area. Once there they were entitled to receive relief by virtue of having resided one night in the parish.[57] It was also claimed that local landlords organised applications to the overseers and pocketed part of the proceeds.[58] Much to the annoyance of Samuel Stevenson, himself an English beggar who appeared before the Mendicity Committee in 1814–15, the Irish seemed to have been aware of their entitlement and 'tell us to our face they have as much right to a settlement as we have ourselves'.[59]

Problems of provision

One of the main problems that London parishes experienced in relation to casual and outdoor relief was how to deal with the fragmentation of jurisdictions and rapid population turnover. These problems were highlighted in 1829 when four paupers were charged with fraudulently claiming relief from different London parishes. One, a man called Paxton, had managed to get money, shoes and clothing from Bishopsgate under a false name, as well as receiving regular relief over a period of years from Holborn, St George Southwark and from Mile End Old Town.[60] His geographical scope ranged across the city and each parish to which he applied was sufficiently distant from the others to avoid the possibility of chance recognition. Nor was this likely to have been an isolated example. Witnesses appearing before the Royal Commission on the Poor Laws in 1834 commented that pauper frauds were as varied as they were numerous.[61] James Corder, vestry clerk for St Paul Covent Garden, told the Commission how Jane Davies, alias Jane Harris, had for several years received relief not only from his parish but also from six neighbouring districts, at times posing as a married woman with a child and at others as a single woman.[62] Similar problems existed in some of

---

55 Ibid., 29 December 1826.

56 PP 1814–15 III Select committee on the state of mendicity in the metropolis, p. 325.

57 PP 1818 V Select committee to consider the poor laws, p. 170. See also PP 1814–15 III Select committee on the state of mendicity in the metropolis, p. 240.

58 PP 1817 VI Select committee to consider the poor laws, pp. 122–3.

59 PP 1814–15 III Select committee on the state of mendicity in the metropolis, p. 284.

60 *The Times*, 26 August 1829.

61 *The Times*, 9 April 1833.

62 PP 1834 XXVIII Royal commission into the administration and practical operation of the poor laws, Appendix A: assistant commissioners' reports, part 1, p. 65.

the larger parishes, particularly where individual overseers were each responsible for specific districts and where the office changed hands annually, as happened frequently with voluntary officials prior to 1834. In Lambeth, one of the largest parishes in London, until the introduction of tickets in place of monetary relief, frauds were said to have been common and on at least one occasion it was claimed that a pauper had managed to obtain relief from each of the eight overseers in the same night.[63] While these instances were not typical of the permanent outdoor poor who received regular weekly allowances from their parishes, nevertheless they illustrate how it was possible for paupers to circumvent the rules of relief. In the context of a crowded city, a multiplicity of authorities and overworked and inexperienced local officers, such opportunities were plentiful.

Geography, in particular, had much to answer for. Prior to 1834, there were over 150 separate poor law authorities in the capital and this situation increased the opportunities for deception. The close proximity of parishes meant that it was relatively easy to seek relief from more than one place, compounded by the fact that different authorities distributed relief on different days of the week.[64] Early in the century, for example, it was possible to apply for relief to a different West End parish each weekday, as Table 2.3 shows. Similar situations existed elsewhere, notably in the City where large numbers of small parishes made coordination of relief particularly difficult.[65] Even in larger parishes where individual overseers had responsibility for separate wards, opportunities for fraud remained. In St Saviour Southwark, mindful of this possibility, the eight overseers in 1833 each met on a weekly basis to review the names of those relieved and from time to time to call them up to check that the same person was not being paid more than once.[66] Elsewhere, in places such as St Marylebone and the City, vestries called for greater coordination between neighbouring parishes over times and days for distributing relief.[67] Without such coordination, paupers well versed in this complex geography of provision could sustain deceptions for several years.

63 Ibid., p.69.

64 PP 1833 XVI Select committee on the removal of Irish vagrants to Ireland, p. 334.

65 PP 1834 XXXV Royal commission on the administration and practical operation of the poor laws, answers to town queries Appendix B, All Hallows, Staining, q. 13.

66 PP 1833 XVI Select committee on the removal of Irish vagrants to Ireland, p. 334.

67 LMA P89/MYR1/512 St Marylebone Directors of the Poor, Minutes, 21 January 1818.

Table 2.3 Distribution of outdoor relief in West End parishes 1818

Weekday	Parish
Monday	St Giles
Tuesday	St George Hanover Square St James Westminster
Wednesday	St George Hanover Square St Ann Westminster St Giles St Pancras
Thursday	St Giles Paddington
Friday	St James Westminster

Source: LMA P89/MYR1/512 St Marylebone Directors of the Poor, Minutes, 21 January 1818.

Whilst lack of coordination between parishes offered opportunities for deception, so too did the absence of paid relieving officers hinder the detection of fraud. Prior to 1834, which marked the professionalisation of many of the functions performed previously by unpaid and often reluctant ratepayers, it was common for relief to be dispensed by overseers appointed for a set period of time, usually a year. The difficulty of persuading these unpaid officials to remain in office hampered the efficient payment of relief. Francis Hobler, chief clerk to the Lord Mayor, acknowledged the severity of the problem:

> Again, we have 97 parishes, with all their complete establishments, all acting differently. Every year they have their new officers, who are subject to continual impositions. Some come in as reformers; others are full of the milk of humankindness, and are imposed upon in proportion. There are vagabonds who go about hunting the new parish officers. I have known as much as £13 or £14 obtained from parishes by fraud of the new overseers in the season.[68]

In St James Westminster, gullible new overseers were said to have been fooled into providing relief as a result of hearing the 'plausible misstatements and piteous tales' of habitual paupers.[69] 'It may be laid down as a general rule', noted Edmund Ludlow, overseer at St Saviours, 'that all overseers on their first entrance to office are extensively imposed upon'.[70]

---

68 *The Times*, 30 December 1833.

69 PP 1834 XXVIII Royal commission on the administration and practical operation of the poor laws, Appendix A: assistant commissioners' reports, p. 70.

70 PP 1834 XXIX Royal commission on the administration and practical operation of the poor laws, Appendix A, assistant commissioners' reports, p. 441.

Where the overseers were shopkeepers or in business, a common dodge was for paupers to apply for relief on a Saturday, the busiest trading day of the week, in the knowledge that a tradesman would rather offer relief than be forced to attend court to explain to a magistrate why it had been denied.[71] When they did so, the chances were that their decision would be questioned and their integrity impugned by paternalistic justices more in sympathy with the poor than the parish. Similarly, paupers applying at overseers' houses for relief not infrequently did so late at night feigning illness or sudden necessity. Quite understandably, overseers themselves often preferred to offer relief as a way of keeping them off their premises at such a late hour.[72]

One way of checking imposition was to employ assistant overseers to investigate and dispense relief, and several parishes, notably the larger ones, had done so prior to 1834. St Marylebone employed five from the early 1800s, including one whose sole responsibility was to deal with the casual poor, and three outdoor inspectors to make enquiries.[73] In St James Westminster, the clerk to the overseers was responsible for relieving the outdoor poor, admitting and discharging paupers from the workhouse and attending the magistrates.[74] In Lambeth, another extensive parish, Luke Teather, the assistant overseer always visited applicants' homes before granting relief:[75]

> A case having been referred to me for inquiry, the course I take is this: I first go their houses, and in nine cases out of ten it is only necessary to see the place to be convinced that they are in distress; the misery or the want of relief is displayed not only in the condition of the place, but in the persons of the applicants or of their children. I think that from experience I can at once determine if the parties are or are not in want. In general the first thing I do is to open the cupboard, it is mostly empty. If any doubt should arise, I make enquiries into the man's character from the place where he has been employed, or from the chandler's shops; the greater part of the money of the poor is spent at the chandler's shop, and there we learn what has been their habits, what sort of good they have been accustomed to buy, and how they have been accustomed to pay for it …[76]

In Spitalfields no casual relief was provided until the poor had been visited in their own homes by an overseer, by which time it became clear that at least half of those

---

71 PP 1834 XXVIII Royal commission on the administration and practical operation of the poor laws, Appendix A, assistant commissioners' reports, p. 86.

72 Ibid., p. 70.

73 Ibid., pp. 68–9.

74 Ibid., p. 70.

75 Ibid., p. 69; PP 1834 XXIX Royal commission on the administration and practical operation of the poor laws, Appendix A, assistant commissioners' reports, p. 427.

76 Ibid., p. 427.

who so applied had given false addresses.[77] A similar system operated in relation to the settled outdoor poor and home visits were always arranged to enquire into their circumstances and character before any form of permanent relief was provided.[78] Such enquiries, however, were time-consuming and there was a balance to be drawn between the numbers of poor who could be visited and the thoroughness of the investigation, particularly where reluctant overseers were involved. The poor knew this, as well as the overseers, and the outcome was always open to an element of negotiation.

Financial crisis and pressures for change

Geographical differences between parishes were important in explaining the complexities of metropolitan pauperism, However, these differences and the emerging structural difficulties of the poor law were accentuated by the financial panic of 1825. Expenditure on relief rose as economic fortunes fell, though the impact was not felt equally throughout the city. In Middlesex costs started to rise in 1824 and continued upward until 1833, the intervening years witnessing an increase in current expenditure of over 31 per cent from £523,387 to £688,161.[79] Few parishes escaped unscathed from the downturn: in the eastern districts of Shoreditch, Bethnal Green, Spitalfields, Mile End and Whitechapel expenditure nearly doubled between 1824 and 1831.[80] In St Marylebone, expenditure rose steeply and by 1828 was more than 50 per cent higher than it had been in 1825. The impact was more muted elsewhere: in the City expenditure peaked in 1828, having risen by nearly 25 per cent whereas in the West End parishes of St George Hanover Square, St James and St Martin in the Fields it hardly rose at all.

At a national level, the deteriorating situation in terms of poor relief was reflected in various attempts at reform and calls even for the total abolition of the poor law itself.[81] Harsher deterrent policies began to appear that focused on reducing outdoor relief and instead providing assistance inside a workhouse, as was the case in Southwell and elsewhere.[82] In London debates focused less around

---

77 PP 1814–15 III Select committee on the state of mendicity in the metropolis, p. 307.

78 PP 1817 VI Select committee to consider the poor laws, p. 45.

79 J. Marshall, *A Digest of All the Accounts*, pp. 36–7.

80 Figures taken from PP 1830–31 XI An account of the money expended for the maintenance and relief of the poor ... for the five years ending 25th March 1825, 1826, 1827, 1828 and 1829; PP 1835 XLVII An account of the money expended for the maintenance and relief of the poor ... for the five years ending 25th March 1830, 1831, 1832, 1833 and 1834.

81 See the Introduction for a summary of these debates, pp. 5–12.

82 See, for example, Peter Searby, 'The Relief of the Poor in Coventry 1830–1863', *Historical Journal*, 20 (1977): 349–50.

the nature of provision than the costs of relief and in this context the discussion was refracted through the lens of geography. Growing social distinctions between wealthy and poor parishes generated calls for some form of redistributing the costs of providing relief. Not surprisingly, support for reform of the rating system and equalising the burden of relief mainly came from eastern districts. The vestry clerk from Bethnal Green, appearing before the Royal Commission on the Poor Laws, argued that only a metropolitan rate arising from union with other wealthier parishes could save it and neighbouring districts from ruin. With the majority of the population teetering on the brink of pauperism, he pleaded 'surely City parishes should contribute a little to ameliorate this state of things'.[83] James Wall, vestry clerk to St Luke, Middlesex, another parish that bordered the City and bore the brunt of its policies, argued in similar vein that 'All the parishes at this end of the metropolis would each be very glad to be united with one of the rich parishes at the west end of the metropolis. One of the great evils of the operation of the Poor Laws is the great inequality with which they press on particular districts.'[84] Such ideas, however, were predicated on the assumption that ratepayers recognised that the city functioned as a single unit, a concept conspicuous by its absence in the fragmented metropolis of the early nineteenth century.

With little or no willingness to accept the common ties that united districts across the city, it was little wonder that the call for rate equalisation was a step too far for most parishes. Instead, steep rate rises to finance the mounting cost of relief focused attention on the inefficiency and corruption of parochial government or the need to impose stricter relief policies. Increasingly anxious ratepayers demanded greater accountability over expenditure and called for reform of parochial administration, notably the abolition of select vestries. Blame for the increase in poor law expenditure was attributed to parochial mismanagement rather than the effects of economic crisis or structural inequality in the ability to raise income. Accusations of maladministration, corruption and inefficiency were heard with increasing frequency, particularly directed against select vestries, many of which had themselves been formed in the late eighteenth century in response to the growing inability of open vestries to function effectively in the face of rapid population growth. The clamour for parochial reform as a way of controlling expenditure had clear parallels with the emerging debate about wider parliamentary reform, in which similar arguments about the rights of representation and taxation were being aired by the middle class. In the aftermath of the economic crisis in London it was this demand rather than rate equalisation or any reform of poor relief *per se* that gathered momentum.

---

83 PP 1834 XXXV Royal commission on the administration and practical operation of the poor laws, answers to town queries, St Matthew Bethnal Green, q. 14.

84 Ibid., St Lukes, q. 14.

Chapter 3
Parish Politics and the Coming of the New System

Introduction

In June 1834 a large gathering of ratepayers and their families from St Marylebone met for a dinner at Chalk Farm to celebrate the third anniversary of the adoption of John Cam Hobhouse's Vestries Act. Toasts were drunk to the monarchy, followed by one to Sir Samuel Whalley, MP for Marylebone, and to the 'ladies' – 300 of whom had apparently voted in the last parochial election for the 'popular cause'. The Poor Law Amendment bill, then being debated in Parliament, came in for harsh criticism not because of any dispute over changes in poor relief *per se* but rather because of the undemocratic franchise proposed for guardian elections.[1] Local democracy rather than poor law expenditure was the issue at stake. Nor were Marylebone ratepayers alone in their concerns. In 1836, when the new poor law was in the process of being introduced in London, ratepayers in neighbouring St Pancras met at White Conduit House where a host of metropolitan radicals and MPs, including Daniel O'Connell and Feargus O' Connor, again denounced the new measure. Loudest cheers were reserved for Thomas Murphy, leader of the parochial reform party, whose toast 'The people – may they soon enjoy their ancient right – local self government' went straight to the heart of the struggle over parochial democracy and the introduction of the new poor law in London.[2]

These dinners and speechmaking were more than just a case of self congratulation by populist parish politicians. Following in the long tradition of radical public dining, they were important pointers to the significance of the struggles between metropolitan parishes and the central state over the legitimacy of the Poor Law Amendment Act in London.[3] As Derek Fraser has remarked, 'To fail to appreciate the political aspect of poor relief is to misunderstand the role of the Poor Law

---

[1] *True Sun*, 25 June 1834. Other dinners were also held in St Marylebone. See *The Times*, 19 July 1837; *London Dispatch*, 12 August 1838. For a rather hostile description of such a dinner see James Grant, *The Great Metropolis* (London, 1837), pp. 103–20.

[2] *The Times*, 29 June 1836.

[3] Radical dining is more fully discussed in James Epstein, *Radical Expression: Political Language, Ritual and Symbol in England, 1790–1850* (Oxford, 1994), pp. 147–67.

in Victorian society.'[4] For those involved, the struggle was less about poor relief itself than about the exercise of legitimate authority. What made this dispute so intractable in London were the political changes that had taken place in the early decades of the nineteenth century and it was in this highly problematic context that Poor Law Commissioners sought to impose their authority. Understanding the relationships between place and policy – a central theme of this book – requires taking into account the emergence of this politicised landscape and the effect it had on the way in which the new poor law was introduced to the capital.

The political landscape

In a formal administrative sense, London did not exist in the early nineteenth century. Its rapid and amorphous growth hindered any easy delineation of metropolitan boundaries: it was not until 1837 and the start of civil registration that any attempts were made to define the city as an administrative unit and only in 1851 did it become a discrete census registration district. In a political sense, too, London was characterised more by the distinctiveness of its parts than by any unity of the whole. Over and above any ideological differences that might have divided one group from another, the size of the city itself and the diversity of its occupational structure hindered the development of any wider metropolitan political consciousness.[5] Speaking of London, Francis Place remarked:

> It has no local or particular interest as a town, not even as to politics. Its several boroughs in this respect are like so many populous places at a distance from one another and the inhabitants of any one of them know nothing, or next to nothing of the proceedings in any other, and not much indeed of those of their own.[6]

London governance was similarly fragmented and remained so for much of the century. There were over 170 parishes in London that varied enormously in both size and wealth. Some, like St Marylebone and St Pancras, were as large if not larger than most provincial cities and growing almost as rapidly. Others were losing population and some, mostly in the City, had barely a handful of residents. Each, however, derived their powers from a bewildering array of local acts that governed the way that vestries provided a range of services including poor relief. Fortified by legal rights and ancient usage, the parishes operated almost as if they were separate ratepayer republics. On the eve of the introduction of the Metropolis

---

4 Derek Fraser, 'The Poor Law as a Political Institution', in Derek Fraser (ed.), *The New Poor Law in the Nineteenth Century* (London, 1976), p. 111.

5 See Eric Hobsbawm, 'Labour in the Great City', *New Left Review*, 166 (1987): 39–51. Hobsbawm's argument is not confined to London alone.

6 Quoted in Francis H. W. Sheppard, *London: The Infernal Wen 1808–1870* (London, 1971), p. 319.

Management Act in 1855, which was the first serious attempt to deal with the infrastructural problems of London, *The Times* noted how the city was 'rent into an infinity of divisions, districts and areas, each with its own jurisdiction, its own officers and its own proper rates'.[7]

It was on this complex landscape of rights and responsibilities that the Poor Law Commissioners after 1834 sought to impose a new administrative map of relief. This was a sufficiently challenging task in itself made even more difficult by the fact that this fragmented administrative landscape was also politicised by competing groups and factions that differed markedly in their ideological orientation as well as their conception of urban governance. The lines on the map demarcating parliamentary constituencies and parish boundaries belied even sharper differences in practice and divisions of opinion that shifted as the city's social composition changed. Neither fixed in stone nor promiscuously fluid, these differences and divisions formed the political context in which the Poor Law Commissioners were forced to operate.

What was of crucial importance in the context of introducing the new poor law to London was the development in the preceding years of what can best be described as a radical turn in metropolitan politics that included both working-class leaders, such as Francis Place and William Lovett, and middle-class reformers, including prominent MPs, such as John Cam Hobhouse and Sir Francis Burdett. In parliamentary terms, this shift is evident from the way in which London constituencies came to support Whig and Radical reformers in the early decades of the century. In the unreformed parliamentary system, the relatively egalitarian franchises of many metropolitan constituencies meant that they were sufficiently large to prevent bribery and patronage from being an effective electoral tool. In the early 1800s, for example, the turbulent Westminster constituency, which had an open householder franchise that allowed many artisans to vote, had an electorate in excess of 15,000 and perhaps as many as 18,000 whilst the number of registered electors in Finsbury and Tower Hamlets in 1832 was nearly 13,000 and 10,000 respectively.[8] Furthermore, the high price of land in London meant that the £10 household franchise of the 1832 Reform Act reached further down the social scale than in other places. As a result, as Edward Thompson noted, the channels between middle-class and working-class reformers remained open and the opportunities for participation in London parliamentary elections were many.[9]

Those constituencies with more liberal franchises, notably Westminster, had developed a tradition of radicalism whilst others with less egalitarian voting

[7] *The Times*, 20 March 1855.

[8] See Charles Dod, *Electoral Facts 1832–1853, Impartially Stated, Constituting a Complete Political Gazetteer* (1853, reprinted Brighton, 1972).

[9] Edward P. Thompson, *The Making of the English Working Class* (Harmondsworth, 1963), pp. 492–513.

qualifications had a more chequered history of support for radical causes.[10] However, from the early years of the century London radicalism flourished at both parliamentary and parish levels. As Figure 3.1 shows, from 1812 metropolitan constituencies returned as many Whigs as Tories, and from 1818 Whig MPs were in the majority, a trend that was at odds with the rest of the country. Indeed, from Lord Liverpool's ministry in 1812 until Wellington's defeat by the Whigs in 1830, the Tories held national power continuously. Of equal or even greater significance, however, is the fact that London Whigs were a far cry from those aristocratic grandees that rallied to the party of order rather than contemplate any drastic reshaping of the political system.[11]

Although one should be wary of ascribing too great a distinction between the parties, nevertheless London Whigs, many of whom like Hobhouse were staunch Benthamite radicals, strongly supported political reform and frequently shared a greater ideological unity with working-class leaders than they did with many of their own party.[12] From 1818, the divergence between the parties was even more pronounced and from then until the late 1830s, by which time the Whigs had also regained power at a national level, the Tories barely mustered more than a token presence in the capital. By contrast, the number of Radical and Whig MPs, in some cases distinguished in little other than name only, increased steadily from 1818. The redistribution of seats following the Reform Act, which doubled the number of London MPs from ten to twenty, was also of clear benefit to this group, particularly the Whigs, who gained most in the 1832 elections, and the Radicals who increased their number from four in that year to seven by 1835. Most notably, this rise in Radical fortunes brought several influential anti-poor law opponents into Parliament including Thomas Wakley in Finsbury, Sir Samuel Whalley in Marylebone and Daniel Whittle Harvey in Southwark. At this level, therefore, London constituencies provided a powerful parliamentary platform for critics of the new poor law.

---

[10] Ibid., pp. 500–514, 669–70. Thompson also makes the point that radicalism was rooted in specific localities – Bethnal Green, Lambeth, Southwark, Finsbury, Islington – from which leaders sometimes emerged.

[11] See Norman McCord, *British History 1815–1906* (Oxford, 1991), p. 6.

[12] Bentham lived in Westminster and was in contact with leading radicals, including Major Cartwright and Francis Place. Although he quarrelled with Hunt and Cobbett, nevertheless he shared with them a commitment to universal suffrage. See Elie Halévy, *The Growth of Philosophic Radicalism* (London, 1928), pp. 249–310, esp. 254–69.

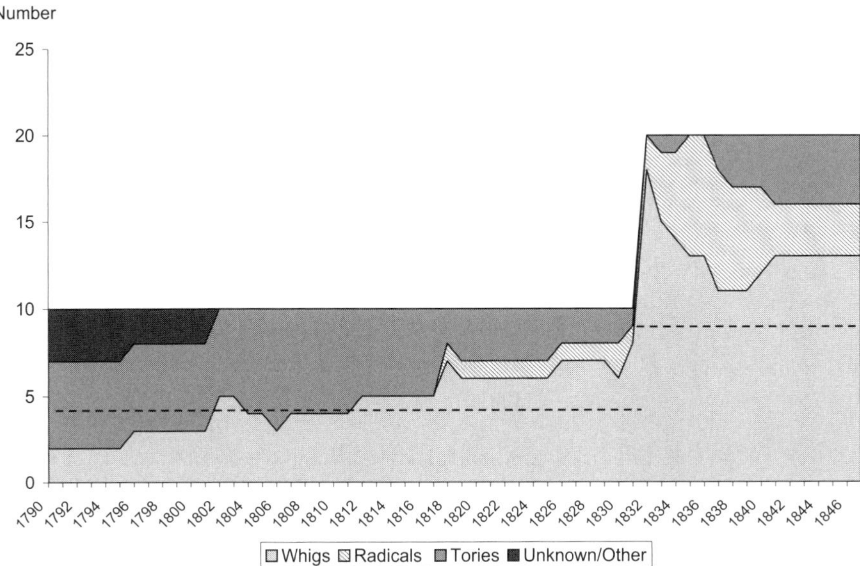

Figure 3.1 Political affiliation of London MPs 1790–1847

Source: Charles Dod, *Electoral Facts 1832–1853*, (1853, reprinted Brighton, 1972).

Whilst parliamentary elections were important in gauging the general tenor of political opinion, it was the parish that was arguably of greater importance as the focus of popular radicalism and extra-parliamentary political activity. Indeed, what took place at a parliamentary level had firm roots in borough and local politics.[13] In London working-class and middle-class radicals cooperated to organise local reform committees based largely on a shared distrust of central authority.[14] Such vestry radicalism emerged as a result of several factors. For most of the war years, the vestries had provided an opportunity for political debate, largely as a result of the exclusion of parish meetings from the Seditious Meetings Act of 1795.[15]

[13] For the former see Rosemary Sweet, 'Freemen and Independence in English Borough Politics c. 1770–1830', *Past and Present*, 161 (1998): 84–115.

[14] A good example of this is contained in the account of the 1831 reform procession in London written by John Powell to Francis Place in which he states 'In Clerkenwell, my own parish, though no housekeeper, we were more successful. We had previously in our character of propagandists converted a *Parochial* reform association held on Clerkenwell Green into a *Political* Reform association, and this was the lever by which we moved into that parish.' See David Rowe (ed.), *London Radicalism 1830–1843: A Selection from the Papers of Francis Place* (London, 1970), p. 42.

[15] Act for the More Effectually Preventing Seditious Meetings and Assemblies (Seditious Meetings Act), 38 Geo. III c. 8. The Seditious Meetings Act of 1795 prohibited

This meant that the vestry became a forum for discussion at a time when other avenues were met with repression. Furthermore, many open vestries still existed in which public participation was common and where working-class politicians could operate freely. As a result, throughout the Napoleonic wars and beyond, the parish frequently provided a platform for political activity for both working-class and middle-class radicals alike. In this sense, the politicisation of the vestries meant that parochial politics in its broader context was not separate to the national scene but constitutive of it.[16]

The links between parish and parliamentary politics are perhaps best exemplified with reference to the individuals involved. Although there were deep schisms within London radicalism, nevertheless links between parish radicals and those who operated on a wider stage were strong. The great radical orator, Henry Hunt, for example, who was active in parish reform and served in various parish offices in Christchurch, Surrey as well as being a vestryman in Lambeth, also became an auditor for the City of London and contested the Westminster election of 1818; Dr Thomas Wakley, crusading editor of the *Lancet*, medical reformer and Middlesex coroner, was elected as the Radical MP for Finsbury in 1835, having previously served as churchwarden of St Giles; Joseph Hume, Radical MP for the Middlesex constituency from 1830 to 1837 was fully involved in parochial elections, proposing a list of anti-poor law candidates in the St Marylebone vestry elections of 1836. A position on the vestry also maintained other MPs hostile to the new poor law, including Sir Samuel Whalley and Benjamin Hall in Marylebone.[17] In the City, too, a vibrant civic associational life provided numerous opportunities for those of relatively humble means to participate and progress in local government and from there to proceed to the national stage. Robert Waithman, for example, who made a living as a linen draper, served in various capacities in the City of London as an alderman, sheriff and Lord Mayor, as well as being an MP there from 1818 to 1820 and again from 1826 to 1833.[18] The links made by this network of metropolitan radicals were expressed clearly at a reform dinner at the Freemasons Tavern held by the churchwardens in St Giles in 1829 where speakers included Thomas Wakley's

---

meetings of more than 50 persons without permission from a magistrate, the only exception being parish meetings. See J. Ann Hone, *For the Cause of Truth: Radicalism in London 1796–1821* (Oxford, 1982).

[16] For a fuller discussion of this point see James Vernon, *Politics and the People: A Study in English Political Culture c. 1815–1867* (Cambridge, 1993), esp. pp. 15–47; Miles Taylor, *The Decline of British Radicalism 1847–1860* (Oxford, 1995), pp. 70–92.

[17] John Belchem, *Orator Hunt: Henry Hunt and English Working-class Radicalism* (Oxford, 1985), pp. 182–3. Election results from F. W. S. Craig, *British Parliamentary Election Results 1832–1885* (London, 1977).

[18] On this topic see Peter Claus, 'Languages of Citizenship in the City of London, 1848–1867', *London Journal*, 24 (1999): 23–37.

friend and business partner William Cobbett as well as Henry Hunt.[19] Describing the dinner, an anonymous opponent expressed better than most the sentiments that bound the strands of parochial and parliamentary reform: 'These gentlemen were of the party; parliamentary reform and parish reform, universal suffrage and open vestries, were considered as equally required to adjust the people's rights.'[20]

If the importance of the parish as a political entity was in part drawn from the circumstances related to their exclusion from the Seditious Meetings Act, it also owed much to the structural conditions of urban growth. The rapid expansion of London's population and infrastructure ushered in new legislative measures that provided vestries with powers to manage the urban environment which ran in parallel with those regulating poor relief. These powers had multiplied and grown in complexity from the mid-eighteenth century as a result of innumerable local acts that had been passed for watching, lighting, cleansing and paving the streets as well as for assessing the rates, administering poor relief and constructing workhouses. Though Benthamites and other social reformers, such as Patrick Colquhoun, argued for greater powers to be vested in central authorities and appointed commissions, nonetheless these powers to regulate the urban environment primarily rested with and were jealously guarded by the vestries.

So, too, was the provision of poor relief. London's growth from the mid-eighteenth century was accompanied by a parallel increase in the number of poor, especially after the end of the Napoleonic wars, and a corresponding increase in local acts regulating poor relief. Reviewing the situation in 1843, the Poor Law Commissioners counted at least 51 local acts governing poor relief in London that had been passed between 1722 and 1795 with a further 54 in the period from 1795 to 1834.[21] In many districts separate local acts existed governing the appointment of directors of the poor, assessments and collection of rates, management of the workhouse and the provision of outdoor relief. Hard-won and jealously guarded parochial autonomy, coupled with the legal labyrinth that had developed to regulate poor relief in the capital, ensured that any attempt to reform the system was bound to generate opposition.

However, the very factors that underpinned the expansion of local government – population growth, the increasing complexity of servicing the urban infrastructure and providing for the growing numbers of poor – also severely strained the ability of vestries and directors of the poor to function effectively. Meetings were

---

19 (St Giles Vestry), *Refutation of Charges against the Select Vestry* ... (1829); pp. 45–6; *Morning Chronicle*, 1 July 1829.

20 Ibid. The anonymous correspondent also noted how 'The aristocracy of the parish was marked out to be trampled down; the resumption of the estates of landed proprietors as a just proceeding because the produce would be sufficient to defray the cost of all poor-rates; the church was reviled as engrossing the wealth destined for charity and the *atrocious* vestry denounced for annihilation.'

21 Poor Law Commission, Ninth Annual Report (1843), Appendix 2, number 2, Report on local acts by Edward Twistelton, pp. 95–115.

often disorderly, particularly where open vestries operated and where substantial ratepayers were too few to have much influence over the crowd. In Bethnal Green, for example, whilst the open vestry operated 'nothing but anarchy and confusion' was said to have reigned whilst in neighbouring Mile End it was claimed that violent disagreements and profligate expenditure characterised the vestry's activities.[22] Business was often carried out haphazardly and the pressure of day-to-day administration, especially regarding poor relief, outstripped the capacity of amateur, unpaid and largely voluntary officers. As traditional forms of dispensing relief waned in the face of larger numbers of the poor and lack of suitable individuals willing to perform the onerous duties of overseers – in itself a result of growing social segregation – so the poor law became increasingly professionalised with paid rate collectors and overseers replacing honorary officers.[23]

In the name of administrative efficiency attempts were made early in the century to reform parish elections. In 1807 Samuel Whitbread had proposed a bill that would have introduced plural voting in elections and although it was withdrawn, the principle of linking votes to property ownership remained. In 1817 the select committee appointed to investigate the poor laws, chaired by William Sturges Bourne, churchwarden and vestryman in St George's Hanover Square, blamed the steep increase in the cost of relief on the inefficiency of the open vestry. The two reforms arising from this report, the Parish Vestries Act of 1818 and the Select Vestry Act of 1819, both of which were drafted by Sturges Bourne, attempted to introduce select vestries comprised of larger ratepayers and to extend the principle of plural voting to parish elections.[24] The first established select vestries elected on a sliding scale of votes according to property ownership, and the second enabled a vestry constituted under the 1818 Act to delegate powers of poor relief to a committee of substantial householders with authority to appoint paid assistant overseers.[25] Under the 1818 Act, resident and non-resident property owners were able to vote in vestry elections on a sliding scale rising from one vote for those assessed up to £50 to 6 votes for those with property valued at £150 or more. In both cases, the legislation effectively transferred power to large property owners whether or not they were resident in the parish, a move calculated to reduce the

---

22 PP 1834 XXXV Royal commission on the administration and practical operation of the poor laws, replies to town queries, responses from Bethnal Green and Mile End Old Town.

23 M. Dorothy George, *London Life in the Eighteenth Century* (Harmondsworth, 1966), p. 22. R. Burn in the *History of the Poor Laws* (1764) had first recommended the employment of a paid overseer. See George Nicholls, *A History of the English Poor Law, vol. 2 1714–1853* (London, 1898), p. 60.

24 Act for the Regulation of Parish vestries (Parish Vestries Act), 58 Geo. III c. 69; Act to Amend the Law for the Relief of the Poor (Select Vestry Act), 59 Geo. III c. 12.

25 See Bryan Keith-Lucas, *The Unreformed Local Government System* (London, 1980), pp. 98–9; David Eastwood, *Governing Rural England: Tradition and Transformation in Local Government 1780–1840* (Oxford, 1994), pp. 131–2.

influence of smaller tradesmen and ratepayers and to dispense altogether with open vestries.

In relation to these reforms, London proved problematic. Concerted opposition from Southwark and the City of London, in which the small size of parishes rendered select vestries superfluous, ensured that both were excluded from the provisions of the 1818 Act. Elsewhere, adoption of the Act depended on whether vestries operated, however poorly, under private local acts, which was the case in many other London districts.[26] Replies from metropolitan parishes to the Royal Commission on the Poor Laws suggested that failure to adopt Sturges Bourne's Parish Vestries Act was precisely because a similar local act operated and that change was therefore unnecessary. As a result, only a small number of London parishes adopted the measure. The same was true of the Select Vestry Act of 1819 and as a result very few metropolitan parishes came under either piece of legislation.[27]

In London, however, it was not just the fact that select vestries operating under local acts had already been introduced that made Sturges Bourne's reforms unpopular. Although there were some supporters of select vestries, especially in those rapidly growing parishes beyond the City where open vestries had proved incapable of governing, opinion was largely hostile – and grew more so as the cost of relief soared in the 1820s.[28] The general principle of select vestries, and more specifically the regressive franchise embodied in the 1818 Parish Vestries Act, was roundly condemned by metropolitan reformers. William Cobbett and Thomas Wakley, amongst others, were staunch opponents.[29] Such criticism, fuelled by sharp rises in rates during the 1820s, focused opposition against select vestries. One anonymous critic who wrote under the pseudonym of 'one of the non-select', described select vestries as nothing more than a 'harpy of corruption, this monster of parochial misrule'. Pointing out some of the worst abuses in St Marylebone, St Paul Covent Garden, St Martin in the Fields and Spitalfields, he castigated such bodies as 'a foul blemish on the fair face of our glorious constitution, tending to render precarious every political privilege which at this moment we enjoy'.[30]

---

26 See, for example, PP 1834 XXXV Royal commission on the administration and practical operation of the poor laws, replies to town queries from St Giles in the Fields, St Anne Limehouse, Paddington, St Mary Whitechapel and Saffron Hill. For fuller discussion see Bryan Keith-Lucas, *The English Local Government Franchise* (Oxford, 1952), pp. 23–31.

27 Ibid., p. 28.

28 Supporters of select vestries on the grounds of efficiency included Joseph Bosworth, *The Practical Means of Reducing the Poor's Rate, Encouraging Virtue and Increasing the Comforts of the Aged, Afflicted and Deserving Poor* (London, 1824), p. 19.

29 See Keith-Lucas, *English Local Government Franchise*, pp. 25–6.

30 ['One of the non-select'], *Considerations on Select Vestries Shewing from the Oppression and Corrupt Practices Now Prevailing in the Different Parishes* (London, 1828), p. 1.

Such language was in some respects justified. In many parishes, expenditure had risen significantly under select and often secretive vestries. In St Marylebone the parochial debt had soared to nearly £250,000 whilst rates had increased by 60 per cent between 1824 and 1827. Enormous amounts had been spent on the parish church, including £159 for a velvet pulpit cover and £213 on a pair of chairs. To make matters worse, accounts appeared sporadically and meetings of the vestry were always held in secret.[31] Accounts were also missing for St Giles in the Fields prior to 1822, where the local act establishing a select vestry was similar to Sturges Bourne's in the sense that it had a sliding scale for voting. There the vestry clerk was said to have received the enormous sum of £1,050 per annum for his work – an extraordinary amount even for a busy parish.[32] In St James Westminster little more than a handful of vestrymen controlled all proceedings whilst in neighbouring St Martin in the Fields vestrymen thought nothing of dining regularly at the parish expense. Extravagance also irked ratepayers in St Pancras where the select vestry dismissed objections to the enormous cost of the new parish church – the most expensive ever built – without leave to appeal.[33] In Spitalfields, concerns about the extravagant repairs to the church financed by some dubious borrowing at unusually high interest also helped direct anger against the select vestry.[34] In Southwark, the United Parishioners Society, led by John Day, a local draper, was founded to check extravagant expenditure, reduce the rates and clear the 'monstrous debt' that that had prevailed under the previous select vestry.[35]

Whilst extravagance and lack of accountability most irked smaller ratepayers, other more general issues were of equal if not greater importance. The main opposition to select vestries came from a close knit group of metropolitan radicals and reformers with strong roots in parish politics. Although members might have differed in their specific ideological viewpoint, nonetheless they shared a

---

31 ['A Churchman'], *A General Statement of the Case of the Parishioners against the Select Vestry of St Mary-le-bone Parish* (London, 1828); ['One of the non-select'], *Considerations on Select Vestries*, p. 55. See also Keith-Lucas, *English Local Government Franchise*, p. 29.

32 Rowland Dobie, *A History of the United Parishes of St Giles in the Fields and St George Bloomsbury* (London, 1829), p. 344.

33 See PP 1830 IV Select committee appointed to inquire into the general operation and effect of the laws and usages under which select and other vestries are constituted, pp. 458, 484, 494, 515–18, 526–7, 560. For the situation in St Marylebone see [Anon], *Copy of Correspondence between the Committee of Parishioners of the Parish of St Marylebone appointed ... to investigate the affairs of the parish ...* (1827); ['A Churchman'], *A General Statement of the Case of the Parishioners Against the Select Vestry of St Mary-le-bone Parish* (1828). For the reform of the St Marylebone vestry see James Brooke, *The Democrats of Marylebone* (London, 1839); Francis H. W. Sheppard, *Local Government in St Marylebone 1688–1835* (London, 1958), pp. 276–314.

34 ['One of the non-select'] *Considerations on Select Vestries*, pp. 30–35.

35 [Anon], *Broadside, United Parishioners of St George the Martyr Southwark, meeting to be held on 31 January 1831.*

commitment to both national and local political reform, understanding the two to be inseparable.[36] This group included some of the most prominent radicals in London: John Cam Hobhouse, who had been imprisoned in 1819 following the Peterloo massacre and elected for Westminster in the following year; George Fall, John Moore and John Grady in Lambeth, the latter of whom was a close friend of Henry Hunt and co-founder of the Friends of Civil and Religious Liberty; John Savage, a Freethinking Christian, Owenite supporter and vestryman in St Marylebone; the Irish Chartist and chairman of the National Political Union, Thomas Murphy, leader of the St Pancras parochial committee; George Rogers, friend and election agent for Thomas Wakley and at one time churchwarden in St Giles in the Fields.[37]

These and other reformers comprised a close network of people for whom parochial and political reform were indistinguishable, a fact perhaps best illustrated by the prominent role played in the National Political Union by Thomas Murphy and Henry Revell, two of the new vestrymen for St Pancras elected after the adoption of Hobhouse's Act.[38] In the ballot for the National Political Union council in 1832, both were elected ahead of Francis Place, along with several of their supporters.[39] Their network of colleagues, which extended beyond the immediate nominees shown in Figure 3.2, included Thomas Potter, one of the reforming vestrymen from neighbouring St Marylebone and George Rogers from St Giles, who was chairman when the new council assembled and who himself had proposed five other delegates, including William Lovett and Thomas Wakley. Only Lovett of this entire network failed to be elected and together this group comprised the main locus of power, confirming the close relationship that existed between parish-based radicals and those active in a wider range of political issues.

---

[36] For further discussion of the ideological divisions within radicalism see John Belchem, 'Republicanism, Popular Constitutionalism and the Radical Platform in Early Nineteenth-Century England', *Social History*, 6 (1981), 1–32; Belchem, *Orator Hunt*; James Epstein, 'The Constitutionalist Idiom: Radical Reasoning, Rhetoric and Action in Early Nineteenth-Century England', *Journal of Social History*, 23 (1990), 553–74; Iorwerth Prothero, *Artisans and Politics in Early Nineteenth-Century London* (London, 1981), pp. 268–99.

[37] For discussions of the activities of these individuals in other spheres of radical politics see Belchem, *Orator Hunt*; Prothero, *Artisans and Politics*; Hone, *For the Cause of Truth* (1982), *passim*. For a hostile contemporary account of these factions see James Grant, *The Great Metropolis* (London, 1837), pp. 67–78.

[38] Both were re-elected in 1833, as were Burnard, Churchill, Longmate, Rogers, Saull, Wakefield and Wright. See Rowe (ed.), *London Radicalism*, pp. 116–17.

[39] Two lists of nominees existed; one for the working class and the other 'not of the working class'. In addition to nominating each other, Murphy proposed six candidates (three from each list) whilst Revell proposed five from the second list. In both cases, all their nominees were elected. See Rowe (ed.), *London Radicalism*, pp. 69–71.

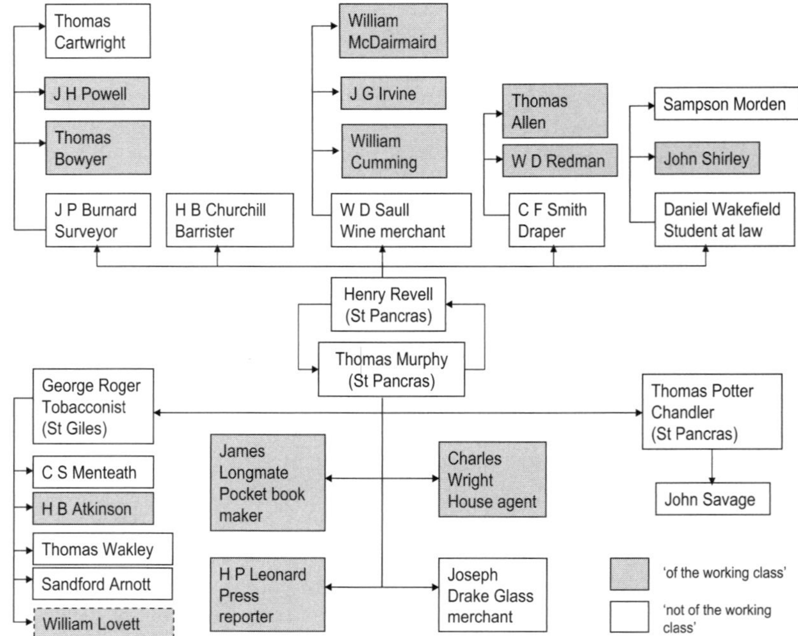

Figure 3.2 Nominations by Thomas Murphy and Henry Revell for the National Political Union, February 1832

Note: Only William Lovett failed to be elected.

Source: Place Papers, British Library, Add. Ms 27791, folio 222, reprinted in David Rowe (ed.), *London Radicalism 1830–1843* (London, 1970) pp. 69–71.

Parochial reform

When the Whigs came to power in 1830 one of the first issues they addressed was reform of the metropolitan vestries, partly because of the difficulties they encountered from Tory dominated select vestries but also as a precursor to other measures of municipal and electoral reform. When Parliament discussed the matter in 1831 both Henry Hunt and Daniel O'Connell supported vestry reform as a step towards full parliamentary representation of the people.[40] Reforming the vestry was therefore not just a question of undermining the power of landowning elites in London's local government, and as such an attack against the Tory establishment, but was also part of the wider movement for electoral reform supported by the radical wing of the Whig administration.

[40] See *Hansard Parliamentary Debates*, 3rd series, 7, 30 September, 8, 13 October 1831.

John Hobhouse was given the task of marshalling the select committee on vestry reform and piloting the measure through Parliament.[41] The ensuing legislation, known as Hobhouse's Act, became law in 1831 and was immediately welcomed in London, particularly in those districts in which abuses had been most blatant. Its main significance was that it widened the franchise to all resident ratepayers not in arrears, including women, who had lived in the parish for one year. It was for that reason that the ladies of Marylebone, discussed above, had been so roundly cheered in 1834. The relatively wide franchise shifted power decisively towards smaller resident ratepayers and laid the foundation for a powerful alliance between the skilled working class and lower middle class against larger property owners. Similarly, the emphasis on occupiers of property as opposed to owners provided smaller local ratepayers with a strong power base whilst a residency clause prevented absentee owners from having any direct say in local elections or acting on the vestry.[42] Fearful of the impact this would have on Tory fortunes in the capital, the Duke of Wellington condemned the measure 'for leaving the property of every man at the disposition of the rabble of the parish'.[43]

As with other similar measures, Hobhouse's Act was permissive rather than mandatory. Provided that two thirds of voters agreed, any parish with over 800 ratepayers could choose to implement the Act. Although it was only adopted in five metropolitan parishes – St George Hanover Square, St James Westminster, St John Westminster, St Marylebone and St Pancras – the agitation surrounding the measure and its subsequent implementation had wider implications for understanding the anti-poor law movement in London. In the first place, these five districts were amongst the largest and wealthiest in the capital. Indeed, in terms of population, they were of national let alone local significance. Second, in those districts in which the Act was adopted, it appeared to be very widely supported: in St Marylebone, 6,509 persons voted for its adoption and only 20 opposed it out of a total electorate of about 8,500; in neighbouring St Pancras, 5,503 voted for and 38 against out of an electorate of about 6,000; in St George Hanover Square the figures were 2,460 for and 25 against; in St James Westminster, 1,152 for and 14 against out of a total electorate of 1,499, and in St John Westminster, 1,036 for and 13 against.[44]

---

41 John Cam Hobhouse was MP for Westminster between 1820 and 1833, and then for Nottingham until 1847.

42 Act for the Better Regulation of Vestries and for the Appointment of Auditors of Accounts in Certain Parishes of England and Wales (Vestries Act), 1 & 2 Will. IV c. 60. At the same time, however, the qualification to act as a vestryman was confined to occupiers of property worth at least £40, thereby ensuring that only substantial local residents, as opposed to absentee owners or the working class, could serve on the vestry.

43 Quoted in John Prest, *Liberty and Locality: Parliament, Permissive Legislation, and Ratepayers' Democracies in the Nineteenth Century* (Oxford, 1990), p. 12.

44 *True Sun*, 19, 27 March, 3, 4, 17, 18 April 1832; CWAC D/1771 St James Westminster Vestry, Minutes, 1 May 1832. It is unclear whether these figures refer to the total number of votes cast or to those that were valid. In St James, the number of votes

Irrespective of any exaggeration in the reported figures, such widespread support by local ratepayers revealed a common dislike of the regressive franchise inherent in metropolitan select vestries and a clear sense of commitment to some measure of political reform.

Under the terms of Hobhouse's Act, the old vestry was to be replaced over a period of three years, which meant that by 1835 the new Hobhouse vestries were in complete control over parish affairs. Authority passed from aristocratic grandees to local tradesmen and *petit bourgeoise* ratepayers who thereafter were as concerned to preserve their new power base as they were to exercise parsimony over poor relief. In St George's Hanover Square, which prior to 1832 had been controlled by a select vestry made up mainly of the gentry and aristocracy, the adoption of Hobhouse's Act ushered in new vestrymen comprising largely of local tradesmen. The same was true in St James Westminster: of the 32 select vestrymen in 1830 no less than 20 were aristocracy, MPs, or noted as 'esquires' whilst only 10 were local tradesmen. In 1835, by which time all vestrymen had been elected under Hobhouse's Act, only one MP remained, whilst 23 were local tradesmen.[45] St Marylebone was similar: in 1829 the vestry contained 18 members of the aristocracy, 50 esquires, 7 MPs but only 18 tradesmen. By 1835 there were at least 43 tradesmen compared to 31 esquires, 3 MPs and only 5 aristocratic vestrymen.[46] In faction-ridden St Pancras, vestry business from 1832 onwards was controlled by radical parochial reform committees which met at various local public houses.[47] For the rowdy supporters of these 'pot-house Jacobin clubs', as James Brooke called them, parochial reform had a wider significance, and 'the question of local taxation had become ... magnified into one of national liberty'.[48]

The new poor law and London

The shift in vestry elections, mirroring that at parliamentary level which had taken place after 1832, moulded the political landscape that faced the new Poor Law Commissioners at precisely the time they began to turn their attention to the capital. It was with somewhat mixed feelings that they set about their mission. Lord Althorp, whose task it was to pilot the Poor Law Amendment bill through

---

reported corresponded to that declared valid by Counsel J Pollock. The voting figures from St John Westminster Vestry, Minutes, 1 May 1832, were 443 for, 8 against, and 594 votes declared invalid. See CWAC E/2470 St James Westminster Vestry, Minutes, 1 May 1832.

45 CWAC D/1774 St James Westminster, List of Vestrymen, 1830, 1835. Occupations and addresses were derived from CWAC D/1771 St James Westminster Vestry, Minutes, 1 May 1830; *Boyles Court and Country Guide*, 1830; *Robsons London Directory*, 1835.

46 CWAC V/8 St Marylebone, *A List of Vestrymen and Auditors of the Parish* 1829, 1835; Occupations were taken from *Robson's London Directory* 1830 and 1835.

47 Brooke, *Democrats of Marylebone*, pp. 30, 59–69.

48 Ibid., p. 30.

Parliament, baulked at the prospect of including London and initially considered leaving out parishes with populations larger than 70,000 from the new arrangements, a move that was calculated to exclude several of the larger metropolitan districts, including those such as St Marylebone and St Pancras in which the parochial reform movement was strongest. However, Edwin Chadwick was reluctant to establish such a precedent and, disregarding the legal and political minefield that London presented, he insisted that such an exclusion be dropped.[49]

Chadwick in particular was hostile to the vestries, questioning their apparent democratic credentials and castigating them as 'juntas', 'petty oligarchies' and 'job-ocracies' which 'maintained their hold over the persons of the pauperised labourers, and the purses of the rate payers by pertinacious blackguardism and every low art'.[50] Answering those who hailed the parish vestry as the fulcrum of local democracy, he argued that 'To talk of this as the self-government characteristics, and the glory of Englishmen, is despicable rant.'[51] Chadwick was especially concerned with the vestry's role in providing poor relief and his views were evident in the Royal Commission's report which described them as 'the most irresponsible bodies that ever were entrusted with the performance of public duties, or the distribution of public money'.[52] Failure to include Hobhouse parishes and those governed by a local act under the Poor Law Amendment Act would, it was argued, permit abuses to continue unchecked by the central commissioners.

Furthermore, most of the 15,000 or so parishes in England and Wales were considered too small to support the cost of a new workhouse whilst poor law officials themselves were often too close to the paupers to allow for the dispassionate provision of relief. As Chadwick noted in relation to a dispute over the constituent districts of Greenwich board of guardians, unions themselves had to be sufficiently large to preclude the possibility of personal knowledge clouding individual judgements:

> The relief of the poor is also found to be administered with greater steadiness of principle and more uniform impartiality by a mixed Board of Guardians of whom a part only have personal knowledge of the applicants for relief than by a Board wholly formed of the fellow parishioners of such applicants.[53]

---

[49] Anthony Brundage, *The Making of the New Poor Law: The Politics of Inquiry, Enactment and Implementation 1832–39* (London, 1978), p. 57.

[50] Edwin Chadwick, 'Extracts from the Information Received by His Majesty's Commissioners as to the Administration and Operation of the Poor Laws…', *Edinburgh Review*, vol. 63, no. 128 (1836): 524.

[51] Ibid., 520.

[52] PP 1834 XXVII Royal commission into the administration and practical operation of poor laws, report, p. 61.

[53] TNA MH12/5092 Local Government Board and predecessors: Correspondence with Poor Law Unions and Other Local Authorities, Greenwich Board of Guardians, 6 March 1838.

The argument against this, of course, was that imposition was more easily detected when applicants for relief were known personally and for that reason local boards were better than those composed largely of strangers. Samuel Bosanquet argued in this fashion that the creation of large districts '... is the most essential evil in the new system of poor law administration'.[54] However, architects of the new poor law argued firmly that unions were necessary in order to provide a more efficient way to administer relief, both by allowing local authorities to capitalise from advantages of scale whilst at the same time minimising the likelihood that local officials would come under undue pressure either from paupers or by smaller ratepayers who themselves were often little removed from pauperism.[55] Such unions, moreover, were necessary in order to construct new, well-regulated workhouses which were to be the cornerstone of the principle of less eligibility.

Chadwick himself had further serious misgivings about the willingness of unreformed vestries to implement changes in poor relief. What concerned him in particular was the fact that in many cases, especially in Hobhouse Act parishes, absentee owners, as opposed to occupiers of property, were ineligible to vote in vestry elections despite the fact that they were still liable to pay the rates. This meant that those mainly responsible for providing the funds for poor relief had little or no control over how it was to be dispensed, resulting inevitably, so he believed, in profligate and irresponsible expenditure. A primary concern, therefore, over and above the formation of new unions, was to reform the franchise for boards of guardians and so shift control over poor relief from the vestry, which usually appointed directors of the poor, to these new directly elected boards.

Under Chadwick's influence, both objectives were included in the Poor Law Amendment Act.[56] The franchise for guardian elections was set to include owners as well as occupiers of property whilst plural voting was re-introduced, giving large owner-occupiers up to six votes each and allowing absentee landlords to vote by proxy. In doing so the Poor Law Amendment Act replicated Sturges Bourne's Vestries Act of 1818 which earlier had been so roundly condemned by reformers. Both plural and proxy voting provided the propertied elite, including gentry and members of the aristocracy who resided only part of the time in London, with a disproportionate influence in guardian elections. In St Martin in the Fields, for example, plural voting in the guardian elections of 1837 accounted for nearly two

---

[54] Samuel Bosanquest, *The Rights of the Poor and Christian Almsgiving Vindicated* (London, 1841), p. 245.

[55] For further discussion see Felix Driver, *Power and Pauperism: The Workhouse System 1834–1884* (Cambridge, 1993), pp. 32–57.

[56] Act for the Amendment and Better Administration of the Laws Relating to the Poor in England and Wales (Poor Law Amendment Act), 4 & 5 Will. IV c. 76. Owners or occupiers of property worth up to £200 were granted one vote, whilst those whose property was worth at least £400 were given three votes. Where the owner was also the occupier, he or she was able to cast two sets of votes up to a maximum of six votes.

thirds of the total votes cast.[57] The measures also meant that guardian elections were in many cases far less egalitarian than those for vestries, which not infrequently resulted in the two bodies being composed of different and potentially conflicting groups.

That the Poor Law Amendment Act threatened to undermine any gains that had been made by the parochial reform movement was not lost on local vestrymen, especially where Hobhouse's Act had recently been implemented. In St Pancras the vestry condemned plural voting as 'unjust' and proxy voting as 'vicious'.[58] Similar objections were raised by the St Marylebone vestrymen. Sir Samuel Whalley called the new measure 'a nefarious infringement on the rights of Englishmen' whilst John Savage, one of those who had been elected to the National Political Union council as part of the network or parish radicals, condemned it thus:

> This bill should be called a bill to repeal the Vestries Act.... it established Sturges Bourne's Act all over the kingdom. It was a bill, not so much for the amendment of the poor laws, as to destroy the liberties of the people.[59]

In neighbouring Holborn, a faction of ratepayers contesting the guardian elections in 1839 issued a handbill entitled 'MANSLAUGHTER under the Poor Law Amendment Act'. Their chief complaint was that the ratepayers themselves were '... treated like cattle under this infamous Act. You have the mockery of a vote, but by a despotic system of voting unjustly given to the landlords, you are entirely disfranchised of the power of returning the Guardians.'[60] This concern over the franchise and the power given to large landowners to influence policy and thereby set the rates, rather than any fundamental disagreement about the relief of poverty, underpinned opposition to the new poor law. Parish radicals and small ratepayers alike therefore rejected the Poor Law Amendment Act as a backward step in the march of democracy and in so doing politicised the struggle against the new poor law in London.

Undeterred by such matters, the Poor Law Commissioners ploughed on with their schemes for implementing the new poor law and establishing unions. The primary consideration in setting the boundaries was that unions should be sufficiently large to support a well regulated workhouse. In rural areas this normally meant a union centred on a market town surrounded by a circular area the maximum radius of which was to be determined by the needs of accessibility. In urban areas, other than a minimum population, such considerations were irrelevant and other criteria were important, including similarities in social and economic conditions. That

---

57 *The Times*, 2 February 1837.

58 CLHC, P/PN1/M/1/16 St Pancras Vestry, Minutes, 1 March 1837.

59 *New Vestryman*, 3 May 1834.

60 TNA MH12/7286 Local Government Board and predecessors: Correspondence, Holborn Board of Guardians, 2 April 1839.

economic efficiency and social compatibility were not the only considerations is clear from that fact that the assistant commissioners were instructed to gather the necessary data for determining which parishes should be combined and to gauge the opinions of any affected parties, including large landowners and parochial authorities. They were also told to identify the obstacles, if any, to the formation of unions, 'whether arising from ignorance, self-interest, or any other cause'.[61] This consideration was essential since, like much legislation, the adoption of the Poor Law Amendment Act was permissive rather than mandatory and depended on acceptance by two thirds of the ratepayers. It was therefore important that the assistant commissioners ensured that the boundaries of the new unions were likely to be agreeable to all parties before proceeding with their recommendations. The union boundaries that emerged thus represented a balance of forces, depending on the influence of local landowners and interested parties, the degree of resistance as well as administrative and economic considerations.

Forming unions

In November 1834 Charles Mott, who as contractor for the Lambeth workhouse already had extensive experience of the London poor law, was appointed assistant poor law commissioner for the city.[62] His first visit was to Clapham workhouse where he was pleased to note that, '… as in most parishes, the alterations are already forcibly felt and all the officers declared what I have heard in several other parishes, that a great alteration is perceptible in the conduct of paupers when applying for relief'.[63] Perhaps buoyed by the prospect of a relatively easy introduction of the new poor law to London, Mott left for a tour of the southwest, only returning in March the following year. Although he complained that the metropolitan district which he had been allocated was too large for one person, nevertheless on his return he made swift progress in forming unions in the southern parishes of Camberwell, Lambeth and St George Southwark, districts with which he was most familiar. The remaining southern parishes, with the exception of St Mary Newington, soon

61 See TNA MH1/1 Poor Law Commission, Minute Books, 4 November 1834.

62 Charles Mott's career as a private contractor for the poor and advocate of strict economy brought him into contact with reformers, including Edwin Chadwick. With the coming of the new poor law, Mott's lucrative contracts ceased. However, his views on strict economy chimed with Chadwick's and he was appointed as an assistant poor law commissioner, a post he held until 1842. He resumed his association with the poor law through his involvement as owner of Haydock lodge lunatic asylum and as a district auditor, though he was never far from controversy and was eventually declared insolvent. Mott's life and career is discussed in D. Hirst, '"A Ticklish Sort of Affair": Charles Mott, Haydock Lodge and the Economics of Asylumdom', *History of Psychiatry*, 16 (2005): 311–32.

63 TNA MH32/56 Local Government Board and predecessors: Assistant Poor Law Commissioners and Inspectors, Correspondence, Charles Mott, 20 November 1834.

followed suit. Similar progress was made in eastern parishes, several of which had recently constructed new workhouses. Where no such improvements had been made, opposition was greatest, as happened in Stepney.[64] Nevertheless, in May 1836, following the first election of guardians in the new unions, Mott wrote in optimistic tones to his superiors at Somerset House:

> ... the new law has been introduced into the metropolitan parishes with much less difficulty than had been anticipated and with a certainty of (a) complete ultimate sweep. Instances are very rare of violent opposition to the new system; prejudices yield to the startling facts brought to light and the extraordinary beneficial effects produced in all districts where the rules and regulations of the Commissioners have been introduced.[65]

Elsewhere, however, progress was somewhat slower. Forming the 98 parishes which comprised the City of London within the walls into a single union was particularly troublesome, especially since it removed an immense source of patronage from the hands of local officials. It also meant that because of the limitation imposed on the size of the new board of guardians, the smaller parishes would not be represented by their own vestrymen. To have allowed all City parishes, even those with fewer than a hundred inhabitants, to have at least one elected guardian would have meant having an impossibly large board.[66] Nevertheless, the need for reform outweighed any opposition and by late 1837 the City of London union had been formed, followed shortly by the East and West London unions comprising the extra-mural City parishes.[67]

The new administrative map of poor relief after 1834 marked a distinct rationalisation of administration. For those places that adopted the Poor Law Amendment Act, although the parish itself remained the basis for rating and settlement, in terms of the provision of relief it was the union that became of paramount importance. By the end of 1837, as Figure 3.3 shows, most metropolitan districts, with the exception of St Mary Newington in the south and a cluster of districts in the north and west, had adopted the Poor Law Amendment Act. In total 28 new unions were created, including 9 single parish unions, and these, together with the 11 vestries which continued to operate under local acts for the relief of the poor, constituted the administrative framework for the new poor law in London. Some further boundary changes took place in subsequent years to accommodate

---

64 TNA MH12/7798 Local Government Board and predecessors: Correspondence, Stepney Board of Guardians, 5 October 1838.

65 TNA MH32/56 Local Government Board and predecessors: Assistant Poor Law Commissioners and Inspectors, Correspondence, Charles Mott, 2 May 1836.

66 Ibid., 21 March, 28 July 1836. See also Andrea Tanner, 'The City of London Poor Law Union 1837–1869', (unpublished Ph.D. thesis, University of London, 1995) pp. 77–82.

67 For the formation of the City of London union see Poor Law Commission, Third Annual Report (1837), pp. 4–5.

population growth and ratepayer discontent. Thus Chelsea, initially included in the Kensington Union, separated in 1841 whilst Fulham and Paddington, also part of Kensington, were divided in 1845. In each case, exceptionally rapid population growth necessitated the changes: Paddington's population for example, almost doubled from 25,173 in 1841 to 46,305 in 1851, a rate of growth unsurpassed anywhere in the city.[68] Other changes included the separation of Hampstead from the Edmonton Union in 1848 and Mile End Old Town from Stepney in 1857. Other than these changes, the map of poor law unions remained the same until the late 1860s.

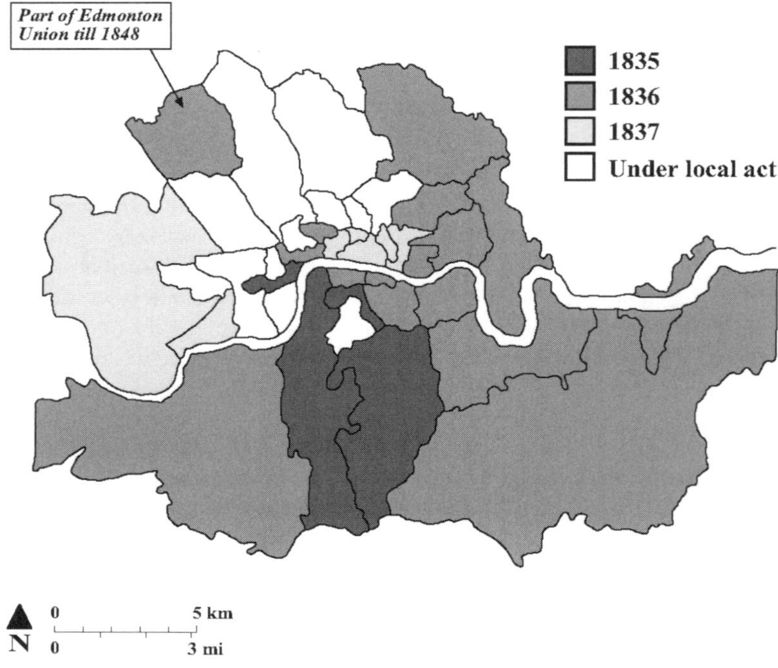

Figure 3.3 Formation of poor law unions in London 1835–1837

Source: Poor Law Commission, Annual Reports 1835–1838.

In the metropolitan context the Poor Law Commissioners had to draw a balance between districts in which the population was inadequate for the purpose of building a new workhouse and those which were so large as to prove impossible to administer. Size itself only became a problem when anonymity afforded 'clever' paupers the opportunity to defraud unsuspecting officials. Nevertheless, whilst the

[68] See R. Price Williams, 'The Population of London, 1801–1881', *Journal of the Statistical Society*, 48 (1885): 399.

average population of the districts that were to comprise the new unions was a little over 47,000 in 1831, there were wide differences in both size and social conditions. The two largest districts in terms of population as well as expenditure were St Marylebone and St Pancras, both of which continued to operate after 1834 under local acts. Lambeth, the largest of the new poor law unions, had a population of 87,856 in 1831 with Kensington, as already mentioned, not far behind. By contrast, the districts that were to form the Lewisham union, the smallest and most rural, consisted of no more than 10,767 persons whilst Rotherhithe's population was only slightly larger at 12,875.

Reorganisation and opposition

In such a complex administrative reorganisation, protests and changes were bound to follow both over points of detail as well as points of principle. Whilst the former were amenable to judicious alterations by the Poor Law Commissioners, the latter proved more problematic. Given the significance of the changes, there were relatively few serious objections amongst those districts that in principle supported the new arrangements. However, complaints over inclusion in specific unions, coupled with demographic change, prompted some hasty reorganisation of union boundaries.

In the west, the Chelsea vestry campaigned vigorously against their inclusion in the Kensington union established in December 1836. Their argument rested on several concerns, notably that the union itself would be too large for relieving officers to enquire into the merits of individual applicants for relief and that their own parish was of a sufficient size to elect a separate board of guardians.[69] Underlying these objections, however, was concern over the additional expenditure incurred as a result of incorporation with the surrounding parishes. Having already sharply reduced costs as a result of the stricter implementation of an outdoor labour task, the Chelsea vestry was hardly in the mood to sanction additional expenditure lightly. Questions were also raised over the precedence of local acts over the Poor Law Commissioners' authority with the situation becoming more confused with the suspension and subsequent reinstatement of the order for new guardian elections in 1837.[70] Recognising the validity of some of these concerns, and taking into account the exceptionally rapid growth of population in these western suburbs, in 1841 the Commissioners separated Chelsea from the other parishes in the Kensington union. Four years later the union was again divided when Fulham was made into a separate poor law district.

Reasons other than population growth underlay the reorganisation of the Greenwich union, which consisted of the parishes of St Paul and St Nicholas in Deptford, Greenwich itself and Woolwich to the east. Chadwick had justified the

69 *The Times*, 4 February 1837, 1 March, 2 November, 1 December 1838.

70 Ibid., 3 March, 1 July 1837.

formation of the union on the grounds that each of the districts was characterised by dockside activities, and that as the best managed parish, Greenwich should be the centre of the new union. The workhouse at Woolwich, he noted, was a 'disgrace to the parish' with weekly per capita costs of 3s 7½d compared to 2s 8¼d in Greenwich.[71] In Woolwich and St Paul objectors countered by arguing that the new union was too large, both in terms of the distance that guardians and paupers alike would have had to travel to attend meetings and receive relief respectively. They also claimed that guardians drawn from such a wide area would have no personal knowledge of the poor. As a result, they argued, '... relief is improperly withheld in many instances and granted without proper investigation in others'.[72] Chadwick, not surprisingly, was dismissive of such objections, arguing that size was of no significance since much larger districts such as Lambeth were well managed.[73] Further objections were also raised in relation to the number of guardians that each of the constituent parishes were allowed on the new board.[74] Woolwich ratepayers complained that they had fewer members than Greenwich despite having a similar population whilst objectors from St Nicholas refused to participate in guardian elections on the grounds that because they only had three members and lacked any *ex officio* representatives, they were effectively unable to influence union policy.[75] Similar complaints were voiced by St Paul's ratepayers whilst in the case of Woolwich local pride as well as a sense of injustice added further fuel to the fire, with objectors there arguing that with its sizeable public establishments the town was large enough and 'of sufficient importance so as not to be rendered a mere suburb of Greenwich or any other parish'.[76] Despite such local difficulties, Greenwich union remained, although those vestries opposed to amalgamation dragged their feet when it came to paying rates and succeeded in delaying the construction of a new workhouse by several years.

Such opposition, however, was just the tip of the iceberg. Much to Chadwick's surprise, even where the Poor Law Amendment Act had been adopted without apparent dissension, there was no guarantee that the newly elected boards of guardians would be sympathetic to the Poor Law Commissioners. In Shoreditch and St George Southwark, anti-poor law campaigners captured the newly elected boards of guardians. In St George Southwark, the United Parishioners' Society,

---

71 TNA MH12/5091 Local Government Board and predecessors: Correspondence, Greenwich Board of Guardians, 15 March 1837.

72 TNA MH12/5091 Ibid., 31 March 1837.

73 TNA MH12/5092 Ibid., 6 March 1838.

74 TNA MH12/5092 Ibid., 6 October, 7, 14, 21 December 1837.

75 TNA MH32/56 Local Government Board and predecessors: Assistant Poor Law Commissioners and Inspectors, Correspondence, Charles Mott, 14 October 1837; TNA MH12/5091 Local Government Board and predecessors: Correspondence, Greenwich Board of Guardians, 18 June, 6 November 1840.

76 TNA MH12/5091 Ibid., 3 November 1836; TNA MH12/5092 Ibid., 6 March 1838.

drawing on support from artisans and small tradesmen and led by John Day and Charles Anderson, both of whom were prominent local radicals, gained control of the vestry in the early 1830s.[77] Day, in particular, kept up a running battle against the Poor Law Commissioners for nearly 20 years, both as a guardian and overseer of the poor, and subsequently as vestry clerk.[78] When guardian elections were first called in 1835, proxy votes ensured that supporters of the new poor law were returned. In the following year, however, the United Parishioners' Society, whose election motto was 'Low rates, no extravagant salaries and mercy at least to the old poor', gained control. From their position of power, these radical guardians defied the Poor Law Commissioners on a variety of issues, ranging from workhouse rules to the way in which the Commissioners themselves calculated rates of pauperism.[79] When they refused to prevent paupers from leaving the workhouse on Sundays, contrary to instructions from Somerset House, assistant poor law commissioner Charles Mott found himself in the uncomfortable position of having to attend their meetings to insist on the strict enforcement of workhouse rules.[80] He received a hostile reception and, finding the board 'perfectly unmanageable', he referred disparagingly to the guardians as 'men of little property and of equal responsibility'.[81] Trouble also flared over the accounts when, as auditor, Mott disallowed the relatively large sum of £233 13s 6d which had been spent on issuing tickets to the outdoor poor for bread.[82] Similar opposition was voiced in Shoreditch. After the guardian elections there in May 1836 Mott noted ruefully that 'At St George Southwark and Shoreditch the right working of the new system is doomed, I am fearful, to still greater delay and many impediments.'[83]

These impediments, though, were minor compared to the battle that began to unfold between the litigious vestrymen of St Pancras and the Poor Law Commissioners. Like many other metropolitan districts, St Pancras was governed

---

77 The Society was founded in 1831 to counter the extravagance and abuse of power of the select vestry. See [Anon] *Rules and Regulations of the Society called the United Parishioners of St George the Martyr Southwark, established 13 January 1831*; [Anon], *To the Worthy Inhabitants of the Parish of St George the Martyr, Southwark* (1831); C. Anderson, *An Account of the Alterations, Reductions, Exposures etc. Effected by the United Parishioners Society of St George the Martyr Southwark* (1833); TNA MH12/12300 Local Government Board and predecessors: Correspondence, St George the Martyr Southwark Overseers of the Poor, 19 August 1835.

78 TNA MH12/12300 Ibid., 18 September 1834, 18 August 1835, 19 March 1836.

79 TNA MH12/12301 Ibid., 25 March 1836, 7 November 1838.

80 TNA MH32/56 Local Government Board and predecessors: Assistant Poor Law Commissioners and Inspectors, Correspondence, Charles Mott, 2, 12, 26 May 1836.

81 TNA MH32/56 ibid., 12 May 1836; TNA MH12/12300 Local Government Board and predecessors: Correspondence, St George the Martyr Southwark Overseers of the Poor, 29 July, 15 December 1836.

82 TNA MH12/12300 Ibid., 11 November 1836.

83 TNA MH12/12300 Ibid., 28 May 1836.

by a local act for poor relief. Under the 1834 legislation, provided a two-thirds majority was reached, ratepayers could vote to dispense with their local act and adopt the Poor Law Amendment Act instead. However, it was unclear whether the Commissioners themselves could force vestries to adopt it against the wishes of local ratepayers. This issue came to the fore in March 1836 when the Commissioners ordered St Pancras vestry to replace its directors of the poor, elected under a local act of 1819, with a newly-elected 21 man board of guardians.[84] Meetings condemning this high handed action took place in St Pancras and the neighbouring parish of St Marylebone.[85] On 23 April, *The Times* reported that about 800 people had assembled at the Riding School in Bidborough Street, St Pancras, at which the familiar constitutional tactic of drawing up a petition to Parliament condemning the Poor Law Amendment Act took place.[86] Despite protests from Henry Bulwer-Lytton and Sir Samuel Whalley, the two Marylebone MPs, the Commissioners nevertheless insisted on fresh elections.[87] A new board was formed but the guardians, all of whom had previously been vestrymen, refused to elect a chairman or to conduct business. In response to this defiant gesture, the Commissioners issued a writ of mandamus forcing the guardians to act, at which point St Pancras vestry appealed to the Court of King's Bench.[88]

Support for St Pancras and condemnation of the Poor Law Commissioners' actions came from several London parishes. In September a large meeting numbering between 1,500 and 2,000 people was held in Shoreditch where a petition to the King was drawn up calling for repeal of the Poor Law Amendment Act.[89] Support came from other districts and memorials and petitions were organised at meetings throughout the city in Holborn, Lambeth, St Giles, St George Southwark, St James Westminster and St Martin in the Fields.[90] As opposition mounted, it appeared that Lord Althorp's concerns about excluding London from the new poor law had finally come to fruition.

Whilst protest meetings took place throughout the city, the Court of King's Bench ruled in January 1837 that the Poor Law Commissioners had no authority to impose a board of guardians on any district in which a suitable body established

[84] CLHC P/PN1/M/1/16 St Pancras Vestry, Minutes, 1 March 1837.

[85] *The Times*, 4 March, 19 April 1836.

[86] Ibid., 23 April 1836. A similar meeting was held at the same place a few months later to protest against the self-elected church trustees. See CLHC P/PN/M/1/16 St Pancras Vestry, Minutes, 17 November 1836.

[87] *True Sun*, 28 April 1834; *The Times*, 4 April 1836.

[88] See CLHC P/PN/M/1/16 St Pancras Vestry Minutes, 17 November 1836, 1 March 1837.

[89] *The Times*, 8 September 1836.

[90] Ibid., 4 March, 4, 19, 23 April, 25 May, 31 August, 8, 30, September, 19, 29 October, 1836; 2, 3, 4, 7, 18, 22 February, 1, 8, 15, 17, 21 March 1837.

under a local act already existed for the provision of poor relief.[91] The implications of this decision rocked the Commissioners and petitions from metropolitan districts seeking the amendment of unions or exemption from the Poor Law Amendment Act itself flooded in. At a meeting of western parishes, Feargus O'Connor condemned the Commissioners and urged Londoners to join northern and midland opposition to the new poor law.[92] Further attempts to form poor law unions in the capital stopped, leaving most northern and western districts, together with Newington in the south, still under local acts governing poor relief. In total 11 districts, accounting for about a third of London's population and expenditure on poor relief, remained outside the Poor Law Amendment Act. As Figure 3.2 shows, this gap in the Commissioners' jurisdiction included some of the largest and wealthiest districts in the capital, such as St George Hanover Square, St Marylebone and St Pancras. In terms of poor relief, these districts were of national let alone local significance.[93] In 1837, for example, poor relief expenditure in St Marylebone was exceeded only by Birmingham, Liverpool and Manchester whilst St Pancras spent more than Bristol and Sheffield.[94] Had these places been outside London, their spirited opposition might have merited more attention but until now their role in the anti-poor law movement has been commented on only in passing.[95]

The St Pancras issue was the catalyst for public meetings throughout the capital and the start of an organised London-wide anti-poor law campaign. In January 1837 a meeting convened by the radical vestrymen of St Pancras was attended by representatives from St Martin in the Fields, St George Southwark, St Giles and St George's, St Marylebone and St Leonard Shoreditch as well as from several smaller parishes in the City. The tone of the meeting, encapsulated in the closing resolution, summarised well their concerns:

---

[91] See Poor Law Commission, Third Annual Report (1838), pp. 3–4; idem., Eighth Annual Report, (1841), pp. 18–20; idem., Ninth Annual Report (1842), pp. 12–16; Anthony Brundage, *The Making of the New Poor Law: The Politics of Inquiry, Enactment and Implementation 1832–39* (London, 1978), p. 156.

[92] *The Times*, 20 January, 3, 4, 7, 9, 15, 18, 23, 27 February, 15, 21, 24 March 1837; TNA MH32/56 Local Government Board and predecessors: Assistant Poor Law Commissioners and Inspectors, Correspondence, Charles Mott, 21 March 1837.

[93] The 11 districts were St George Hanover Square, St Giles and St George Bloomsbury, St Luke Middlesex, St James Clerkenwell, St James Westminster, St Leonard Shoreditch, St Margaret and St John Westminster, St Marylebone, St Mary Islington, St Mary Newington and St Pancras.

[94] The figure for Birmingham was £43,868; Liverpool was £36,564; Manchester was £29,763; Bristol was £15,294 and Sheffield was £14,687 compared to £27,803 for St Marylebone and £19,920 for St Pancras. See Poor Law Commission, Seventh Annual Report, Appendix D, Poor Rate Returns for year ending 25 March 1838.

[95] For St Marylebone and St Pancras see Brooke, *The Democrats of Marylebone*; David Owen, *The Government of Victorian London 1855–1889: The Metropolitan Board of Works, the Vestries and the City Corporation* (London, 1982), pp. 260–62, 276–82, 286–9, 296–8.

> That the extent of the powers vested in the commissioners are most arbitrary and unconstitutional; that the giving of votes to owners of property not occupiers is destructive of the principle of self-government; that the scale of voting is unjust, and the mode of voting by proxy is most vicious....[96]

A second meeting one month later took place at the Crown and Anchor tavern on the Strand, presided over by Earl Stanhope and attended by representatives from vestries hostile to the new poor law. Thomas Murphy from St Pancras was a prominent speaker, as too was Sir Samuel Whalley who had earlier sought to have metropolitan parishes excluded from the Poor Law Amendment Act. Representatives from other London districts, including St Leonard Shoreditch, St George Southwark, Kensington and the City of London, roundly condemned the new poor law as arbitrary and unconstitutional and called for its immediate repeal.[97]

With anti-poor law feelings running high and parochial elections looming, the Poor Law Commissioners were forced to rescind regulations for the populous districts of Shoreditch, Kensington and Islington.[98] In Shoreditch, the order setting up a board of guardians in March 1836 was revoked and control of poor relief returned to the trustees appointed under the local act governing the parish.[99] In Bethnal Green internal disputes broke out amongst the guardians whilst in Whitechapel union parish officers of the Old Artillery Ground refused to cooperate with the new guardians. A similar situation threatened to disrupt business in the neighbouring district of Stepney.[100] Meetings also took place south of the river in Woolwich and St Paul Deptford, where inhabitants opposed a union with Greenwich.[101] In February 1837 commissioners and trustees of the poor in Woolwich sought to avail themselves of the St Pancras judgement and applied to the Court of King's Bench to be allowed to withdraw from the Greenwich Union.[102] Mott wrote to the Poor Law Commissioners that letters were needed 'to prevent unpleasant proceedings on their part and perhaps prevent the expression of similar

---

96 CLHC P/PN1/M/1/17 St Pancras Vestry, Minutes, 1 March 1837; *The Times*, 20 January 1837.

97 Ibid., 28 February 1837.

98 TNA MH32/56 Local Government Board and predecessors: Assistant Poor Law Commissioners and Inspectors, Correspondence, Charles Mott, 3 May 1837.

99 TNA MH32/56 Ibid., 21 March 1837; CLHC P/PN1/M/1/16 St Pancras Vestry, Minutes, 2, 9 March, 17 November 1836, 9 February, 1 March 1837; LMA P91/LEN/3 St Leonard Shoreditch Vestry, Minutes, 20 March 1837.

100 TNA MH32/56 Local Government Board and predecessors: Assistant Poor Law Commissioners and Inspectors, Correspondence, Charles Mott, 3 May 1837.

101 TNA MH12/5091 Local Government Board and predecessors: Correspondence with Poor Law Unions and Other Local Authorities, Greenwich Board of Guardians, 3 November 1836.

102 TNA MH12/5091 Ibid., 15 March 1837.

discontent by some of the London parishes under local acts'.[103] However, by that time it was too late to halt the tide of anti-poor law sentiment and in March 1837 he again wrote to the Commissioners:

> Gentlemen, the very unsettled state of some of the London parishes renders my position just now anxious and harrowing in the extreme ... no foresight or exertion of mine could have prevented the angry feeling which has lately been exhibited in some of the London parishes.[104]

A few weeks later he wrote disconsolately to his superiors at Somerset House: 'the Board will pardon me for representing how disheartening it is to know that all my efforts are rendered ineffective'.[105]

Anti-poor law feelings continued to run high and campaigners from London and the provinces maintained close contact. Several prominent London campaigners, including Earl Stanhope, Daniel Whittle Harvey and John Walter were invited to the large anti-poor law meeting in Huddersfield in May 1837, and although none was able to attend each sent letters of support.[106] In December campaigners led by John Day of Southwark agreed to form a metropolitan association for 'the amelioration or extinction of the Poor Law Amendment Act'.[107] Day himself had been instrumental in forming a local anti-poor law association in Southwark which had successfully contested guardian elections. A second meeting was convened at the Crown and Anchor in February 1838 to establish a Central Anti-Poor Law Association, the objects of which were to coordinate local opposition in London and to forge links with anti-poor law campaigners outside the capital. Earl Stanhope again presided, Thomas Murphy from St Pancras was also there, as was Dr Wade and Thomas Wakley, by now the Radical MP for Finsbury and a staunch opponent of the new poor law both in his previous capacity as vestryman of St Giles and later as the Middlesex coroner.[108] A further meeting was held the following week at the Freemasons Tavern in Lincoln's Inn, where Tory and Radical representatives from anti-poor law associations across the country as well as from London attended, including Richard Oastler from Yorkshire, John Fielden, the Oldham MP, John Cobbett and John Walter, proprietor of *The Times* and long time adversary of Chadwick's reforms.[109] Earl Stanhope chaired the meeting and in an attempt to

---

103 TNA MH12/5091 Ibid., 9 February 1837.

104 TNA MH32/56 Local Government Board and predecessors: Assistant Poor Law Commissioners and Inspectors, Correspondence, Charles Mott, 21 March 1837.

105 TNA MH32/56 Ibid., 3 May 1837.

106 *The Times*, 18 May 1837.

107 Ibid., 16 December 1837.

108 Ibid., 20 February 1838.

109 John Walter, owner of *The Times*, was a vociferous opponent and provided the anti-poor law movement in London with a platform to express its views. See TNA MH32/56 Local Government Board and predecessors: Assistant Poor Law Commissioners and

preserve unity amongst such a diverse political group, called on speakers to avoid mention of party politics. As the meeting drew to a close, 'amid loud and continued cheering' those assembled agreed to establish a Central Anti-Poor Law Association based in London. Though little more was heard from the Association, nevertheless those involved in its initial organisation continued to make their case. In May 1839 the Southwark vestry led by John Day even petitioned Queen Victoria, arguing that the Whig government had 'by the introduction and obstinate maintenance of the wretched new poor law endangered the peace and security of the Empire and the stability of the Crown and brought this Kingdom upon the verge of disorder, confusion and insurrection'.[110]

A central part of this argument was that the new centralised administration would subvert the wishes of local ratepayers and as such was an attack on the traditional rights and liberties of free born Englishmen.[111] This fear was voiced by a deputation to Parliament from 11 parishes, including most of those that had adopted Hobhouse's Act, which argued that the new measures were an alarming attempt to subvert that 'most useful and beneficial principle of the British Constitution ... that which secures to the tax and rate-payers the government and control of their own affairs'.[112] Others also voiced similar concerns. The *New Vestryman*, a mouthpiece for the anti-poor law campaigners in St Marylebone and St Pancras, condemned the Poor Law Amendment Act as an attack on 'The system of local and popular government, which was the foundation of the well-regulated liberty of England.'[113] Drawing on the myth and folklore of Anglo-Saxon libertarian history, and couching their opposition in terms of a constitutionalist discourse of English nationalism, opponents such as the antiquarian City lawyer, Joshua Toulmin Smith, bitterly condemned all forms of government by commission.[114] Upholding the parish as

---

Inspectors, Correspondence, Charles Mott, 21 March 1837. For Walter's campaign against the New Poor Law see Brundage, *Making of the New Poor Law*, pp. 38–42, 159–61.

110 SLSC St George the Martyr Southwark Vestry, Minutes, 29 May 1839.

111 Similar arguments were made in relation to borough politics in provincial towns, particularly where anti-aristocratic sentiment was strong. See Sweet, 'Freemen and Independence'.

112 CWAC TI/53/ St Marylebone Vestry, Minutes, 26 July 1834.

113 *New Vestryman*, 8 March 1834.

114 See Joshua Toulmin Smith, *A Letter to the Metropolitan Sanatory Commissioners* (London, 1848), Joshua Toulmin Smith, *Government by Commission: Illegal and Pernicious* (London, 1849); Joshua Toulmin Smith, *Local Self Government and Centralisation* (London, 1851); Joshua Toulmin Smith, *The Metropolis and its Municipal Administration* (London, 1852); Joshua Toulmin Smith, *The People and The Parish* (London, 1853); Joshua Toulmin Smith, *Local Self Government Unmystified* (London, 1857) . For further discussion of Toulmin Smith's ideas see W. H. Greenleaf, 'Toulmin Smith and the British Political Tradition', *Public Administration*, 53 (1975): 25–44. The constitutionalist debate in which Toulmin Smith's ideas were grounded is discussed further in Keith-Lucas, *English Local Government Franchise*, pp. 25–26; Edward P. Thompson, *The Making of the English Working Class* (Harmondsworth, 1968), pp. 84–110; James Vernon, *Politics and the*

the historic offspring of the Anglo-Saxon tradition of self government, Smith vilified the 'French system' of centralisation as the handmaiden of despotism. Commenting on the tendency towards centralisation, he warned that

> On one pretext or another the enemy has made already very many approaches and wrapped the coils of Centralization round the whole land.... Today the Poor-law may be made the specious pretext; tomorrow, Public Health, next day Police; till one by one – each step riveting the bondage firmer....[115]

In like manner, Thomas Walker, barrister and London magistrate echoed a common belief that 'Parochial self government is the very element upon which all other government in England depends, and as long as it is out of order, everything must be out of order, representation – legislation – police.'[116] Neglect this principle, he argued, and all progress and prosperity would cease.

Critics argued that by allocating to the central state executive powers over legally constituted locally elected authorities, the Poor Law Amendment Act breached two important principles: that those responsible for local administration should have a community of interest with those over whom they were placed and that control of expenditure should be the prerogative of those charged with raising revenue. For metropolitan vestries, such arguments had particular resonance in relation to the introduction of the new poor law. That implacable foe of the new system, John Day, put the argument clearer than most:

> Now then, let Englishmen, tax-payers and ratepayers see how they are degraded under this new poor law, and say will they be content that this scheme of wholesale taxation without representation should continue any longer? And will they be satisfied that their lawful and ancient right to control the expenditure of their own funds shall be taken away for ever, and that the comforts and even the lives of their poor shall be placed in the hands of a set of theoretical speculators, hired government officers, who are to them comparatively aliens and foreigners instead of neighbours and friends?[117]

In many London parishes the answer to these questions was a resounding No! What was abundantly clear was that these parishes were sufficiently powerful to have resisted any unwelcome attempts to impose the new poor law in their

---

People (Cambridge, 1993), pp. 295–330; James Vernon (ed.) *Re-reading the Constitution* (Cambridge, 1996), esp. pp. 9–13.

115 Toulmin Smith, *The People and The Parish*, p. 20.

116 Thomas Walker, *Suggestions for a Constitutional and Efficient Reform of Parochial Government* (London, 1834), p. 3.

117 John Day, *A Few Practical Observations on the New Poor Law Showing the Demoralizing and Enslaving Effects of this Anti-Christian Enactment* (London, 1838), p. 8.

districts. In this respect, and without the violence associated with the movement elsewhere, the London anti-poor law campaigners were successful in keeping centralised control at bay.[118]

Rhetoric and practice: the impact of failure?

In January 1839 James Kay, the newly appointed assistant poor law commissioner for London, reported that the city 'is distinguished from other districts with which I am acquainted by a greater jealousy of central authority', noting that public opposition had prevented the construction of workhouses in several districts, including Bethnal Green, Kensington, Whitechapel, Stepney, and Greenwich.[119] Though muted in relation to the hostile reception the new poor law had received elsewhere, nevertheless opposition in London continued. In February 1841 and 1842, Southwark guardians petitioned against the continuation of the new poor law condemning it as 'harsh, cruel and arbitrary', and noting also how '... the whole principle of the proposed measure is at variance with the right of representation; and the lawful right of the poor, centralising in its effects, and that must drive to a remedy by fearful convulsion or submission to sheer and open despotism'.[120] Such sentiments were echoed by others opposed to the Poor Law Commissioners, irrespective of whether or not they agreed with the harsher attitudes to relief associated with the new poor law.

Running battles continued between the parishes and the central authorities. A few years later in 1846, in a blatant attempt to circumvent parochial autonomy, Chadwick tried to establish district asylums to deal with the casual poor, thereby removing responsibility for their relief from individual unions. His proposals were once again met with widespread hostility and the newly constituted district asylum boards collectively refused to act.[121] According to those opposed to the measure,

---

118 The apparent lack of overt protests has diverted attention from the strength of anti-poor law feeling in London with the result that it has received relatively little attention in the literature. For further discussion of the anti-poor law movement see Nicholas Edsall, *The Anti-Poor Law Movement 1834–44* (Manchester, 1971); see also Ann Digby, *Pauper Palaces* (1978), pp. 215–28; Felix Driver, *Power and Pauperism* (Cambridge, 1993), pp. 112–30; John Knott, *Popular Opposition to the 1834 Poor Law* (London, 1986); Michael Rose, 'The Anti-Poor Law Movement in the North of England', *Northern History* 1 (1966): 70–91; Michael Rose, 'The Anti-Poor Law Movement', in John T. Ward (ed.), *Popular Movements 1830–1851* (1970), pp. 78–84. Brundage, *The Making of the New Poor Law*, pp. 145–80 has drawn attention to the importance of different forms of protest, including those in London.

119 TNA MH32/50 Local Government Board and predecessors: Assistant Poor Law Commissioners and Inspectors, Correspondence, James Kay, 14 January 1839.

120 SLSC St George the Martyr Southwark Vestry, Minutes, 22 February 1841.

121 See PP 1846 VII Select committee on establishment of district asylums for houseless poor in metropolis, *passim*. See also TNA MH17/32 Poor Law Commission

it was not merely a question of unnecessary additional expense but also that the removal of local control over expenditure was yet again a fundamental breach of the principles of local self government.[122] Nor were they alone in their views. In the wake of the furore the Poor Man's Guardian Society was formed by some of the staunchest opponents of the new poor law, including Thomas Wakley, John Walter and John Day, to expose examples of neglect and cruelty and to ensure that the poor were granted their legal rights to relief.[123] More than ten years after the introduction of the new poor law in the rest of the country, this Society could still contemplate the formation of a metropolitan Anti-Poor Law Union – evidence that opposition in the capital remained strong. Mindful of the depth of feeling, and taking account of the precarious situation that the Poor Law Commissioners found themselves in 1847 in the wake of the Andover scandal, the scheme was dropped. In the struggle for London, at least insofar as the administration of the poor law was concerned, metropolitan opposition proved too strong, even for Chadwick's reforming zeal.

But other than being an administrative inconvenience and a source of irritation to Somerset House, did the ongoing failure to incorporate parishes under the Poor Law Amendment Act have any material consequences? Were the relief policies adopted in the recalcitrant parishes any different to those places that chose to adopt the Act? Since overseers' actions led directly to ratepayers' pockets, the pattern of expenditure provides an answer to this question. Figures available from 1825 allow us to compare the total cost of relief between adopting and non-adopting parishes in the years leading up to and following the changes, and here the evidence tells a consistent story. In relation to expenditure, both sets of parishes essentially followed the same pattern, shown most clearly in Figure 3.4 by the annual rate of change at current prices. Whether or not vestries adopted the Poor Law Amendment Act appeared to have made little difference to patterns of expenditure. From a peak in 1826–27, when relief expenditure rose by over 10 per cent in a year, annual rates of change fell continuously in both adopting and non-adopting parishes and by the early 1830s most places experienced an absolute decline in the cost of poor relief.

---

and successors: Correspondence with Asylum Districts and Boards, Metropolitan Asylum District, 1845–61.

122 PP 1846 VII Select committee on district asylums, pp. 359, 457, 465, 481; *Weekly News*, 15 February, 1, 8 March 1846.

123 Poor Man's Guardian Society, First Annual Report (1846). Charles Dickens was also involved along with others, including John Fielden.

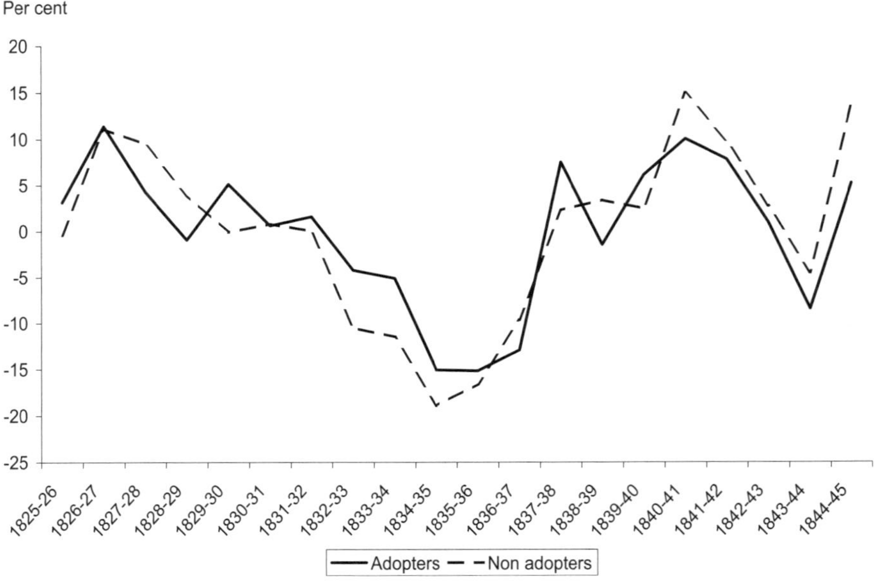

Figure 3.4 Annual rate of change in expenditure on poor relief at current prices in adopting and non-adopting districts in London 1825–1845

Note: Adopting unions: Bermondsey, Bethnal Green, Camberwell, City of London, East London, Greenwich, Hackney, Hampstead, Holborn, Kensington, Lambeth, Lewisham, Poplar, Rotherhithe, St George Southwark, St Martin in the Fields, St Olave Southwark, St Saviour Southwark, Stepney, Wandsworth, West London, Whitechapel.
Non-adopting parishes: St George Hanover Square, St Giles in the Fields, St James Clerkenwell, St James Westminster, St John and St Margaret, St Leonard Shoreditch, St Lukes, St Mary Islington, St Mary Newington, St Marylebone, St Pancras.

Source: PP 1830–31 XI An account of the money expended for the maintenance and relief of the poor ... for the five years ending 25th March 1825, 1826, 1827, 1828 and 1829; PP 1835 XLVII An account of the money expended for the maintenance and relief of the poor ... for the five years ending 25th March 1830, 1831, 1832, 1833 and 1834; Poor Law Commission, Annual Reports, 1834–45.

If anything, the decline in expenditure was steeper in the non-adopting parishes in the years leading up to 1834, suggesting that greater attention was paid in these places to trimming the costs of relief. This was certainly the case in St Giles, which was governed by a local act passed in 1830 and was typical of the non-adopting parishes. There expenditure on poor relief fell from over £27,000 in 1830 to £20,900 by 1834, largely accounted for by sharp cuts in outdoor relief, which fell from over three-quarters to just over 42 per cent of the total relief budget.[124] This fall was made possible by a large reduction in the numbers of poor supported on weekly pensions from 2,239 in 1830 to 345 in 1834.[125] Other cost-cutting measures were also implemented that predated the recommendations of the Royal Commission on the Poor Laws. In St Marylebone in 1833, scales of payments for illegitimate children were reduced and non-resident casual relief to settled paupers living within 12 miles of the parish was stopped.[126] In the neighbouring parish of St George Hanover Square, a report to the vestry from the workhouse committee in May 1833 recommended '... that it is an imperative duty to subject the able-bodied, the sturdy and the refractory to a more rigid discipline'.[127] In the following year, the vestry clerk wrote to Edwin Chadwick, recording how the new workhouse regime had succeeded in reducing the number of inmates from 903 to 740. Other measures had also succeeded in reducing the number of casual poor from 848 cases a week to 280.[128] Poor rates fell accordingly from 3s 4d in 1831 to 1s in 1834.[129]

Vestries in non-adopting parishes acted entirely in accordance with the sentiments of the new poor law and to all intents and purposes implemented policies that were identical to those which prevailed in parishes that had adopted the Poor Law Amendment Act. Failure to adopt the Act may have been a political and administrative disappointment to the Commissioners but it did nothing to affect the willingness of vestries to implement the changes in policy even before the new poor law itself had arrived on the statute books. In that sense, at least, failure was immaterial.

---

124 St Giles in the Fields and St George's Bloomsbury, *Annual abstract account of the receipts and expenditure for the relief of the Poor in the year ending 1830*; St Giles in the Fields and St George's Bloomsbury, *Annual abstract account of the receipts and expenditure for the relief of the Poor in the year ending 1834*.

125 St Giles in the Fields and St George's Bloomsbury, *An Abstract of the Expenditure of the Parishes in the years from 1828 to 1835*. The numbers supported assumed that each family consisted of three persons.

126 LMA P89/MYR1/521 St Marylebone Directors of the Poor, Minutes, 1 March, 15 November 1833.

127 CWAC C/781/ St George Hanover Square Vestry, Minutes, 25 May 1833.

128 TNA MH12/7127 Local Government Board and predecessors: Correspondence, St George Hanover Square Overseers of the Poor, 15 October 1834.

129 John Leslie, *Remarks on the Present State of the Poor Law Question with Illustrations of the Advantages Arising to the Poor by Means of the Workhouse System of Relief* (London, 1834).

Chapter 4
Building the Workhouse System

The workhouse system

In November 1834 the Poor Law Commissioners issued instructions that 'the only remedy which can be entirely depended on for the mitigation and ultimate extinction of the various evils which have been generated by the faulty administration of the poor laws is *The Workhouse System*'.[1] Mindful of the iconic significance of the new general workhouse and its crucial role in relation to the classification of paupers and the policy of deterrence, the early years of the Poor Law Commission were spent both criticising the disorderly state of old workhouses and encouraging the construction of new ones. From the outset these new union workhouses were the most visible and iconic features of the change in policy, translating into bricks and mortar the zeal and ideology of Benthamite reformers. The Commissioners were acutely aware not just of the functional importance of the new workhouses in the regulation and management of relief but also their symbolic role as a demonstration of the state's authority. The scale of construction provided evidence of the permanent changes introduced by the Poor Law Amendment Act. Their location, often on the edge of towns or along main roads, no less than the high walls that enclosed them or their internal spatial arrangement, emphasised the principle and practice of the strict separation of paupers from the rest of society, whilst the opening of such places provided theatrical opportunities for the public affirmation of those policies. As William Sclater observed in 1836, 'The institution of the Union Workhouse presents as prominent a feature in the new system as the building itself displays in the landscape of the country where it has been erected.'[2]

In unions without a workhouse, the Poor Law Amendment Act allowed the Commissioners, with the consent of a majority of guardians or ratepayers, to order a new one to be built. They could also order an existing workhouse to be enlarged without such consent, providing that the sum expended did not exceed one tenth of the annual rate.[3] Although the Royal Commission report in 1834 had initially anticipated that separate categories of pauper would be housed in different institutions, in practice this was difficult to achieve either because places were

---

1 TNA MH1/1 Poor Law Commission, Minute Books, 4 November 1834, p. 55.

2 William Sclater, *A Letter to the Poor Law Commissioners of England and Wales on the Working of the New System* (Basingstoke, 1836), p. 9.

3 James Mahon, *The Poor Laws as They Were and as They Are, or Recent Alterations in the Poor Laws by the Statute 4 & 5 William IV Cap 76* (London, 1835), pp. 56–7.

too distant from each other or because they were not large enough to warrant constructing entirely separate buildings. Also, because the assistant poor law commissioners had to travel between places for the purposes of inspection, it made little sense to have separate institutions spread throughout a union. As a result, the central Commissioners accepted that a single, general workhouse was the best solution and by 1841 at least 320 of these new institutions had been built.[4]

The iconic significance of these new workhouses was not lost on the working class, particularly outside London. In East Anglia and elsewhere attacks on workhouses and assaults on officers were only the most obvious indication of antipathy towards the new poor law.[5] Almost as soon as the new union workhouses were erected they acquired the epithet of bastilles on the grounds that they reflected not only the unjust incarceration of the poor but also the exercise of what many considered was the despotic power of the centrally appointed Poor Law Commissioners to override the wishes of local ratepayers.[6] Just as the storming of the Bastille had proved to be a symbolic rallying cry against the French monarchy, so the attacks on workhouses and intimidation of poor law officials in various parts of the country hinted at larger political concerns about representation of the people. Those links were made clear at the huge anti-poor law demonstrations that took place in Yorkshire and other northern counties in 1837 where placards calling for universal suffrage were as prominent as those condemning the new poor law.[7]

In London, however, as the previous chapter demonstrated, opposition was directed less at buildings and officials than the changes associated with the exercise of political power. The iconographic significance of the new poor law workhouse was of less importance there by virtue of the fact that fewer new buildings were constructed. It was also different because of the range of new types of institutions that were built. The close proximity of unions and the relatively large numbers of different categories of pauper meant that economies of scale could be achieved that made it possible to construct separate institutions for each category of pauper rather than having to construct new workhouses. As well as the workhouse itself, county asylums, licensed madhouses, children's establishments and district schools

---

4 Felix Driver, *Power and Pauperism: The Workhouse System 1834–1884* (Cambridge, 1993), p. 59. At that point there were 536 unions in England and Wales. See also Margaret Crowther, *The Workhouse System 1834–1929: The History of an English Social Institution* (London, 1981), pp. 30–53. Crowther makes the point that because the Commissioners expected relatively high standards of provision inside the new workhouses, they took a keen interest in enforcing strict discipline.

5 For general discussions of these protests see A. Digby, *Pauper Palaces: The Economy and Poor Law of Nineteenth-Century Norfolk* (London, 1978), pp. 215–24; J. Knott, *Popular Opposition to the 1834 Poor Law* (London, 1986).

6 See *The Times*, 9 October 1836; Ibid., 13 November 1838. See also W. R. Baxter, *The Book of the Bastilles, or the History of the Working of the New Poor Law* (London, 1841).

7 See F. Driver, *Power and Pauperism*, p. 121.

comprised a system of institutions to deal with the able-bodied, aged, infirm, sick and casual paupers, and also children and lunatics for whom the parish similarly had a responsibility of care. Only the reluctance of guardians to develop shared provision with other districts hindered this possibility. In London, therefore, new workhouse construction was delayed whilst separate types of institution for different categories of pauper were constructed. Both helped diffuse anti-poor law sentiment in the capital by removing the physical reminder of the new relief regime that underpinned working-class resentment elsewhere. Discovering the way in which this range of institutional provision operated is the key, therefore, not just to understanding the pattern of workhouse construction in London but also to explaining the absence of concerted working-class opposition in the capital to the new 'bastilles'.

Designing the new poor law workhouse

From the start of the new poor law, the ability to enforce strict discipline and separation of paupers rested on the availability of space in a workhouse. As such the state of existing institutions occupied much of the assistant commissioners' time. They were instructed to visit each workhouse in their region to 'examine their construction, means of classification, dietary management, expenditure and report to the Board the defects which he finds'.[8] The workhouse had to be sufficiently large not merely to enable the classification of paupers but also to allow the 'entire and absolute separation between the sexes, who are to live, sleep, and take their meals in totally distinct and separate parts of the building, with enclosed yards for each'.[9] If the existing parish workhouse was large enough to allow for the satisfactory classification of paupers, then forming a union was thought unnecessary. If not, the assistant commissioners' task was to establish which parishes should combine in order to build a new workhouse suitable for the task of classifying and separating pauper inmates.

From the outset the Poor Law Commissioners took a keen interest in the construction of new workhouses. It was not just that they thought they would be more efficient but that they would also be an impressive reminder of the permanence of the reforms. They published four model designs in their first annual report and another in their second, one by assistant commissioner Sir Francis Head and the rest by a relatively young architect called Samuel Kempthorne. Kempthorne's model plans, which were praised in the *Architectural Magazine* for the attention paid 'to the principles of separation and classification, to clean lines, to ventilation and to general convenience', were variations of radial and square designs for different

8 TNA MH1/1 Poor Law Commission, Minute Books, 4 November 1834, p. 72.

9 Ibid.

sized institutions.[10] They were based on panopticon principles with a central tower from which the master could observe activities elsewhere in the workhouse. The principles of separation were achieved by the internal arrangement of spaces for different categories of pauper, the high walls that enclosed the workhouse and its physical separation where possible from other buildings.

In the early rush of construction many of the new plans followed or adapted Kempthorne's designs for radial and square workhouses.[11] However, the designs themselves allowed for fairly generous amounts of open space for exercise yards, which might have been suitable in rural areas with low land values but which were impractical in London, especially in already crowded central districts. Whilst lack of space was important in dictating the shape and scale of new construction, other considerations, notably relating to ventilation, were taken into account. As a result, from the 1840s new corridor plan workhouses became more popular. Instead of wings radiating from a central tower, as had been the case with earlier designs, workhouses were generally constructed with separate blocks for specific functions, usually consisting of an entrance containing various offices, a main building to accommodate the different wards and workrooms, and a separate infirmary. Corridors running the length of the main buildings were designed to increase ventilation and light, although they had the disadvantage of allowing freer mixing of paupers. Where space permitted, exercise yards for different categories of pauper separated one block from another.[12] This arrangement proved to be more flexible in relation to the restrictions of site that arose in urban locations and between 1840 and 1870 about 150 of these corridor-plan workhouses were built.[13]

Such designs, which still emphasised classification and segregation but avoided the prison-like appearance of the earlier plans, characterised workhouses built in London after 1834. The first of these was built in Greenwich and completed in 1840. The site chosen was about a mile to the east of the town, on the main road between Greenwich

---

10 See the comments made on these plans in the *Architectural Magazine*, 2 (1835), 511. Not all were so enamoured with the plans. Augustus Pugin in the second edition of *Contrasts: or, a Parallel Between the Noble Edifices of the Middle Ages, and Corresponding Buildings of the Present Day; Shewing the Present Decay of Taste*, published in 1841, compared the 'modern poor house' with its medieval equivalent, using it to illustrate what he considered to have been the degeneration of English values of care and charity. In the wake of the Andover workhouse scandal of 1845–46, an anonymous article in the *Illustrated London News* also criticised Kempthorne himself for having traced his plans from the designs of American prisons, adding that it was hardly surprising that the buildings themselves had been denounced as 'Bastilles'. See *Illustrated London News*, 7 November 1846.

11 Kathryn Morrison, *The Workhouse: A Study of Poor-Law Buildings in England* (Swindon, 1999), pp. 46–84. See also Anna Dickens, 'Architects and the Union Workhouses of the New Poor Law', (unpublished Ph.D. thesis, Brighton Polytechnic, 1982).

12 For a fuller discussion see Morrison, *The Workhouse*, pp. 85–102; Kathryn Morrison, 'The New Poor Law Workhouses of George Gilbert Scott and William Bonython Moffatt', *Architectural History*, 4 (1997): 190.

13 See Morrison, *The Workhouse*, pp. 85–102.

and Woolwich and, although prominently located, was somewhat peripheral to the main concentration of population in the district. The building shown in Figure 4.1 was designed by a relatively obscure architect, R. P. Browne, and consisted of an administrative block with a central archway, behind which was the main three-storey building that could accommodate up to 700 inmates. To the south a separate wing housed the infirmary, with space for some 200 paupers, the laundry and other activities. The workhouse was one of the first to have been planned with a central corridor which ran the length of the main block, with iron gates preventing the mixing of different types of paupers.[14] Various workrooms, the master's office and refractory wards were located on the ground floor, whilst the two upper storeys contained workrooms and dormitories housing the different categories of paupers, including space for children. The external exercise and work areas were enclosed by high walls which separated children, the elderly and adult men and women.

Several other London workhouses built in the 1840s followed a similar arrangement. Browne's plan in Greenwich was virtually repeated in Fulham and Hammersmith, shown in Figure 4.2, albeit on a smaller scale, but so similar were the designs that *The Builder* accused the architect there of copying.[15] Figure 4.3 shows the City of London's workhouse built on the Bow Road and opened in 1849. There the buildings were arranged in perpendicular alignment to the street rather than horizontal but the plan was otherwise essentially the same. Other workhouses also constructed in the 1840s and 1850s followed more or less similar lines, differing only in scale and architectural detail according to fashion, local need and the depth of ratepayers' pockets.

Whilst function largely dictated the internal arrangements of the workhouse, its external appearance was also important in conveying an image – be it civic pride or parochial parsimony – to those beyond its walls. Whilst Kempthorne's designs had been austere with little external decoration, preference soon shifted for workhouses built in a neo-Jacobean or Tudor style, with gables and stone mullioned windows. The Greenwich workhouse was designed in the Elizabethan style with white Suffolk brick and stone tills and lintels. Figure 4.4 shows the new workhouse in Kensington opened in 1848 which was a handsome red brick building in neo-Jacobean style decorated in stone with blue and white brick patterning.[16] More ornate designs were sometimes Italianate, with gables, pinnacles, projecting bays and Venetian windows, such as that in Fulham and in particular the most expensive workhouse of all belonging to the City of London.[17] By contrast, the Bethnal Green workhouse, shown in Figure 4.5, was far more austere, consisting of a low three-storey brick building unrelieved by decoration and reflecting the relative poverty of the area as well as parochial parsimony in providing relief.

14 Morrison, *The Workhouse*, pp. 86–8.

15 *Illustrated London News*, 4 August 1849; *The Builder*, 6 (1848), p. 245.

16 Ibid., 5 (1847), pp. 5, 73, 88, 102; Ibid., 6 (1848), pp. 6–7.

17 See *Illustrated London News*, 4 August 1849; *The Builder*, 7 (1849), pp. 378–9, 400.

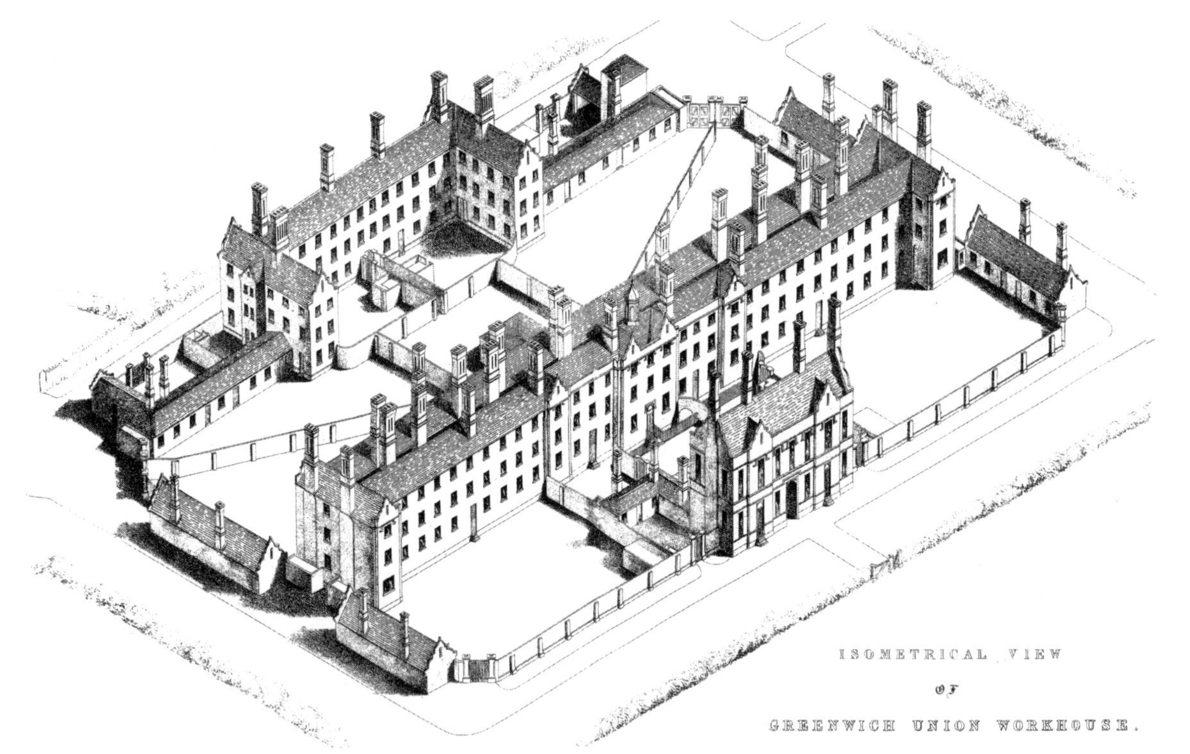

Figure 4.1 Greenwich union workhouse 1843

Source: R. P. Browne, 'Greenwich Union Poorhouse', *Quarterly Papers in Architecture*, 1 (1843): 7.

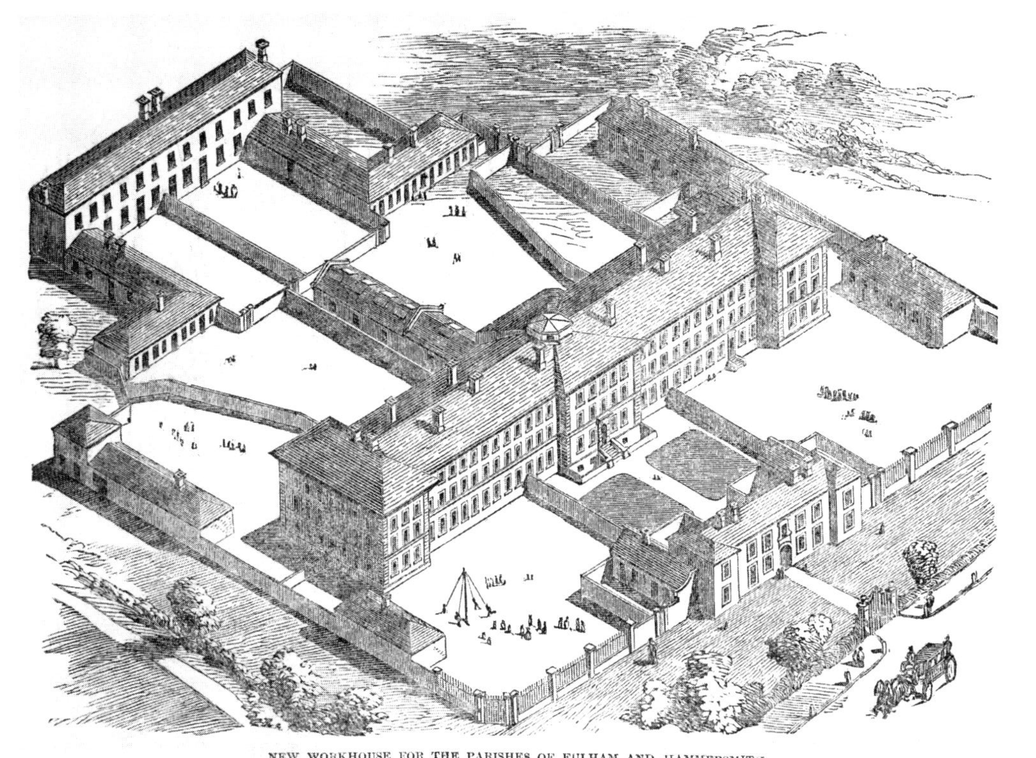

NEW WORKHOUSE FOR THE PARISHES OF FULHAM AND HAMMERSMITH.

Figure 4.2 Fulham and Hammersmith union workhouse 1849

Source: *Illustrated London News*, 4 August 1849. Reproduced with kind permission of the Senate House Library, University of London.

Figure 4.3 City of London union workhouse 1848

Source: *The Builder*, 11 August 1849. Reproduced with kind permission of the City of London, London Metropolitan Archives.

Figure 4.4 Kensington union workhouse 1848

Source: *The Builder*, 1 January 1848. Reproduced with kind permission of the City of London, London Metropolitan Archives.

Figure 4.5 Bethnal Green union workhouse, Waterloo Road c. 1935

Reproduced with kind permission of Peter Higginbotham.

The symbolic importance of these new workhouses was matched by the theatricality of their opening, which provided occasions for the public legitimation of the new poor law. Individual authorities veered between grand civic openings and much quieter, less extravagant celebrations. The Bishop of London presided over the foundation ceremony of the new Fulham and Hammersmith workhouse in 1849, which included guardians, parish officers, clergy and pauper children, together with a crowd said to number 800, 'a large portion of whom were ladies'. The guests were entertained by the children who sang a hymn specially composed for the occasion, followed by a convivial dinner for the main dignitaries which started at 5 pm and finished at 'a late hour'.[18] Larger institutions warranted even grander ceremonies. As the first of its kind, the opening of the North Surrey Industrial School at Annerly in November 1850 boasted a guest list that included the Archbishop of Canterbury, along with several bishops, MPs, magistrates, guardians from the constituent districts and other local dignitaries. After a chance to inspect the buildings and a sermon from the Bishop of Winchester, guests were treated to the sight of the children tucking in to a hearty dinner of roast beef and plum pudding. Clearly, the magnificence of the buildings and the largesse of the occasion, which included the guests' own feast at the Freemasons Tavern, helped to reinforce public affirmation for the benevolence of the new poor law.[19]

Workhouse expenditure

Despite these early successes, building new workhouses in London proved to be more difficult than the Poor Law Commissioners first imagined. Charles Mott, the first assistant poor law commissioner for London, had a good idea of what was required. He already had extensive experience as a private contractor for the poor in Gosport and Newington, and from 1831 in Lambeth. His attention to workhouse dietaries which, it was claimed, had reduced the cost of relief in Lambeth by several thousand pounds, had much impressed Edwin Chadwick.[20] He was also

---

18 *Illustrated London News*, 4 August 1849.

19 *The Times*, 21 November 1850.

20 TNA MH32/56 Local Government Board and predecessors: Assistant Poor Law Commissioners and Inspectors, Correspondence, Charles Mott, 3 November 1834. See also PP 1834 XXIX Royal commission on the administration and practical operation of the poor laws, Appendix A, reports of the Assistant Commissioners, Appendix A, *Examination of Mr Charles Mott, Contractor for the Maintenance of the Poor of Lambeth by E. Chadwick, Esq.*, pp. 444–6. For a detailed history of Mott's activities both before and after his appointment and subsequent resignation see Andrew Roberts, 1990. *England's Poor Law Commissioners and the Trade in Pauper Lunacy 1834–1847*. [Online]. Available at: http://www.mdx.ac.uk/www/study/mott.htm [accessed: 18 September 2008]. See also David Hirst, 2004. 'Mott, Charles (*bap.* 1788, *d.* 1851)', *Oxford Dictionary of National Biography*. [Online]. Available at: http://www.oxforddnb.com/view/article/42189 [accessed: 18 September 2008].

joint proprietor of the Peckham House asylum which took lunatic paupers from several London parishes. Familiar with the benefits of strict management and in tune with Chadwick's desire to enforce a strict workhouse test, Mott was in a good position to assess the adequacies or otherwise of London workhouses as the new poor law was being introduced to the city.

The early months of Mott's office entailed visits to most London parishes, starting with familiar territory south of the Thames and then extending to districts to the north. He encountered very different conditions in the various workhouses he visited. In 1836 he noted that

> The separation (sic) of man and wife which has given rise to much opposition in some parts of the country, has always been strictly enforced in the London parishes and in the best regulation of their workhouses it has invariably been held as a sure sign of incompetency on the part of the master when the male and female paupers have been suffered to be associated together, even in the day time.[21]

In his 1838 report on the state of London workhouses, Mott considered that despite the fact that many buildings were old, the workhouse test was an effective deterrent in half the places he visited.[22] In the Strand, for example, he reported that 'this union for correctness and management and strict adherence to the rules cannot be surpassed by any union in England'.[23] Some districts, however, came in for more criticism. When Mott visited St Nicholas Deptford, he found the workhouse in a deplorable state 'with a total absence of good order, cleanliness and management'.[24] The old Bethnal Green workhouse was little better and in 1839 it was described by the Poor Law Commissioners as 'the most inconvenient, crowded and in all respects the worst premises now occupied by any Board of Guardians acting under the Commissioners' regulations'.[25] Evidently, the state of London workhouses varied considerably, a situation that owed as much to historical accident as to the strictness with which local guardians and overseers implemented poor law policy.

Despite a handful of early new poor law workhouses in London, for reasons to do with the scale of existing provision, the refusal in some districts to adopt the Poor Law Amendment Act, and the reluctance of ratepayers to spend money unless absolutely necessary, the city lagged behind the rest of the country in terms of new

---

21 TNA MH32/56 Local Government Board and predecessors: Assistant Poor Law Commissioners and Inspectors, Correspondence, Charles Mott, 28 May 1836.

22 TNA MH32/57 Ibid., Quarterly return showing the state of the workhouses, 31 March 1838.

23 Ibid.

24 Ibid., 14 October 1837.

25 LMA BE/BG/2 Bethnal Green Board of Guardians, Minutes, 17 April 1837; BE/BG/4, Ibid., 19 August 1839.

building. In relation to expenditure on workhouse construction in the country as a whole, Felix Driver notes that before 1850 London accounted for less than 11 per cent of the authorised total, rising to 26 per cent from 1851 to 1866 and 41 per cent from 1867 to 1883.[26] However, the pattern of expenditure in London varied both in timing and geography. Figure 4.7 and Figure 4.8 shows the number of unions authorised by the Poor Law Commissioners to spend money on building, enlarging or altering their workhouse and the amount of expenditure.[27] In contrast to the rush of construction that occurred elsewhere soon after 1834, only three London unions sought permission to build new workhouses in the first ten years of the new poor law: Wandsworth and Greenwich in 1838 and Bethnal Green in 1841. By 1847 only eight unions had been authorised by the Commissioners to build new workhouses, although a far larger number had spent money on alterations which in some cases were so extensive as to almost constitute an entire rebuilding.

The rate of construction increased following the depression of the late 1840s and the ensuing rise in pauperism. However, rather than build new workhouses several unions chose instead to construct separate parochial schools whilst others joined in the newly formed school districts, removing most children from existing buildings and thereby leaving more space for adult paupers. Nevertheless, even taking into account the increased expenditure on school building in the 1850s, the rate of construction was slow and by 1854 less than half the metropolitan unions had built a new workhouse. In 1861 Henry Farnall, the poor law inspector for London, reported that 16 of the 42 existing workhouses were still inadequate both in terms of size and internal arrangements.[28] Partly because of increased demands on the poor law during the economic downturn of the early 1860s, and partly because of renewed central pressure to stem the tide of outdoor relief, authorisations for workhouse expenditure increased sharply after 1864 reaching a peak of £208, 258 in 1868. However, even by that date ten unions, including several in the centre, were still without a new workhouse.

---

26 Driver, *Power and Pauperism*, p. 77.

27 Authorisations for workhouse expenditure were published in the annual reports of the Poor Law Commission and the Poor Law Board.

28 PP 1861 IX Select committee to inquire into the laws and administration of relief of the poor under orders, rules and regulations of the Poor Law Commissioners and Poor Law Board, p. 116.

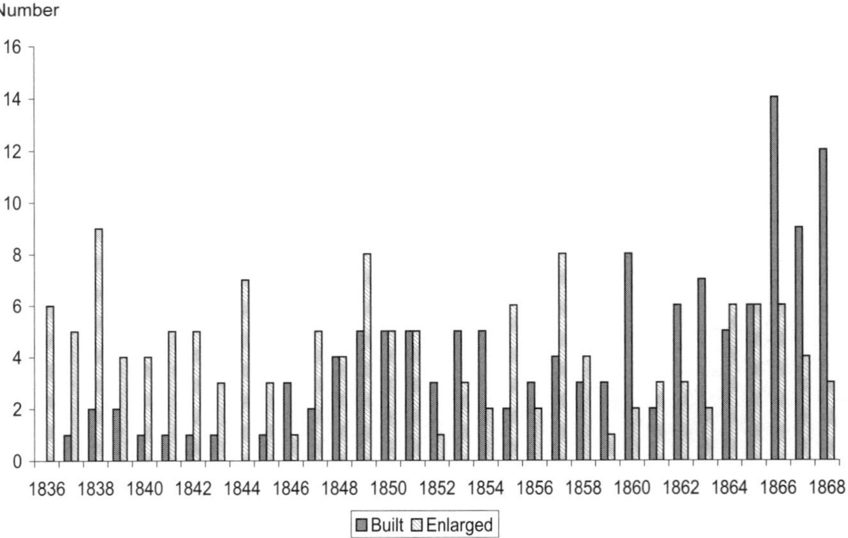

Figure 4.6 Number of poor law unions building or enlarging workhouses and schools, 1836–1868

Source: Poor Law Commission, Annual Reports, 1836–47, Poor Law Board, Annual Reports, 1848–68.

Apart from the general reluctance of many London guardians to cooperate with the Poor Law Commissioners, and the fact that several parishes had already built new workhouses in the relatively recent past, the main factor explaining the slow pace of construction was expense. The Royal Commission on the Poor Laws had estimated that the cost of building a new workhouse would be in the region of £10 per head, but in most cases the figure was higher and it was significantly so in London.[29] In 1840 authorised expenditure for the Greenwich workhouse, one of the first to be built, was £22,700 for about 1,000 paupers, equivalent to approximately £23 per head, whilst in Kensington the new workhouse built in 1848 at an eventual outlay of £17,000 compared to the original tender of £11,020, cost about £42 per head.[30] However, the most expensive workhouse was the City of London's in Bow Road which was built to accommodate up to 1,000 paupers. The elaborate Italianate design proved exceptionally costly and after the initial approval of £40,000 in 1847 the Poor Law Commissioners were forced to authorise an additional £10,000 to cover the expense. By the time it was finished, the final cost had risen to over

---

[29] Morrison, *The Workhouse*, p. 48.

[30] *The Builder*, 6 (1848), pp. 6–7; PP 1866 LXI Statement showing as respects workhouses authorised by orders of the Poor Law Board to be built in the Metropolitan District. The numbers of paupers refers to the figure provided by the Poor Law Commissioners at the time of their approval of the loan for construction and noted in their annual reports.

£55,000, making it the most expensive workhouse in London both in absolute and relative terms.[31] City ratepayers, perhaps, could afford this outlay more than most, but others baulked at this level of expenditure.

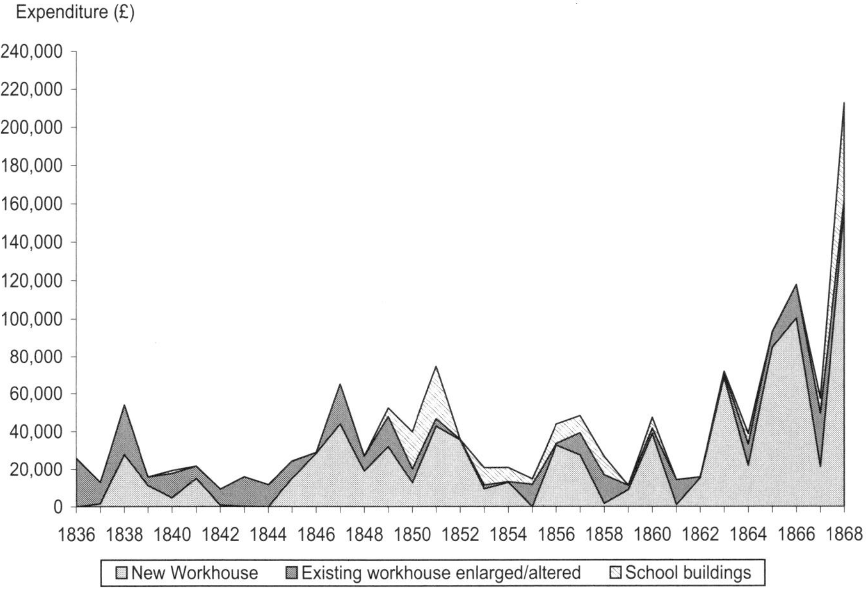

Figure 4.7 Authorised expenditure on building and enlarging new workhouses and schools, 1836–1868

Source: Poor Law Commission, Annual Reports, 1836–47, Poor Law Board, Annual Reports, 1848–68.

Geographies of construction

The slow rate of construction was reflected in the limited geography of new building that took place in the years after 1834, shown in Figures 4.8 to 4.11. In the first few years after 1834, most workhouse building and enlargement took place south of the river, notably in Greenwich and Wandsworth, where new workhouses were authorised, and in Lambeth, where £20,000 had been agreed for extensive enlargements that effectively created what Charles Mott called 'a

[31] *The Builder*, 7 (1849) pp. 378–9, 400. Authorised expenditure is taken from Poor Law Board, First Annual Report (1848); Ibid., Second Annual Report (1849). See also Andrea Tanner, 'The City of London Poor Law Union, 1837–1869', (unpublished Ph.D. thesis, University of London, 1995), pp. 167–8. The number authorised by the Poor Law Board was 1,000, although *The Builder* claimed that it would accommodate 1,200 paupers.

splendid new workhouse'.[32] This early concentration was in part due to the speed with which unions had been established south of the Thames, a situation that had much to do with Mott's familiarity with the area. However, administrative expediency, no less than architectural considerations of form and function, was an important consideration in constructing the new workhouse system. These early workhouses reflected not just civic commitment to the new poor law but also the central Commissioners' concerns to tie sometimes reluctant parishes into a closer embrace with the new union structure. They also served as a concrete reminder to Londoners that, despite their reluctant adoption of the new poor law, the reforms were a permanent feature of life.

The new workhouse in Greenwich illustrated well some of these broader considerations. The new union formed in November 1836 was fractious from the start. It comprised four neighbouring parishes thrown together in a somewhat reluctant and hasty embrace: Greenwich, Woolwich, St Paul Deptford and St Nicholas Deptford. Almost immediately its workings were blocked by ratepayers from St Nicholas and St Paul Deptford who objected to the arrangements, and those in Woolwich, who sought to form their own union with neighbouring Charlton and Plumstead.[33] Whilst the Poor Law Commissioners recognised the argument put forward by the Woolwich guardians, they refused to countenance objections from other parishes in the new union.[34] Mindful of the difficulties that the Commissioners thought were likely to occur when full guardian elections were due to be held in 1839, they tried to forestall any attempt to break up the union by hastily authorising the construction of a new workhouse, thereby binding the districts together by virtue of a shared institution.[35] Initially, the Commissioners authorised a loan of £18,000 for the workhouse, but when tenders were received the cheapest was £27,000. After some pruning, costs were brought down to £22,000 and although they still considered the design expensive for the number of paupers to be housed, they nevertheless agreed to proceed.

---

32 TNA MH32/57 Local Government Board and predecessors: Assistant Poor Law Commissioners and Inspectors, Correspondence, Charles Mott, Quarterly return showing the state of the workhouses, 31 March 1838.

33 TNA MH12/5091 Local Government Board and predecessors: Correspondence, Greenwich Board of Guardians, 3 November 1836, 9 February, 15, 31 March 1837; TNA MH12/5092 Ibid., 1 February, 22 December 1838; TNA HO/73/51/38, ff. 280–83, Copy of reply from Poor Law Commissioners for Lord John Russell to resolutions passed by inhabitants of St Nicholas Deptford, maintaining that the union with St Paul Deptford, Greenwich and Woolwich stands, 17 November 1836; TNA HO/73/52/24, ff. 174–5 Letter from clerk to the guardians of Greenwich union to Poor Law Commission explaining problems with parishes of Woolwich and St Paul Deptford; concerns about case pending in King's Bench to declare union invalid, 13 May 1837.

34 TNA MH32/56 Local Government Board and predecessors: Assistant Poor Law Commissioners and Inspectors, Correspondence, Charles Mott, 14 October 1837.

35 TNA MH12/5092 Local Government Board and predecessors: Correspondence, Greenwich Board of Guardians, 18 November 1838.

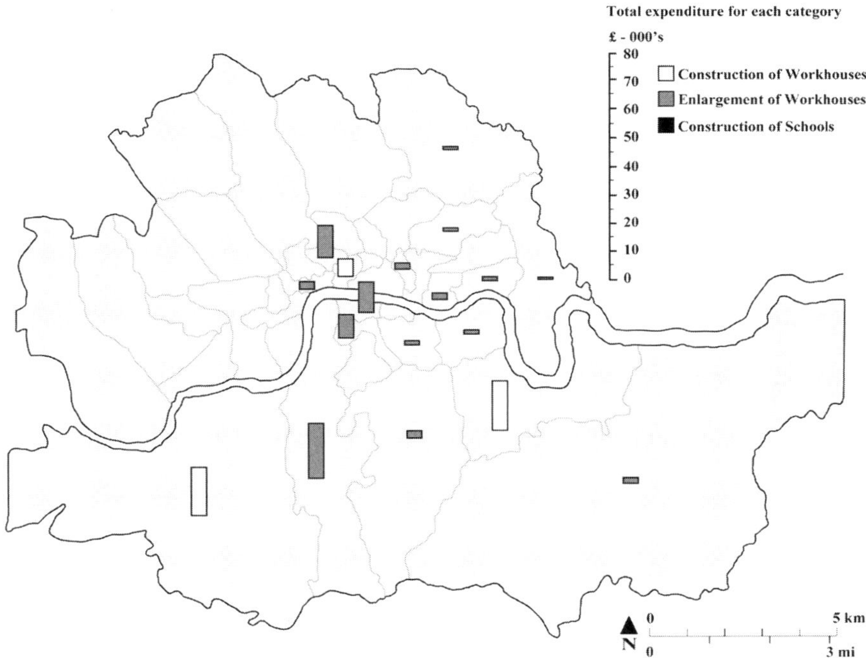

Figure 4.8 Workhouse and school construction 1835–1839

Source: Poor Law Commission, Annual Reports, 1836–39.

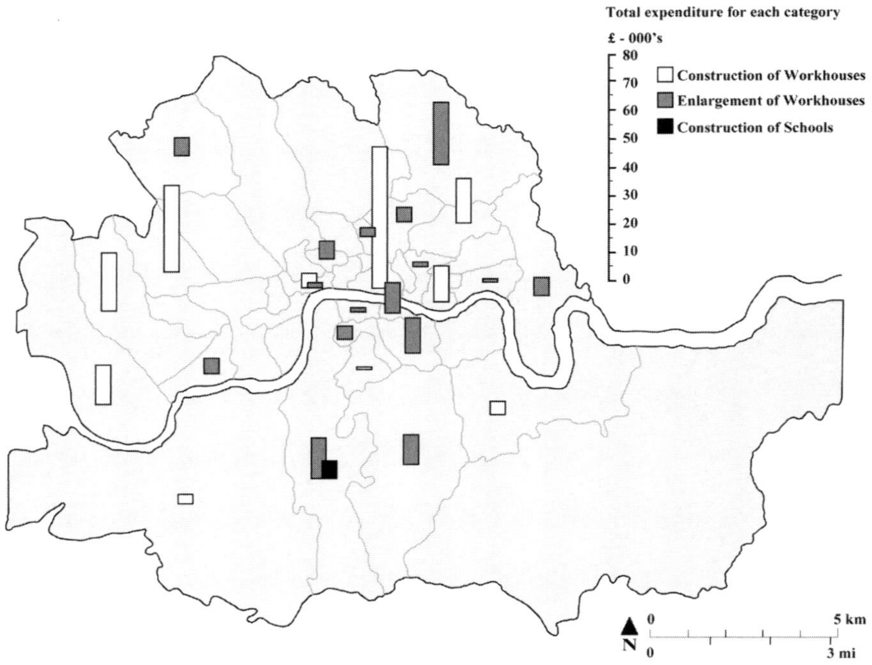

Figure 4.9 Workhouse and school construction 1840–1849

Source: Poor Law Commission, Annual Reports, 1840–47; Poor Law Board, Annual Reports, 1848–49.

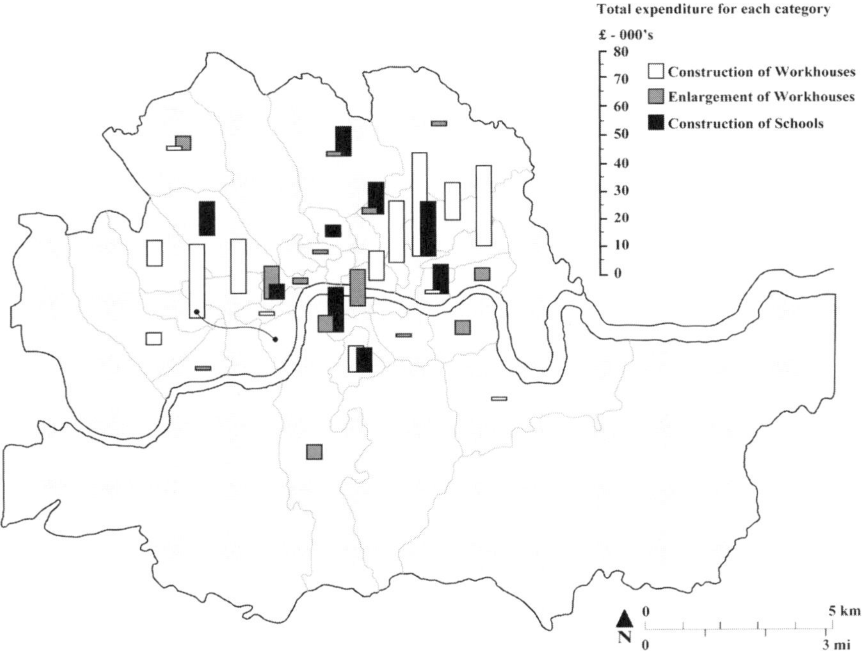

Figure 4.10 Workhouse and school construction 1850–1859

Source: Poor Law Board, Annual Reports, 1850–59.

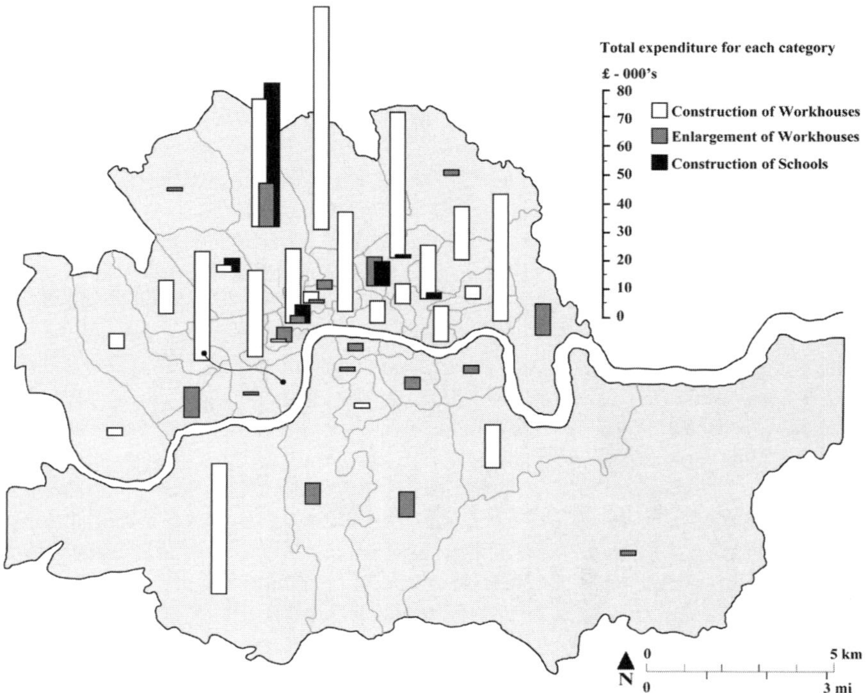

Figure 4.11 Workhouse and school construction 1860–1868

Source: Poor Law Board, Annual Reports, 1860–68.

The case for building a new workhouse in Greenwich, however, was far from clear. Each of the constituent parishes already had their own building. When Charles Mott visited the district in late 1836 he condemned the St Nicholas workhouse as 'deplorable' yet found that in neighbouring St Paul Deptford, which had only recently been enlarged, 'exceedingly clean and well arranged' – which partially explains why ratepayers from that district were so hostile to the new union in the first place and firmly objected to having to pay some £5,000 or £6,000 for a new building.[36] Edwin Chadwick himself intervened in the dispute arguing that the existing workhouses were inadequate to allow proper classification of paupers and that a new building was needed in order to administer relief efficiently.[37] Within two months, and before forthcoming guardian elections could took place, new

36 TNA MH12/5091 Local Government Board and predecessors: Correspondence, Greenwich Board of Guardians, 5 October 1837; TNA MH12/5092 Ibid., 22 December 1838.

37 TNA MH12/5092 Ibid., 1 January 1839.

tenders had been received and the architect had been appointed. However reluctant guardians were to accept the situation, construction of the new workhouse started immediately and was completed by 1840, although relationships between the constituent parishes remained strained.[38]

The fractious context of the Greenwich workhouse was perhaps unusual and construction in the following decade was generally less contentious. In eastern districts new building took place in Bethnal Green with extensive alterations also to the workhouse in neighbouring St George in the East. In Bethnal Green ratepayers and guardians enthusiastically embraced the new poor law which made the decision to build an easy one. The new workhouse in Waterloo Road was a relatively modest three-storey brick building with little exterior decoration (See Figure 4.5). The site itself was confined and the amount of space devoted to exercise yards was accordingly much smaller than at Greenwich. Designed to accommodate 800 paupers, it was completed in 1842 at a comparatively low cost of £15,000.[39] As already noted, the City of London's new workhouse in Bow Road built in 1849 was a much grander affair costing more than three times as much. Until then City paupers had been relieved in three separate establishments: the casual poor, men and couples at Peckham; women in a place at Stepney and children at a contractor in Norwood. However, pressure arising from the large number of casual poor relieved in the City and the virtual ending of pauper farming lent urgency to the need for a new and closer workhouse, although even the Poor Law Commissioners blanched at the eventual cost.[40] The other workhouses built in the 1840s were erected in western districts. The break up of the Kensington union in 1848 resulted in the construction of workhouses in the new districts of Fulham, Paddington and Kensington itself, with the old workhouse in Chelsea remaining in use.[41] The only other district in the west of London to build a new workhouse in the 1840s was St Margaret and St John, although in this case the building was confined to housing the casual poor.

The slow pace of building in London continued into the 1850s: by the start of that decade only nine unions had built a new workhouse and by the end only another five had been added. Construction was mainly concentrated in eastern districts and by the end of the decade, most unions there had new workhouses, the exceptions being Shoreditch, which built a large parish school instead; Stepney, which only separated from Mile End in 1857 and which had a workhouse adequate for local needs; and Poplar, which similarly had built a large workhouse earlier in the century. New pauper schools were also added in Whitechapel and St George in the East, which helped relieve pressure on space in their existing

38 TNA MH12/5092 Ibid., 3 January, 19 February 1839.

39 Poor Law Commission, Seventh Annual Report, Appendix A, number 6 (1841), pp. 27–9.

40 Poor Law Commission, Second Annual Report, (1836), p. 17. See also Tanner, 'The City of London Poor Law Union', pp. 102–27.

41 See *The Builder*, 5 (1847), pp. 73, 88, 102; Ibid., 6 (1848), pp. 6–7.

workhouses, and this policy was also followed in several other parts of the city as an alternative to expanding the workhouse itself. Indeed, as discussed below, this approach to solving the problem of overcrowding in the workhouse proved to be extremely important in London. Elsewhere, especially in central areas, it proved impossible to find space for a new workhouse and guardians were often forced to look outside their district for suitable sites. The guardians of St Margaret and St John Westminster, for example, acquired a plot in Kensington to the south of that district's own workhouse and a new building was erected there in 1852. By the late 1850s, therefore, the City, together with most eastern and southern districts, and the newly formed unions arising from the break up of Kensington, had acquired a new workhouse or at least had spent considerable sums enlarging their old one or building a parochial school.

Although the map of new workhouse construction had filled out considerably, significant gaps remained. Some of the largest parishes together with the more crowded central districts, several of which had refused to be included under the Poor Law Amendment Act, conspicuously failed to build new workhouses. To some extent this can be explained in relation to existing supply and anticipated need: several central districts were losing population and the demolition of insanitary housing in such places meant that many of the poor had been forced to move elsewhere. However, continued population growth in other areas, coupled with patently inadequate workhouse accommodation, meant that sooner or later the need for extra space became urgent and in the 1860s several substantial workhouses were built to address this situation. This was certainly true in Islington, where population growth had been exceptionally rapid and where the capacity of the old workhouse in Upper Barnsbury Lane had been exceeded for some time. At the time of Henry Farnall's visit there in 1857, he found the building old and, although well managed, he considered it inadequate.[42] The new workhouse, which was authorised in 1865 at a cost of £51,500, was eventually completed in 1869 on the outskirts of the district, leaving the old one to function for a short while as a smallpox and fever hospital.[43] Elsewhere, in Stepney and Shoreditch, the last two eastern districts which still had pre-1834 workhouses in operation, relatively large and expensive workhouses were authorised. In Stepney the new workhouse was opened in 1863 at a cost of over £30,000 whilst in Shoreditch a workhouse and infirmary for 1,200 paupers was opened in 1866 at a cost of £47,750. By the late 1860s, then, much progress had been made although gaps still remained, notably in central districts.

---

[42] TNA MH32/24 Local Government Board and predecessors: Assistant Poor Law Commissioners and Inspectors, Correspondence, Henry Farnall, Report on London Workhouses, 16 February 1857.

[43] Poor Law Board, Eighteenth Annual Report (1866), p. 308.

Expanding the system: from private contractors to district schools

The failure to construct new workhouses needs to be understood in the context of other forms of institutional provision for the poor and in this respect district schools were of prime importance. Building a new workhouse was not the only way of expanding indoor provision, especially where economies of scale made it possible to support specialist institutions for different categories of pauper. This was particularly important in relation to children. An enquiry showed that in England and Wales in 1836 there were more than 42,000 children under 16 years of age in workhouses and by 1840 this number had risen to 68,000.[44] Outside London and other large urban areas, separate provision for parish children was hampered by the geographical dispersal of unions, making it impractical to create separate establishments and forcing guardians to keep such children together with adults in the workhouse. In London, however, children comprised nearly a third of those receiving indoor relief throughout the period and therefore economies of scale made it possible to build separate poor law schools.

Given the large numbers of children supported by the poor law, the creation of separate schools was of particular importance, not only allowing authorities to remove them from the contaminating influence of habitual indoor paupers but also making more space available for adults in often overcrowded workhouses. Providing separate accommodation for parish children, therefore, was one means by which metropolitan unions could create more space for adult paupers without the need to rebuild or enlarge the workhouse. Given the pressures on space in central areas, and the possibility of building children's schools in the countryside, this was an attractive option. The issue in London, therefore, was not whether to make separate arrangements for children but how and in this case the choice was whether to use private contractors or public provision.[45]

The difficulties of dealing with pauper children in London reflected the peculiar circumstances of the city. Concern for the high death rate of children in eighteenth-century London workhouses had prompted legislation which required parishes to remove their infants to nurses or private contractors in the countryside.[46] Children below two were to be farmed out to nurses at least five miles away, whilst those between two and six had to be sent at least three miles from the city.

---

44 Frank Compton, *Workhouse Children* (Thrupp, 1997), p. 46.

45 For general discussion of this issue see Michael Horsbaugh, '"No Sufficient Security": The Reaction of the Poor Law Authorities to Boarding Out', *Journal of Social History*, 12 (1983): 51–73.

46 Act for the Keeping Regular, Uniform and Annual Registers of all Parish Poor Infants under a certain Age, Within the Bills of Mortality, 2 Geo. III c. 22 and Act for the Better Protection of Parish Poor Children (Hanway's Act), 7 Geo. III c. 39. See George Nicholls, *A History of the English Poor Law* (London, 1898), vol. 2, pp. 62–4; Compton, *Workhouse Children*, p. 5; Alysa Levene, 'Children, Childhood and the Workhouse: St Marylebone, 1769–1781', *London Journal*, 33 (2008), p. 48.

These arrangements seemed to have been common practice in London prior to 1834.[47] In St James Westminster, for example, children were sent to 'women of character' in Wimbledon, each one having up to 12 or 14 in their care, and those nurses who could keep their charges alive for at least 12 months received a premium of 10 shillings. St Luke's sent an average of 50 children to three wet nurses in Southgate whilst other parishes used nurses in Ealing, Edmonton, Enfield, Finchley, Ilford and Lewisham. Several districts used Frederick Aubin's establishment at West Hill in Norwood, including some City parishes as well as larger districts such as Clerkenwell and St Saviour's Southwark.[48]

If children survived this experience and reached the age of seven, parishes were faced with the problem of what next to do with them. Prior to 1816 it had been common practice to send these pauper children to work in mills in Derbyshire and Lancashire but legislation in that year prohibited parishes from sending children more than 40 miles away.[49] Such measures appeared to have made an immediate impact. In St George Hanover Square, for example, the parish ceased to send its children to mills from 1816, the parish clerk noting that 'We cannot dispose of our children now, there will be more of them kept in the workhouse and brought up in the workhouse to be men and women.'[50] Other parishes followed suit and problems mounted over how to deal with the new excess of children in the workhouse.

Further difficulties also arose over apprenticing pauper children. The new regulations prohibited parishes apprenticing children aged less than nine and, perhaps most importantly, stated that no settlement was to be established by the child unless the terms of the law had been adhered to.[51] This meant that overseers had to rely more on finding apprenticeships in London and this too proved problematic. Many London trades which typically had taken apprentices, such as shoemaking and silk weaving, were in structural decline and masters were increasingly reluctant to take on apprentices or if they did, maintain them for their

---

47 For further discussion see M. Dorothy George, *London Life in the Eighteenth Century* (Harmondsworth, 1966), pp. 236–61.

48 PP 1834 XXXV Royal commission on the administration and practical operation of the poor laws, answers to town queries. Districts using Aubin's included St James Clerkenwell, St Giles in the Fields, St Paul Covent Garden, Christchurch and St Savoiur's Southwark, and the City parishes of St Anne and St Agnes, St Anne Blackfriars, St Dionis Backchurch, St Leonard Foster Lane, St Martin Ludgate, St Michael Cornhill, St Michael Crooked Lane, St Dunstan in the West. See also Thomas Pettigrew, *The Pauper Farming System: A Letter to the Rt Hon Lord John Russell on the Condition of the Pauper Children of St James Westminster* (London, 1836), p. 15.

49 Act to Regulate the Binding of Parish Apprentices (Parish Apprentices Act) 56 Geo. III c. 139. See Nicholls, *A History of the English Poor Law, vol. 2 1714–1853*, pp. 156–8.

50 PP 1817 VI Select committee to consider the poor laws, p. 66.

51 Parish apprenticeship in the eighteenth and early nineteenth century is discussed in more detail in George, *London Life in the Eighteenth Century*, pp. 213–61 and Levene, 'Children, Childhood and the Workhouse', pp. 51–2.

full term of service.[52] 'It is a very rare instance now', noted the parish clerk of Mile End Old Town in 1832, 'for a respectable, or even a decent tradesman, to take a parish apprentice.'[53] There were, of course, opportunities in less skilled branches and in other trades, including chimney sweeping and domestic service, both of which were important in London, but even here opportunities also appeared to be shrinking and parishes were forced into paying ever higher premiums to masters for taking on apprentices.[54] Furthermore, public opinion was turning from pauper apprenticeship towards general education as a way of better providing children's long term welfare and independence from the poor law.[55] Without suitable education and training, which experience showed hardly ever flowed from parish apprenticeships, it was felt that children of the poor would never escape from the vicious cycle of pauperism.

These mounting difficulties and concerns continued after 1834 but although the Poor Law Commissioners found parish apprenticeship 'productive of great evils and mischief', they hesitated to make any significant changes until they had gathered more information. Assistant commissioner James Kay's reports on the training of pauper children in 1838 and 1839 recommended the establishment of district schools rather than a continuation of parish apprenticeship and although the Commissioners again did not seek to abolish apprenticeship entirely, nevertheless they tightened the regulatory framework and in so doing further limited the practice.[56] Regulations issued in 1844 both curtailed the freedom of guardians to apprentice their children in other parishes and tightened considerably the conditions under which apprenticeship could take place. In particular, where children were to be apprenticed to a master outside a parish, the guardians in the receiving union had to be informed and could object to the arrangements. Premiums, too, were limited to part money and part clothing, thereby reducing the financial incentive to accept apprentices.[57] The outcome was that what little inducement remained for employers to take on pauper apprentices all but ceased, leaving parishes to care for their children within the confines of their own institutions, and this had significant implications for the workhouse system.

---

52 For a discussion of the economic pressures in this period and the impact on apprenticeship see David R. Green, *From Artisans to Paupers: Economic Change and Poverty in London 1790–1860* (Aldershot, 1995), pp. 73–84, 122–5.

53 PP 1834 XXVII Royal commission on the administration and practical operation of the poor laws, report, p. 88.

54 See George, *London Life in the Eighteenth Century*, pp. 256–7.

55 Ibid., pp. 260–61.

56 Poor Law Commission, Fourth Annual Report (1838), Appendix B no. 3, pp. 140–61; Ibid., Fifth Annual Report (1839), Appendix C no. 1, pp. 84–100. Kay's experiences in East Anglia were described in James Kay 'On the Establishment of County or District Schools for the Training of Pauper Children Maintained in Union Workhouses, Part 1', *Journal of the Statistical Society*, 1 (1838), pp. 14–27.

57 Poor Law Commission, Twelfth Annual Report (1846), Appendix A no. 3, p. 41.

The gradual ending of parish apprenticeship exacerbated the problems for London unions since it removed one of the main means by which the burden of responsibility for pauper children could be shifted elsewhere. In the absence of alternative arrangements, children either had to be kept in the workhouse or farmed out to private contractors. The Poor Law Commissioners noted in their second annual report that London workhouses were typically occupied by adults and children 'above the age of nurture' and this situation continued in the following years.[58] Where they remained in the workhouse, as was the case in districts such as Bethnal Green, Fulham, St Giles, St Pancras and St Marylebone, they typically comprised about a third of indoor paupers. In Bethnal Green, for example, there were 300 children out of a total of 1,050 inmates whilst in St Marylebone, they comprised some 550 of over 1,800 indoor paupers.[59] Figure 4.12 shows that this proportion was fairly typical of London as whole. Where parishes had more than one workhouse, as was the case in Stepney which had three, children could be housed separately. However, where only one existed they had to be accommodated together with other paupers, which then created serious problems of segregation and raised deep concerns about the contaminating influence of the workhouse on children's character, particularly in relation to girls.[60] As William Lee, master of St Pancras workhouse, reported to the Royal Commission on the Poor Laws:

> As little or no classification can take place, the younger soon acquire all the bad habits of the older, and become for the most part as vitiated. This is peculiarly the case with respect to young girls. We are obliged to have many young prostitutes among our inmates; they decoy the young girls with whom they have met in the house to leave it, and addict themselves to the same abandoned course.[61]

---

[58] Ibid., Second Annual Report (1836), p. 10. The age of nurture was below seven years old.

[59] TNA MH32/24 Local Government Board and predecessors: Assistant Poor Law Commissioners and Inspectors, Correspondence, Henry Farnall, Report on London Workhouses, 16 February 1857.

[60] *The Times*, 26 December 1842.

[61] PP 1834 XXVII Royal commission on the administration and practical operation of the poor laws, report, p. 29.

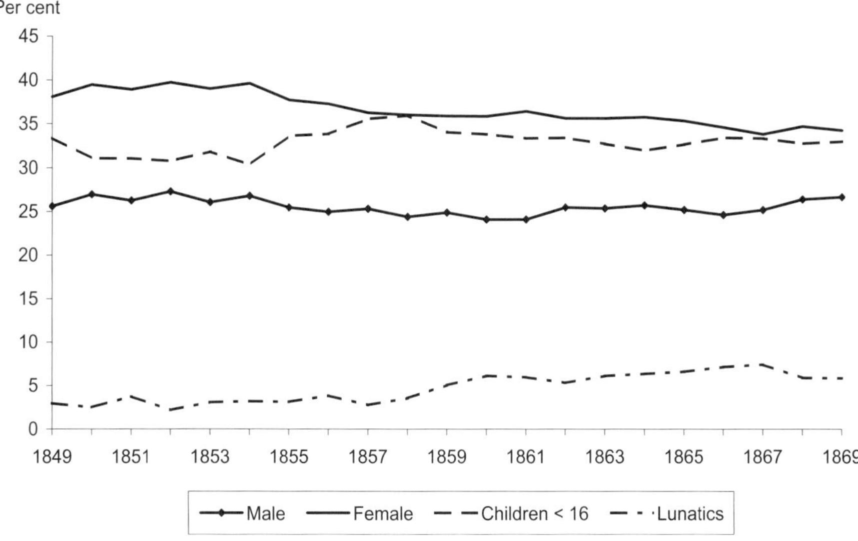

Figure 4.12 Indoor paupers relieved in London on 1 January 1849–1869 (% total paupers)

Source: Poor Law Board, Annual Reports 1849–69. Figures for 1849 to 1858 refer to Middlesex and from 1859–69 to metropolitan parishes in Middlesex, Surrey and Kent.

Such concerns, as well as pragmatic reasons relating to space, prompted guardians to make alternative arrangements for their pauper children. One solution to workhouse overcrowding noted by the assistant poor law commissioners was the removal of children to separate establishments on the outskirts of the city.[62] The West London and Islington unions, for example, sent children to a place in Edmonton whilst Shoreditch had a parochial school in Enfield.[63] In other cases, guardians made use of private contractors. Two of the largest establishments for pauper children were Frederick Aubin's in Norwood and George Drouett's at Brixton and Tooting. Both Aubin's and Drouett's businesses grew rapidly after 1834. In 1836, Dr Neil Arnott reported that Aubin's establishment accommodated 650 children and Drouett's 150.[64] However, demand evidently rose and by 1839 Aubin's had grown to accommodate 1,100 children and Douett's Grove House establishment in Brixton housed 300. In addition, Drouett had opened another

[62] See Pettigrew, *The Pauper Farming System*, p. 15.

[63] *The Times*, 25 December 1844.

[64] Poor Law Commission, Second Annual Report (1836), Appendix C, no. 1a, pp. 488–9. In 1836 a report in *The Times* of an inquest on George Coster, a young boy who had died at Aubin's establishment, noted that there were between 300 and 500 children there. See *The Times*, 21 March 1836.

establishment in Tooting which by 1842 could take up to 800 children.[65] Demand continued to grow and by 1848 Aubin's school contained 1,240 children from 11 unions and Drouett housed 1,370 from 13 unions.[66] From 1834 onwards the pauper children business clearly thrived.

Such rapid expansion, of course, came at a price and concerns were voiced about conditions at both contractors' establishments. The St James' directors of the poor noted that the mortality rate of children who had previously been nursed by women in Wimbledon had quadrupled within a year of them having been removed to Aubin's school. Although there was some doubt as to whether the St James' children sent there were healthy or not when they arrived, conditions were grossly overcrowded, with children sleeping two and three to a bed. When Dr Arnott inspected the place on behalf of the Poor Law Commissioners, he found both the ventilation and heating inadequate. 'When I entered the great school-room, containing some 300 to 400 boys', he recorded, 'I was instantly struck by the strong odour, namely the concentrated breath and exhalations of the crowd of human beings.'[67] Noting the prevalence of ringworm, scabies and fever, particularly amongst the younger children, a visiting committee in 1835 commented that 'this place is unfit for children of tender years', an opinion subsequently reiterated by various other visitors including Dr Tweedale, physician to the Royal Metropolitan Infirmary and Royal Naval School.[68]

Whilst conditions were generally poor in these private institutions, they were no worse than in many workhouses and in some cases were demonstrably better. James Kay's report on the training of pauper children in London in 1839 pointed to some improvements in education and discipline in Aubin's establishment that followed closely plans for district schools prepared by the Poor Law Commissioners. Prior to his investigation, religious instruction was inadequate and moral training 'in every respect extremely defective'.[69] Boys were occupied sorting bristles and making hooks and eyes, useless in Kay's opinion for providing them with any skills with which to earn their own living, and 'pernicious because they disgusted them with labour'. Girls fared little better, also carrying out these tasks as well as learning needlework and doing domestic chores. Following instructions and regular inspection by the assistant commissioners, however, some improvements seemed to have taken place at Aubin's. Kay also noted how similar improvements had been made in several workhouse schools, where sound religious, moral and

---

65 Poor Law Commission, Fifth Annual Report (1839), p. 147; *The Times*, 25 December 1844.

66 TNA MH32/37 Local Government Board and predecessors: Assistant Poor Law Commissioners and Inspectors, Correspondence, Richard Hall, 29 December 1848.

67 Poor Law Commissioner, Second Annual Report (1836), Report by Dr Neil Arnott on the metropolitan houses for the reception of pauper children, p. 490.

68 Pettigrew, *Pauper Farming*, pp. 19–21.

69 Poor Law Commission, Fifth Annual Report (1839), Appendix C, no. 1, Training of pauper children second report, p. 146.

industrial training was seen as the means of eradicating the 'germs of pauperism in the rising generation'.[70] Not so at Drouett's, however, where the girls regularly spent triple the amount of time sewing shirts than they did at lessons.[71] Without clear authority to regulate standards of education and care in contractors' institutions and individual poor law unions, it was clear that no uniformity in the treatment or training of children could emerge. As a result, Kay concluded,

> My experience leads me to say, that the defects apparently inseparable from contractors' establishments, are such as to render their extension in the highest degree impolitic; and to induce me to add that a right regulation of such houses can generally be secured only by incessant and painful vigilance.[72]

Failing such vigilance, he suggested, the training of pauper children would continue to be ineffective.

Kay's recommendation, borne out of his previous experience in East Anglia, was to establish district schools separated from all associations with the workhouse. They were to be located in rural settings away from the corrupting influence of the city. By combining the children from several unions, the schools themselves could be of sufficient size to allow efficient regulation with due regard to economies of scale. Training children in large district schools was attractive for two other reasons. First, relatively small numbers of children in individual workhouses meant that it was difficult to justify the cost of employing qualified teachers. Furthermore, the constant coming and going of those children belonging to families that entered and left the workhouse disrupted education. The result was that what little teaching children received in the workhouse was almost always inadequate. Second, for children, work was seen more as a means of promoting habits of industry but for able-bodied adults in the workhouse itself it was viewed primarily as a form of deterrence. Separating these two meanings of work proved difficult when both were performed in the same physical space.

District schools addressed both sets of issues. By virtue of their size and physical separation from the workhouse they allowed a more efficient and economical way of training children. Their physical separation meant that children tended to remain at the school until they reached the age at which they could begin work. At the same time, education in district schools emphasised the utility of work rather than its deterrent nature. Girls were taught cooking, washing and other domestic skills whilst boys typically learned various types of industrial and agricultural work.

---

70 Ibid., Fourth Annual Report (1838), Appendix B, no. 3, Report on the training of pauper children, p. 229.

71 PP 1847 XLIX Workhouse schools: copies of extracts of all reports made by assistant commissioners on the subject of workhouse schools since the 1st day of January 1846, pp. 168–74.

72 Poor Law Commission, Fifth Annual Report (1839), Appendix C, no. 1, Training of pauper children second report, p. 158.

For the latter, music was also seen as a particularly effective form of training, allowing boys to acquire enough skill to enter regimental bands after only six to seven months' training compared to the two or more years needed for tailoring or shoemaking.[73]

The financial penalties arising from the failure to provide an adequate training for pauper children were clear. Ratepayers would have to continue to support those who could not provide for themselves because they lacked training, whilst premiums would still have to be paid to persuade employers to take on parish apprentices. The better the training, Kay noted, the more likely it was that paupers could be transformed to self-supporting individuals, and the more desirable would parish apprentices be to employers.[74] The outcome of failure to separate children from the influence of habitual paupers and to provide adequate training, he argued, was continued dependency on poor relief with inevitable consequences for ratepayers.

Kay's views echoed those of others, including Charles Dickens. In the character of *Oliver Twist*, first published in 1837–38, Dickens highlighted the failure not just of the workhouse to provide a suitable setting for the education for pauper children but also the inadequate nature of parish apprenticeships. Oliver's failure as an apprentice to Sowerberry, the local undertaker, led inexorably to a life of crime as a pickpocket on London's streets. In an unusual show of agreement, *The Times* and the Poor Law Commissioners also concurred that the workhouse was not a suitable place for children. *The Times* noted that 'Experience has abundantly shown that there was no hope for the mental or moral culture of the youthful pauper while contact with the adult was permitted.'[75] Henry Farnall, the assistant poor law inspector, agreed. Children educated in the workhouse, he argued, were reared in 'the midst of wickedness and want' and left without 'an acquaintance with either order, cleanliness or industry.... Parish loaves and parish clothing; alms and a compulsory rate, penal codes and active police will never reduce this moral evil'. Rather, early education and early occupation, especially in separate district schools, would suffice to break the cycle of pauperism for these 'outcast children'.[76] Others, such as Jellinger Symons, the inspector of workhouse schools, and Mary Carpenter, suggested that education in state-run pauper schools where industrial training could be combined with moral reform, which should also be open to children of the poor as day pupils, could reform both the bodies and minds of pauper children.[77] Concerns about the means of providing that education –

---

[73] Ibid., Fourth Annual Report (1838), Appendix B, no. 3, Report on the training of pauper children, p. 237. See also PP 1857–58 XLV Reports by Her Majesty's Inspectors of Schools on workhouse schools, 1857–58, pp. 37–9.

[74] Poor Law Commission, Fifth Annual Report (1839), Appendix C, no. 1, Training of pauper children second report, p. 156.

[75] *The Times*, 22 August 1855.

[76] TNA MH32/24 Local Government Board and predecessors: Assistant Poor Law Commissioners and Inspectors, Correspondence, Henry Farnall, 25 April 1859.

[77] Jellinger C. Symons, *Tactics for the Times as regards the Condition and Treatment of the Dangerous Classes* (London 1849), pp. 183–4; Mary Carpenter, *Reformatory Schools*

whether in large establishments or smaller homes – did not mask the fact that there was broad agreement that some form of collective provision was required that would remove pauper children altogether from the workhouse.[78]

Such views struck a chord with the Poor Law Commissioners and guardians alike – the former keen to exert some control over pauper education and the latter equally keen to reduce overcrowding in the workhouse which had been exacerbated by the decline of pauper apprenticeship. These concerns were compounded by the difficulties of regulating both workhouse schools and private institutions. As a result, the Commissioners sought new legislation to establish district schools from scratch. The 1844 Poor Law Act included measures to repeal earlier legislation relating to parish children which, as they themselves noted, 'had for the most part been disregarded in practice'.[79] The new legislation included provisions by which groups of poor law unions could combine for the purpose of building large district schools. For the new school districts, the contribution of each union was to be based on the average expenditure on poor relief in the previous year, later extended to three years. However, mindful of the difficulties in forcing parishes to act against their will, the legislation exempted local act parishes with populations greater than 20,000 from the need to combine in a school district unless by consent of the majority of guardians.

The formation of district schools initially aroused little enthusiasm, though unlike the proposal for the creation of district asylums for the casual poor, it did not provoke outright opposition.[80] Since several districts had already made their own arrangements to educate pauper children within the workhouse or other parish run institutions, or, more likely, in separate establishments run by private contractors, there was no immediate pressure to implement reforms. In 1848 only four out of 34 parishes responded favourably to a questionnaire from Richard Hall, assistant commissioner for London, about district schools. The remainder, he noted, were keen either to continue their arrangements with Aubin and Drouett or to maintain schools in their own parishes and under those circumstances he thought it would be impossible to make a 'general and systematic' arrangement work.[81] The reason for this reluctance, according to the Poor Law Commissioners, lay in the fact that the act setting up district schools failed to make sufficient financial allowance for the schools themselves to be built.[82] Metropolitan individualism appeared to be too

---

for the Children of the Perishing and Dangerous Classes and for Juvenile Offenders (London, 1851).

[78] [Anon], *Workhouses and Women's Work* (London, 1858), pp. 9–25.

[79] Act for the Further Amendment of the Laws Relating to the Poor in England and Wales (Poor Law Amendment Act), 7 & 8 Vict. c. 101; see also Poor Law Commissioners, *Official Circular of public documents and information* vol. IV, 147, 30 September 1844.

[80] TNA MH32/36 Local Government Board and predecessors: Assistant Poor Law Commissioners and Inspectors, Correspondence, Richard Hall, 1 February 1845, 1 January 1847.

[81] TNA MH32/36 Ibid., 1 January 1847; TNA MH32/37 Ibid., 29 December 1848.

[82] Poor Law Commission, Eleventh Annual Report (1845), pp. 18–19.

strong and there was no hope, Hall concluded, of persuading parishes to unite for the purpose of opening district schools.[83]

The formation of district schools

From the Commissioners' perspective, the difficulty was that control over the private children's establishments was even weaker than that over individual boards of guardians, and although they had a duty of inspection, they had no powers to enforce any changes.[84] The Commissioners had some control at Aubin's where they paid for part of the teachers' salaries but no such arrangement existed with respect to Drouett's establishment and as such they were powerless to influence change.

Cholera precipitated the crisis that eventually resulted in the creation of district schools in London. In December 1848 there was a serious outbreak in Drouett's school in Tooting which resulted in the death of 180 children.[85] Inquests on the deaths of pauper children from Holborn and Chelsea unions presided over by Dr Thomas Wakley heard evidence from a range of witnesses that defective arrangements in the school had worsened the outbreak: the food was poor, clothing insufficient, ventilation inadequate and overcrowding severe. Several children called as witnesses complained about the amount and poor quality of the food, especially the black and watery potatoes. Anyone who complained was likely to be beaten, and those who tried to escape were birched and humiliated by Drouett and other staff.[86] Once the epidemic had started, the medical response was totally inadequate: there were insufficient nurses and many children, having been taken ill, were left to lie in their own vomit and excrement. Healthy children were drafted in to act as auxiliary nurses, a course of action which itself placed them in danger of contracting the disease.[87] To make matters worse, when children had died they had been buried hastily without their parents' knowledge. The catalogue of neglect proved too much: the various juries each passed a verdict of manslaughter on Drouett.[88] But before he could be arrested he himself contracted cholera, declaring just before his death that he was 'a murdered man' on account of the various prosecutions initiated by Wakley.[89]

The outbreak prompted several parishes to withdraw their children and the question of what to do with them therefore took on added urgency. In a report by William Lumley to the St Pancras Directors of the Poor, the point was made that by sending their children

83 TNA MH32/37 Local Government Board and predecessors: Assistant Poor Law Commissioners and Inspectors, Correspondence, Richard Hall, 29 December 1848.

84 *The Times*, 24 January 1849.

85 TNA MH32/37 Local Government Board and predecessors: Assistant Poor Law Commissioners and Inspectors, Correspondence, Richard Hall, 6 October 1849.

86 *The Times*, 29 January 1849.

87 Ibid., 13 January 1849.

88 Ibid., 24 January, 1 February 1849.

89 Ibid., 15 February 1849.

to Drouett's, parishes had effectively agreed to the principle of combining resources.[90] The question, therefore, was not whether to combine but how and once this point had been accepted the path was clear to the creation of district schools. Within a couple of months of the cholera outbreak plans had been drawn up for the formation of separate school districts paid for collectively by poor law unions.[91] By August 1849 three school districts had been formed in London: the Central London district which comprised the City, East London and St Saviour; the South Metropolitan which included St Olave's, Bermondsey, Camberwell and Rotherhithe; and the North Surrey District incorporating Wandsworth and Clapham, Lewisham as well as Kingston, Richmond and Croydon. Other unions were added to these districts in the coming years. The Central London district took over Aubin's establishment at Norwood, retaining him as supervisor, and after alterations costing some £17,000 it could accommodate 800 children. Even this, however, soon proved too small, and a new school was opened at Hanwell in 1857 which by the time it had been completed in 1861 could accommodate 1,200 children.[92] The first purpose built district school to open was in Annerly in November 1850 belonging to the North Surrey Industrial School District and shown in Figure 4.13. The opening ceremony, described in detail in *The Times*, was a grand affair attended by over 200 guests including the Archbishop of Canterbury, several bishops, local clergy, MPs and a host of other dignitaries.[93] Slightly smaller than the Central London school, there was space for some 800 children.[94] The South Metropolitan School District purchased 60 acres of land at Sutton in 1850 and opened a school there in 1855 at a cost of nearly £44,000 (see Figure 4.14).[95] Although a fire destroyed the south wing very soon after its opening, by 1857 the school had some 755 children.[96] In total, nearly 3,000 places for children were created within a space of ten years, equivalent to the total numbers of paupers relieved in St Marylebone and St Pancras workhouses combined.

---

90 Ibid., 24 January 1849.

91 TNA MH32/37 Local Government Board and predecessors: Assistant Poor Law Commissioners and Inspectors, Correspondence, Richard Hall, 19 February, 3 March, 20 April 1849.

92 *The Times*, 26 December 1857; TNA HLG 26/1 Records created or inherited by the Ministry of Housing and Local Government, and of successor and related bodies, Poor Law Commission and successors: Legal Department and successors: Orders, Central London, South Metropolitan and North Surrey School Districts 14 April 1856; 11 March 1859; PP 1857–58 Part I LXIX Return of district schools established under orders of the Poor Law Board, relating to cost, number of paid officers and expenditure, 1856–57, p. 2.

93 *The Times*, 21 November 1850.

94 Ibid., 22 August 1855.

95 TNA HLG 26/1 Records created or inherited by the Ministry of Housing and Local Government ..., Legal Department and successors: Orders, Central London, South Metropolitan and North Surrey School Districts, 5 April 1850; 6 July 1852; TNA HLG 26/3 Ibid., 29 November 1870.

96 PP 1857–58 Part I LXIX Return of the average number of inmates in district union schools in England and Wales, p. 1.

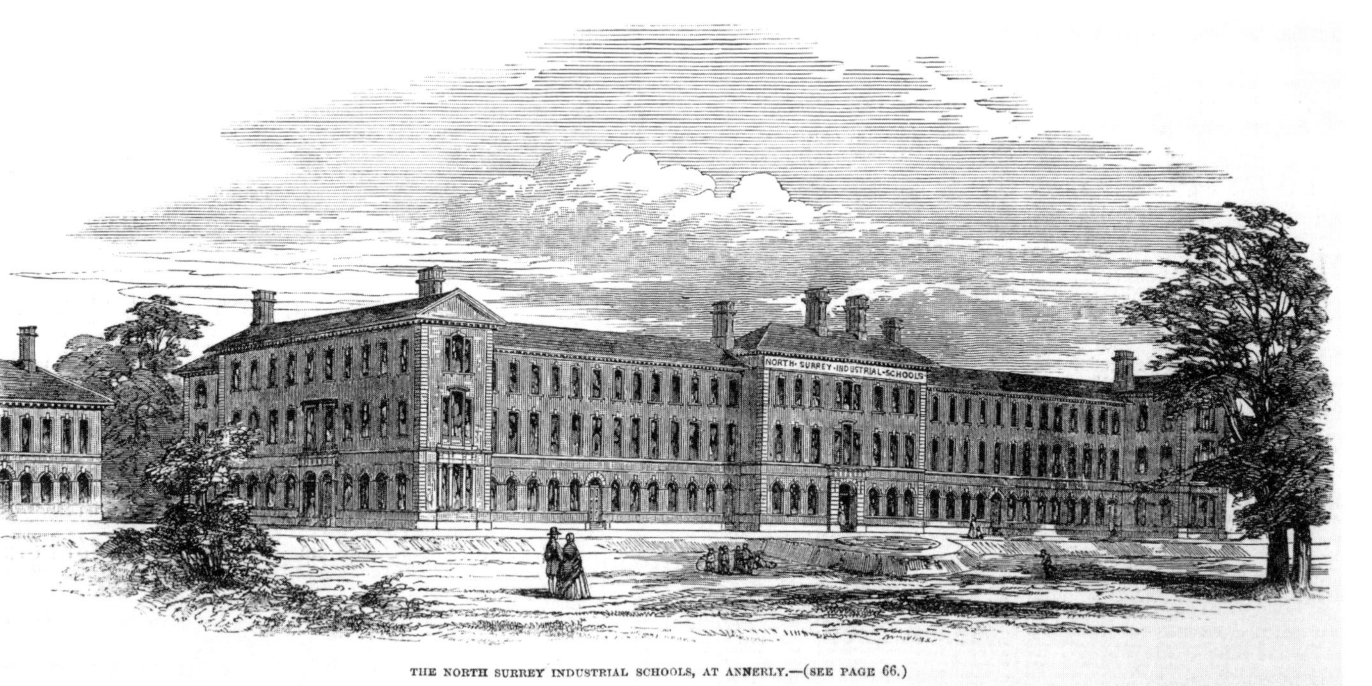

Figure 4.13 The North Surrey Industrial School at Annerly 1850

Source: *Illustrated London News*, 20 July 1850. Reproduced with kind permission of the Senate House Library, University of London.

Figure 4.14 The South Metropolitan Industrial School at Sutton 1854

Source: *Illustrated London News*, 18 March 1854. Reproduced with kind permission of the Senate House Library, University of London.

The new schools were not only physically but also symbolically separate from London workhouses. Although the Central London district had taken over Aubin's establishment, the new schools built for the South Metropolitan and North Surrey districts were both located in rural surroundings in Surrey at some distance from London. The physical separation was also reinforced by the moral separation from the workhouse proper. As *The Times* noted in its report on the Annerly school 'The establishment is strictly industrial, and no pauper officers or servants are allowed on the premises, so that the contamination consequent on contact with adult paupers may be prevented.' The aim was to provide '... not only what is generally known as school education but such industrial education as shall form valuable servants and induce respectable masters to employ the children or as shall fit them for migration'.[97] Directions for the management of the Central London school noted that in addition to lessons in reading, writing and arithmetic, 'such other instruction shall be imparted to them as may be calculated to produce in them habits of industry and virtue'.[98] Not everyone welcomed the scale of provision, arguing that large establishments could never provide a 'home' for pauper children. However, although conditions varied, and in some cases were clearly inadequate, nevertheless in 1861 Mary Carpenter could write

> Under judicious inspection, and with efficient aid, the Workhouse Schools which were formerly a disgrace to the nation, have become models of excellent training, perhaps nowhere surpassed, wherever guardians have themselves been willing to avail themselves of the Act for establishing District Industrial Workhouse Schools'.[99]

Not all unions chose to collaborate in forming district schools and several either opted to retain children in their own workhouse or to build new schools themselves, as the expenditure figures discussed above show. Where they remained in the workhouse, children typically comprised about a third of indoor paupers.[100] However, it became more common for guardians to send children to separate schools and several were built from the late 1840s in the outskirts of London. In 1849 the Strand union opened an industrial school in Edmonton that could accommodate at least 200 children; St George in the East built one at Plashett in Essex in 1851 and

---

[97] *The Times*, 21 November 1850.

[98] TNA HLG 26/1 Records created or inherited by the Ministry of Housing and Local Government..., Legal Department and successors: Orders, Central London, South Metropolitan and North Surrey School Districts, 23 February 1852.

[99] Mary Carpenter, 'On Educational Help from Government for the Destitute and Neglected Children of Great Britain', *Journal of the Statistical Society*, 24 (1861): 28. See also [Anon], *Workhouses and Women's Work* (1858), pp. 9–10; Strand Board of Guardians, *The Strand Union Pauper Children at Edmonton* (London, 1852).

[100] TNA MH32/24 Local Government Board and predecessors: Assistant Poor Law Commissioners and Inspectors, Correspondence, Henry Farnall, 16 February 1857.

Whitechapel's industrial school at Forest Gate opened in 1854. Other unions also sent their children to these schools: Kensington used Plashett school whilst Poplar sent children to Forest Gate.[101] In each case, rural locations ensured both a physical as well as a moral separation from the city in keeping with the sentiments that underpinned the construction of the larger district schools elsewhere.

In relation to the amount of space available in London workhouses, the scale of school provision was significant. By 1860, about 5,200 of the 6,900 or so children aged over seven who were the responsibility of London unions were cared for outside the workhouse itself, with roughly equal numbers in new districts schools and separate children's establishments opened by individual unions.[102] This figure represented about 20 per cent of indoor paupers, although the amount of space made available as a result of removing children was less.[103] Whether or not the new district and workhouse schools provided an adequate education to allow children to escape the clutches of poverty is not the main issue here. In relation to the poor law as a whole, the schools' significance was that by removing children from the workhouse they provided much needed space in often overcrowded institutions and this allowed guardians in some cases to escape the pressing need to rebuild or make enlargements. The fact that parishes had to combine in order to finance the construction and running of the new schools also provided an important precedent for later forms of cooperation. Though London boards of guardians may have been criticised for being insular and self interested, when the benefits were tangible, mutual interest clearly could overcome mutual distrust.

The lunatic poor

The last and in numerical terms the least significant category of pauper catered for in separate institutions in London was the lunatic poor. In the first half of the century, pauper lunatics were cared for by a mixture of private enterprise in licensed madhouses, public provision in county asylums, and in some cases within the workhouse itself, sometimes in special wards for the insane. This public-private mixture of provision had emerged early in the century as a response to concerns about the treatment of lunatics in the care of the state. Over time, however, just as had been the case with children's establishments, private provision gave way to

---

101 Ibid.

102 *Workhouse Papers*, 1 May 1860, p. 2. All but nine London unions sent their children to one of the three new district schools.

103 In 1860 the average number of indoor paupers in metropolitan unions was 24,348. Figures are taken from the day count of indoor paupers on 1st January and 1st July 1860. See Poor Law Board, Twelfth Annual Report (1860); Ibid., Thirteenth Annual Report (1861). See also Frederic Mouat, 'On the Education and Training of the Children of the Poor', *Journal of the Statistical Society*, 43 (1880): 236.

the state, albeit controlled not by the central poor law itself but rather by separate Lunacy Commissioners.[104]

Until the construction of county asylums, insane paupers were either kept in the workhouse or, quite commonly in London, in licensed madhouses, which grew in number from 17 in 1806, to 24 by 1816 rising to 42 by 1837.[105] The number of pauper lunatics also rose in line with increasing provision from 110 in Middlesex in 1816 to 2,048 by 1828.[106] In practice, however, the business of pauper lunacy was confined to a small number of relatively large establishments and by the late 1820s and 1830s between 1,200 and 1,400 paupers a year were cared for in a handful of licensed establishments: two in Bethnal Green, one in nearby Hoxton and a fourth in Peckham.[107] Whilst the Metropolitan Lunacy Commissioners were worried about the cramped conditions in the first three, which were in densely populated areas, they were particularly concerned at the poor diet at Peckham, an institution that had been owned by Charles Mott, the first assistant poor law commissioner for London, and in 1844 they considered withholding the licence for its operation on those grounds.[108]

By this time, however, the construction of county asylums paid for by the rates was becoming more prominent in the treatment of pauper lunatics. From 1808 county asylums began to be built to which poor law officers could send their lunatic paupers with the approval of local justices. The first Middlesex asylum was built at Hanwell in 1831, with that for Kent constructed in 1833 and Surrey in 1841. At Hanwell, as a means of ensuring some equity in admissions, each parish was entitled to send one

---

[104] For broader discussions of the provision for pauper lunatics see Peter Bartlett, *The Poor Law of Lunacy: the Administration of Pauper Lunatics in Mid-nineteenth Century England* (Leicester, 1999); Andrew Scull, *Museums of Madness: The Social Organisation of Insanity in Nineteenth-Century England* (Harmondsworth, 1979).

[105] See PP 1807 II Select committee on the state of criminal and pauper lunatics in England and Wales, pp. 74, 79, 93; Andrew Roberts, *The Lunacy Commission: A Study of its Origin, Emergence and Character*. [Online]. Available at: http://www.mdx.ac.uk/www/study/01.htm [accessed: 18 September 2009]. See Elaine Murphy, 'Mad Farming in the Metropolis, Part 2: The Administration of the Old Poor Law of Insanity in the City and East London 1800–1834', *History of Psychiatry* 12 (2001): 405–30.

[106] See PP 1807 II Select committee on pauper lunatics, p. 79; PP 1830 XXX Report from the Metropolitan Commissioners in Lunacy to the Secretary of State for the Home Department, 1829, p. 277.

[107] PP 1830–31 XIV Return of the number of public and private asylums and houses licensed for the reception of lunatics in each county in England and Wales, p. 34; PP 1841 Session 2 VI Metropolitan Commissioners in Lunacy, annual reports, 1835–41, to the Lord Chancellor; PP 1844 XXVI Metropolitan Commissioners in Lunacy, report to the Lord Chancellor, pp. 47–9. See also Murphy, 'Mad Farming in the Metropolis Part 2'; W. H. Sykes, 'Statistics of the Metropolitan Commission in Lunacy', *Journal of the Royal Statistical Society*, 3 (1840), p. 151.

[108] PP 1844 XXVI Metropolitan Commissioners in Lunacy, report to the Lord Chancellor, pp. 48–9.

pauper per £7,000 of its rateable value.[109] However, the asylum there soon proved too small and it was enlarged from its original size of 300 places to 800 within two years of its opening. By 1844 it contained nearly 1,000 pauper inmates, although its size caused some concern to the Lunacy Commissioners who considered it too large to ensure the effective treatment of patients. Even this increase, however, was inadequate to deal with the demand for places and over 400 lunatic paupers remained in Middlesex workhouses.[110] Within a few years, pressure on space necessitated the construction of a second county asylum at Colney Hatch which was opened in 1851 to cater for up to 1,200 patients. The Kent asylum, which was some distance from London at Maidstone, could accommodate about 250 patients whilst the Surrey asylum at Wandsworth had space for 385 lunatics.[111] Although such institutions were ostensibly regulated by the Metropolitan Commissioners for Lunacy, which had been established in 1828, and by the Lunacy Commissioners from 1845 onwards, since they consisted entirely of pauper inmates they were in effect poor law institutions in all but name.

The mixed institutional provision for lunatic paupers continued in the early years of the new poor law, although the relative importance of different arrangements shifted.[112] The Poor Law Amendment Act paid little attention to the treatment of the lunatic poor, stating only that the insane should not be detained in a workhouse for longer than 14 days but removed to an asylum. The imprecise terminology of the instructions allowed guardians considerable leeway in the way they interpreted the requirement to provide care for their lunatic poor and this latitude, together with differing levels of institutional provision, resulted in variations in practice across the country, as well as in London.[113] In the early 1840s, just over 42 per cent of pauper lunatics in the England and Wales were housed in asylums or licensed madhouses, the remainder being cared for primarily in workhouses or by relatives.[114]

However, this masked significant differences between places. In general, London differed from other parts of the country in its reliance on institutional rather than personal care of the insane poor. Table 4.1 shows this clearly, with between one and two per cent of lunatic paupers in Middlesex cared for by relatives and other individuals compared to over 20 per cent in the rest of the country. The relatively early construction of county asylums in Middlesex, Kent and Surrey

---

109 Ibid., p. 91.

110 Ibid., pp. 28, 89–91, 99–101.

111 Ibid., p. 95.

112 For a discussion of these arrangements in East London see Elaine Murphy, 'The New Poor Law Guardians and the Administration of Insanity in East London, 1834–44', *Bulletin of the History of Medicine*, 77 (2003): 45–74; Elaine Murphy, 'The Lunacy Commissioners and the East London Guardians, 1845–1867', *Medical History*, 46 (2002): 495–524.

113 Elaine Murphy, 'The New Poor Law Guardians and the Administration of Insanity', pp. 54–5.

114 Ibid., 55.

meant that by 1847 a greater proportion of the insane poor were cared for in these institutions, although ten years later the rest of the country had more or less closed the gap. Even so, the failure to provide adequate accommodation for the insane poor in Middlesex before 1851 ensured that private contractors remained important up to that date. Once the Colney Hatch asylum was built, however, pauper lunatics from Middlesex parishes were sent there rather than to the licensed madhouses and although private contractors maintained approximately the same numbers in their establishments, nevertheless their relative importance for the care of pauper lunatics declined.[115] Even so, private provision was still between two and three times more important in Middlesex compared to the rest of England and Wales, reflecting perhaps the need to bridge the gap arising from the lack of relatives and others who could provide personal care for the insane poor.

By the late 1860s the importance of the county asylums had increased further and about two thirds of lunatic paupers in London were inmates there compared to 20 per cent in workhouses and about 12 per cent in private licensed madhouses.[116] Although the care of lunatic paupers still left much to be desired, the growing importance of public provision reflected the belief that specialist institutions regulated by the state could provide a more effective and economical form of treatment than was possible through the use of private contractors. In that sense, at least, specialist provision for lunatic paupers in large institutions paid for collectively through the rates followed a similar path to that adopted for the care of pauper children.

---

[115] Poor Law Board, Eleventh Annual Report, (1859), p. 175; PP 1859 Session 2 XIV Commissioners in Lunacy: thirteenth annual report to the Lord Chancellor, Appendix A, pp. 630–31. Figures for London unions do not exist for earlier years. For 1859, however, separate figures are given for individual unions and these show that of the 4,566 lunatic paupers relieved 2,581(56.5%) were in a county asylum, 626 in a licensed house (13.7%), 1,297 in a workhouse (28.4%) and 62 cared for by relatives or others (1.4%). These private madhouses also accepted pauper lunatics from outside London and this supply of patients may have helped to maintain their viability. See Chris Philo, 'Journey to Asylum: A Medical–Geographical Idea in Historical Context', *Journal of Historical Geography*, 21 (1995): 159–61.

[116] PP 1870 XXXIV Commissioners in Lunacy: twenty-fourth annual report to the Lord Chancellor, pp. 92, 96, 252–68.

Table 4.1 Care of the lunatic poor 1847 and 1858 (per cent of total)

	County asylums		**Licensed houses**		**Workhouses**		**Relatives and elsewhere**	
	1847	1858	1847	1858	1847	1858	1847	1858
Middlesex	42.3	56.4	38.7	16.8	17.1	25.9	1.9	1.0
Kent	50.0	56.6	12.6	7.2	22.3	31.7	15.0	4.6
Surrey	49.8	59.5	21.9	5.1	21.6	29.7	6.6	5.6
Rest of England and Wales	25.3	46.6	19.3	5.6	27.9	25.1	27.5	22.7

Source: PP 1847–48 XXXII Commissioners in Lunacy: further report to the Lord Chancellor, 1847, p. 763; PP 1859 Session 2 XIV Commissioners in Lunacy: thirteenth annual report to the Lord Chancellor, Appendix E, abstract of annual returns of pauper lunatics and idiots, pp. 651–75.

Conclusion: institutional provision for the poor

Constructing in bricks and mortar the institutional system of poor relief in London after 1834 was more than just a question of building new workhouses. Indeed, arguably what was different in London compared to the rest of the country was the failure to construct new workhouses and this can only be understood in the context of existing as well as alternative forms of institutional provision for the various categories of paupers. Nor was it simply a matter of more public provision, although over time this is in fact what happened. Rather, the question was whether and how to balance public with private provision, and in what kind of buildings. Although central to this issue, the workhouse itself was only one element, the others consisting primarily of schools and lunatic asylums of one sort or another. Decisions to build new workhouses or enlarge existing ones were taken in the light of these additional institutions, particularly schools which in terms of the number of paupers involved were far more significant than separate asylums.

The shifting balance of institutional provision reflected the possibilities offered by the size of the city and the scale of pauperism. London unions, though large enough in their right, could by virtue of spatial proximity take advantage of economies of scale to create specialist institutions for the poor. In this way, children could be removed from the workhouse to separate schools with professional and better qualified staff than would otherwise have been the case. Similarly, the relatively early provision of county asylums and the existence of licensed madhouses in London, also meant that workhouse provision for the insane was, in the early stages of the new poor law, of lesser importance compared to other parts of the country. In similar ways, scale and geographical proximity created opportunities for private contractors to fill gaps in poor law provision. That they did so to a greater extent than elsewhere, particularly in relation to lunatic paupers, reflects this fact at least as much as the absence of family and friends in the care of the insane.

The reliance on private contractors brought its own problems, not least in the ability to regulate standards of treatment, and there was some concern both in relation to district schools and county asylums that large size inevitably meant poor quality provision. However, it is not the place here to debate whether or not the increasing scale of provision resulted in better education or care for pauper lunatics. Rather, what is important is to note how economies of scale in London allowed for different institutional solutions to the problem of workhouse overcrowding. In the case of children this involved constructing a system of district schools that emerged from the poor law itself. In the care of the insane, the new county asylums and licensed madhouses were ostensibly separate from the poor law, though the former in particular catered almost exclusively for paupers. In both cases this mixed form of provision meant that the need to build new workhouses *per se* was less pressing and it was for that reason, rather than any deeply held antipathy to the tenets of the new poor law, that London districts lagged behind construction elsewhere in the country.

Chapter 5
Negotiating Relief: Pauper Encounters with the Poor Law

Bargaining for relief

Recent histories of the poor law have drawn attention to the ways in which paupers bargained for relief and although this book is primarily about the relationships between place and policy, nevertheless the voice of the poor was an important element in the way that assistance was negotiated.[1] The English poor law conferred a set of rights and obligations on those who received and those who provided relief. Encounters between the poor and officials were therefore embedded in a set of rules and expectations that influenced their respective patterns of behaviour. Paupers were by no means powerless to influence the kinds and amounts of help they received, and strategic considerations guided their actions no less than those of relieving officers, overseers and others responsible for dispensing relief whilst at the same time seeking to protect the parish purse. They wrote letters and sent petitions to the Poor Law Commissioners.[2] They brought complaints about their treatment to the notice of the courts and others in the public realm, underpinned by the idea that paternalistic authority – the monarch, parliament and the magistracy – should intercede on their behalf against the tyranny of local officials.[3] At times they threatened and fought with officers inside and outside the workhouse. They destroyed parish property, they lied and they stole. In short, they bargained for relief.

---

1 The importance of these negotiations has been discussed by Lynn Lees, *The Solidarities of Strangers: The English Poor Laws and the People, 1700–1948* (Cambridge, 1998), pp. 153–76. See also Steven King and Alannah Tomkins (eds), *The Poor in England 1700–1850: An Economy of Makeshifts*, (Manchester, 2003), and Tim Hitchcock, Peter King and Pamela Sharpe (eds), *Chronicling Poverty – The Voices and Strategies of the English Poor 1640–1840*, (Houndmills, 1997).

2 Pauper letters have been the subject of much recent research. See Thomas Sokoll, 'Negotiating a Living: Essex Pauper Letters from London 1800–1834', *International Review of Social History*, 45 (2000), 19–46; Thomas Sokoll, *Essex Pauper Letters 1731–1837* (Oxford, 2001); James Taylor, 'Voices in the Crowd: The Kirkby Lonsdale Letters, 1809–1834', in Hitchcock, King and Sharpe (eds), *Chronicling Poverty*, pp. 109–26.

3 See Gregory Smith, '"The Poor in Blindness": Letters from Mildenhall, Wiltshire, 1835–36', in Hitchcock, King and Sharpe (eds), *Chronicling Poverty*, pp. 222–3.

For the poor, the outcome of encounters with officials had material consequences in terms of the kinds and amounts of help received. Knowing how the system worked and how best to elicit relief, as Peter Mandler has pointed out, was essential for survival.[4] Whether it was by being deferential in the hope of receiving better treatment, becoming a nuisance by breaking windows or damaging property, or appealing to the magistrates in the hope of their benign intervention, the poor needed to know how to exert their right to relief. An awareness of how those negotiations proceeded, the issues that were at stake and the resources that each of the participants could bring to bear on the outcome is therefore an essential part of understanding how the poor law operated on a day to day basis.

Elizabeth Maybon's story is an example of one such encounter. She was a troublesome pauper typical of many young women who applied to the London poor law. Her father was a pauper and for years had received an allowance from the overseers of St George Hanover Square. She was admitted to the workhouse there in May 1833, at a time when relief practices were being tightened, and had a baby in August. In the following April she discharged herself but very shortly was re-admitted, having been removed from the neighbouring parish of St Ann Westminster. She remained in the workhouse until October when on account of her misconduct and violent temper, she was sent to Fry's pauper farm, a common punishment for difficult or refractory paupers. Her child died there some months later after which she left. In October 1835, by which time she was again pregnant, she sought admittance to the St George's workhouse but was refused because of her previous misconduct. One week later she re-applied, this time well dressed and deferential, but was again turned away – her efforts to look presentable suggesting to the relieving officer that she had some resources of her own. Two days later, she again asked for relief but was refused and this time she threatened to break the workhouse windows unless her request was granted. The following day she made another attempt to get help and was offered a token sum of one shilling. Later that evening she carried out her threat and broke three windows at the workhouse, at which point she was prosecuted and sent to jail for one week. It was only after she was released and re-applied for relief that she got her way and was finally admitted to the workhouse.[5]

Elizabeth's story illustrates well the kinds of daily encounters that took place between applicants and officials. As a young woman with an illegitimate child, she

---

4 See Peter Mandler, 'Introduction', in Peter Mandler (ed.), *The Uses of Charity* (Philadelphia, 1990), pp. 12–23. In this context see also Tim Hitchcock, *Down and Out in Eighteenth-Century London*, (London, 2007), pp. 125–49.

5 TNA MH12/7127 Local Government Board and predecessors: Correspondence with Poor Law Unions and Other Local Authorities, St George Hanover Square Overseers of the Poor, 22 June 1835. Elizabeth Maybon was not dissimilar to the paupers who were inmates of the neighbouring St Martin in the Fields workhouse discussed in Lynn MacKay, 'A Culture of Poverty? The St Martin in the Fields Workhouse 1817', *Journal of Interdisciplinary History*, 26 (1995): 209–31.

was typical of one of the main groups of paupers who sought help. She may have been by nature troublesome but her actions also reflected the fact that she expected to receive some assistance and when it was not forthcoming was prepared to take matters into her own hands. Upon such encounters were relief decisions made.

For both outdoor and indoor paupers bargains could be struck over the amounts and types of relief and the kinds of work and behaviour expected in return. That such negotiations sometimes, perhaps often, merged into insubordination was evident in the frequent problems that officials had in maintaining discipline inside the workhouse, particularly in the early years of the new poor law. Paupers used a repertoire of tactics, ranging from assaults to petitions, to challenge authority and negotiate the terms of relief. Some behaviour was clearly opportunistic, stemming more from a sense of personal frustration or individual resentment. But other actions were part of a more considered strategy of resistance that drew upon notions of moral legitimacy and social justice. Irrespective of the reasons, however, it was clear that paupers challenged authority and that they did so both behind workhouse doors as well as in the full glare of the public gaze. As William Osbaldeston, vestry clerk to St Margaret Pattens in the City, noted in his response to the Royal Commission on the Poor Laws in 1834, 'officers make the best bargain they can, and so does the pauper'. The question is what resources could the poor muster with which to negotiate relief. To answer this we need to understand not just the characteristics of the paupers themselves but also the rules of relief and the contexts in which they operated.[6]

London paupers

A working-class life was often lived close to the margins of poverty. Life cycle factors together with personal misfortune and adverse labour market conditions could easily tip individuals and households below the poverty line.[7] However, not all of the poor necessarily became paupers. At the end of the century Charles Booth estimated that over 30 per cent of London's population was living in poverty but the proportion that were actually paupers was little more than two per cent.[8] People drifted in and out of poverty just as they drifted in and out of the workhouse, and

[6] Further discussion of this issue is contained in David R. Green, 'Pauper Protests: Power and Resistance in Early Nineteenth-Century London Workhouses', *Social History*, 31 (2006): 137–59.

[7] For a discussion of urban poverty see Carl Chinn, *Poverty Amidst Prosperity: The Urban Poor in England, 1834–1914* (Manchester, 1995); John Treble, *Urban Poverty in Britain* (London, 1979).

[8] Charles Booth, *Life and Labour of the People of London: First Series, Poverty, vol. 2* (London, 1902), p. 21; Local Government Board, Thirty Second Annual Report (1902), Appendix E, pp. 380–81. The average number of paupers relieved in London during 1901 was 103,089.

the poor and the destitute who beat a path to the overseers' door or the workhouse gates, illustrated in Sir Luke Fildes', *Applications to a Casual Ward*, painted in 1874, reflected a wide diversity of individuals and conditions, from the newly widowed to the unemployed mechanic, from the very young to the very old, and from the broken down tradesman to the disabled old soldier and professional beggar. Each group posed a particular set of problems for the poor law.

Applications for poor relief, as opposed to those to whom it was granted, provide a clearer picture of who sought assistance in London. Lynn Lees' research based on applications to Hammersmith, St Pancras and St Giles, shows that at mid-century men and women applied for poor relief in roughly equal proportions: 57 and 43 per cent respectively.[9] These figures are borne out by more detailed evidence drawn from settlement and examination registers. In St Giles, for example, between 1832 and 1862 men comprised 46 per cent and women 54 of all applicants for relief.[10] The majority of applicants were aged between 20 and 60, though as Figure 5.2 shows, those between 20 and 44 were under-represented in comparison to the population as a whole. By contrast, old age significantly increased the risks of poverty and those aged 60 years and above were more than twice as likely to apply for relief than their share of the population would suggest.[11] Nevertheless, the majority of applicants were aged below 44, almost all of whom were of working age.

Those who applied for assistance, however, were by no means the same as those who received it and considerations of age, sex and personal circumstances dictated whether and what kind of relief was granted. Between applying for and receiving relief lay a whole series of barriers through which the poor had to pass in order to be granted help of one sort or another. For men, especially those considered capable of work, those barriers were particularly difficult to cross and the terms of relief they could expect were stricter compared to women and the non-able-bodied poor.

---

9 Lees, *Solidarities of Strangers*, p. 194.

10 LMA P82/GIS/14-132 St Giles and St George's Bloomsbury, Directors of the Poor, Settlement and Examination Books, 1832–1862. This figure is based on a 1 in 20 sample of all applications for relief between 1832 and 1862 (N=1,401). See David R Green and Alan Parton, 'Slums and Slum Life in Victorian England: London and Birmingham at Mid-Century', in Martin Gaskell (ed.), *Slums* (Leicester, 1990), p. 75.

11 Using non-able-bodied paupers as a surrogate measure for paupers aged over 65, Pat Thane has tentatively estimated that approximately 42 per cent of the population in England and Wales over 65 were in receipt of poor relief. See Pat Thane, *Old Age in English History; Past Experiences, Present Issues* (Oxford, 2000), p. 171. See also George Boyer and Timothy P. Schmidle, 'Poverty Amongst the Elderly in Victorian England', *Economic History Review*, 61 (2008): 1–30.

Figure 5.1 Sir Luke Fildes, Applications to a Casual Ward (1874)

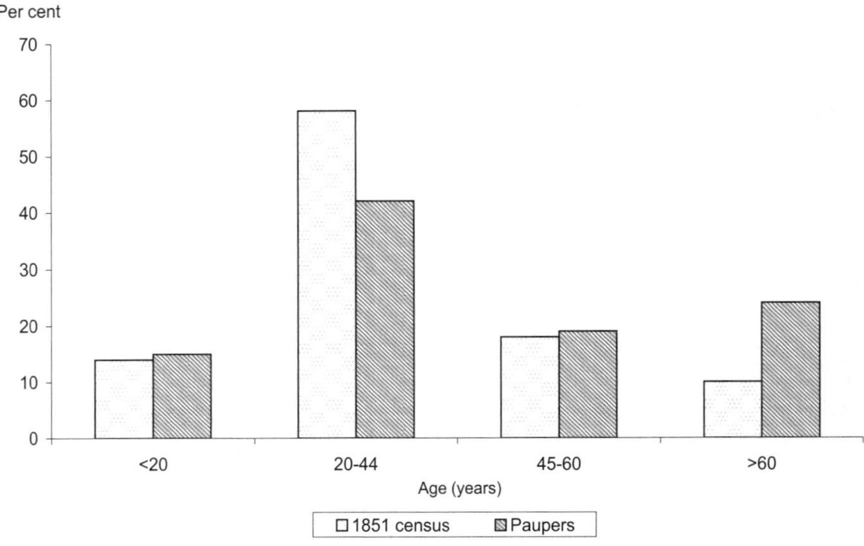

Figure 5.2 Age structure of applicants for relief in London c. 1850

Note: Figures for paupers refer to individual applications based on a 1 in 10 sample of three London parishes – Hammersmith, St Giles in the Fields and St Pancras N=274. Figures for the population are taken from the 1851 census.

Source: Lynn Lees, *Solidarities of Strangers*, p. 194.

An idea of the main groups of paupers can be gauged from aggregate figures published in the Poor Law Commissioners' annual reports that provide information on gender, condition and type of relief. The figures, however, must be treated with caution. The definition of able and non-able-bodied paupers was unclear and applied inconsistently even within unions let alone between them and little reliance can therefore be placed on this particular distinction.[12] Further classification separated out children below the age of 16, lunatics and vagrants. Other than children, no further information is given about age until much later in the century. Separate counts of specific categories of paupers exist for some years but there is no consistency in the information provided. Using this evidence to compare differences between places and over time, therefore, is difficult and limited to a few basic characteristics. Despite these shortcomings, the aggregate totals shed light both on who received relief and the policies adopted in relation to each different category of pauper.

Perhaps the most basic yet arguably the most significant characteristic of those who received relief was gender. Women were twice as likely to receive relief as men and

---

[12] See Paul F. Aschrott, *The English Poor Law System: Past and Present* (London 1888, reprinted 2006), p. 283.

they comprised nearly 69 per cent of adult paupers relieved in London between 1849 and 1869. Taking into account all ages, Figures 5.3 and 5.4 show that women accounted for over a third of both indoor and outdoor paupers.[13] Many of these women would have applied for relief on account of abandonment or death of a male breadwinner and a significant proportion of these were likely to have been accompanied by their family, which accounts for the large number of children who were included in the totals. Many women also gave birth in the workhouse, which often functioned as a lying in hospital for the poor. In St Giles, for example, one in five women who applied for relief did so on account of childbirth. The example of Elizabeth Maybon, discussed above, was typical of this group. Male paupers were more likely to have been offered indoor relief: they comprised over a quarter of the indoor poor compared to only 14 per cent of outdoor paupers, a fact that reflected the importance of the workhouse as a deterrent for able-bodied men considered capable of work.

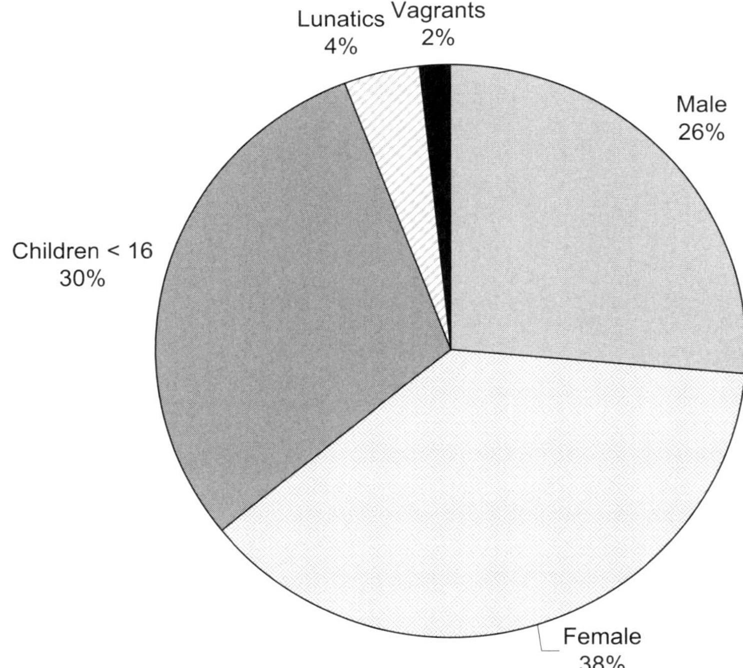

Figure 5.3 Paupers relieved indoors on 1 January 1849–1869

Source: Poor Law Board, Annual Reports, 1849–69.

[13] Indoor paupers were those relieved in establishments under the administration of boards of guardians including the workhouse, district school, infirmaries and sick asylums. The remainder were categorised as outdoor paupers. Lunatics relieved in county asylums and other places not under the control of the guardians fell into this category.

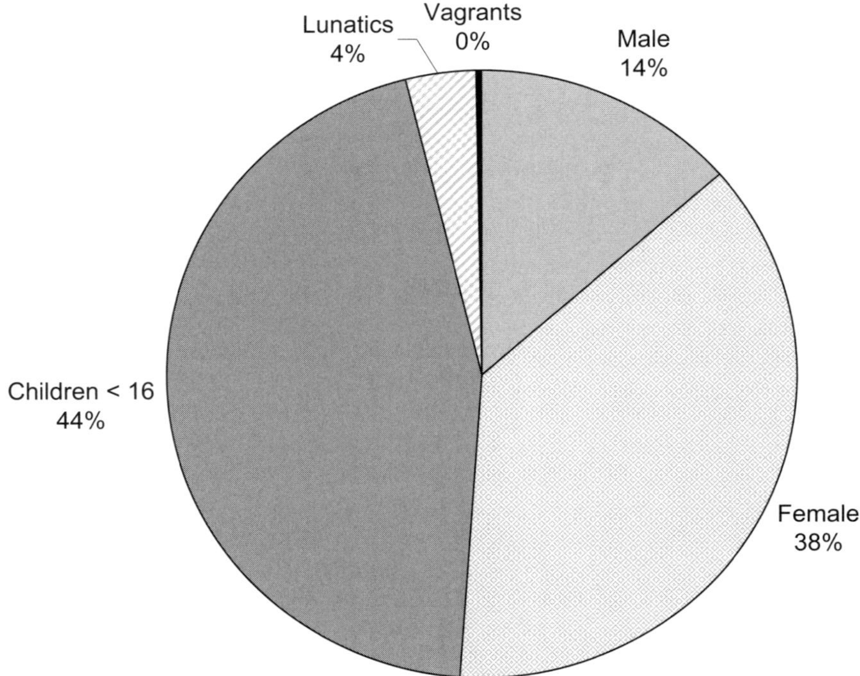

Figure 5.4 Paupers relieved outdoors on 1 January 1849–1869

Source: Poor Law Board, Annual Reports, 1849–69.

Differences in treatment, however, also depended on the vagaries of place and local circumstances could make a considerable impact on the kinds of assistance provided. In 1840, for example, *The Times* reported that the poor who were taken to the City of London relieving officers by the police were likely to have been given bread or money rather than an offer of the workhouse while virtually no one taken to the neighbouring West London and East London unions received anything but an offer of the house.[14] Similar variations existed between Bethnal Green, where the workhouse was offered as a matter of course, and the surrounding unions which were far more likely to provide outdoor relief. When Richard Hall, the assistant poor law inspector for London, investigated the types of outdoor relief given in 1852, he found enormous variations between districts: the City of London provided 90 per cent of relief in money and 10 per cent in kind, whilst

[14] Of the 375 poor taken to the City of London Union, 272 were provided with bread or money and only 83 offered the workhouse. Of the 355 poor relieved in the West London Union, 300 were offered the house and only 32 received bread or money. See *The Times*, 30 December 1840.

in districts such as Bethnal Green, Hampstead, Lewisham and St Martin in the Fields, the majority of relief was given in kind rather than money.[15] Aggregate figures therefore often hid very different experiences depending on the way that policy was interpreted and enacted on the ground.

Negotiating relief in the public gaze: paupers and the police courts

Experiences of relief were coloured not just by the depth of the parish purse, the policies adopted by the overseers and the way the relieving officers interpreted their duties, but also by the characteristics, personal circumstances and behaviour of paupers themselves. Understanding the kinds of negotiations that took place on a daily basis between the poor and relieving officers provides an insight into these differences and ultimately into the meaning behind the aggregate numbers of paupers and amounts of expenditure published in the Commissioners' annual reports.

Negotiating relief was never just a question of applying to an overseer or relieving officer, or seeking a night's shelter at the workhouse. It involved a theatrical display of needs, rights and obligations that sometimes took place in the public gaze. Officials, albeit in a powerful position to influence relief, could not do so without taking into account the law, the state of the parish coffers, the watchful gaze of the press and public opinion and, from 1834, the Poor Law Commissioners. Magistrates, many of whom were sympathetic to the poor, played a particularly important role in overseeing officers' behaviour. Although constant encounters with the poor did not necessarily breed sympathy and understanding, as David Eastwood has pointed out, it did nevertheless heighten magistrates' awareness of social extremes and perhaps persuade them of the need to remind poor law officers of their legal obligations regarding relief.[16] In many cases such encounters also undoubtedly helped to loosen the hinges of the poor box. Similarly, the Poor Law Commissioners themselves scrutinised the behaviour of guardians and officials and not infrequently responded to complaints about niggardly or unjust treatment, though action was rarer than investigation. Mindful of parliamentary concern and public opinion, particularly after the Andover scandal in 1846, the Commissioners also reined in authorities that they considered had overstepped the mark either by acts of unwarranted generosity or by the overzealous actions of penny pinching officials.[17]

---

15 TNA MH32/37 Local Government Board and predecessors: Assistant Poor Law Commissioners and Inspectors, Correspondence, Richard Hall, 2 November 1852.

16 David Eastwood, *Governing Rural England: Tradition and Transformation in Local Government 1780–1840* (Oxford, 1994), pp. 76, 100–187.

17 PP 1834 XXXVI Royal commission on the administration and practical operation of the poor laws, answers to town queries, St Margaret Patterns, q. 32.

These encounters frequently spilled over into the public domain. The importance of the public gaze reminds us that in poorer districts, where endemic poverty affected large numbers of people, individuals were more likely to have known paupers first hand or had themselves at one time or another received relief. Because the poor law in such places touched a far greater number than those who appeared on the relief registers at any one time, it was therefore of concern to the wider local community. Other individuals and institutions also hostile to the new poor law, notably *The Times*, were equally keen to highlight stories of paupers who had suffered harsh treatment. Cases of neglect leading to death were investigated by the coroners and frequently reported in the press, whilst other less serious cases were also recorded. Though *The Times* was the most vociferous of newspapers when it came to monitoring the poor law, it was by no means alone. Other individuals and organisations such as the radical MP and coroner, Thomas Wakley, and the Poor Man's Guardian Society which he helped to found in 1846, also seized on every opportunity to discredit its workings.[18] Perhaps with some justification, the Poor Law Commissioners believed that such adverse publicity merely encouraged paupers to commit further acts of insubordination in the knowledge that they were likely to receive a sympathetic hearing.[19]

The frequency with which the poor negotiated the terms of relief in the public gaze is best illustrated by reports of cases that came before the London police courts. The fact that poor relief was governed by statute meant that disputes between paupers and relieving officers, and between parishes themselves, were often settled in court. For the poor attendance at court cost nothing and promised much. Though many paupers accepted their lot without questioning authority, others were clearly not so passive in their encounters with the poor law and sought redress through the courts. Paternalistic magistrates could be relatively sympathetic to a pauper's plight and were often critical of uncooperative poor law officers keen to protect the parish purse. Once in the public realm cases of neglect or cruelty were frequently the subject of further investigation by a hostile press. Not surprisingly relations between magistrates, the press and local officials were frequently strained, as the churchwardens of St Nicholas Coleabby in the City remarked in 1834: 'we believe that parish officers are very often improperly summonsed, much misrepresented by the public press and that the interference of magistrates is productive of more evil than good'.[20]

The unique role of the London police courts stemmed from the Middlesex Justice Act of 1792 which established stipendiary magistrates sitting in separate courts to replace the notoriously corrupt 'trading justices' that had existed throughout the

---

18 *Poor Man's Guardian*, 5 December 1847.

19 This was a particular concern in relation to the casual poor. See Poor Law Commission, Eighth Annual Report (1841), pp. 24–5.

20 PP 1834 XXXVI Royal commission on the administration and practical operation of the poor laws, answers to town queries, St Mary Coleabby, q. 47.

eighteenth century. By 1800 there were nine such courts, in addition to the two that already existed in the City and by the 1840s this number had risen to 13 to incorporate the growth of new suburbs.[21] The magistrates themselves were paid salaries of up to 1,200 guineas, and were expected to attend the courts on a daily basis from 10 in the morning until 5 in the afternoon, although many complained that their hours extended well beyond this time. The boundaries of the courts, which after 1829 corresponded to the new police districts rather than to ancient parochial boundaries, meant that the magistrates themselves had little if any allegiance to a particular parish. This was especially important when dealing with the poor law since it meant that justices operated independently of any particular parish interest. Freed from the need to justify their actions to local ratepayers, magistrates could be generous in ordering relief and this no doubt helped to attract many poor persons seeking redress in the courts. As Justice Ballantine from Limehouse noted in 1837, 'the paupers had a perfect right to come before a magistrate if they had any just cause of complaint. Good God, if the poor creatures reduced to a workhouse were not to complain to the magistracy, who were they to complain to?'[22]

In providing a 'poor man's system of justice', these courts played a far greater role than just the investigation and prosecution of petty criminals.[23] Numbers alone hint at their importance: in 1838, they dealt with over 64,000 cases, and by 1855 this had risen to 97,090.[24] Magistrates provided a means of redress for the working class against individuals, families, neighbours, landlords and employers, as well as poor law officials. They arbitrated personal disputes, investigated complaints and provided advice. Most significantly in the context of the poor law, they had the authority to question the conduct of poor law officers and guardians, to adjudicate on questions of settlement and removal, and to order that relief be provided. Where they felt so inclined, magistrates could themselves dispense money from the poor box.[25]

How magistrates dealt with claims for poor relief varied considerably. They had neither the time nor the resources to investigate individual claims for relief

---

21 Joseph Fletcher, 'The Metropolis: Its Boundaries, Extent and Divisions for Local Government', *Journal of the Society*, 7 (1844): 124–7; Joseph Fletcher, 'Statistical Account of the Constitution and Operation of the Police Courts of the Metropolis', *Journal of the Statistical Society*, 9 (1846): 289–309.

22 *The Times*, 29 November 1837.

23 For a full discussion see Jennifer Davis, 'A Poor Man's System of Justice: The London Police Courts in the Second Half of the Nineteenth Century', *Historical Journal*, 27 (1984): 309–35.

24 Fletcher, 'Statistical Account of the Constitution and Operation of the Police Courts', p. 295; Davis, 'A Poor Man's System of Justice', p. 312.

25 Few records survive of the range of cases dealt with by magistrates. One rare example from the north east of England in the mid-eighteenth century suggests that poor law cases accounted for about 12 per cent of cases heard. See Gwenda Morgan and Peter Rushton, 'The Magistrate, the Community and the Maintenance of an Orderly Society in Eighteenth-Century England', *Historical Research*, 76 (2003): 61, 68.

and therefore they often had to weigh up the word of the poor against that of the relieving officer. As a result, concepts of need and respectability based on appearance, demeanour and character played an important part in constructing an image of who was or was not a deserving case.

Appearances were important and descriptions of the poor who attended the police courts frequently mentioned their state of dress and looks, although the evidence could be a double-edged sword. Too well dressed and the poor could be accused of deception; too ragged and they might have been mistaken for vagrants. When the Stepney union relieving officer refused to provide relief for Charlotte Spriggs, for example, despite the fact that she had been taken to the workhouse in a feeble state by the police, the excuse he gave was that she had a small amount of money on her and appeared to be 'tolerably well dressed' – hardly the image of a poor, destitute woman.[26]

Personal appearance could suggest past respectability, as hinted at by some of the figures in Sir Luke Fildes *Applications for a Casual Ward*. Those shabby genteel poor, especially widows, who had fallen on hard times but who previously had led a respectable life, frequently elicited sympathetic treatment from magistrates. Decayed housekeepers who had at one time paid the rates also demanded sympathy. When Susan Miller, a middle-aged widow who had seen better times, appeared before Mr Norton at Lambeth Street police court in December 1838 in pursuit of a claim to relief from St George in the East, she made much of the fact that she and her deceased husband had previously paid rates and taxes and that despite her best efforts to find work, she was still unable to support herself. By despatching a policeman to remonstrate with the relieving officer at the workhouse, it was clear where Norton's sympathies lay.[27]

The poor could also use the courts in more overt ways to press their claims for relief. Smashing windows and lamps as a means of either forcing officers to provide assistance or being sent to jail was common, especially during the winter months, with food shops, relieving officers' homes and workhouses the most frequent targets. During 1845, the Lord Mayor noted that he had dealt with 140 persons who had been refused relief and who had then broken windows, often at the Mansion House itself.[28] There was a seasonal rhythm to such activities that mirrored applications for relief. In St Giles and Bethnal Green, as Figure 5.5 shows, applications peaked in the winter months and during January and February they were twice as high compared to the summer months. Window smashing proceeded likewise and, noting the seasonal rhythm of such protests, *The Times* commented in December 1864 that 'As surely as the numbers of these destitute increase, so surely does the window-breaking season set in.'[29]

---

26 *The Times*, 26 January 1838.

27 Ibid., 19 January 1838.

28 Ibid., 6 January 1846.

29 Ibid., 21 December 1864.

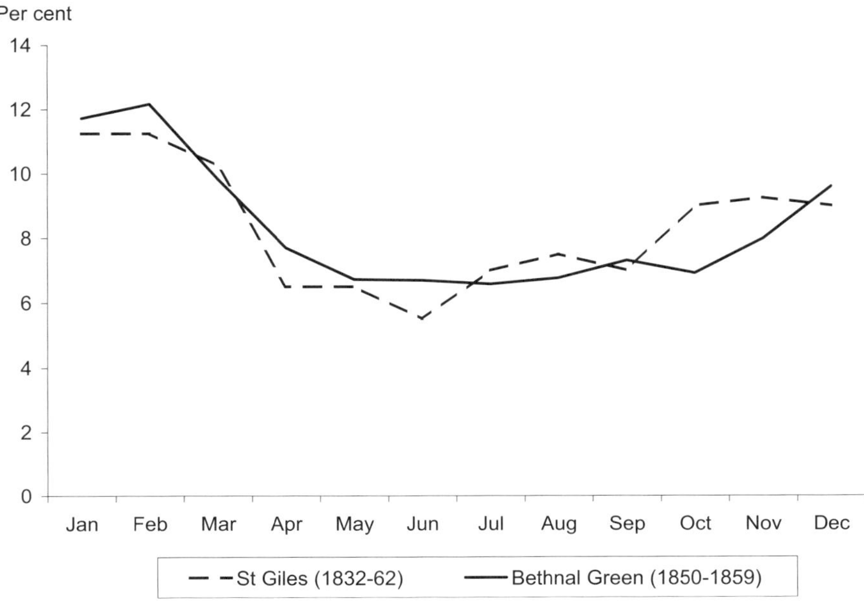

Figure 5.5 Monthly applications for poor relief to St Giles 1832–1862 and Bethnal Green 1850–1859 (% total)

Source: LMA/P82/GIS/014–132 St Giles and St George's Bloomsbury, Settlement and Examination Books, 1832–1862 (1 in 20 sample); LMA BE/BG/13–23 Bethnal Green Board of Guardians, Minutes, 1850–1859.

Such acts of desperation seemed to have been more common amongst those without clear settlements in the city whom officials were reluctant to assist.[30] Arthur O'Keefe, an Irish man who had served for several years as a soldier in the East India Company but who had been discharged on grounds of ill health, was typical of this group. He appeared before magistrates in May 1837 accused of repeatedly breaking gas lamps. He had applied to the Whitechapel guardians to be removed back to Ireland but had been refused, whereupon he had smashed a lamp in an attempt to force the relieving officer's hand. He was sentenced to a week in jail but on his release he promptly re-applied for a pass and, having again been refused, repeated the offence. On this occasion, the magistrate urged the guardians to reconsider since further refusal would likely have lead to another offence, and on those grounds they finally agreed to his request.[31]

30 See, for example, Ibid., 30 November 1841; 29 September, 19 November 1842.

31 Ibid., 15 May 1837.

Smashing windows sometimes took on the form of collective action, as was the case with four miserably clad youths who appeared in 1842 before Mr Cottingham at Union Hall police court. All had come from the country and were accused of damaging property at the Christchurch workhouse. The porter there told the court how a crowd of about 30 casual poor had assembled outside the workhouse on the previous night. When they were refused relief on the grounds that the casual wards were full, two of the ringleaders had hurled stones through the windows and urged the others to follow suit.[32] Under the circumstances, the parish had little option but to call the police and prosecute the window smashers. Jail, in their case, was an alternative to the workhouse.

A large number of complaints arose from the reluctance of relieving officers to accept applications late at night and this was a frequent bone of contention with the magistrates. Mr Bennett, the justice at Worship Street, complained to the Royal Commission on the Poor Laws that he had been forced at times to deal with over 100 applicants a day and, because of the refusal of the Shoreditch overseers to provide relief for the casual poor who applied late at night, it was not unusual for him to have to sit until 10 or 11 p.m. issuing orders for relief.[33] Magistrates at the other police courts also voiced similar complaints.[34] One of these poor people who fell foul of this situation was Mary Davis, a Welsh woman who had been taken by a constable late at night to Mr Dossett, the Hackney relieving officer. Despite the late hour, his servant claimed he was not at home and without an order for relief she was unable to obtain a place in the workhouse. At that point the policeman was forced to take her back to the station house where she spent the night. This same rigmarole occurred the following day at which point the inspector of N division complained to the Poor Law Commissioners at the amount of time taken up as a result of Dossett's refusal to deal with the application.[35] In his defence, Dossett argued that it was unreasonable to expect that relieving officers should remain awake at all hours to deal with applications. A compromise was eventually reached by which any person found destitute in the streets after 11 p.m. was to be taken to the station house first, rather than to the relieving officer or workhouse.[36]

'The remedy is worse than the disease': magistrates and the poor law

As far as guardians and relieving officers were concerned, the most irksome role that magistrates performed was their interference in matters relating to poor relief. Prior to the Select Vestries Act of 1819 a single magistrate was permitted to order

---

32 Ibid., 9 November 1844.

33 Ibid., 11 January 1834. See PP XXIX Royal commission on the administration and practical operation of the poor laws, Appendix A, pp. 354–6.

34 See, for example, *The Times*, 29 November 1837.

35 Ibid., 1 November 1839.

36 Ibid., 18 February 1840.

relief for a period of up to three months, although the amount was limited to three shillings or three quarters of the cost of maintaining a pauper in the workhouse.[37] After that date their power was limited to ordering relief for no more than 14 days in cases of emergency and urgent distress and it appeared that this power was widely exercised. However, what constituted an emergency or urgent distress was left to the discretion of the magistrate and parishes were never sure of how they would react. This situation was compounded in the City of London where the constant rotation of magistrates meant that there was no uniform interpretation of the law. As William Payne, secretary to the Guildhall police court, noted in his evidence to the 1834 Royal Commission:

> We have no uniform practice in the city, there being 26 magistrates; that is a great evil. Every week there is a new magistrate, and therefore a new law; for as each magistrate had his own views of the law, and commonly acts upon a different system, we may be said to have 26 different systems of poor law administered with in our district.[38]

Nor could officials attending court ever be sure when their case would be heard, since magistrates often failed to adhere to set times and when they did appear dealt first with appeals from the poor leaving parish business to the end of the day. The unpleasantness of the surroundings and lengthy claims on their time no doubt added further to the courts' unpopularity with officials.

The most persistent criticism of the magistrates was that they ordered relief almost as indiscriminately as they summonsed officials and this placed the overseers at the mercy of justices 'whom misdirected benevolence, or desire of popularity, or timidity, leads to be profuse distributors of other people's property'.[39] Voicing a common concern to the Royal Commission on the Poor Laws, officials from St Mary at Hill in the City noted that 'The conduct of magistrates is such … that the pauper is always attended to, let him be known by the local authorities to be never so disreputable a character.'[40] Several officials agreed that it was better to provide

---

37 Act to Amend the Law for the Relief of the Poor (Select Vestry Act), 59 Geo. III c. 12. See George Nicholls, *A History of the English Poor Law, vol. 2 1714–1853* (London, 1898), pp. 153–4.

38 *The Times*, 30 December 1833. See also PP 1834 XXIX Royal commission on the administration and practical operation of the poor laws, Appendix A, p. 340.

39 PP 1834 XXVII Royal commission on the administration and practical operation of the poor laws, first report, p. 78. See also Samuel Miller, *Pauper Police: Letters Addressed, through 'The Times', to the Churchwardens, Overseers and Parishioners of the Several Parishes in the City of London*, (London, 1831).

40 PP 1834 XXXV, Royal commission on the administration and practical operation of the poor laws, answers to town queries, St Mary at Hill, q. 29; see also replies from St Dionis Backchurch, St Edmund Martyr, St Lawrence Pountney, St Helen Bishopsgate; *The Times*, 30 December 1833.

outrelief to the able-bodied poor in order to prevent an appeal to the magistrate, 'by which the pauper is too much protected'.[41] St James Smith, overseer from St Lawrence Pountney in the City, noted that where magistrates issued an order for relief against the wishes of the local poor law, 'the parish have no redress unless they choose to go to law; then the remedy is worse than the disease'.[42] In the knowledge that magistrates were likely to take the side of a pauper, parish officers, reluctant to lay themselves open to reprimand by the one and insults by the other, frequently ordered relief to be given even where the pauper in question was thought to be undeserving or ineligible.[43]

Not surprisingly, these opinions helped to confirm the Royal Commission's view that the power of unelected officials, such as the magistrates, to dispense relief should be curtailed. As a result the Poor Law Amendment Act contained several clauses which limited magistrates' power to order relief, confining it mainly to situations where an official ignored his legal responsibility to provide assistance. Given the desire of relieving officers and guardians to avoid having to appear in court, this change was important since it gave them greater freedom to act in the knowledge that they would not have to justify their actions before a magistrate. James Corder, vestry clerk to the Strand Union, noted how although the spirit of the Poor Law Amendment Act had been implemented in the parish prior to 1834, '… it was not until the parochial authorities found themselves strengthened and encouraged by the provisions of the Poor Law Amendment act that they ventured to make the change in the mode of administrating relief'.[44] The change in question related to the provision of outdoor relief which after 1834 was tightly restricted and commonly refused to able-bodied applicants. As Corder explained:

> This reduction (in outdoor relief) could never have been effected had the magistrates retained the almost unlimited power they formerly possessed of ordering relief. Numerous cases of idle drunken able-bodied persons have been wholly got rid of who had been receiving relief some permanently and others occasionally for years – who were known to the officers to be unfit and undeserving objects – but who the moment relief was refused repaired to the magistrates and generally succeeded in obtaining orders for relief.[45]

Magistrates were clearly aware of their changed responsibilities in relation to their power to authorise outdoor relief, although interpretations of their freedom to act

---

41 PP 1834 XXXV, Royal commission on the administration and practical operation of the poor laws, answers to town queries, St Mary at Hill, q. 30.

42 Ibid., answers to town queries, St Lawrence Pountney, q. 29.

43 Ibid., answers to town queries, St James Westminster, q. 29.

44 TNA MH12/7834 Local Government Board and predecessors: Correspondence with Poor Law Unions and Other Local Authorities, Strand Board of Guardians, 11 January 1837.

45 Ibid. Parentheses added.

differed. In 1839, Harrison Codd from the Worship Street police court argued that it was unquestionably the case that magistrates could order relief under section 54 of the Poor Law Amendment Act, which empowered any magistrate 'to order the said overseer, by writing under his hand and seal, to give temporary relief in articles of absolute necessity, as the case shall require, but not in money'.[46] The point at issue, however, was what constituted a case of sudden and urgent necessity, and what comprised articles of absolute necessity. The latter, as Codd pointed out, was dependent on the time of year since, during the winter months, shelter was a necessity no less than food. Other magistrates thought that they had little authority to order any relief, although they could do all in their power to persuade local officials of the need to make provision. In early 1838, Mr Norton, the magistrate from Lambeth Street police court, observed that

> it appeared to him that the object and scope of the Poor Law Bill was to take the power out of the hands of the magistrates of administering relief to the poor, and to place it in the hands of the guardians, and that any powers to be exercised by the former were very limited indeed. It was only in cases of urgent necessity that they could interfere at all, and they could only order temporary relief.[47]

Mr Greenwood, from the Thames Police Court, generally sent a policeman to the relieving officers to accompany the poor with verbal instructions to afford relief, a course of action which according to one officer was bound to lead to irregularities.[48] William Bennett, one of the more liberal magistrates at Hatton Garden with over 20 years' experience, did likewise noting that 'I have no power to act as a magistrate but I have a right to recommend; and I frequently send persons to the workhouses of the different parishes, sometimes with a verbal recommendation, frequently with a note.'[49]

Although after 1834 the magistrates themselves might have had relatively little power to intervene directly in the provision of relief, they could dispense money from the poor box and this alone was likely to have attracted the poor to their court.[50] During 1844, for example, the Marlborough Street magistrates claimed to have given £355 to at least 903 applicants. It was noted that 'In the great majority of cases it was found that the applicants either obtained no relief, at least, no substantial relief, from their parishes, or that they entertained an invincible repugnance to accept the parish relief, in the form in which it was offered.'[51]

---

[46] Act for the Amendment and Better Administration of the Laws Relating to the Poor in England and Wales (Poor Law Amendment Act), 4 & 5 Will. IV c. 76.

[47] *The Times*, 26 January 1838.

[48] Ibid., 23 April 1839.

[49] PP 1837–38 XV Select committee on metropolis police offices, p. 514.

[50] Money for the poor box came both from fines and donations, especially, it was claimed, from readers of *The Times*. See *The Times*, 2 January 1843, 14 January 1846.

[51] Ibid., 4 January 1845.

In Greenwich over the same period, 169 persons received money from the poor box at a cost of a little over £40, making the average there 4s 10d per person, a relatively generous amount compared to that provided to outdoor paupers.[52]

During periods of severe distress, the courts were sometimes besieged by applicants seeking help. In January 1855 *The Times* reported that so large was the number of people seeking relief from the Lambeth Street magistrates that at times the court resembled less a place of law than the office of a relieving office of a large parish or union. In January Mr Norton, the sitting magistrate, was kept fully occupied in listening to complaints from the poor about the lack of assistance from the Newington officers. He noted that it was a magistrate's duty

> to hear the complaints of all persons requesting his advice, let them be paupers or others. At the same time he wished to state that there was no person less willing to interfere with the duties of the guardians or the parish officers, so long as those very onerous duties were discharged in a humane and proper spirit.[53]

But his patience ran thin and having been forced to hear complaints from 27 people on the same day, he accused the parish of neglecting its duty of care. This accusation brought a swift response from Mr Burgess, chair of the Newington guardians who accused Norton of being overgenerous with the poor box and thereby encouraging applications for relief. The court, he argued, had been made into a place of imaginary grievances and, while he would normally have been happy to comply with the magistrate's request, 'The deception practised by the applicants to the magistrates, in order to get some of the poor-box money, was such that the slightest reliance could not in many instances be placed in it.'[54]

There may indeed have been some truth in the accusation. In neighbouring Southwark, pressure on the relieving officers was enormous. Mr Caslake, St George's relieving officer, stated that he was at that time dealing with over 700 applications for relief, many of whom he claimed were imposters, and that many who did not have a settlement in the district had to wait their turn to be seen.[55] As a result delays inevitably occurred and a large number of the poor appealed to the courts for assistance.[56] Again in January 1861, John Hollingshead described how during the sharp frost that prevailed, thousands waited outside the courts for handouts from the magistrates. In that month alone some 3,000 poor received help from the Mansion House magistrates and in Westminster, the justices assisted some 2,000 applicants. Gatherings of the poor took place around all the metropolitan police courts and magistrates dealt with the throng well beyond their allotted

---

52 Ibid., 1 January 1845.

53 Ibid., 1, 19 January 1855.

54 Ibid., 19 January 1855.

55 Ibid., 19 February 1855.

56 Ibid., 15 February 1855.

time.[57] Although help from the poor box could only be temporary and provided in cases of urgent necessity, clearly it came at critical periods and at those times functioned as an alternative to poor relief.

The shift in magistrates' responsibilities under the new poor law also resulted in changes in the way that the police dealt with those found destitute in the streets. Prior to 1834 the practice had been for police to bring any poor persons found in the street to the courts. However, this practice became ineffective because magistrates no longer had the power to order relief until a person had actually been turned away from the workhouse.[58] For this reason, in November 1838 the Lord Mayor instructed police constables in the first instance to take destitute people found in the streets suffering from 'sudden and urgent necessity' to the relieving officer of the local parish.[59] The precise location where a destitute person was found, therefore, became crucial since it then determined which parish was initially responsible for providing support. In theory, it was the duty of the relieving officer to provide applicants with relief until the next meeting of the board of guardians. In turn, the fact that poor law officials were obliged to offer relief to anyone who claimed to be destitute, albeit in the workhouse in many instances, meant that in the eyes of the law no one should have had recourse to begging. Anyone found begging, therefore, could be considered a vagrant and dealt with accordingly.[60] By the same token, officials who ignored their responsibilities and refused relief could be summonsed for neglect and possibly fined by the magistrates, although such sanctions were rarely enforced.

Magistrates not only arbitrated between paupers and poor law officials but also between parishes in dispute over relief. The settlement laws in particular were a constant source of contention between parishes keen to shift their financial responsibilities elsewhere and magistrates had an important role in adjudicating cases and sanctioning removals. They were also called on to establish equity between neighbouring parishes. In the early 1840s this occurred frequently in the City of London where there were large differences between places in the availability of workhouse space and where wide disparities in treatment existed.[61] Magistrates there frequently came into conflict with the West and East London unions over their reluctance to offer assistance to the destitute. Officials from these two unions complained bitterly of the 'intolerable grievance' they faced by virtue of the fact that the neighbouring City union did not have a workhouse of its own in the vicinity.[62] Rather than be forced to walk several miles to the City's workhouse at Peckham, it was claimed that the poor instead applied to neighbouring unions

---

57 John Hollingshead, *Ragged London in 1861* (London, 1861, reprinted 1986), pp. 178–92.

58 *The Times*, 29 November 1839.

59 Ibid., 20 November 1838.

60 Ibid., 30 December 1840.

61 Ibid., 30 December, 31 December 1840.

62 Ibid., 25 February 1841.

for relief. In 1842, Mr Miller, the West London relieving officer, claimed that upwards of 6,000 casual poor had been relieved and Mr Pontifex, one of the guardians, complained that 'if the doors of the West London union were left open for a short time the whole house would be soon crammed with paupers from all parts of the city'. It was to protect themselves against this situation that restrictions had been placed on when the poor could apply at the workhouse and who was to be relieved.[63] In turn, of course, the impact of such restrictions rippled out to other neighbouring districts, such as nearby Holborn, where officials complained of being forced to shoulder the burden of the casual poor turned away from the West London union.[64] In these situations, magistrates could advise and cajole but had no real powers to alter the situation.

Negotiating relief inside the workhouse

The new poor law workhouse, according to Edwin Chadwick, was designed to be 'an uninviting place of wholesome restraint … thus making the parish fund the last resource for the pauper, and rendering the person who administers the relief the hardest task-master and the worst paymaster that the idle and dissolute can apply to'.[65] Classification of paupers according to their personal circumstances, the imposition of strict rules and rigid discipline, and overbearing monotony, were central facets of this policy of deterrence. Inside the workhouse the authority of the master and the decisions made by boards of guardians under the watchful gaze of the Poor Law Commissioners apparently provided little room for negotiation or discretion between paupers and officials. Indoor paupers were taught to know their place, from the ritual of initial application through to the medical examination that confirmed their status as able-bodied or infirm and determined their physical separation in separate spaces inside the workhouse. Once there, life followed a set of rules and expectations that governed the daily routine, broken only on special occasions such as public holidays. However, even within the workhouse bargains were struck between inmates and officials. Indeed, the very functioning of such institutions rested on the tacit agreement between inmates and officials to conform to the rules. The bargain struck by each side depended on the willingness of both parties not to transgress accepted norms of behaviour, be they deference on the part of the poor and humanity on the part of officials. Without such cooperation, as some boards of guardians found to their cost, the workhouse could become a place of discontent and trouble.

---

63 Ibid., 27 February 1841, 4 January 1842.

64 TNA MH12/7286 Local Government Board and predecessors: Correspondence with Poor Law Unions and Other Local Authorities, Holborn Board of Guardians, 18 March, 2 April 1841.

65 PP 1834 XXIX Royal commission on the administration and practical operation of the poor laws, Appendix A: part 3, p. 277.

Maintaining discipline in the workhouse was a fundamental tenet of the new poor law and an essential aspect of enforcing deterrence. The early years of the new poor law were particularly difficult in this respect: between 1835 and 1842 over 10,500 paupers were summarily tried for offences inside a workhouse, of which nearly 2,000 came from metropolitan parishes and unions.[66] Aware of the importance of imposing strict discipline in the workhouse, in February 1842 the Poor Law Commissioners issued the General Workhouse Regulations. These dealt with all aspects of indoor relief, including various forms of misbehaviour and the rights of the workhouse master to punish disorderly and refractory paupers.[67] Disorderly behaviour included relatively trivial offences such as making noise, swearing, refusing to work, absconding or disobeying orders, and was punishable by imposing a diet of just bread or potatoes and the withholding of all 'luxuries' such as broth, butter or tea. Paupers who transgressed were deemed disorderly on the first offence, and refractory if the behaviour was repeated within a week.[68] Refractory behaviour also referred to more serious or repeated offences, including insulting a member of the workhouse staff, assaulting another person, damaging property, being drunk, and acting or writing in an indecent manner. Punishments were more severe, and the master was empowered to confine paupers for up to 24 hours and impose a reduction in diet. Serious and more persistent offenders could be prosecuted and magistrates could impose prison sentences of up to 21 days' hard labour.

Despite these powers, workhouses were anything but tranquil institutions in the early years of the new poor law, especially in London. The demise of pauper farming after 1834 meant that troublesome paupers were more likely to have remained in the workhouse and this, coupled with stricter indoor policies, also meant that relations between inmates and staff were often strained. London appeared to have had some particularly difficult workhouses, associated mainly but not exclusively with the large number of casual poor that filled the city's vagrant wards. During the first decade of the new poor law, London accounted for about a fifth of all paupers convicted for offences in the workhouse and this trend continued. In 1852, London paupers accounted for 356 out of a total of 1,788 committals for breaches of workhouse discipline in England and Wales, a figure that would have been higher had several large metropolitan unions bothered to complete their returns.[69] Prosecutions continued throughout the following years. In the six months leading up to March 1874, the Local Government Board reported that some 524 casual

---

66 PP 1843 XLV, Return of the number, names, and ages of all persons committed to any prison in England and Wales for any offence in a union workhouse, pp. 343–61. See also Margaret Crowther, *The Workhouse System 1834–1929: The History of an English Social Institution* (London, 1981), p. 209.

67 *The Times*, 21 May, 3, 20 June 1842.

68 Ibid., 16 December 1846.

69 PP 1852–53 LXXXIV Number of inmates of workhouses who were committed to prison during the year 1852 for offences committed while they were inmates, p. 973.

paupers and 152 indoor poor were sent to prison from London workhouses out of a total of 1,408 and 632 respectively for England and Wales, proportions not dissimilar to the situation in earlier years.[70]

Maintaining discipline in London workhouses seemed to have been a perennial problem and the offences committed took various forms. As *The Times* noted in 1866 in relation to the casual poor:

> The paupers' favourite mode of evincing a mutinous spirit is the destruction of their own clothing, but there is a pleasing variety in their attempts to annoy those who have sheltered them. Some obstinately refuse to get up in the morning; others become violent on being requested to break stones or to pick oakum in return for their night's lodging; others, and especially women, assail the superintendents and matrons with the foulest language, out of pure malevolence. These breaches of discipline are becoming so common as to call for stringent measures of repression, and to suggest some doubt whether our sympathy with vagrants has not been a great deal too indiscriminate.[71]

Table 5.1 shows this assessment was not far off the mark. The destruction of clothing was certainly important, although reasons other than just a 'mutinous spirit' may have been responsible. So common was this practice that in some workhouses cheap canvass trousers were provided to those who deliberately destroyed their own clothing.[72] In desperation Camberwell Union provided casual paupers with jackets imprinted with large characters stating 'Camberwell Parish' and 'Stop it' – a mode of dress that provoked curiosity and ridicule on the streets, and was in fact later prohibited by the Poor Law Commissioners.[73] Although some paupers undoubtedly used the opportunity of getting a new set of shoes and clothes to make a little money outside, others claimed in their defence that being decently dressed, as opposed to wandering around in rags, was necessary to find employment.[74] Either way, officials were caught between overstepping the bounds of common decency and allowing casual paupers to leave the workhouse semi-naked, and turning the parish into the pauper's tailor. Other than prosecute those who destroyed their clothes, there was little else they could do.

---

70 PP 1875 LXII Return of the number of persons (inmates and casuals) committed to prison from each union workhouse (England and Wales) for the half year ending on 25 day of March 1874, p. 393.

71 *The Times*, 27 January 1866.

72 LMA C/BG/15 West London Board of Guardians, Minutes, 13 February 1849. See also *The Times*, 6 April 1843.

73 Ibid., 6 September 1843.

74 Ibid., 18 November 1865.

Table 5.1 Committals to prison for offences in London workhouses for the half year ending 25 May 1874

	Casuals	**Inmates**
Refusal to work; neglecting work	296	40
Tearing own clothing; tearing own clothing and refusal to work	160	–
Disorderly or Refractory	21	21
Drunkenness; drunkenness and disorderly behaviour	18	27
False statements to obtain relief	11	1
Assaults on workhouse official	5	9
Absconding	3	10
Theft	–	7
Damaging workhouse property	2	6
Assaults on workhouse inmates	1	3
Abusive or threatening language	1	2
Absconding with workhouse clothing	3	21
Others	3	5
TOTAL	524	152

Source: PP 1875 LXII Return of the number of persons (inmates and casuals) committed to prison from each union workhouse (England and Wales) for the half year ending on 25 day of March 1874, p. 393.

Without doubt, the casual poor were the most difficult to manage, partly because of the relatively large numbers who applied to London workhouses and partly because many of them were young and able-bodied. In January 1846, for example, *The Times* reported that at least 57 paupers had been committed for various acts of insubordination in several workhouses, including 27 casual poor who had been involved in a riot at the Christchurch workhouse.[75] In St George Southwark, the workhouse master complained of the nightly rowdiness with fighting, singing, and the destruction of bedding and furniture commonplace. When offenders were prosecuted, he claimed, magistrates acted too leniently.[76] In the following year, magistrates themselves complained at the number of committals for similar offences from Bethnal Green, recommending that instead of recourse to the courts, local officials should consider some mode of prevention by way of 'educational discipline' in the workhouse itself.[77] Nor was the situation unique. In the half year

[75] Ibid., 6, 8, 13, 14, 19 January 1846.

[76] PP 1846, VII Select committee on establishment of district asylums for houseless poor in the metropolis, pp. 264, 269.

[77] LMA BE/BG/11 Bethnal Green Board of Guardians, Minutes, 29 March 1847.

ending Lady Day 1866, at least 96 casual paupers were committed for offences in the St Marylebone workhouse and in one week alone in January 1866 *The Times* reported on similar committals from several workhouses including the West London Union, St Giles, Bermondsey, Rotherhithe, St Marylebone, Westminster and Clerkenwell.[78] Not even the introduction of police constables to assist relieving officers could stem the tide of misbehaviour that characterised casual wards throughout London workhouses.

The main problem that faced officials was in enforcing a task of work. Over and above the punitive nature of the labour test, which normally involved breaking stones, working at a pump or picking oakum, it was the relationship between food and work that was the most frequent bone of contention. Casual paupers had a right to be fed, irrespective of whether or not they performed a task of work. Where supper was provided, they were expected to perform work the following morning prior to receiving breakfast. However, many arrived too late at night and under these circumstances officials were required to provide breakfast the next day before demanding any work. Staff who tried to insist on work in the morning prior to breakfast, however, were the source of frequent complaints and where this was proved to have taken place they were liable to be on the receiving end of an official reprimand from the Poor Law Commissioners.[79]

The problem was that once food had been provided, there was little incentive for paupers to complete their task of work and in this situation workhouse staff were faced with the decision either to release those who refused or to haul them before the courts as idle and disorderly persons.[80] But their chance of success was limited. When the Whitechapel guardians prosecuted Thomas Reader for refusing to break stones before breakfast, Mr Norton, the Lambeth Street magistrate, who was by no means sympathetic to the plight of the casual poor, was forced to dismiss the case on the grounds that although lodging had been provided, breakfast had not. Similar dismissals also occurred in Greenwich, where the magistrate refused to sentence paupers who had failed to complete work on the grounds that they had received insufficient food.[81] All that officials could do was to detain paupers for up to four hours, after which time they either had to be discharged or taken to court. If food had been provided, the situation was different, as Isaac Baker, who was committed by the same Greenwich magistrate, found to his cost.[82] Under those circumstances, refusal to work could be punished by sentences of up to 21 days,

78 *The Times*, 27 January, 14 April 1866.

79 Ibid., 14 January 1846. See also TNA MH12/7288 Local Government Board and predecessors: Correspondence with Poor Law Unions and Other Local Authorities, Holborn Board of Guardians, 16 July 1847; LMA G/BG/005 Greenwich Board of Guardians, Minutes, 28 October, 11 November 1841.

80 Poor Law Commission, Official Circular, vol. 7, no. 13, 19 February 1848.

81 LMA G/BG/006 Greenwich Board of Guardians, Minutes, 29 September 1842.

82 *The Times*, 1 November 1842.

a term that was later increased to three months hard labour.[83] Workhouse officers were therefore in a difficult position – unable to enforce a labour test effectively but at the same time unable to withhold food. Either way, unless officials were prepared to spend the time and effort in detaining and then prosecuting those who refused to work, there was little they could do to enforce the regulations. Knowing these limitations, it was hardly surprising that once they had been fed and housed, the casual poor flouted workhouse authority so openly, so frequently and with such impunity.

As a test of destitution, the requirement to perform a task of work in return for relief was a crucial part of the new poor law and as such the work was deliberately designed to be monotonous, arduous and unpleasant. Prior to 1834 some parishes had already recognised the disciplinary role that work could perform. In St Marylebone in 1826, for example, the directors of the poor agreed to set the casual Irish poor work 'of the most laborious kind', paid at rates considerably lower than that which they could normally get outside.[84] For the Marylebone overseers, the deterrent effect of employment was more important than the possibility of making a profit. Breaking stones and picking oakum were also used to discipline incorrigible paupers. As in so many parishes up and down the country, the overseers at St Andrew Holborn found oakum picking 'a very excellent way of correcting the lazy and undeserving' whilst in St Pancras 'dissolute' paupers were sent to the stone yard.[85]

Such experiments were adopted by the Poor Law Commissioners who made a deterrent labour test a central part of relief policy. The work was to be of a 'laborious and undesirable nature' at rates of pay less than could be earned by an independent labourer.[86] For able-bodied males, stone breaking was recommended but where paupers were incapable of this task they were often required to pick oakum. By all accounts, this was a hard and dirty task that tore the fingers. It consisted of unpicking old rigging that was subsequently used in caulking a ship. As an alternative to stone breaking, casual paupers were normally expected to pick between 1 and 2 lbs of oakum in return for food and a night's lodging. Those permanently in the workhouse picked more – 3 lbs was the normal amount but this could be doubled as a punishment. Indeed, oakum picking was sometimes used punitively for disorderly and refractory paupers. Depending on the quality of

---

83 Act to Continue until the Thirty-first Day of July One thousand eight hundred and forty-seven, and to the End of the then next Session of Parliament, the Poor Law Commission; and for the further Amendment of the Laws relating to the Poor in England (Poor Law Continuation Act) 5 & 6 Vict. c. 57. See *The Times*, 18 October 1842.

84 LMA P89/MYRI/517 St Marylebone Directors of the Poor, Minutes, 10 March 1826.

85 See PP 1834 XXXV Royal commission on the administration and practical operation of the poor laws, answers to town queries St Andrews Holborn, St Pancras.

86 Poor Law Commission, Second Annual Report (1836), p. 45.

the oakum and the skill of the picker, it could take anything up to three hours to complete 1 lb of work.[87]

However, the conditions under which applicants were offered work in return for outdoor relief as opposed to relief inside the workhouse were unclear. Faced with an increase in the number of paupers granted outdoor relief, the Commissioners issued the Outdoor Labour Test Order in 1841 which directed the kinds of labour test required in return for support. Metropolitan unions were excluded from this order, as they were from the Outdoor Relief Prohibitory Order of 1844 which imposed stiffer regulations but which also exempted certain categories of poor, notably widows with children and able-bodied men suffering from temporary illness, from being forced to undertake work in return for relief.[88] The difficulties that exclusion presented, however, remained and in 1852 the Commissioners sought to bring London unions closer to the regulations that prevailed elsewhere. A new Outdoor Relief Regulation Order was issued to several London unions, though not to those local act parishes that had failed to adopt the Poor Law Amendment Act, which recognised that outdoor relief to able-bodied men was necessary in some cases but that it should only be given in return for work, though guardians were allowed some discretion as to the nature of the task. For male able-bodied paupers, the most common task was stone breaking and sometimes pumping water or grinding corn. Oakum picking was done by female paupers, as well as men who were unable to do any heavier work. Women were also sometimes employed in making clothes as well as doing domestic chores in the workhouse, although in these cases the deterrent aspect was less well defined.[89] Exceptions were made only for cases of 'sudden and urgent necessity' provided that cases were reported to the Poor Law Board within 15 days.

Conflicts relating to the labour test revolved both around the nature of the task and the amount of relief provided in return. Paupers continually complained that they were forced to do work for which they were physically incapable in direct contravention of instructions issued by the Poor Law Commissioners. In Spitalfields, silk weavers complained bitterly on several occasions that stone breaking ruined their hands and made it impossible for them to return to their work. They petitioned the Commissioners to be exempted from this kind of work and at a large meeting in 1842 stated that they were

---

[87] This information has been pieced together from accounts given by workhouse officials and paupers brought before the courts for refusing to undertake work. See *The Times*, 19 November 1842, 22 April, 9 September 1843, 18 November 1865. See also Poor Law Commission, Official Circular, vol. 9, no. 44, 24 December 1850.

[88] The only exception was Poplar. See W. C. Glen, *The General Orders of the Poor Law Commissioners, the Poor Law Board, and the Local Government Board Relating to the Poor Law* (London, 1898), pp. 488–510.

[89] Poor Law Commission, Official Circular, vol. 2, no. 42, 18 February 1842.

> disgusted with the practice (stone breaking), and further, were of the opinion that it is unconstitutional and unchristian, and from the knowledge of the effect that it has on the hands of the silk weaver, by disabling him from working, do pledge themselves to oppose this horrible system to the utmost.[90]

The Commissioners' response was that the nature of work should be unpleasant and act as a deterrent. Not surprisingly, therefore, such complaints brought little sympathy or change of policy. In neighbouring Bethnal Green in 1849 a group of indoor paupers collectively petitioned the Commissioners about the water pump – 'the everlasting pump with a cistern that is never satisfied … the men positively declare it to be a system of murder from which it appears neither age nor affliction will excuse them'.[91] Their complaints evidently bore little fruit since similar protests were voiced in subsequent years. Writing to the Poor Law Commissioners in 1850, six mechanics kept on bread and water in the Bethnal Green workhouse for refusing to break stones complained that 'The cruelty going on in this place is beyond description, it is a disgrace to a Christian land boasting of humanity.'[92] Such protests rarely ended in a reprimand but in questioning the morality of enforcing tasks for which they were physically incapable, paupers nevertheless challenged not only the authority of local officials but also the moral legitimacy of the poor law itself.

While the nature of the work was a common source of complaint, questions about what constituted a fair rate of pay also prompted objections. In the 1840s, London unions typically paid outdoor able-bodied male paupers 1d per hundredweight (cwt) of stones and 1½d for married men with families. On these rates it was claimed that a good worker might have been able to earn up to 2s 6d a day, though this was the exception rather than the rule. Most of those who appeared before the courts for refusal to work or who complained about their treatment earned nowhere near this and it was clear that a sense of what was a just and fair return infused such protests.[93] Typical of these complaints were those voiced by Marylebone paupers in 1847 and 1848. In November 1847, in an attempt to reduce their deficit of £8,000, the parish overseers had lowered rates of pay in the stone yard, eliciting a complaint by 107 able-bodied outdoor paupers about the meagre rates of relief. According to the stonebreakers, rates had been cut from 4s a yard to 2s, and were well below that paid in other neighbouring parishes.[94] When in the following year, the Marylebone authorities further ordered that stones should

90 *The Times*, 22 December 1841, January 17 1842. For similar complaints see Poor Law Commissioners, Fourth Annual Report, (1838), Appendix A, number 3, p. 157.

91 TNA MH12/6845 Local Government Board and predecessors: Correspondence with Poor Law Unions and Other Local Authorities, Bethnal Green Board of Guardians, 22 August 1849.

92 TNA MH12/6845 Ibid., 6 February 1850.

93 *The Times*, 22 February, 4 September 1841, 18 January 1842, 1 February 1843.

94 *Poor Man's Guardian*, 13, 27 November 1847.

be broken into smaller fragments for the same pay, a second petition was sent in which the paupers claimed that they could only earn 1s 6d a day, an amount totally inadequate to maintain a family. They sought nothing more than for the overseers to 'cogitate on the matter with humanity and Christian sympathy … and give a fair price for fair labour'.[95]

Legitimacy also lay at the heart of other forms of protest within the workhouse. Armed with knowledge of their rights and an awareness of the limitations imposed on officials by the workhouse regulations, paupers could challenge those who overstepped their authority. It was his treatment as a casual paper and the harsh enforcement of a labour test that brought John Vezey, a 33-year-old labourer, into conflict with the Greenwich guardians. Vezey, who had a settlement in the parish, initially applied for relief in 1842 and was placed in the vagrant ward, made to break stones and only provided with bread and water – treatment normally reserved for the casual poor. When he re-applied for admission to the workhouse he was again offered the vagrant ward, a course of action that he considered unlawful on the grounds that he had a settlement in the district and therefore should not have been treated as if he was a casual pauper.

It was at that point that Vezey smashed the workhouse windows which precipitated his arrest. When he appeared in court, Mr Grove, the magistrate, who had dealt with similar claims in the past, admonished the guardians for treating him like one of the casual poor. Their defence was that he was able-bodied and therefore should have been able to get his own living, an opinion called into question when Vezey himself was admitted to the infirmary a week or so after the incident had occurred. Both Grove and the guardians then sought the opinion of the Poor Law Commissioners, the latter complaining that this has been the third case of window breakers that had been discharged by the court. Echoing a common belief on the part of officials, they argued that the leniency with which the magistrates dealt with refractory paupers encouraged insubordination in the workhouse. Much to the guardians' concern, however, the Commissioners concurred with the court noting that the treatment offered was not appropriate for the settled poor.[96] When next winter arrived, Vezey again challenged the guardians' authority by refusing to work at the water pump, and when prosecuted was once more discharged by Grove, a result which the guardians claimed had led to yet more insubordination in the workhouse.[97] Evidently, Vezey's first window smashing exploits and subsequent encounter with the law had emboldened him and others to demand their rights to appropriate treatment within the workhouse. That those rights were upheld clearly indicated the legal limits within which officials were expected to operate.

---

95 *The Times*, 21 October 1848.

96 TNA MH12/5093 Local Government Board and predecessors: Correspondence with Poor Law Unions and Other Local Authorities, Greenwich Board of Guardians, 20 January, 5 February 1842; *The Times*, 18, 21, 22, 28 January 1842.

97 TNA MH12/5094 Ibid., 23 January 1843.

If John Vezey was a difficult pauper because he knew his rights, then Daniel Thompson was even more so. Arguably, he may have been the most troublesome pauper in London. Thompson appeared to have been a well educated man: over a 20-year period he peppered the Home Secretary, the Poor Law Commissioners , the Lord Mayor and others with complaints about his treatment in the City of London workhouse. By his own reckoning he had been in and out of the workhouse at least 300 times. He appeared regularly before the courts and was quite capable of conducting his own defence. In 1857 he summonsed the workhouse master and porter before the Guildhall magistrates for confiscating his papers and for refusing relief. The master complained that the content of the papers was contrary to workhouse regulations, adding that Thompson was exceptionally troublesome and had already been committed on numerous occasions for being refractory. More importantly, however, by reading the papers aloud and encouraging inmates to send petitions to the Poor Law Commissioners he had managed 'to render the paupers dissatisfied, and to create a great deal of insubordination'.[98] This battle evidently continued and in 1863 Thompson himself was prosecuted for refusing to pick oakum. He argued in his defence that

> He objected to the tyranny and oppression of the menials in the union house, as a violation of the rights and liberties of a British subject. He protested against being compelled to pick oakum. It was felon's work, and had been so described by Mr Selfe (the magistrate) before a committee of the House of Commons.[99]

Despite being sent to jail for his refusal to work, he continued to defy the authorities and appeared in court on further occasions, each time questioning the legitimacy and authority of the poor law to dictate the terms and conditions of relief.[100]

Complaints made by workhouse inmates who had previously been in respectable circumstances posed particular problems for the Poor Law Commissioners and although accusations were often difficult to uphold, nevertheless where clear evidence existed that officials had breached their terms of office they sometimes took action. In Lambeth where a culture of confrontation seemed to have prevailed in the workhouse, they upheld a series of complaints by inmates about illegal punishments and forced the resignation of the master, George Day.[101] The workhouse there had a troubled history and, prompted by a series of complaints organised by James Nicholls, an inmate who had formerly been a solicitor, the Commissioners

98 *The Times*, 27 November 1857.

99 Ibid., 11 September 1863. Parentheses added.

100 Ibid., 24 June 1868, 1 September 1869.

101 Ibid., 6 November 1866. Lambeth continued to be a particularly troublesome workhouse. See Samuel Shaen, *Workhouse Management and Workhouse Justice: A Further Letter to the President of the Poor Law Board* (London, 1869) and Crowther, *The Workhouse System*, pp. 121–2, 134, 209, 224, 236.

had already intervened on previous occasions of alleged misconduct by officials.[102] In 1866 18 indoor paupers were brought before the magistrates for attempting to injure Charles Chambers, an unpopular warder who, they claimed, had acted in an arbitrary and unjust manner. The inmates, some of whom were elderly and several of which had been in 'a respectable position of life', including James Nicholls, complained about being subjected to the tyranny of someone who had previously been convicted of theft, and when the Lambeth guardians failed to intervene they had taken matters into their own hands. Although the magistrate, Mr Elliott, could not reach a judgement, his recommendation that 'a person of better temper and character should be appointed as wardsman' made it clear with whom his sympathy lay.

Those paupers who questioned the legitimacy of relief decisions, such as Daniel Thompson or the elderly inmates in the Lambeth workhouse, need to be understood in the context of shifting poor law practice and expectations. Faced with mounting pressure on relief budgets, guardians were always likely to try to reduce the burden by imposing stricter conditions of relief. In the 1850s, for example, several east London unions were forced to tighten policies. In Bethnal Green this resulted in a series of complaints by indoor paupers regarding insufficient food, excessive labour tasks and unwarranted punishments, leading to a visit by Henry Farnall, the poor law inspector.[103] A similar set of complaints in neighbouring St George in the East, where the guardians had implemented a stricter regime in an attempt to reduce overcrowding, also resulted in a visit and meeting with the indoor poor.[104] Elderly inmates there complained about reductions in visiting times and the discontinuation of their 'rightful liberty day' once a month. The guardians responded by stating that since the workhouse was overcrowded, measures were needed to deal with the situation and pointing out that as a result of the changes, the number of indoor paupers had fallen from 883 to 717. Although Farnall failed to substantiate the concerns, complaints persisted about the poor quality of food, inadequate medical treatment and the harsh work regime imposed on elderly inmates and an internal investigation later in the year found some truth in the claims, particularly regarding the diet. Further petitions and complaints from the relatives and friends of elderly inmates clearly worried the Poor Law Commissioners and Farnall was again sent to investigate, meeting with both guardians and inmates to resolve the problems.[105] Clearly, achieving a

---

102 Nicholls was sufficiently well known to have warranted an obituary in the *South London Press*. See Crowther, *The Workhouse System*, p. 236.

103 TNA MH12/6847 Local Government Board and predecessors: Correspondence with Poor Law Unions and Other Local Authorities, Bethnal Green Board of Guardians, 30 October, 10 November 1857; 4 February, 22 March, 19 April, 26 July 1858.

104 TNA MH12/7105 Local Government Board and predecessors: Correspondence with Poor Law Unions and Other Local Authorities, St George in the East Board of Guardians, 27, 29 June, 17, 27 July, 2 September, 14, 17 October 1857.

105 TNA MH12/7105 Ibid., 21 November, 5 December 1857.

legitimate balance between deterrence and humanity in relation to both indoor and outdoor relief was always open to interpretation and negotiation.

Conclusion

Not all paupers were able to make a case as eloquently as Daniel Thompson or James Nicholls but as their situations demonstrated, the rules of relief and patterns of behaviour were open to question. The numerous complaints and court cases noted above, the resignation or dismissal of officials who overstepped the mark and the persistent and petty infringements of workhouse rules all hint at the contested nature of encounters between paupers and the poor law. At first sight such encounters might appear to have been little more than attempts by paupers to better their lot with no thought as to the wider consequences or issues. Some forms of defiance were clearly opportunistic, the actions of troublesome individuals and stemming more from little more than a sense of personal frustration. Others were part of a more considered strategy relating to workhouse rules that drew upon notions of moral legitimacy and social justice. They may well have been a continuation of anti-poor law sentiment from behind the workhouse walls. While we should be wary of imputing too much to these pauper protests, it would also be wrong to view their actions merely as calculative attempts to squeeze more relief from miserly officials. Misbehaviour was more complex than just that. It involved an understanding of customary rights and expectations in relation to poor relief. It also involved symbolic forms of protest based on concepts of respectability and self esteem in the face of institutional efforts to shape the pauper's character and mould their social relations. As Patrick Joyce has noted, in the context of an apparently fatalistic and conservative popular working class 'the need for dignity and respect … also led to claims for justice, equality and fraternity'.[106] Given the fluidity of the boundary between poverty and pauperism, it would have been surprising indeed if these notions did not extend to paupers whose encounters with the poor law drew on a set of customary expectations, adopted a language of rights and enlisted concepts of Christian morality to challenge the legitimacy and authority of the terms of relief.

[106] Patrick Joyce, *Visions of the People. Industrial England and the Question of Class, 1848–1914* (Cambridge, 1994) p. 155. For discussions of working-class respectability see, for example, Peter Bailey, '"Will the Real Bill Banks Please Stand Up?" Towards a Role Analysis of mid-Victorian Working-Class Respectability', *Journal of Social History*, 12 (1979): 336–53; Marc Brodie, *The Politics of the Poor: The East End of London 1885–1914* (Oxford, 2004), pp. 75–88.

Chapter 6
Paying for Pauperism: Urban Change and Fiscal Stress

From encounters to expenditure

The outcome of the pauper encounters discussed in the previous chapter etched a line directly from the relieving officer's hand to ratepayers' pockets and from there to the figures on pauperism recorded in the Poor Law Commissioners' annual reports. The number and types of paupers relieved and the amounts spent on assistance were the culmination of thousands of bargains struck daily between paupers and relieving officers. Beyond these individual experiences, however, lay a combination of factors that influenced the overall number of paupers and pattern of expenditure: longer term structural shifts in the demand for relief arising from economic change and demographic growth; shorter term fluctuations arising from cyclical and seasonal factors, and shifts in national and local poor law policy.

The impact of these wider processes were filtered by regional patterns of growth and the peculiarities of place and in this context London came to play a much more prominent role in the national pattern of poor relief.[1] In the decades after 1834 its share of poor law expenditure increased, albeit at different rates depending on the state of the economy. Behind this trend, however, was a much more complex set of relationships that depended on individual circumstances in each of the city's constituent unions and parishes. Being aware of this more local geography of provision, as well as London's status as *the* pauper capital, helps to explain how those pressures were manifested in the metropolitan context.

Counting the poor: the evidence of numbers

Establishing the dimensions of pauperism first requires an understanding of how pauper encounters were translated into the tables published in the annual reports of the Poor Law Commissioners. On those pages the success or otherwise of poor law policy could be measured with reference to the number and types of paupers and the amounts expended on their relief. But herein lay the problem. What precisely could be measured and how did it reflect the state of pauperism?

---

[1] The regional dimensions of poor relief are discussed more fully in Steven King, *Poverty and Welfare in England 1700–1850: A Regional Perspective* (Manchester, 2000).

On expenditure the Poor Law Commissioners were on relatively strong grounds, the annual figure for each union having been inspected by independent auditors before being sent to Somerset House. But on numbers and types of paupers confusion reigned.[2]

The main problem was the way that annual numbers of paupers were recorded. Up until 1848 the only count of paupers consisted of those relieved in the quarter ending 25 March or Lady Day. The Commissioners acknowledged the deficiency of these figures in 1845 when they estimated that at least another half a million more paupers received relief than the figure of 1.47 million noted in the annual report for that year. They recognised that instead of the nine per cent of the population who were recorded as having received relief, the true proportion was probably closer to 12 per cent.[3] Even this figure was thought to be inaccurate and when the Poor Law Board was established in 1848 one of the first changes it made was to replace these quarterly totals with two daily counts of paupers taken on 1st January and 1st July each year. When using these daily counts to estimate levels of pauperism two problems arise. First, the dates did not necessarily reflect the highest and lowest points of the annual variation in applications, which tended to occur in late January or February and August respectively.[4] This inevitably introduces inaccuracies when using the counts to estimate average pauperism, although according to MacKinnon the distortion is relatively minor.[5] Second, no account was taken of the length of time paupers received relief, nor of those who applied on other days or more than once. This problem would not have been so significant if paupers had received relief continuously throughout the year, as was the case with many of the chronically sick, elderly and infirm who increasingly filled the workhouses. However, in many cases paupers applied repeatedly for relief, often staying in the workhouse for relatively short periods of time, and this seemed to be a relatively common experience in London. In Holborn over one in eight paupers admitted to the workhouse during 1867 had made more than one application for relief in that year. Younger inmates were especially likely to have been admitted on several occasions, using the workhouse as a temporary refuge rather than as a permanent place to stay.[6] This situation continued and counts of those relieved in London during the year ending 25 March 1892 suggest that paupers aged between 16 and 64 tended to receive relief for shorter periods compared

---

[2] See Karel Williams, *From Pauperism to Poverty* (London, 1981), pp. 68–73, 145–234.

[3] See Poor Law Commission, Eleventh Annual Report (1845) p. 4.

[4] See Paul F. Aschrott, *The English Poor Law System: Past and Present* (London 1888, reprinted 2006), p. 281.

[5] Mary MacKinnon, 'The Use and Misuse of Poor Law Statistics, 1857 to 1912', *Historical Methods*, 21 (1988): 11.

[6] Margaret Crowther, *The Workhouse System 1834–1929: the History of an English Social Institution* (London, 1981), pp. 227–9.

to other regions of the country.[7] Where this was the case, averaging the daily counts is likely to have been more inaccurate as an estimate of annual rates of pauperism.

Some attempt to estimate the extent of this under-counting was made by Robert Pashley in 1850 who thought that the real number of paupers was at least three times higher than the daily counts, and in 1857 Francis Purdy, at the time principal of the statistical department of the Poor Law Board, thought the ratio to be closer to three and a half. Figures for Holborn workhouse in 1867 also confirm that the number of persons who passed through its doors during that year was about two and a half times larger than those who were resident there on 1st January.[8] For later decades Robert Giffen and the Webbs thought that a ratio of 2.24 would provide a better picture since there were relatively more indoor paupers who were more likely to have been permanently relieved.[9] More recently Lynn Lees has used this multiplier to estimate the likely proportion of paupers in England and Wales.[10] However, in London where so much relief was for relatively short periods, even this multiplier is likely to have seriously underestimated the real number of paupers that were supported by the poor law in the course of a year.

Landscapes of pauperism: London and the nation

Counting paupers may be an inexact science, as MacKinnon notes, but we must make do with what is available to shed light on trends over time and regional differences in poor relief. In this respect, the daily counts starting in 1849 provide an indication of the ebb and flow of pauperism in England and Wales. Figure 6.1, which uses a multiplier of 2.24 to inflate the average daily totals, shows that the number of paupers remained relatively stable during the 1850s, rising sharply in response to the Lancashire cotton famine in the early 1860s and again later in the decade. Rates of pauperism fluctuated between about 10 and 12 per cent of the population.[11] The situation in London, however, was quite different. Figure 6.2 shows that both the number of paupers and rate

---

7 MacKinnon, 'The Use and Misuse of Poor Law Statistics', p. 14.

8 Crowther, *The Workhouse System*, p. 232.

9 See Robert Pashley, *Pauperism and the Poor Laws* (London, 1852), pp. 36–7; Robert Giffen, *Statistics* (London, 1913), p. 398; Sidney and Beatrice Webb, *English Poor Law History Part II: The Last Hundred Years, vol. 2* (London, 1929), p. 1051.

10 Lynn Lees, *The Solidarities of Strangers: The English Poor Laws and the People, 1700–1948* (Cambridge, 1998), pp. 179–85.

11 Figures based entirely on the daily counts are much lower, closer to 5.3 per cent in the 1850s and 4.4 per cent in the 1860s. See Nigel Goose, 'Poverty, Old Age and Gender in Nineteenth Century England: The Case of Hertfordshire', *Continuity and Change*, 20 (2005): 354–5.

of pauperism increased steadily from the mid-1850s, rising steeply in the late 1860s in response to the severe economic downturn that struck the capital.[12] Indeed, over a third of the increase in the total number of paupers in England and Wales in those years was attributable to London alone and, as indicated in Figure 6.3, this helped to fuel the city's overall share of the national total of pauperism from around 6 per cent in the early 1850s to nearly 15 per cent by 1870.

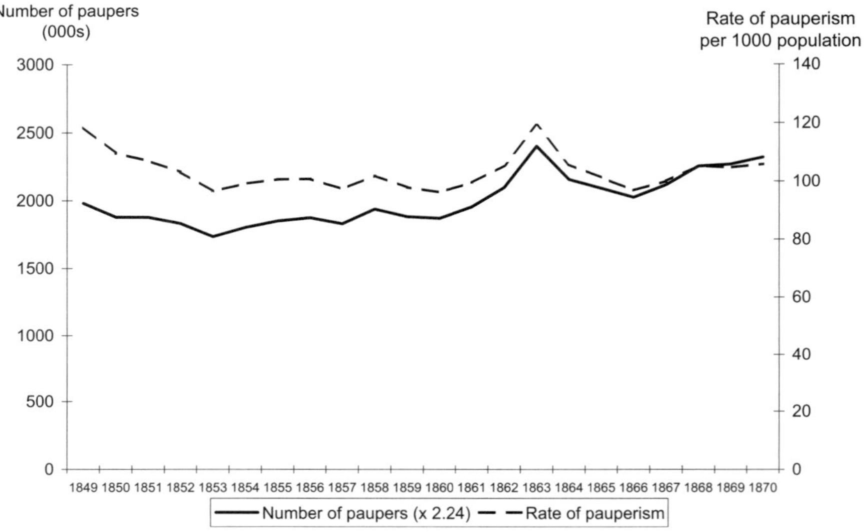

Figure 6.1 Pauperism in England and Wales 1849–1870

Note: The total number of paupers recorded is an average of the daily counts taken on 1st January and 1st July using a multiplier of 2.24

Source: Poor Law Board, Annual Reports, 1849–70.

12 London only appeared as a separate geographical region in the Poor Law Board annual reports from 1858 onwards. Prior to that date counts of paupers are only available for individual counties. The figures for London between 1849 and 1857 have been compiled by averaging out the share of the metropolitan unions in Middlesex, Kent and Surrey for 1858 to 1860 as a percentage of the county totals. This denominator is then used to determine the average number of paupers in each of those counties that could be accounted for by the metropolitan unions. The total for each of the counties has then been added to give a figure for London.

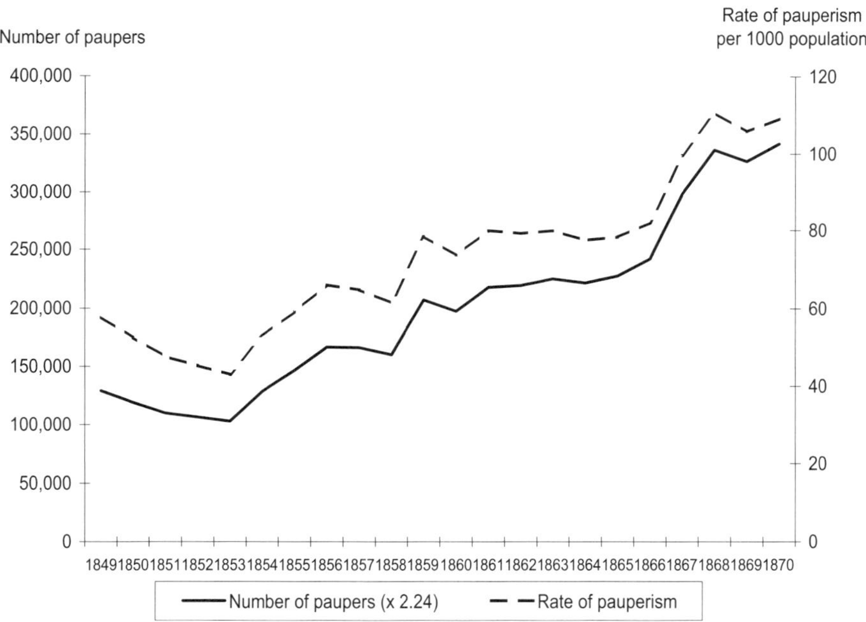

Figure 6.2 Pauperism in London 1849–1870

Note: the total number of paupers recorded is an average of the daily counts taken on 1st January and 1st July using a multiplier of 2.24

Source: Poor Law Board, Annual Reports, 1849–70.

Figure 6.3 London pauperism 1849–1870 (% of total paupers in England and Wales)

Note: the total number of paupers recorded is an average of the daily counts taken on 1st January and 1st July using a multiplier of 2.24

Source: Poor Law Board, Annual Reports, 1849–70.

The increase in pauperism was matched by rising levels of expenditure and Figure 6.4 shows that by 1870 London unions accounted for close to 20 per cent of the total expenditure on poor relief in England and Wales. Indeed, it would not be an exaggeration to say that from the 1850s and 1860s problems of the national poor law were increasingly identified as problems in London. In part this situation was driven by population growth but it was also a result of the way in which poor relief itself was provided. The sharp falls in expenditure after 1834 in the country as a whole were primarily the result of reductions in the provision of outdoor relief. However, although the Poor Law Commissioners were keen to reduce outdoor relief it was difficult to achieve in practice. Far larger numbers of the poor continued to be relieved outside the workhouse and as a result the cost of outdoor relief tended to dominate poor law budgets. This is very clear from expenditure totals between 1850 and 1870 for England and Wales compared to London, shown in Figure 6.5. At a national level, the cost of outdoor relief always remained about three times larger than that for indoor. However, in London the opposite held true and from the 1850s until the crisis years from 1867 onwards, the cost of indoor pauperism exceeded that of outdoor relief.

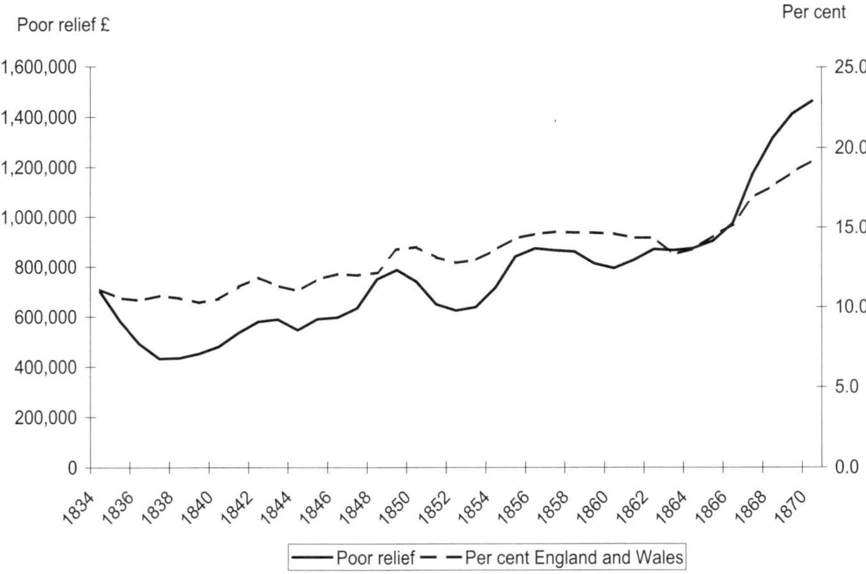

Figure 6.4 Poor Law expenditure in London 1825–1870

Source: Poor Law Commission, Annual Reports, 1835–47; Poor Law Board, Annual Reports, 1848–70; Local Government Board, Annual Report, 1871.

The significance of the workhouse in London – which was as much a feature at the start as it was towards the end of the nineteenth century – is further highlighted by the geographical pattern of indoor relief for 1851 shown in Figure 6.6.[13] In that year, which was by no means untypical of the long term pattern, indoor relief accounted for nearly a third of the total expenditure in Kent, over 40 per cent in Surrey and nearly 48 per cent in Middlesex, compared to 24 per cent in Lancashire and 12 per cent in the West Riding.[14] These disparities reflected different policy responses to contrasting types of labour markets. In industrialising regions, such as Lancashire and Yorkshire, for example, large employers used outdoor relief as a means of retaining their workforce during cyclical downturns and thereby spreading the cost of unemployment among ratepayers as a whole.[15] Outdoor relief was similarly important in agricultural areas where low wages continued to be supplemented by hand-outs from the poor law.

---

[13] MacKinnon notes that in 1906–1907 long term indoor relief in London was at least twice as important as in other urban and rural districts. See MacKinnon, 'The Use and Misuse of Poor Law Statistics', p. 14.

[14] These figures refer only to the total expenditure on indoor and outdoor relief.

[15] George Boyer, *An Economic History of the English Poor Law, 1750–1850* (Cambridge, 1990), pp. 233–64.

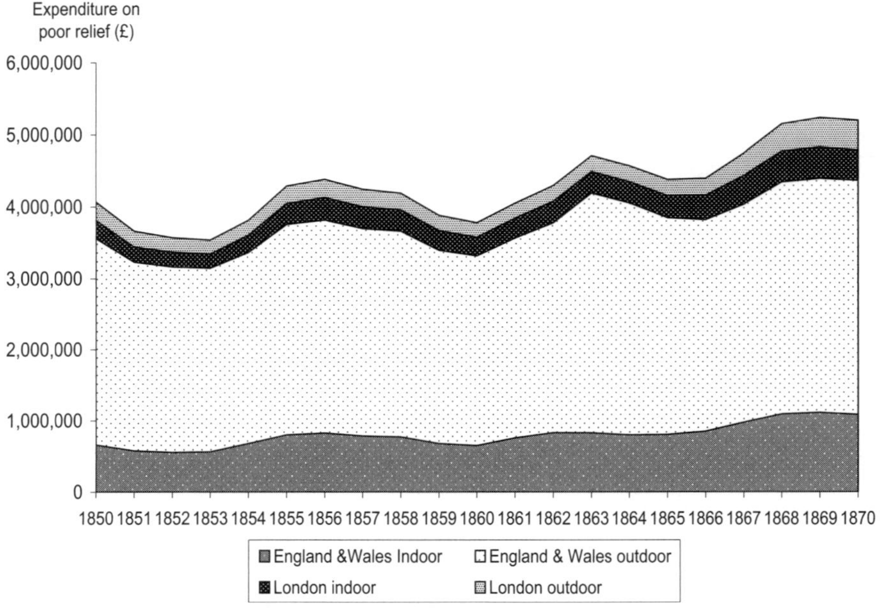

Figure 6.5 Expenditure on indoor and outdoor relief in England and Wales and London 1850–1870

Note: The total for England and Wales excludes the amount for London.

Source: Poor Law Board, Annual Reports, 1850–70.

The outcome was that in both these types of places the balance of indoor to outdoor relief was heavily weighted towards the latter.[16] By contrast, in London there were relatively few large employers and, more significantly, there was a permanent glut of unskilled and casual labour. As a result there was little incentive for employers to rely on poor relief as a way of retaining a workforce during seasonal or cyclical downturns. In addition, given the proximity of separate poor law unions, there was no guarantee that those able-bodied persons who received outdoor relief in one district would necessarily have worked in the same place. Providing temporary outdoor relief would therefore potentially have meant subsidising workers employed elsewhere, a course of action that made little economic sense to already hard pressed ratepayers.

---

[16] In Norfolk, for example, after 1843 the proportion of outdoor relief increased. See Anne Digby, *Pauper Palaces: The Economy and Poor Law of Nineteenth-Century Norfolk* (London, 1978), pp. 110–14.

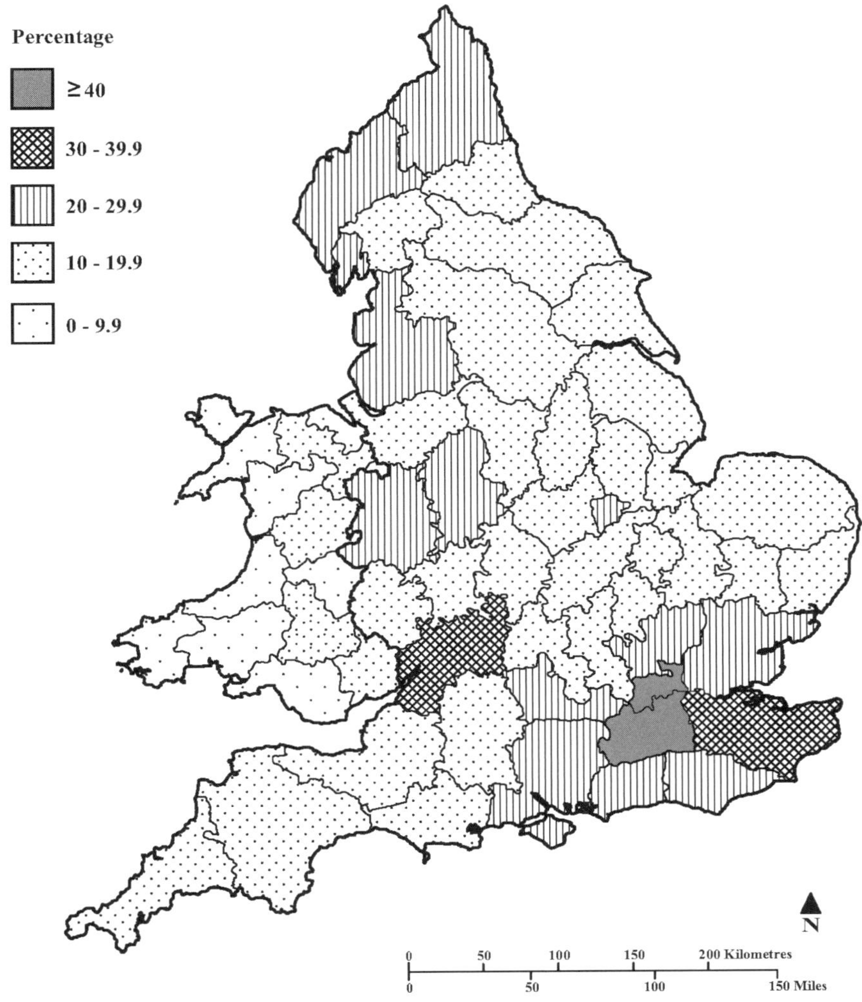

Figure 6.6 Expenditure on indoor relief in England and Wales 1851 (% total relief)

Source: Poor Law Board, Annual Report, 1851.

Metropolitan landscapes of pauperism: indoor and outdoor relief expenditure

In relation to poor law expenditure, to speak of a London as whole is to risk blurring the increasingly sharp divisions that began to emerge between metropolitan districts. Different rates of growth, rapid social change, shifts in economic fortunes and large scale urban redevelopment meant that important differences existed which had a significant impact on the demand for poor relief. At the same time, overseers and boards of guardians themselves chose to implement relief policies in distinctive ways, adding a further layer of complexity to the pattern of poor relief in the city. Understanding the relationships between the peculiarities of place and the implementation of policy is the key to unravelling the patterns of relief.

In the absence of figures on the number of paupers in individual poor law unions, differences in the balance of indoor or outdoor expenditure provides an insight to this complex landscape of pauperism. This pattern, shown in Figure 6.7, illustrates how indoor relief was the norm in some of the wealthy West End parishes and suburbs together with several poorer districts in the inner industrial perimeter surrounding the central core. In the more affluent districts a relatively small working-class population meant that demand for poor relief was comparatively low. By contrast, districts in the inner industrial perimeter contained a large and increasingly impoverished population, many of whom were being squeezed out of the central core by street clearances and demolitions. St Giles, Holborn and St Luke's each contained pockets of intense poverty as well as significant concentrations of wealthier residents and although none of these districts built new workhouses, expenditure on indoor relief was relatively high throughout the period. St Giles in particular kept to a strict indoor policy throughout, its guardians mindful of the large number of poor living in the Church Lane rookery and Seven Dials.[17] Guardians in Southwark, equally mindful of the demands made on their increasingly hard pressed ratepayers, also operated a strict indoor policy, as did those in the East London union.

The last set of indoor unions, and in many ways the most significant, comprised the relatively poor eastern districts of Bethnal Green, St George in the East, Stepney and Mile End. As discussed previously, even prior to 1834 eastern parishes had been amongst the strongest advocates of indoor relief and several had already erected comparatively large workhouses.[18] Local ratepayers and vestrymen there had enthusiastically embraced the new poor law and had been some of the earliest to enforce stricter implementation of the workhouse test. However, unlike indoor unions in the wealthier West End, this group of districts had the common problem of balancing a rising demand for poor relief with a relatively small and ever diminishing ratepayer base. Pinched by poverty, boards of guardians in these places followed the new poor law to the letter, and sometimes beyond, and used the workhouse test as a way of achieving economy.

---

17 See David R. Green and Alan Parton, 'Slums and Slum Life in Victorian England: London and Birmingham at Mid-Century', in Martin Gaskell (ed.), *Slums* (Leicester, 1990), pp. 61–82.

18 TNA MH12/7799 Local Government Board and predecessors: Correspondence with Poor Law Unions and Other Local Authorities, Stepney Board of Guardians, 11 October 1838.

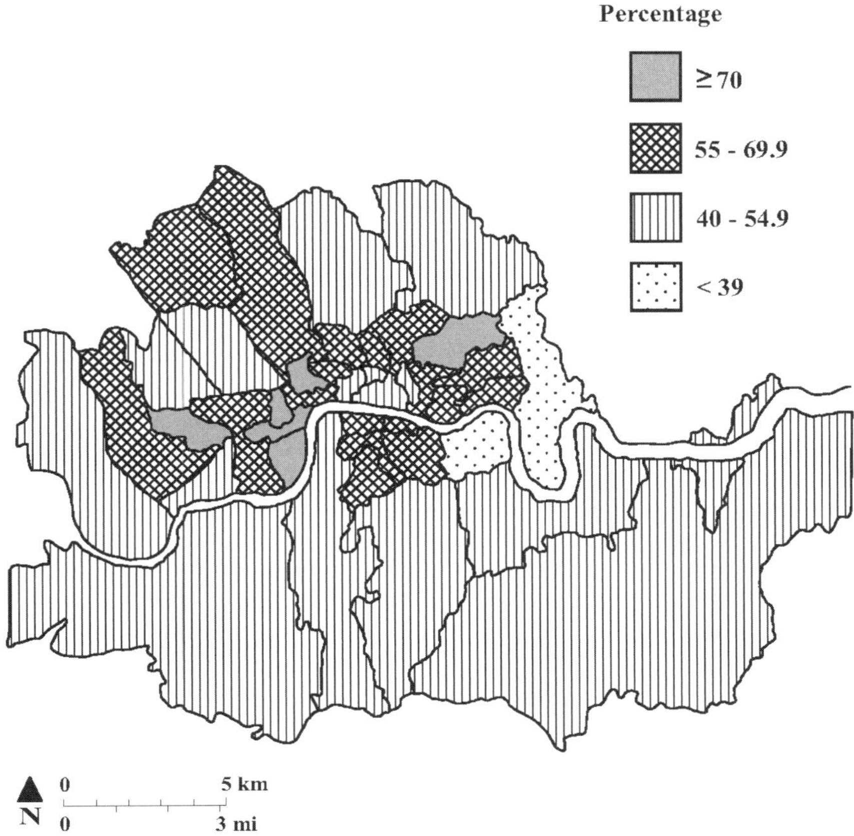

Figure 6.7 Expenditure on indoor relief in London 1849–1868 (% total relief)

Source: Poor Law Board, Annual Reports, 1849–68.

Of this group, Bethnal Green stood out by virtue of the rigour with which its guardians embraced this deterrent policy. Indeed, they had the dubious reputation of being the strictest in London, a view borne out by the figures. Between 1854 and 1866, with the exception of one year, indoor expenditure in the district was always more than four times higher than outdoor relief.[19] To the extent that the population was so poor and the ratepayer base was shrinking, there was justification in Bethnal Green, as in other eastern districts, for exercising prudence over expenditure. However, the reputation for harshness and penny-pinching gained by the Bethnal Green guardians far exceeded even the bounds of prudence as the many letters of

[19] Figures are taken from the Poor Law Board, Annual Reports, 1854–66.

complaint sent by paupers to the Poor Law Commissioners testify.[20] Typical of these was a letter from an elderly silk weaver called Daniel Bush, one of a large number of workers in that declining industry, who in 1851 complained bitterly to the Commissioners about the guardians' refusal to grant him outdoor relief. 'I was once cast away in Africa in the Caffers Country and traveled 1,000 miles and found more humanity among the Caffers and Hottentots than I find among thies Jacks in office', he wrote.[21] Nor was his complaint an isolated incident as other letters about miserly relief, damp and overcrowded accommodation, lack of heating, unwholesome food and restriction of liberties also testify.[22] In August 1849 indoor paupers in Bethnal Green petitioned the Poor Law Commissioners about poor food, restrictions on liberty and above all the strict work requirements.[23] It appears that little was done to address these complaints and in 1858 the Poor Law Board was told that as a result of continued cruelties, 'A general feeling of discontent prevails throughout the house.'[24] In each case the guardians justified their strict indoor policy pleading 'that if they were to deviate from the rule, in one case, a vast influx of similar applications would soon be the "order of the day"'.[25] The comparatively low rate of pauperism in the district hinted at the success of that policy.[26]

As long as the Bethnal Green guardians behaved in this manner, neighbouring unions could ill afford to waver from a similarly strict policy. It was the epitome of a 'beggar thy neighbour' approach in which none dared deviate for fear of being swamped by a flood of paupers. Moreover, even a strict policy was liable to be tightened as a result of the need to reduce overcrowding in the workhouse. So, when the Poor Law Board instructed guardians in St George in the East to reduce numbers in the workhouse, they followed Bethnal Green's example by tightening rules, restricting visiting hours, removing pauper indulgences and

20 TNA MH12/6845 Local Government Board and predecessors: Correspondence with Poor Law Unions and Other Local Authorities, Bethnal Green Board of Guardians, 14 January 1848, 22 August 1849, 6 February 1850.

21 TNA MH12/6846 Ibid., 3 August 1851. Spelling as in the original.

22 TNA MH12/6845 Ibid., 6, 15 February 1850; TNA MH12/6847 Ibid., 30 October, 10 November 1857, 22 March, 19 April, 26 July 1858; TNA MH12/7916 Local Government Board and predecessors: Correspondence with Poor Law Unions and Other Local Authorities, Whitechapel Board of Guardians, 29 June 1849; TNA MH12/7919 Ibid., 14 December 1855; TNA MH12/7920 Ibid., 12 October 1856.

23 TNA MH12/6845 Local Government Board and predecessors: Correspondence with Poor Law Unions and Other Local Authorities, Bethnal Green Board of Guardians, 22 August 1849.

24 TNA MH12/6847 Ibid., 22 March 1858.

25 TNA MH12/6846 Ibid., 8 March 1853.

26 PP 1861 IX Select committee to inquire into the laws and administration of relief of the poor under orders, rules and regulations of the Poor Law Commissioners and Poor Law Board, pp. 118, 176.

forcing even elderly inmates to break stones, chop wood and pick oakum, eliciting in the process a flurry of complaints from inmates and their relatives.[27]

Whilst indoor relief was the norm in most districts, some preferred to provide outdoor relief. Between 1850 and 1870 several places, especially the more suburban districts, continued to spend more on outdoor relief than on indoor. In Poplar, which was geographically peripheral to the rest of the city and where employment was dominated by shipbuilding and dock labour, the guardians normally spent between 50 and 75 per cent more on outdoor relief than indoor, rising to over 300 per cent during the crisis years of 1867 and 1868. In Rotherhithe and Lewisham, both relatively small districts, similar outdoor policies prevailed. The only other place in which outdoor relief was of major significance was the City of London, and here specific reasons existed which made this necessary.[28] By the 1850s, the City was losing population and most of the poor with a settlement there actually lived beyond its boundaries. City guardians continued to grant non-resident outdoor relief to these poor persons, irrespective of where they lived in London and for that reason the cost of such relief remained high. But these were the exceptions rather than the rule and elsewhere indoor relief continued to be the norm.

The emerging crisis

In London as a whole, as shown in Figure 6.3 above, trends in poor law expenditure mirrored closely the ebb and flow of economic fortunes. Economic difficulties in the early 1840s and again in 1848–49 were reflected in higher levels of expenditure. Relatively mild winters together with falling prices, helped dampen the impact of depression and in both sets of years, although there was some localised distress, there was no general city-wide crisis. A few isolated attacks on bread shops occurred in the winter of 1842 but they were confined to the City and petered out relatively quickly, helped no doubt by harsh sentences of transportation imposed on the ringleaders.[29] The depression of 1848–49, exacerbated by the cholera epidemic and the influx of Irish migrants fleeing the famine, also caused some distress but the impact was again highly localised.

27 TNA MH12/7105 Local Government Board and predecessors: Correspondence with Poor Law Unions and Other Local Authorities, St George in the East Board of Guardians, 27, 29 June, 17, 27 July, 2 September, 14, 17 October, 21 November, 5 December 1857.

28 For further discussion of the City of London union relief policies see Andrea Tanner, 'The Casual Poor and the City of London Poor Law Union, 1837–1869', *Historical Journal*, 42 (1999): 183–206.

29 *The Times*, 14 January 1842.

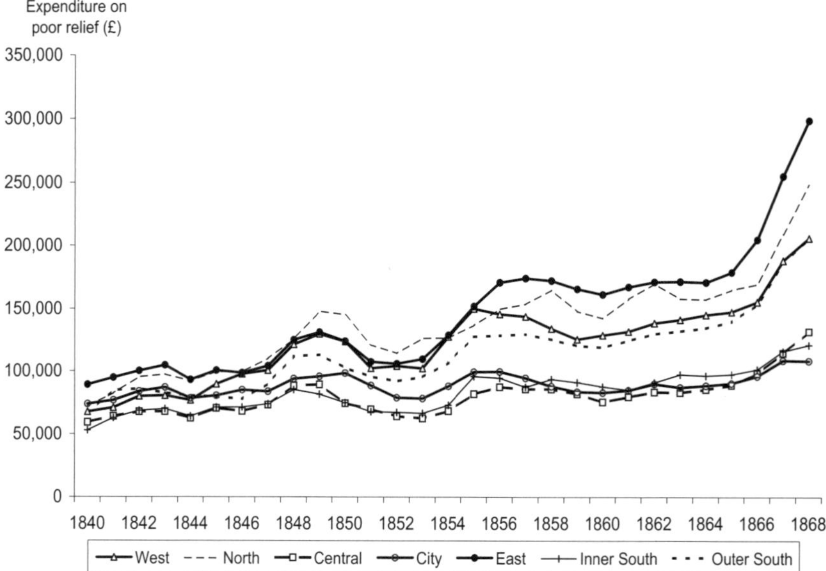

Figure 6.8 Regional expenditure on poor relief in London 1825–1868

Source: Poor Law Commission, Annual Reports, 1840–47; Poor Law Board, Annual Reports, 1848–68.

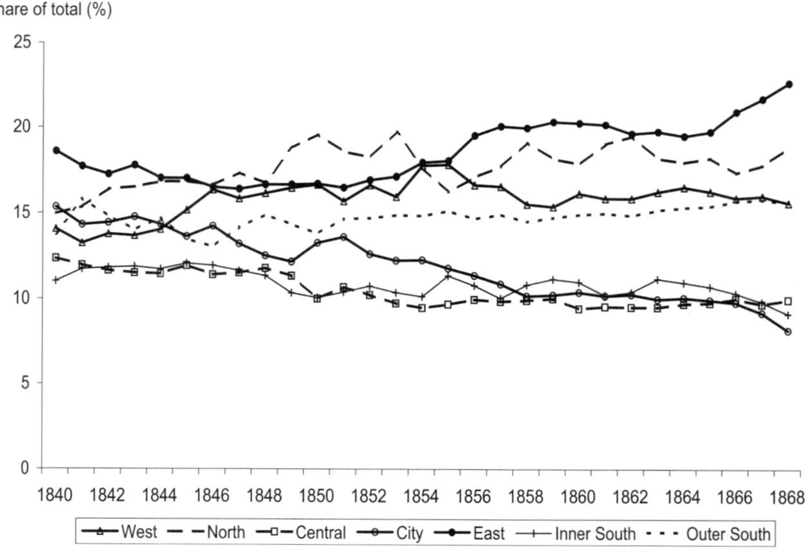

Figure 6.9 Percentage share of poor law expenditure in London regions 1825–1868

Source: Poor Law Commission, Annual Reports, 1840–47; Poor Law Board, Annual Reports, 1848–68.

However, closer inspection of expenditure reveals that experiences were beginning to diverge and in the 1850s the differences between districts became more marked, driven by changes in the distribution of population and by shifts in the city's social geography. In central districts that had been losing population, such as St Martin in the Fields and most notably the City itself, poor law expenditure began to fall. Elsewhere costs were rising, driven largely by rapid population growth in new suburban districts and, more significantly, by growing impoverishment in eastern districts.

From the 1850s these divergent experiences become more pronounced as the absolute totals and relative share of relief expenditure shown in Figures 6.8 and 6.9 demonstrate. By then it was becoming clear that some central, eastern and riverside districts were beginning to experience severe structural problems in providing relief during periods of exceptional hardship and these problems grew worse as the period progressed. A poor harvest in 1853, followed by the outbreak of the Crimean War in 1854, fuelled steep price rises and heralded a period of sharply rising expenditure. The total number of outdoor paupers in Middlesex on 1st January rose by nearly 40 per cent from 33,869 in 1853 to 47,097 in 1855, with the steepest increases in eastern and some riverside districts.[30] The winter of that year was exceptionally severe and in February the Thames froze over, stopping all traffic on the river and halting work at the docks. A report in *Reynolds Newspaper* noted that '... there are not fewer than 50,000 men out of employ, who have been for several days past subsisting on the scanty relief doled out by the parishes and unions'.[31] In early February the St George in the East workhouse ran out of bread and a few days later, upon being refused relief at the Whitechapel workhouse, a crowd ransacked food shops in the vicinity.[32] Food riots broke out in other eastern districts and also in Bermondsey and for a week the situation remained tense.[33] Extra police were drafted in and several of those who were arrested for stealing a few loaves of bread received sentences of up to six months hard labour.[34] Meanwhile donations from the West End bourgeoisie flowed into charities for distribution in the distressed eastern districts.[35] Although a thaw brought a sudden end to the immediate difficulties, it had become abundantly clear that under a combination of adverse circumstances guardians in the poorer districts were unable to cope.

---

30 Poor Law Board, Fifth Annual Report (1852–53), pp. 102–3; Ibid., Seventh Annual Report (1854–55), pp. 112–13.

31 *Reynolds Newspaper*, 25 February 1855.

32 LMA ST/BG/SG/005 St George in the East, Board of Guardians, Minutes, 16 February 1855.

33 *The Times*, 23 February 1855; *Reynolds Newspaper*, 25 February 1855.

34 *The Times*, 12 March 1855; *Reynolds Newspaper*, 18 March 1855.

35 *The Times*, 23 February 1855; Association for the Promotion of the Relief of Destitution in the Metropolis, Thirty Seventh Annual Report (1855), pp. 14–15.

Figure 6.10 Waiting for relief outside Whitechapel union workhouse, winter 1855

Source: *Illustrated London News*, 3 March 1855. Reproduced with kind permission of the Senate House Library, University of London.

For the remainder of the decade, warm winters and cheap bread alleviated the pressure of distress. In 1857 mass applications for outdoor relief throughout London were coordinated by the National Association of Unemployed Operatives but failed to engender any comparable crisis.[36] In early February the relieving officer in St Marylebone struggled under the daily burden of between 2,000 and 4,000 applicants and in neighbouring St Pancras the labour yard was swamped with applications for work and the casual wards were overfilled.[37] Other mass applications took place at workhouses in Islington, Clerkenwell, St Lukes and St Giles and also spread to southern and eastern unions.[38] But unlike the situation in 1855, the winter was mild and bread prices were falling and as a result there was no repetition of the previous shortages or riots.[39] Reports of disorder were limited to isolated attacks on food shops in the East End and Clerkenwell and, except for a handful of extra police stationed at workhouse gates, no extra precautions were taken.[40] Peace was preserved, poor law officials coped and the crisis passed.

The respite was brief. In eastern districts competition from the newly opened Royal Victoria Docks in Poplar had begun to erode the profitability of the older St Katharine's and London Docks, resulting in reduced work for casual labourers throughout the area.[41] This situation was exacerbated in December 1860 when the Thames again froze over, stopping all navigation. The dock companies immediately reduced their workforce: out of a total of 30,000 men that were usually employed, only between 4,000 and 5,000 remained at work.[42] Matters worsened when the collapse of the contractor engaged in building the new mains sewer in east London threw at least 3,000 men out of work. The outbreak of the American Civil War, which was so disastrous for the Lancashire cotton industry, further disrupted trade in the London docks and reduced the demand for shipbuilding. In May 1861 barely 900 men out of a normal workforce of 2,500 were employed at the Thames Iron Works in Poplar and in the course of the year unemployment spread to other trades.[43] Through a combination of poor weather and economic difficulties, outdoor work ground to a halt and the prospect of another flood of pauperism resurfaced.

---

36 The National Association of Unemployed Operatives consisted mainly of building workers. See *Reynolds Newspaper*, 11, 18, 25 January 1857.

37 *The Times*, 3, 6 February 1857.

38 *Reynolds Newspaper*, 1, 8, 19, 22 February, 1 March 1857; *The Times* 3, 5, 6, 19 February 1857.

39 Ibid., 6 February 1857.

40 *Reynolds Newspaper*, 8 February 1857.

41 PP 1861 IX Select committee to inquire into the laws and administration of relief of the poor, p. 136; Charles Capper, *The Port and Trade of London: Historical, Statistical, Local and General* (London, 1862), pp. 161–3, 179.

42 John Hollingshead, *Ragged London in 1861* (London, 1861, reprinted, 1986), pp. 46, 63, 89.

43 PP 1861 IX, Select committee to inquire into the laws and administration of relief of the poor, pp. 136–37, 176–7, 835. Poor Law Board, Fourteenth Annual Report (1861–62),

That flood was not slow in coming. In London as a whole the number of outdoor paupers relieved on 1 January rose by over ten per cent between 1860 and 1861. It was reported that in the third week of January 1861, at the height of the crisis, over 130,000 persons had received parochial relief.[44] The Mendicity Society was swamped by a three-fold increase in the number of applicants seeking assistance. Eastern districts were hardest hit: crowds of unemployed dockers besieged police courts awaiting handouts from the poor box and bread shops were again ransacked.[45] But it was the poor law that bore the brunt of the problem. Workhouses rapidly filled to capacity and sheer pressure of numbers restricted the application of any labour test for outdoor relief.[46] In St George in the East, Reverend George MacGill claimed that a quarter of the population was in need of relief and that the poor law was unable to cope.

Difficulties persisted in eastern districts for the remainder of 1861 and 1862. Falling food prices helped to stave off immediate collapse of the poor law but as MacGill and others recognised, the respite was temporary. A series of milder winters, low bread prices and the availability of work reduced levels of distress but in 1865 the situation again deteriorated. Bread prices began to rise and the outbreak of cattle plague resulted in sharp increases in the price of meat. Buoyant employment initially masked the effects of these price rises but in the summer of 1866 the collapse of Peto and Betts, one of the largest building firms in London, followed shortly after by the failure of the finance house of Overend and Gurney, signalled the onset of widespread commercial panic. The tightening of credit, coupled with growing provincial competition, hastened the collapse of the Thames shipbuilding industry. By September, the main shipbuilding districts of Millwall, Poplar and Deptford had been plunged into depression and by the end of the year shipbuilding in London had all but ceased.[47] In January 1867 as much as a half of the male labour force in eastern districts was without work. By June only one gunboat was being built in the Poplar shipyards and an eerie silence had settled over the district. As one visitor remarked, 'If any person were to walk around the Isle of Dogs and Millwall during the working hours they would almost fancy it

---

p. 14; Poor Law Board, Fifteenth Annual Report (1862–63), p. 148.

44 Poor Law Board, Thirteenth Annual Report (1860–61), p. 185; Poor Law Board, Fourteenth Annual Report (1861–62), pp. 185–6. The total number of paupers relieved on 1 January 1860 was 94,774 and 103,936 in 1861. The number of outdoor paupers was 67,601 and 74,500 respectively. See also *The Times*, 18 January 1861; *Reynolds Newspaper*, 20 January 1861.

45 Ibid., 20 January 1861; *The Times* 19, 21, 22, 23 January 1861.

46 PP 1861 IX Select committee to inquire into the laws and administration of relief of the poor, pp. 125–30; *The Times*, 11, 23 January 1861.

47 *Reynolds Newspaper*, 23 September, 21 October 1866; *East London Observer*, 8 December 1866; Sidney Pollard, 'The Decline of Shipbuilding on the Thames', *Economic History Review*, 3 (1950): 72–89.

was Sunday as there is hardly the sound of a hammer to be heard and nothing but the bare scaffold poles to be seen in most of the shipbuilding yards.'[48]

As the second winter of hardship approached, those who had managed to subsist on their savings and credit were forced to seek relief. Counts of the number of paupers relieved on the last day of the Christmas quarter, shown in Table 6.1 reveal the extent of the problem. Between 1865 and 1867 pauper numbers rose by over 43 per cent and in eastern districts the increase was nearly double that for the city as a whole. In Poplar, the district most affected by the collapse of shipbuilding, the number of paupers rose from 3,462 in 1865 to 9,617 in 1867.[49] In St George in the East over 4,000 able-bodied men applied for out relief in the last two weeks of January and the guardians admitted that were unable to cope.[50] Workhouses throughout eastern and southern riverside districts were soon filled making enforcement of the workhouse test impossible.[51] The costs of relief in London soared, from £905,640 in 1865 to £1,316,759 in 1868, an increase of over 45 per cent, nearly all of which was accounted for by the rise in expenditure in eastern districts.[52] Relieving officers were swamped by the numbers of applicants and on this occasion the crisis overwhelmed the local poor law.

Table 6.1 Paupers relieved in London on the last day of the Christmas quarter 1865–1867

	1865	**1866**	**1867**
West	13,633	15,597	21,005
North	19,241	23,186	26,448
Central*	17,538	19,139	21,953
East	19,988	27,508	36,407
South**	32,792	37,839	41,797
TOTAL	103,192	123,269	147,610

Note: * Includes City of London; **Includes Inner South and Outer South.

Source: Poor Law Board, Annual Reports, 1865–68.

In many districts, and not just those in east London, balancing the books became an increasingly challenging task and few guardians, if any, could rest easy

48 *Reynolds Newspaper*, 20 January, 2 June 1867. See also Poor Law Board, Twentieth Annual Report (1867–68), pp. 28–30, 119–22.

49 Figures refer to the last day of the Christmas quarter. See Poor Law Board, Nineteenth Annual Report (1866–67), p. 347; Poor Law Board, Twentieth Annual Report (1867–68), p. 365.

50 LMA ST/BG/SG/010 St George in the East Board of Guardians, Minutes, 18, 25 January, 1 February 1867.

51 Ibid., pp. 14, 126.

52 *Reynolds Newspaper*, 5, 12 January 1868.

in the knowledge that from one year to the next their rate income would cover the costs of relief. The extent to which their concerns were borne out can be gauged by comparing relief expenditure with income raised from the rates. Although by no means a perfect indication of the difficulties in financing the poor law, not least because rate income was used for a variety of other purposes over and above relief itself, nevertheless the balance between rate income and relief expenditure yields an insight to the extent of the fiscal crisis that threatened to overwhelm London poor law unions.

Higher rateable values allowed guardians to raise more money but, even so, there was a limit as to how far expenditure could exceed income. The ebb and flow of fiscal stress is shown in Table 6.2, which measures the total surplus or deficit in London unions by decade based on the balance of rateable income and poor law expenditure. During the 1840s, the number of deficit and surplus unions was exactly the same and in the 1850s, when the economy was relatively buoyant, the balance moved strongly towards those in surplus. Only four districts in that decade spent more on relief than they raised through the rates. However, as noted above the situation changed in the following decade and between 1860 and 1867 no less than 28 poor law unions spent more on relief than they raised from the rates. The most severe problems were largely concentrated in the riverside districts of St George in the East and Poplar together with Southwark. Other districts where expenditure significantly exceeded income included St Margaret and St John in Westminster, and Hackney, although in both places relatively high rateable values made raising extra funds comparatively easy. In other eastern districts a combination of strict relief regimes, as in Bethnal Green, and higher rates as in Mile End and Stepney, ensured that expenditure never exceeded income. Although it could be argued that the surpluses amassed in the previous decade were being used by guardians to subsidise this additional expenditure, it was clear from the number of unions that remained in deficit that the cost of relief in some areas had outstripped the capacity of local ratepayers to fund the increase.

Table 6.2 Fiscal stress and poor law unions 1840–1867

	Deficit		**Surplus**		**Balance**
	Number	£	Number	£	£
1840–49	18*	94,409	18	151,456	57,047
1850–59	4	18,243	34	310,337	292,094
1860–67	28	159,509	10	34,556	(-124,953)

Note: *Excludes Holborn for which faulty accounts were submitted in three years and St Lukes which broke even.

Source: Poor Law Commission, Annual Reports, 1840–47; Poor Law Board, Annual Reports, 1848–68.

Shouldering the burden

For ratepayers rising expenditure normally meant higher rates but the burden was distributed unequally. Social change had robbed several inner and eastern districts of their ratepaying middle class who were in turn replaced by the poor. By mid-century the delicate social balance that once had prevailed in such places had been eroded with serious consequences for raising money through the rates.

In central areas clearances and demolitions worsened overcrowding and denuded districts of their resident middle class.[53] Between 1831 and 1861, with the exception of Holborn and Clerkenwell, all central districts lost housing. In the West London registration district, for example, nearly a third of the housing stock disappeared between these years.[54] In neighbouring Clerkenwell in 1857 Reverend Warwick Wroth noted ruefully that 'The richer classes are continually moving to other localities and the poorer are taking their place. Houses which formerly were filled with tolerably well-to-do, are now let out in lodgings and the lodgers, instead of being able to aid others, sometimes need aid themselves.'[55] In the centre those that were left included a scattering of tradesmen together with large numbers of casual labourers – 'people who do not know, when they rise in the morning by what chance jobs in the streets or the markets they are to get food for the day'.[56] In eastern districts what few middle-class families had been present were also leaving and in Bethnal Green Henry Morley claimed that 'there was not one resident that the world would call respectable (and) not more than about half a dozen families able to keep a servant'.[57] A few years later, in 1866 the Reverend George MacGill, the incumbent in St George in the East, complained that

> Most of the better class of tradesman have migrated to the suburbs – to Stratford, Bow, Hackney, and elsewhere, and the difficulty of obtaining funds for the various charities is increasing each year, whilst every year the need for them is increased, for as the better class go the poor fill their place. Few will be left soon

---

[53] D. M. Evans, *The City, or the Physiology of London Business* (London, 1845), p. 190.

[54] See David R. Green, *From Artisans to Paupers: Economic Change and Poverty in London, 1790–1870* (Aldershot, 1995). p. 185.

[55] Association for Promoting the Relief of Destitution in the Metropolis, Fourteenth Annual Report (1858), p. 6.

[56] Joseph Fletcher, 'The Metropolis: Its Boundaries, Extent and Divisions for Local Government', *Journal of the Statistical Society*, 7 (1844) p. 70. This topic is further discussed by Gareth Stedman Jones, *Outcast London: A Study of the Relationships Between Classes in Victorian Society* (Oxford, 1971), pp. 159–78; Anthony Wohl, *The Eternal Slum: Housing and Social Policy in Victorian London* (London, 1977), pp. 1–44.

[57] Henry Morley, 'The Quiet Poor', *Household Words*, 9 (1854), cited in Kate Flint (ed.), *The Victorian Novelist* (London, 1987), p. 207.

> besides the poor, the poor rate collector, the relieving officer, the policeman and the parson.[58]

Whilst those who could afford it fled the central areas by choice, the working class were pushed out by necessity and the direction of this flow was largely determined by the availability of cheap housing. High rents in western districts limited the extent to which the poor could live in those areas. An investigation by the Statistical Society of London in 1843 found that in St George's Hanover Square, the average weekly rent paid by working-class households was 4s 3d compared to 3s 7d in St George in the East. As the Society's investigators discovered, where rents were high families were forced to economise on space: approximately 63 per cent of families in the Hanover Square district lived in one room compared to just over 35 per cent of families in St George in the East.[59]

These stark differences, coupled with demolition of housing in central areas to make way for railways, roads and commercial premises, underlay the movement of large numbers of the poor into eastern and southern riverside districts, in many cases taking over houses that had been vacated by the migratory middle class. Similar stories were heard throughout the belt of impoverished districts that ringed the City. In Bethnal Green in 1848 Hector Gavin noted how the construction of the Eastern Counties Railway had exacerbated overcrowding and encouraged poor quality and insanitary dwellings to be hastily erected in back gardens and other open spaces.[60] In Southwark Edward Collinson, chairman of the board of guardians, reported that 'Unquestionably improvements in the City at first tended very much to make poor persons' houses, which were formerly shop and dwelling houses, be let out in tenements and as lodging houses…'. By the 1860s, over half the housing stock in the area was said to have been subdivided and let out as single rooms and ratepayers had difficulties in coping with the inexorable rise in the demand for relief.[61]

---

58 Association for Promoting the Relief of Destitution in the Metropolis, Twenty First Annual Report (1866), p. 6.

59 C. R. Weld, 'On the Condition of the Working Classes in the Inner Ward of St George's Parish, Hanover Square', *Journal of the Statistical Society*, 6 (1843): 20, 23; H. Hallam and R. A. Slaney, 'Report to the Council of the Statistical Society of London from a Committee of its Fellows Appointed to Make an Investigation into the State of the Poorer Classes in St. George's in the East', *Journal of the Statistical Society*, 11 (1848): 209, 211.

60 Hector Gavin, *Sanitary Ramblings: Being Sketches and Illustrations of Bethnal Green* (London, 1848), pp. 34, 109.

61 PP 1862 X Select committee to inquire into the laws and administration of relief of the poor under orders, rules and regulations of the Poor Law Commissioners and the Poor Law Board, pp. 511, 527–9, 531, 536–9; PP 1866 XXXIII Eighth report of the Medical Officer to the Privy Council, p. 504.

The outcome of this social transformation was that the rating burden for relief increased sharply in areas into which the poor had moved. As costs mounted and population changes began to erode the capacity of some districts to meet their obligations, serious anxieties over the level of rating inequality began to be voiced. Such concerns had existed for several years but economic crisis and residential separation lent urgency to the situation. Further pressure was added by legal changes to the entitlement to relief brought about by the 1846 Poor Removal Act, which made five years' residence in a district the grounds for claiming relief.[62] Suspicion existed that as a result of the new legislation, ratepayers in wealthy districts had become keener to displace the poor as a means of shifting the burden of relief.[63] Surveying the situation in 1855, Robert Warwick, a City of London guardian and active supporter of rate equalisation, noted that as a result of the act 'the burdens of supporting the poor have been removed from one class of ratepayers to another, and that the class which are sufferers are those who occupy property in those parishes where the labouring man can obtain a residence'.[64] When the City of London guardians therefore chose to discontinue relief to their non-resident paupers in 1857, the burden thrown onto surrounding districts into which the poor had moved was considerable and added significantly to the mounting difficulties faced by ratepayers in such places.[65]

The outcome of these various transformations was increasing disparities in rating levels between different districts in London as the evidence on rates in 1860 shown in Figure 6.11 illustrates. By that time eastern and southern riverside districts had rates three to four times higher than most western and suburban district and in these places it took little to overwhelm the capacity of the poor law to deal with the demand for relief. As the Reverend George MacGill noted at a period of peak distress at the end of January 1861:

> The history of the last month shows that the Poor law has broken down, that it is utterly incompetent under its present constitution to relieve the London poor. It has no powers of expansion to meet an emergency which is almost certain to occur every winter season ...[66]

---

62 Act to Amend the Laws Relating, to the Removal of the Poor, until the First Day of October One thousand eight hundred and forty-eight (Poor Removal Act), 10 & 11 Vict. c. 110. See Chapter 7 for further discussion of this topic.

63 William Gilbert, *On the Present System of Rating for the Relief of the Poor in the Metropolis* (London, 1857a), p. 19.

64 Robert E. Warwick, *Observations on the Laws of Settlements, Poor Removals and the Equalization of the Poor Rates*, (London, 1855), p.13.

65 Andrea Tanner, 'The City of London Poor Law Union 1837–1869', unpublished Ph.D. thesis, University of London, 1995, pp. 223–52.

66 *The Times*, 23 January 1861.

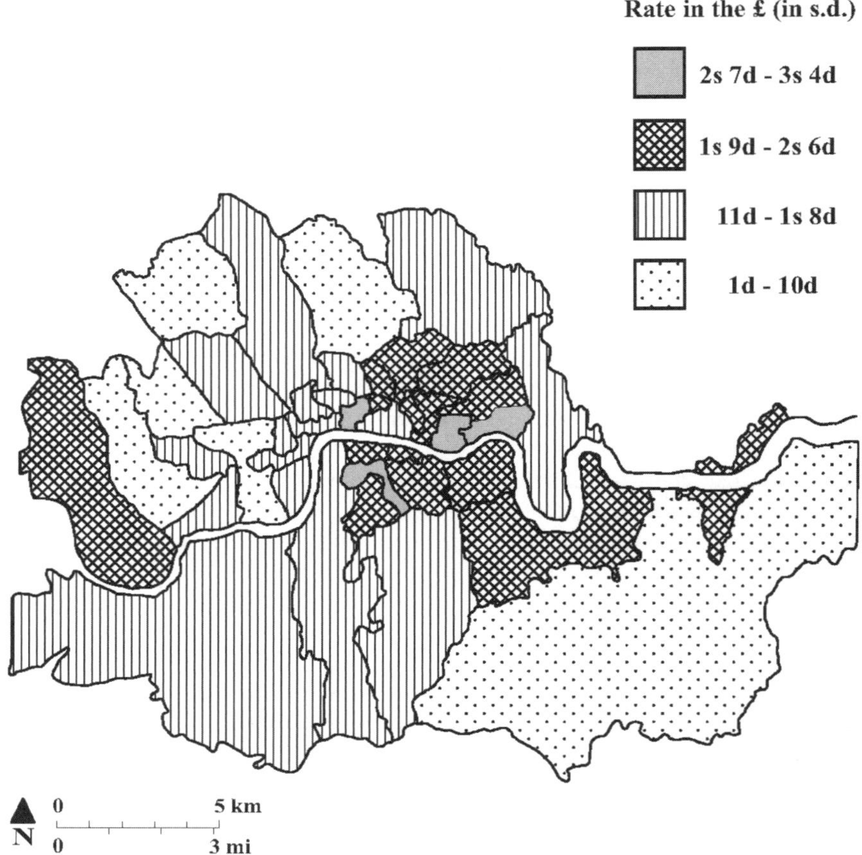

Figure 6.11 Rate in the £ for poor relief in London 1860

Source: PP 1867 LX Return from unions and parishes in the metropolitan district of the amount expended for relief to the poor, 1857–66, Rateable value and rate in pound.

How the burden of poor relief could be redistributed and how powers of expansion could be created to deal with the emerging crisis of expenditure were pressing problems. The fact that London occupied an inceasingly prominent position in relation to the national pattern of poor law expenditure meant that the problem had much wider significance than just that relating to the city itself. Indeed, many of the subsequent reforms to the way the poor law operated in the country as a whole were in reality attempts to tackle problems that were specific to London.

Chapter 7
Reforming Relief: From Removals to Redistribution

Removals and redistribution

Preserving the equilibrium between ratepayer income and relief expenditure depended on a variety of factors: a semblance of social balance in each district, economic growth commensurate with population increase and a means by which to redistribute the cost of relief for those without a legal settlement in a district. From mid-century onwards changes that widened class separation had begun to erode the social balance necessary to maintain the solvency of the local poor law in specific places. This situation, however, was exacerbated by economic downturn in the 1860s and changes in legislation that undermined the possibility of redistributing costs. Of these the last was arguably the most important since without any redistributive mechanism that could spread the cost of pauperism, poorer districts would always struggle to make ends meet. Given the importance of the non-settled poor in London, this problem was particularly acute and understanding the way that authorities dealt with this group, which mainly consisted of migrants to the city, helps to explain how the poor law changed from the 1850s onwards.

Two possible solutions existed to deal with the non-settled poor: the first was to move people and the second was to move money. Guardians wishing to avoid the costs of relief could remove non-settled paupers to their legal place of settlement. Although this was expensive, in some cases it was worthwhile. Alternatively, guardians could choose to pay relief to their own non-settled poor living in other districts and therefore preclude the possibility that such poor persons might be removed back to their own district.[1] For a variety of reasons, these options were both difficult and impractical to operate in London.

The second solution was more radical and that was to recognise the unequal burden placed on poorer districts and to remedy this through some form of redistribution of the rates. As Patrick Colquhoun had suggested in 1799 'Why should inhabitants of rich parishes not contribute to relief of the poor…. Nothing can exceed the inequality of the weight for the support of the poor in the metropolis, since where the demand is greatest, the means of supply are always most deficient

[1] The mechanics of paying outrelief are discussed in Steven King, '"It is Impossible for Our Vestry to Judge His Case into Perfection From Here": Managing the Distance Dimensions of Poor Relief, 1800–40', *Rural History*, 16 (2005): 161–89.

and inadequate.'[2] That this problem was recognised so early in London, yet took so long to remedy, highlighted the difficulties of overcoming the fragmented nature of local government and the failure to conceive of ways in which to reconcile collective provision of relief with the concerns of local ratepayers. Ultimately, however, redistribution proved to be a more effective way than removals of resolving the growing crisis of poor law expenditure.

Redistributing paupers: the role of settlement and removals

Deterrence through the imposition of a strict workhouse or labour test was one means by which parishes could try to limit the numbers of their own settled poor or encourage those without a settlement to seek relief elsewhere. In Bethnal Green, where deterrence was pursued most vigorously, this policy proved effective. However, since harsh treatment in one district was always likely to generate similar responses in neighbouring parishes, deterrence clearly had its limitations. In the absence of redistribution of funds through the rates, the only other avenue by which costs could be shifted elsewhere was to remove non-settled paupers back to their place of settlement or come to some financial arrangement with their home parish. Though the settlement laws were widely criticised as hindering the free flow of labour, nevertheless the Royal Commission of 1834 had left them in place, choosing only to tinker with some of the grounds by which a settlement could be obtained, notably relating to bastardy.[3] Although the removal of non-settled paupers could be cumbersome and expensive to execute, nevertheless it served to deter would-be applicants and was the only means by which guardians could shift the burden of relief elsewhere.

In gaining a settlement, a person became entitled to receive relief from his or her parish and therefore could not be removed. However, the grounds for establishing a settlement were exceptionally complex and costly to prove, depending on birth, parentage, marriage, hiring and service, apprenticeship, renting property, paying rates, serving a parochial office or acquiring an estate. The Poor Law Amendment Act did little to alter the grounds for obtaining a settlement, making only two

---

2 Patrick Colquhoun, *The State of Indigence and the Situation of the Casual Poor in the Metropolis* (London, 1799), p. 30.

3 For a discussion of the settlement laws see David Feldman, 'Migrants, Immigrants and Welfare from the Old Poor Law to the Welfare State', *Transactions of the Royal Historical Society*, 13 (2003): 79–104; Norma Landau, 'The Laws of Settlement and the Surveillance of Immigration in Eighteenth-Century Kent', *Continuity and Change*, 3 (1988): 391–420; Norma Landau, 'The Eighteenth Century Context of the Law of Settlement', *Continuity and Change*, 6 (1991): 417–39; Keith Snell, 'Pauper Settlement and Poor Relief', *Continuity and Change*, 6 (1991): 375–415; James Taylor, 'The Impact of Pauper Settlement 1691–1834', *Past and Present*, 73 (1976): 42–73; James Taylor, *Poverty, Migration and Settlement in the Industrial Revolution* (Palo Alto, 1989).

significant changes in relation to illegitimate children and hiring and service. After 1834 illegitimate children took their mother's settlement until the age of 16, after which time they acquired the settlement of their place of birth unless they had established another in the meantime.[4] Under these circumstances, if guardians wanted to avoid the future costs of supporting illegitimate children, it was clearly important to do everything in their power to prevent unmarried women giving birth in their parish. The only other significant change made in 1834 related to the abolition of hiring and service as a means of gaining a settlement. From that date on employment for a year as a domestic servant ceased to be a means to obtaining a settlement, an important change in London, particularly for women for whom service was one of the main sources of employment.

The diversity by which settlements could be obtained is demonstrated in Figure 7.1, which shows the grounds on which removal orders were issued in London for the year ending 25 March 1857. Derivative settlements obtained by parentage, through marriage or by birth, were the most important reasons by which individuals gained a legal settlement, accounting for nearly two thirds of the total. Paying for a tenement worth £10 a year, equivalent to a rent of 4s a week, was also particularly important in London where the cost of housing was relatively high compared to the rest of the country. In St George in the East in the 1840s, for example, which was by no means a wealthy district or one noted for the high rents, about a third of families rented accommodation worth at least that much.[5] Other grounds included hiring and service, which because of its abolition under the new poor law must by 1857 have included only those relatively elderly persons who had managed to establish their settlements in this way before 1834. Apprenticeship also provided a route to a settlement, although its decline in London meant that it was of diminishing significance as the period progressed.

---

[4] For further discussion of the bastardy clauses in the Poor Law Amendment Act, see Lisa Forman Cody, 'The Politics of Illegitimacy in an Age of Reform: Women, Reproduction, and Political Economy in England's New Poor Law of 1834', *Journal of Women's History*, 11 (2000): 131–56 and Ursula Henriques, 'Bastardy and the New Poor Law', *Past and Present*, 37 (1967): 103–29.

[5] See H. Hallam and R. A. Slaney, 'Report to the Council of the Statistical Society of London from a Committee of its Fellows Appointed to Make an Investigation into the State of the Poorer Classes in St. George's in the East', *Journal of the Statistical Society*, 11 (1848): 208. Out of 1,954 families, 675 paid this amount or more.

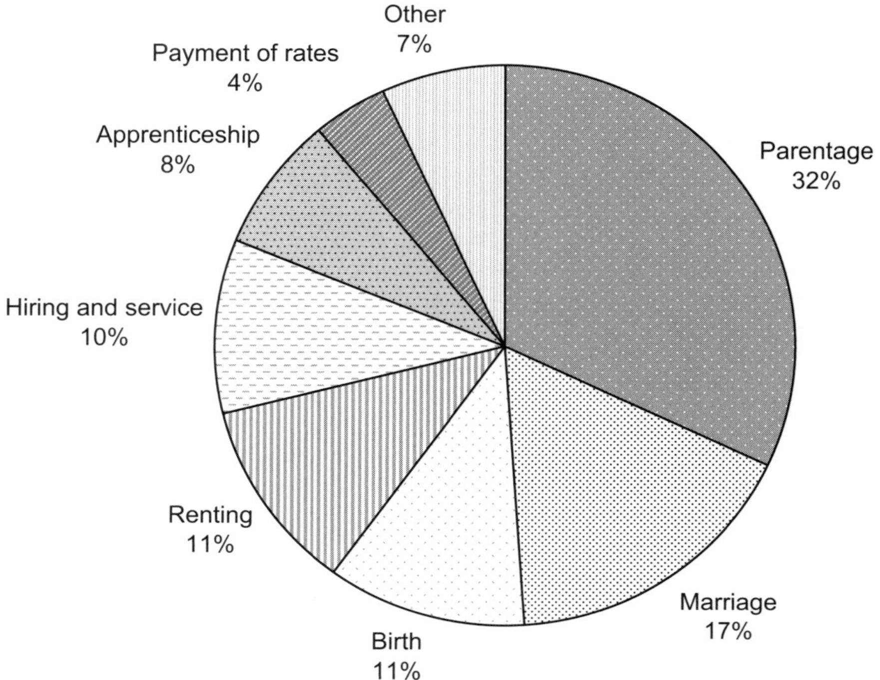

Figure 7.1 Grounds of settlement for persons removed from London in year ending 25 March 1857

Source: PP 1857–58 Part I XLIX Grounds of settlement for persons removed from London in year ending 25 March 1857, p. 507.

Whilst various grounds for establishing a settlement existed, proving which one took precedence was more complex. Over time an individual could establish by accident or design several different grounds for a settlement. Given the complexity of the settlement laws, the reluctance or inability of paupers themselves to give the correct information and the difficulty of communicating with authorities from distant parishes, proving which one was the last, and which therefore took precedence, was by no means straightforward. Even when a settlement could be established, in many instances the grounds hinged on half remembered events and dubious evidence, and officials could waste large amounts of time as well as money trying to prove their case.[6]

[6] An indication of the efforts made to determine settlements early in the century was given by Edward Wittington, who was employed by the St Marylebone overseers to investigate claims, attend appeals and execute orders of removal. He estimated that in the five years he was employed, he travelled between 60,000 and 70,000 miles, at a cost of between

Given these problems, it was little wonder that appeals against removals by disgruntled parishes were so common. In 1845, for example, when the overseers of the poor from St Katherine Cree Church in the City questioned the settlement of George and Elizabeth Durrant, an elderly couple who had become chargeable in the nearby parish of St Dionis, they did so on the basis of the cost of a rental that had taken place over 30 years before in 1812. The issue at the centre of the dispute was whether or not the couple had ever rented property to the value of £10 a year, equivalent to 4s a week, which would have been sufficient for them to have established a legal settlement in the parish. The couple thought that they had done so but the landlady who had originally let the property, Ann Da Costa, claimed that the rent had only been 3s 6d a week, which placed them below the threshold. In the event legal counsel suggested that objections to the settlement should be dropped because Da Costa's memory was poor 'and her character is not quite such as to entitle her to credit for as we are informed she had kept a brothel for many years'.[7] The St Katherine's overseers were forced not only to pick up the bill for supporting the couple but also for their unsuccessful appeal – a situation that was repeated on many occasions in the various London courts.

Establishing a settlement was only the first stage in the complex business of initiating a removal. Officials then had to appear before a magistrate to seek permission to execute the removal. In practice, the delay in obtaining an order of removal often meant that paupers disappeared before they could be removed. In the case of Irish and Scottish paupers this cumbersome process was revised in 1845 when officials were allowed to dispense with prior investigations before appealing for a removal order. However, the impracticality of operating even this simplified procedure in London and other large towns was obvious and in 1847 relieving officers were given further powers to apply for a removal order more speedily. Even so, the process still remained cumbersome and wherever possible officials sought to circumvent the legal process of removal. Savings in time and money could be made by avoiding this entire process but not without a separate agreement between the sending and receiving parish. These so called 'friendly orders' between reciprocal pairs of parishes rendered unnecessary the expensive and time consuming process of applying to the magistrates. Where they operated, they seemed to have been important.[8] In St George in the East in 1848, for example, there were nearly three times more friendly order removals than those sanctioned

£450 and £500 each year. See PP1834 XXVIII Royal commission on the administration and practical operation of the poor laws, Appendix A, assistant commissioners' reports.

[7] CLRO MS 19236/1 Overseers of the Poor of the Parish of St Dionis Backchurch, papers relating to the removal of George and Elizabeth Durrant.

[8] At the start of the century, for example, Christchurch, Spitalfields operated such friendly orders with the neighbouring parishes of Mile End, Bethnal Green, Shoreditch, Bishopsgate and Whitechapel. See PP 1817 VI Select committee to consider the poor laws, p. 32.

by the court.[9] Neverthless, given the large number of parishes, the practical difficulties in making such arrangements inevitably restricted their usage.[10]

Irrespective of whether such arrangements existed, the possibilities of fraud and the disadvantages of distance remained and these considerations further limited the use of removals. The financial arrangements that lubricated removals were open to widespread abuse. Passmasters responsible for conveying paupers were paid a set rate by distance, usually between 2d and 3d a mile in the early 1830s, and the paupers themselves were given a daily rate of between 4d and 6d a day subsistence. However, paupers and passmasters sometimes colluded to split the money rather than continue with the removal. Forged passes for removal were also said to have been a frequent means by which the poor were able to elicit relief from passmasters.[11]

To a large extent, however, the main cost of removal was determined by distance and in this respect geography conspired against London parishes. Early in the century Patrick Colquhoun, who as a magistrate and philanthropist was in a good position to know the problems first hand, noted how removals from London to western counties and those north of the Trent were scarce on account of their expense, a view also echoed by John Leigh, clerk to the St George Hanover Square directors of the poor, where paupers were often relieved temporarily rather than removed to distant parishes.[12] Similar concerns over costs were also said to have limited the removal of Irish and Scottish paupers.[13] Depending on which route was taken, in the early 1830s the cost of removing paupers back to Ireland varied from £1 3s 7d to £1 17s 11½ d.[14] Little had changed by the 1860s when the cost of removing Irish paupers from districts north of the Thames was between £1 2s and £1 18s, and to Scotland between £1 2s and £3, equivalent to the cost of between about four and ten months' outdoor relief respectively.[15]

---

9 LMA ST/BG/SG/003 St George in the East Board of Guardians, Minutes, 3 March 1848.

10 An alternative scheme was adopted by Directors of the Poor in St Margaret and St John in the 1830s which provided paupers with a document to be presented to the removing agent at their place of settlement in return for relief on arrival, thereby saving the cost of transport and limiting the occasions when a parish officer was required to accompany a pauper. See CWAC E/5028 St Margaret and St John Directors of the Poor, Minutes, 20 May 1830.

11 PP1834 XXVIII Royal commission of inquiry into the administration and practical operation of the poor laws, Appendix E, pp. 247–8. See also PP 1833 XVI Select committee on the removal of Irish vagrants to Ireland, pp. 330, 336, 344.

12 PP 1814–15 III Select committee on the state of mendicity in the metropolis, p. 285; PP 1817 VI Select committee to consider the poor laws, p. 64.

13 PP 1814–15 Select committee on the state of mendicity, pp. 240, 283.

14 PP1834 XXVIII Royal commission of inquiry into the administration and practical operation of the poor laws, Appendix E, pp. 247–8. See also PP 1833 XVI Select committee on the removal of Irish vagrants to Ireland, pp. 330, 336, 344.

15 PP 1861 IX Select committee to inquire into the laws and administration of relief of the poor under orders, rules and regulations of the Poor Law Commissioners and Poor

In southern metropolitan unions the practice of transporting Irish paupers overland to a seaport, usually Bristol, rather than placing them directly on a ship in London, was thought to have doubled the cost.[16]

Removing Irish paupers in particular could be a large drain on parish finances. Although the initial cost of obtaining a pass fell on the parish, the majority of the expenses associated with executing the removal itself were paid by the county. In the early decades some parishes in which large numbers of Irish resided took advantage of this arrangement to implement removals. Between 1820 and 1827 Sir Robert Baker, treasurer to Middlesex, calculated that at least 14,433 Irish vagrants had been passed by the county compared to 1,564 Scottish poor. During the early 1830s in St Giles an average of 800 Irish families were passed and at least 3,000 Irish vagrants were also removed from the City of London.[17]

In 1845, however, an important change occurred which limited the removal of Irish and Scottish paupers. In that year, for districts with a population larger than 30,000, the cost of passing a pauper back to his or her place of settlement was transferred from the county to the individual parish.[18] All but four metropolitan unions – Fulham, Lewisham, Rotherhithe and St Martin in the Fields – had larger populations and therefore this change was important. At the same time, the failure of the potato crop in Ireland meant that conditions there worsened dramatically. The combination of these two factors meant that the number of removals from London to Ireland and Scotland declined sharply. In the 12 months prior to 1845 the St George in the East guardians removed 819 Irish and Scottish paupers but in the following year they removed none. A similar situation existed in several other unions, notably the City, East London, Shoreditch and Whitechapel north of the Thames, and Camberwell and St George Southwark to the south, all of which became known after 1845 as non-removing parishes.[19] Some parishes, such as St Marylebone, continued to enforce removals whilst others, including St Martin in the Fields, which by virtue of its small size was able to defray the costs of removal to the county, did likewise.[20]

Law Board, pp. 119–20. In 1861 the average per capita cost of indoor relief in London was estimated to have been 4s ½d. a week compared to outdoor relief of 1s 4½d.

16 PP 1847 XI Select committee to inquire into the operation of the law of settlement, and Poor Removal Act, sixth report, pp. 636–37; CLHC P/GG/PO/8 St Giles in the Fields Directors of the Poor, Minutes, 6th July 1852.

17 PP 1833 XVI Select committee on the removal of Irish vagrants to Ireland, pp. 330, 336, 338, 344.

18 The only exceptions were those parishes which had a population of less than 30,000. The costs in this situation were still borne by the county rate.

19 PP 1847 XI Select committee to inquire into the operation of the law of settlement, and Poor Removal Act, pp. 246, 637; PP 1854 XVII Select committee on poor removal. Report, Minutes of Evidence, Appendix, Index, p.547.

20 Ibid., pp. 547, 561.

Despite the many problems associated with enforcing removals, they were exceptionally important in London where migrants formed a relatively large proportion of the population. Evidence on the number of removals, shown in Table 7.1, was published sporadically in parliamentary papers from the 1850s onwards. At that point London unions accounted for about a quarter of the total number of persons removed in England and Wales and by the 1860s this had risen to between 30 and 50 per cent, figures which were far in excess of the relative size of the city or its share of the total number of paupers relieved. However, the costs and practical difficulties of enforcing removals meant that they were used selectively, primarily for paupers that potentially represented a long term drain on the rates, notably large families, widows, single women, female-headed households, orphans, the elderly, lunatics and the chronically ill, rather than the male able-bodied poor. As the figures in Tables 7.2, 7.3 and 7.4 show, single women and female-headed households were more likely to be removed than men, largely because of the potential costs involved in supporting illegitimate children born in the parish. In St Margaret and St John in the 1830s these groups, rather than single men, comprised the majority of those removed back to the parish from elsewhere. A similar situation occurred in Bethnal Green and St George Southwark in the 1840s. Clearly, when long term costs outweighed the short term inconvenience, removals were seen as a useful way of limiting the drain on parish finances.

Table 7.1 Number of persons removed in London and England and Wales 1853–1868

Year ending 25 March	London	England and Wales	London as percentage of England and Wales
1853	2,371	10,032	23.6
1854	2,897	11,113	26.1
1857	5,337	16,546	32.2
1863	4,298	13,989	30.7
1868	4,320	8,351	51.7

Note: The figures for 1853 and 1854 are imperfect with several London districts failing to submit returns.

Source: PP 1854 LV Poor Law (orders of removal). Returns showing the number of orders of removal from parishes, signed by justices, and executed in England and Wales, during the year ending 25 March 1853; PP 1854 LV Poor removal. Return showing the number of orders of removal from parishes, signed by justices and executed in England and Wales, during the year ending 25th day of March 1854; PP 1865 XLVIII Orders of removal. Return showing the number of orders of removal from parishes, signed by justices and executed in England and Wales, during the year ending the 25th day of March 1863; PP 1867–68 LX Orders of removal. Return showing the number of orders of removal from unions and parishes, signed by justices and executed in England and Wales, during the year ending 25th March 1868.

Table 7.2 Social status of paupers removed to St Margaret and St John Westminster in 1830 and 1838

Category	1830		1838	
	Number	Per cent	Number	Per cent
Male – single	15	12.3	11	11.5
Female – single	57	46.7	23	24.0
Dual headed household	32	26.2	30	31.2
Female headed household	15	12.3	19	19.8
Orphans, bastard/abandoned children	3	2.5	13	13.5
TOTAL	122	100.0	96	100.0

Source: CWAC E/5208 St Margaret and St John Directors of the Poor, Minutes, 1830, 1838.

Table 7.3 Social status of paupers removed to Bethnal Green 1843–1848

Category	Number	Per cent
Male – single	25	11.5
Female – single	49	22.5
Dual headed household	66	30.3
Female headed household	51	23.4
Male headed household	5	2.3
Orphans, bastard/abandoned children	22	10.0
TOTAL	218	100.0

Source: LMA B/BG/271 Bethnal Green Board of Guardians, Notices of orders of removal from sundry parishes to Bethnal Green, 1843–48.

Table 7.4 Social status of paupers removed from St George Southwark August 1843 to June 1846

Category	Number	Per cent
Male – single	27	29.0
Female – single	25	26.9
Dual headed household	9	9.7
Female headed household	24	25.8
Male headed household	2	2.2
Orphans, bastard/abandoned children	6	6.5
TOTAL	93	100.0

Source: LMA SO/BG/27 St George Southwark Board of Guardians, Removals to various parishes, 1843–46.

Given the complexities of establishing a settlement and the potential savings that could be made when the burden could be shifted elsewhere, disputes between parishes over the legality of removals were common, as the case of Florence Fletcher, a pauper in the City of London workhouse, illustrates. In March 1865 at the request of the City of London guardians, she was examined by Henry Farnall, the assistant poor law inspector for London, on the grounds of having been wrongfully refused relief from the Shoreditch workhouse.[21] She originally came from Wigan where she had worked as a servant, milliner and dressmaker. In 1861 she left for Bolton and then Manchester, where she had been employed as a servant. Two years later she came to London and earned her living at needlework until the birth of an illegitimate child in December 1864. Between then and March 1865 she sought help four times at three different workhouses: Whitechapel for one week, the City of London union for a short time in the casual ward, followed by Shoreditch, where the relieving officer allowed her some broth before telling her to leave despite the fact that she was too weak to walk. She finally returned to the City of London workhouse where she remained for three months. Officials there, keen to avoid what was potentially a large and long term cost, tried to send her back to Shoreditch, complaining that the relieving officer had acted illegally in forcing her to move when she was in no fit state to do so. In the event, Henry Farnall thought otherwise and overruled their complaint, thereby forcing the City guardians to foot the bill for relief. The case, however, illustrated two points. First, relieving officers were under an obligation to provide assistance in cases of urgent and sudden need and were not allowed to harry the pauper into moving on. Second, it demonstrated the difficulties associated with establishing the legality of removals, which as this case illustrated, could hang on something as tenuous as an interpretation of the pauper's physical state. Little wonder, then, that disputes between districts were so common.

Florence Fletcher's story also highlights a further characteristic of removals in London, namely that they tended to be short distance and as such had a limited impact as a deterrent. In the 1830s, between 88 and 93 per cent of paupers removed to St Margaret and St John Westminster came from elsewhere in London, about a third of which came from the nearby parish of Lambeth.[22] The same was true for removals in other London districts. In Southwark over 80 per cent of removals in the 1840s were to other London parishes and of the 217 removal orders of paupers to Bethnal Green between 1843 and 1848, all but 15 came from other metropolitan districts with the majority coming from adjoining unions.[23]

---

[21] TNA MH12/7462 Local Government Board and predecessors: Correspondence with Poor Law Unions and Other Local Authorities, City of London Board of Guardians, deposition of Florence Fletcher before Henry Farnall, 10 March 1865.

[22] These figures are taken from the number of persons recorded as having been removed to the district from other districts in 1830 and 1838. See CWAC E/5208 St Margaret and St John Directors of the Poor, Minutes, 1830 and 1838.

[23] LMA SO/BG/27 St George Southwark, Removals from St George's Southwark to various parishes 8 August 1843 to 18 June 1846; LMA BE/BG/271 Bethnal Green Board

Figure 7.2 shows the spatial pattern of removals from Camberwell, Lambeth, Islington and Bethnal Green between 1840 and 1846. With the exception of Bethnal Green, paupers tended to be removed to and from places within five miles of each other. On average 45 per cent of those removed went less than 20 miles and in Lambeth over 78 per cent of removals to other parishes involved distances of less than five miles. Bethnal Green, which was noted as a particularly harsh poor law union, was different in the sense that the guardians there not only removed relatively large numbers of paupers but also sent them much longer distances with over half travelling to places more than 20 miles away. However, this was the exception and removals to and from London parishes tended to take place over much shorter distances. Although the number of removals fell in subsequent years, even in the 1860s the majority of removal orders executed in London were to other districts in the city.[24] For some paupers removal may have been a traumatic experience and could have acted as a deterrent. But the fact that it tended to be used selectively for certain groups of applicants within relatively short distances meant that as an effective means of deterrence and of redistributing the cost of relief, it clearly had its limitations.

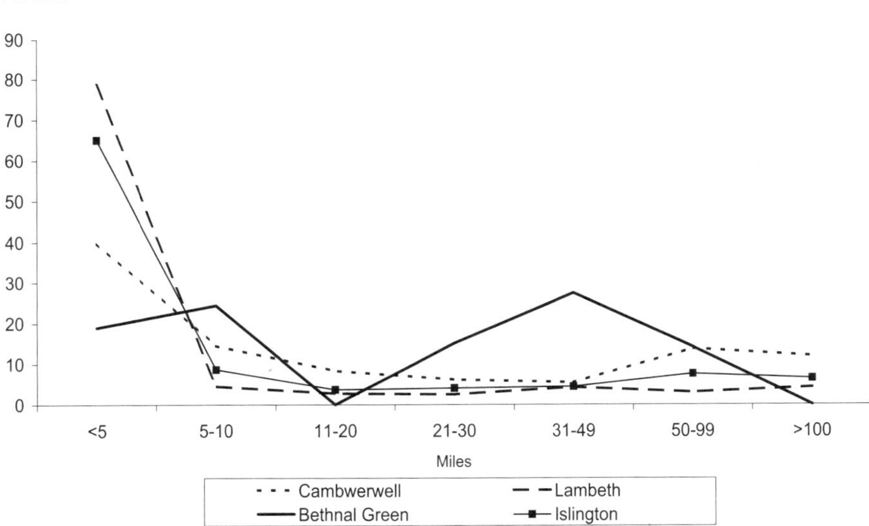

Figure 7.2 Removals from selected London parishes 1843–1846 (% by distance)

Source: 1847 XI Select committee to inquire into the operation of the law of settlement and Poor Removal Act: fourth report, pp. 27–8, 94–5.

of Guardians, notices of orders of removal from sundry parishes to Bethnal Green, 1843–1848. A removal order may have referred to several individuals in a family and therefore the number of persons involved was higher than the total number of orders.

[24] PP 1864 LII Return showing the number of orders for the removal of paupers executed and the number of persons removed ... during the years ended 31 day of December 1861 and the 31 day of December 1863, p. 303.

These short distance removals also help to explain another apparent paradox in London, namely that whilst parishes spent relatively little on removals and the necessary legalities, officials in the early years of the new poor law nevertheless remarked how frequently paupers were removed.[25] In 1847 Richard Hall, then London's assistant poor law commissioner, noted that 'greater attention has been paid in London than in other parts of my district to removing the poor and getting rid of the burden of supporting them'.[26] The explanation for this view lies in the geography of removals noted above, namely that the majority tended to take place between metropolitan unions and were therefore relatively cheap to arrange. Friendly orders and other forms of mutual cooperation between parishes further helped to reduce the costs of removal and in so doing made it more likely that parish officers would resort to this practice as a way of relieving ratepayers of the burden of supporting non-settled paupers, albeit selectively.

Redistribution threatened: irremovability and the 1846 Poor Removal Act

Despite the various problems involved in enforcing removals, in the absence of other means they were the only way that guardians could legally rid themselves of the burden of supporting the non-settled poor. However, in 1846 even this option was withdrawn as a result of the Poor Removal Act which had particularly serious consequences for London.[27] This measure, passed largely as a sop to the landed interest to compensate for any shortfall in profits arising from repeal of the Corn Laws, created a new category of non-settled but irremovable pauper. This new status was conferred on widows within a year of their husband's death and most significantly on those paupers who could prove that they had been resident in a parish for five continuous years. Although the introduction of irremovability did not dispense with removals entirely, since paupers who could not prove continuous residence for five years were still liable to be removed, it nevertheless limited their significance. More importantly in relation to London and other cities, because large numbers of the poor were rural migrants the Act in effect transferred the cost of relief from rural to urban areas.[28]

---

25 Between 1835 and 1837, when figures are available for the cost of removals compared to the total relief expenditure, Middlesex parishes spent on average just over two per cent of their total expenditure on removals compared to 2.9 per cent for the rest of the country.

26 PP 1847 XI Select committee to inquire into the operation of the law of settlement, and Poor Removal Act, fourth report, p. 69; Ibid., sixth report, p. 247.

27 Act to Amend the Laws Relating to the Removal of the Poor (Poor Removal Act), 9 & 10 Vict. c. 66.

28 See Robert Pashley, *Pauperism and the Poor Laws* (London, 1852), p. 275; Michael Rose (ed.), *The Poor and the City: The English Poor Law in Its Urban Context, 1834–1914* (Leicester, 1985), p. 9.

In London, irremovability had an additional impact since it shifted the cost of pauperism from richer districts to poorer ones that contained large amounts of cheap housing. Because much working-class residential mobility in cities was typically short distance, it was relatively easy for the urban poor to remain within the same parish for long periods of time despite changing addresses frequently and in that situation they were able to claim relief without fear of being removed.[29] Once the Act came into force, any district into which large numbers of the poor had moved was therefore liable to have faced an increasing bill for their support.

The implementation of the Poor Removal Act, although initially surrounded by confusion about whether the five year clause applied retrospectively and if it included Scottish and Irish paupers, was accompanied by reductions in removals and a consequent rise in the numbers eligible for poor relief.[30] In the year ending March 1857, for example, 5,333 persons were removed from metropolitan unions but by the 1860s, by which time the period of residence conferring irremovability had been reduced from five to three years, this total had fallen to just over 4,000.[31] With the further reduction of the qualifying period to one year in 1865, removals virtually ceased and settlement became secondary to residence as the grounds for being able to claim relief.

Where trust between parishes was apparent and reciprocal arrangements could be agreed, guardians continued to pay relief to their own non-resident poor living outside the district, though there were some notable exceptions to this policy, such as St James Westminster and Whitechapel.[32] Nevertheless, guardians in several inner districts were faced with an immediate increase in the number of irremovable

---

[29] PP 1859 Session 2 VII Select committee on the irremovable poor, p. 105. See also David R. Green, and Alan Parton, 'Slums and Slum Life in Victorian England: London and Birmingham at Mid-Century', in Martin Gaskell (ed.), *Slums* (Leicester: 1990), pp. 76–82.

[30] TNA MH32/36 Local Government Board and predecessors: Assistant Poor Law Commissioners and Inspectors, Correspondence, Richard Hall, 19 March 1847. See also [Anon], *The Settlement and Removal of the Poor Considered* (London, 1847), pp. 23–5.

[31] PP 1857–58 Part I XLIX Return showing the number of orders of removal from parishes signed by judges and executed in England and Wales during the year ending 25 day of March 1857. See also PP 1864 LII Returns showing the number of orders for the removal of paupers executed and the number of persons removed during the years ended 31 day of December 1861 and the 31 day of December 1863. In the year ending March 1868, 4,320 persons were removed from London unions. See PP 1867–68 LX Return of number of orders of removal from parishes signed by justices and executed in England and Wales, 1867–68, p. 278.

[32] TNA MH12/7916 Local Government Board and predecessors: Correspondence with Poor Law Unions and Other Local Authorities, Whitechapel Board of Guardians, 20 October 1846; LMA ST/BG/SG/003 St George in the East Board of Guardians, Minutes, 9, 30 October, 20 November 1846; CLHC P/GG/PO/1/6 St Giles and St George Directors of the Poor, Minutes, 15 December 1846; PP 1847 XI Select committee to inquire into the operation of the law of settlement, and Poor Removal Act, first report, minutes of evidence,

poor which was further exacerbated by a rush of Irish applicants fleeing the potato famine. In St George Southwark, for example, an estimated 900 additional paupers were relieved as a result of this influx and the operation of the Poor Removal Act.[33] Elsewhere the numbers were even higher. Between 1850 and 1852 the East London and neighbouring Whitechapel unions relieved over 18,600 and 24,200 irremovable paupers respectively, accounting for nearly 20 per cent of expenditure in each district.[34]

Faced with these potentially huge increases, the Poor Law Commissioners took two further steps. First, they framed legislation that transferred the cost of the irremovable poor from the parish to the whole union.[35] Until that time each parish had been responsible for paying for its own poor. Where unions consisted of several parishes, especially when these included both rich and poor districts, this change helped to spread the additional cost to all ratepayers rather than just those in the poorer areas. However, for single parish unions, several of which existed in London, this made no difference to the expense of maintaining the irremovable poor. Second, the Commissioners speedily advised unions that although the initial legislation applied to Irish and Scottish paupers it was not retrospective and therefore the residency requirement would only come into effect five years hence.[36] This ruling removed some of the immediate pressure and allowed guardians to withdraw relief to many non-settled but resident poor. But the reprieve was temporary and the message was clear: once the five year clause came into operation, districts in which the poor resided could expect a huge increase in the burden of relief. Guardians in these unions braced themselves for the deluge.

---

pp. 20–21. Given the proximity of London parishes, the difficulties that distance imposed in arranging non-resident relief were likely to have been relatively minor.

[33] Ibid., pp. 41, 43. See also George Nicholls, *History of the English Poor Law, vol. 2* (London, 1898), pp. 372–4.

[34] PP 1852–53 LXXXIV Returns showing the total number of persons who have become chargeable on any parishes and unions in England and Wales under the operation of the Poor Removal Act of 1846 and of the subsequent acts relating to the enactment for the past three years.

[35] Act to Amend the Laws Relating to the Removal of the Poor, until the First Day of October One thousand eight hundred and forty-eight (Poor Removal Act), 10 & 11 Vict. c. 110. The Act was also known as Bodkin's Act.

[36] Poor Law Commission, Thirteenth Annual Report (1846), p. 9; Sidney Webb and Beatrice Webb, *English Local Government: English Poor Law History, Part 2: The Last Hundred Years* (London, 1929), pp. 423–4.

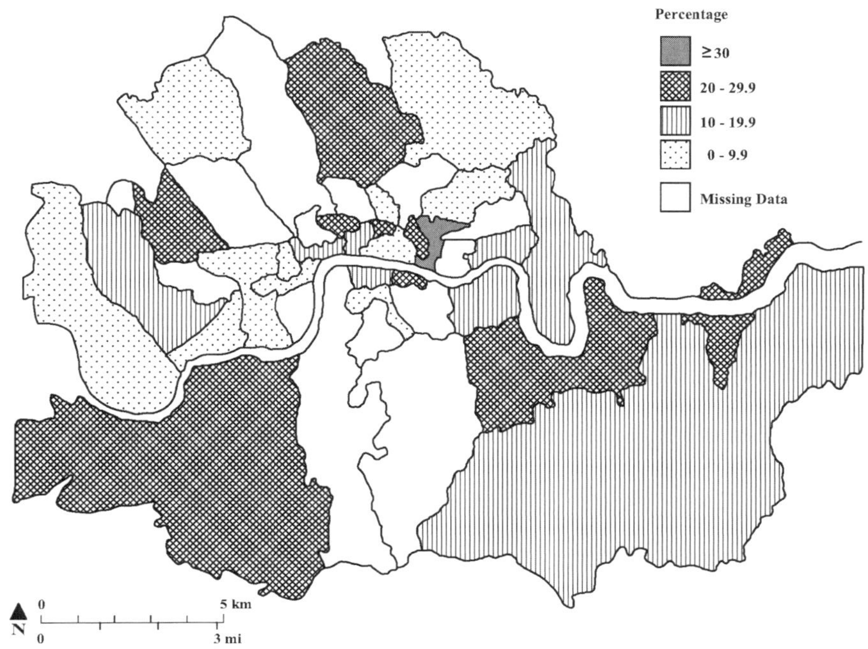

Figure 7.3 Expenditure on relief to the irremovable poor 1850–1852 (% total relief)

Source: PP 1852–3 LXXXIV Returns showing the total number of persons who have become chargeable on any parishes and unions in England and Wales under the operation of the Poor Removal Act of 1846 and of the subsequent acts relating to the enactment for the past three years.

From the early 1850s, as the Poor Removal Act took effect, the delicate balance between relief expenditure and rate income was overturned. In western areas, where working-class housing was in short supply, the proportion of irremovable poor was small and the problems created by irremovability were less important. In central areas, such as the Strand, St Martin in the Fields and the City, all of which were losing population, the irremovable poor also constituted only a small proportion of the total number of paupers and the changes made little difference.[37] Between 1850 and 1858 in the Strand, for example, the irremovable poor constituted no more than about ten per cent of paupers relieved.[38] In the City, John Rowsell, clerk to the guardians, estimated that there were no more than 40 irremovable, non-settled poor in the district compared to between 1,500 and 1,600 paupers with settlements

[37] PP 1859 Session 2 VII Select committee on the irremovable poor, pp. 44, 70, 83.

[38] Ibid., p. 82.

there but resident in adjacent parishes.[39] Thus, the decision of the City guardians to continue to pay for their own non-resident poor was of enormous significance and when the policy changed in the late 1850s it had important repercussions for the surrounding areas.[40]

The situation was different, however, in districts in which the poor lived or into which they had moved as a result of clearances and these areas experienced sudden increases in the number of irremovable paupers and correspondingly sharp rises in expenditure.[41] In eastern districts, notably Whitechapel, Poplar, and in the southern districts of St George Southwark, St Olave and St Saviour, a third or more of the total poor law expenditure from the mid-1850s was committed to relief of the irremovable poor.[42] In the East London union over 43 per cent of the total number of paupers relieved were irremovable under the terms of the Poor Removal Act.[43] A similar situation existed in Bethnal Green where complaints that large numbers of removable poor were being supported at the ratepayers' expense proved unfounded. Although an investigation showed that there were 243 poor in the workhouse without settlements in the union, only 22 were legally removable, the rest having the right to receive relief as a result of the 1846 Act.[44]

Further changes to the residency requirements were made and in 1865 the Union Chargeability Act reduced the period of irremovability to one year's continuous residence in a union, as opposed to a parish.[45] By then, however, relief

---

39 PP 1847 XI Select committee to inquire into the operation of the law of settlement, and Poor Removal Act, first report, p. 20. For the early nineteenth century James Taylor found that non-resident relief was mainly associated with northern industrial districts. See James Taylor, 'A Different Kind of Speenhamland: Nonresident Relief in the Industrial Revolution', *Journal of British Studies*, 30 (1991): 183–208.

40 Ibid.

41 See Thomas Thwaites, *The Poor Laws Unmasked Being a General Exposition of our Workhouse Institutions with Especial Reference to the Law of Settlement and Removal of the Poor* (London, 1859), pp. 26–8.

42 PP 1859 Session 2 VII Select committee on the irremovable poor, pp.76–8, 89, 99–100, 105; PP 1860 XVII Select committee on the irremovable poor, p. 116; W. G. Lumley, 'On the Present State of the Administration of the Relief to the Poor in the Metropolis', *Journal of the Statistical Society*, 21 (1858): 195. Steven King also found that in some Lancashire parishes earlier in the century, out-relief to non-resident poor accounted for between 33 and 39 per cent of relief expenditure. Although not all non-resident poor would have been irremovable under the terms of the Poor Removal Act, these figures give an indication of the likely extent of the problem elsewhere. See King, '"It is Impossible for our Vestry to Judge his Case into Perfection From Here"', p. 167.

43 PP 1859 Session 2 VII Select committee on the irremovable poor, pp. 76, 78.

44 LMA BE/BG/18 Bethnal Green, Board of Guardians, Minutes, 31 November 1855.

45 Act to Provide for the Better Distribution of the Charge for the Relief of the Poor in Unions (Union [Poor Law] Chargeability Act), 28 & 29 Vict. c. 79. At first the cost of providing this additional relief had been borne by individual parishes but the Act to Amend

at the place of residence had become the rule and removals ceased to be of much significance as an effective way of redistributing the costs of poor relief. Guardians found that wherever the poor found accommodation, the outcome was the same: rapidly increasing numbers of paupers with a right to claim relief, higher levels of overcrowding in workhouses and sharply rising expenditure.

Redistributing money: the path to rating reform

The effective cessation of removals focused attention on alternative ways of equalising the burden of poor relief. This took two main forms: union chargeability and rate equalisation – the one leaving intact the holy grail of local self government and the other posing a direct threat to parochial autonomy.

The question of union chargeability had initially been raised in London during the 1840s in relation to the Poor Removal Act.[46] Whilst confirming the parish as the unit of administration insofar as removals were concerned, it was unclear whether the increased burden of relief for the irremovable poor should fall on the parish or union. At first the cost of providing this additional relief had been borne by individual parishes but Bodkin's Act of 1847 shifted the burden to the common fund of the union according to the relative expenditure of each parish, a proposal that had first been made in 1844 by Sir James Graham, the Home Secretary, in conjunction with the initial reform of settlement and removals.[47] Payment of the new union charges, however, was based on average poor law expenditure over the previous three years and therefore fell more heavily on poorer parishes within a union. It was, in effect, a tax on poverty rather than property and as such ratepayers in poorer parishes strongly objected to its operation. But the true significance of

the Laws Relating, to the Removal of the Poor… (Poor Removal Act), 10 & 11 Vict. c. 110, also known as Bodkin's Act, shifted the burden to the common fund of the union according to the relative expenditure of each parish. Poorer parishes with higher expenditure thus paid more for the support of the irremovable poor than their wealthier neighbours with which they were in union. Under the Act to Amend the Laws Regarding the Removal of the Poor and the Contribution of Parishes to the Common Fund in Unions (Poor Removal Act), 24 & 25 Vict. c. 55, the basis on which the cost of supporting the additional numbers of irremovable paupers was levied changed from expenditure to rateable value. This transferred the burden of relief from poorer to wealthier parishes in a union.

46 See, for example, Edmund Head, 'Seventh and Eighth Reports from the Select Committee on Settlement and Poor Removal', *Edinburgh Review* vol. 87 no. 176 (1848): 451–72; G. L. Hutchinson, *A Proposed Plan for the Equalization of the Poor Rates Throughout the United Kingdom* (London, 1846). For a detailed discussion see Maurice Caplan, 'The New Poor Law and the Struggle for Union Chargeability', *International Review of Social History*, 23 (1978): 267–300.

47 Act to Amend the Laws Relating, to the Removal of the Poor, until the First Day of October One thousand eight hundred and forty-eight (Poor Removal Act), 10 & 11 Vict. c. 110.

Bodkin's Act was that it set a precedent for union chargeability more generally and thus represented an important breach in the struggle over the parochial system of rating.[48]

In 1848 Charles Buller, chairman of the newly created Poor Law Board, again suggested shifting the basis for relieving the irremovable poor from expenditure to rateable value. As on previous occasions, when the matter came before Parliament it was opposed by country MPs who feared that it would undermine the system of closed parishes and Buller was forced to withdraw the proposal.[49] For a few years the issue was laid to one side but in 1854 the new President of the Poor Law Board, Matthew Baines, reopened the topic of union chargeability by introducing a bill to abolish removals and establish the union as the area for rating. Some feared that London would fare badly under the proposal since removals still represented one of the only ways metropolitan parishes, especially the poorer ones, could rid themselves of non-settled paupers. Faced with concerted opposition, the bill was dropped.[50]

However, the problem would not disappear and soon re-emerged in the debates about irremovability aired in the select committee set up in 1859 to examine the operation of the Poor Removal Act. Two important changes emerged. First, in 1861the period of irremovability was reduced from five to three years. Second, to protect poorer parishes from again being submerged by a flood of newly irremovable paupers, the cost of their relief was transferred to a charge based on the union using rateable values rather than expenditure as the basis upon which parishes should contribute to a common poor fund. Although the change was irrelevant for single union parishes and the need for full metropolitan equalisation was still pressing, nevertheless the alteration succeeded in establishing the principle of union chargeability and thereby created an important precedent for subsequent and more wide reaching reform.[51]

Despite these changes, the failure of union chargeability to spread the costs of other categories of relief more equitably, and the fact that a third of London unions

---

[48] Caplan, 'The New Poor Law and the Struggle for Union Chargeability', p. 276.

[49] Ibid., pp. 277–8. Closed parishes were those in which one or a small number of landowners could prevent the poor from residing, thereby reducing the cost of poor relief. Provided that expenditure remained the basis for determining the cost of irremovable relief, ratepayers in such parishes faced little or no extra expense. The proposal to alter the basis for determining the cost from expenditure to rateable value would have meant substantially higher expenditure in these parishes.

[50] See [A Metropolitan Poor Law Officer], *Remarks on the Laws of Settlement and Removal* (London, 1854), pp. 17–18; Michael Rose, 'Settlement, Removal and the New Poor Law', in Derek Fraser (ed.) *The New Poor Law in the Nineteenth Century* (London, 1976), p. 30.

[51] On this point see the evidence of John Day, assistant overseer of St George Southwark, in PP 1862 X Select committee to inquire into the laws and administration of relief of the poor under orders, rules and regulations of the Poor Law Commissioners and the Poor Law Board, third report, pp. 536–44.

consisted of single parishes, encouraged further discussion about redistribution which focused on the issue of rate equalisation.[52] For poor, single parish unions the reduction of the period of irremovability merely meant an increased burden of support without the possibility of spreading the cost. Ratepayers in these poorer districts, particularly in eastern areas and inner southern parishes, where what little semblance of a social balance between rich and poor had all but disappeared, argued for rating reform with increasing urgency. A deputation to the Poor Law Board in 1857 led by East End clergy complained that the West End and City parishes were 'elbowing out the poor' who then settled in eastern districts around the docks, noting further that 'as the poor flowed in the rich flowed out'.[53] The inevitable outcome was rapidly rising costs that the remaining hard-pressed ratepayers had difficulty in paying.

Demands for reform coalesced around the newly formed Metropolitan Association for the Abolition of Poor Removals and the Equalization of the Poor Rates, which in 1857, in recognition of the declining importance of removals, changed its name to the Association for Promoting the Equalization of the Poor Rate and Uniformity of Assessments throughout the Metropolitan Districts.[54] Support came primarily from the poorer districts such as Shoreditch, Southwark and Whitechapel, whilst similar associations were formed in Stepney and St George in the East.[55] Meanwhile, opponents of any form of equalisation of the rates or the abolition of removals, notably from wealthier parishes, argued that it would lead inevitably to the destruction of the parish and the centralisation of power. [56] As one MP Mr Brooke, remarked:

---

52 Mary MacKinnon argues that elsewhere in the country union chargeability laid the basis for the subsequent expansion of workhouse capacity that made the crusade against outdoor relief in the 1870s possible. See Mary MacKinnon, 'English Poor Law Policy and the Crusade Against Outdoor Relief', *Journal of Economic History*, 47 (1987): 603–25.

53 *The Times*, 7 May 1857.

54 The earliest reference to the Society for the Equalization of the Poor Rate occurs in a letter to the St George in the East Board of Guardians. See LMA ST/BG/SG/005 St George in the East Board of Guardians, Minutes, 10 February 1854. See also *The Times*, 16 February 1854; Robert E. Warwick, *Observations on the Laws of Settlements, Poor Removals and the Equalization of the Poor Rates*, (London: 1855); William, Gilbert, *Address* (London: Association for Promoting the Equalization of the Poor Rate on an Equal Assessment over the Metropolitan District, 1857b).

55 *The Times*, 23 February 1857; *East London Observer*, 5, 19 December 1857; G. L. Hutchinson, *The Equalization of the Poors' Rate of the United Kingdom of Great Britain and Ireland* (London, 1858); William Gilbert, *Poor Law Reform – Proceedings of the Metropolitan and County Association for the Equalization of the Poor Rate* (London, 1860), p .4.

56 *The Times*, 16 February 1854. See also F. W. Knight, *The Parochial System versus Centralization. Statistics of 'Close and Open Parishes'* (London, 1854), pp. 20–24. Knight had previously been secretary to the Poor Law Board.

> They would commence by union rating, then proceed to district rating, then to metropolitan rating and finally they would arrive at national rating, which would be nothing less than centralization and coercion.[57]

In 1857 a large number of these ratepayers' associations, notably but not exclusively from poorer eastern districts, petitioned Parliament to introduce some form of equalisation.[58] With the recent bread riots in eastern districts fresh in mind, the Reverend George McGill from St George in the East, warned that 'if the richer parishes were allowed to escape, the peace of London would not continue to be safe. The men who went about parading the streets and demanding bread, would not respect parochial bounds.'[59] Such alarmist visions, however, were not shared by Edward Bouverie, President of the Poor Law Board, who argued that policy should not be determined '*ad terrorem*'. More importantly, he was concerned that equalisation could lead to extravagance since it would undermine the principle that local expenditure should always be determined by local ratepayers. Would ratepayers in wealthy West End districts, he asked, agree to guardians elsewhere 'having the privilege of putting their hands in the pockets of the whole metropolis?'[60] Given the concerns about self-serving guardians and lax administration of the poor law in eastern districts, the answer was clearly no! And when a bill to promote rate equalisation in London was introduced in 1858 by A. S. Ayrton, the Radical MP for Tower Hamlets, it had to be withdrawn when it became apparent that it had no support from the Poor Law Board or the government.[61]

The issue, however, did not disappear and spurred by the growing problem of pauperism in the early 1860s, the campaign for rating equalisation gathered strength.[62] Pressure resulted in two important pieces of legislation. The first, the Union Chargeability Act Union of 1865, which made the union rather than the parish the basic unit for all purposes relating to rating and poor law expenditure, was a significant step on the way to wider rate equalisation. By also reducing the period for irremovability to one year, which effectively put an end to removals, it

---

57 *The Times*, 30 April 1857.

58 Petitions in favour of rate equalisation came from Bermondsey, Chelsea, City of London, Fulham, Lambeth, Mile End, St Andrew Holborn, St George in the East, St George Southwark, St Marylebone, Shadwell and West London. Counter petitions were sent by St Ann Westminster, St George Hanover Square, St Giles and St Georges, and St Mary Islington. See *The Times*, 11, 12 May 1857.

59 Ibid., 7 May 1857.

60 Ibid., *Reynolds Newspaper*, 16 May 1858; According to Reverend George MacGill, 70,000 signatures were collected. See George MacGill, *The London Poor and the Inequality of the Rates Raised for Their Relief*, (London, 1858), p. 30.

61 *The Times*, 5, 12 May 1858.

62 Ibid., 26 April 1861, 22 January 1866. *East London Observer*, 27 April 1861. See also J. C. Parkinson, 'On a Uniform Poor Rate for London', *Fortnightly Review*, 4 (1866): 184–92.

was, as Maurice Caplan has argued, 'a milestone on the road to social justice'.[63] However, because of the number of single parish unions in London, it was seen as a necessary but not sufficient step towards the greater goal of metropolitan rate equalisation. Pressure brought other rewards in 1864 when the Metropolitan Board of Works was temporarily given limited powers to reimburse boards of guardians for the cost of building casual wards and in 1865 these arrangements were made permanent by the Metropolitan Houseless Poor Act.[64] It was not the total amount of money involved that was significant, however, but rather the fact that a precedent had been set for the redistribution of funds by a centralised metropolitan authority for certain categories of poor relief. Within a year, all but one union had built or enlarged accommodation for casual paupers.[65] At a meeting of metropolitan guardians in December 1865, amidst claims that measures provided under the Houseless Poor Act had broken down, Henry Farnall, the poor law inspector for London, claimed that 'It was to remedy the injustice of poverty stricken parishes having a burden from which rich parishes were free that the legislature passed the Act.' The audience cheered enthusiastically when he stated that as a result of the changes 'payment for the houseless was spread over the whole of the metropolis instead of some poor parishes being burdened and others getting off'.[66]

The growing crisis of pauperism in the late 1860s also coincided with mounting concern about the poor quality of medical care inside workhouses. By that time London workhouses had primarily become places for the care of the sick and elderly, with nearly 90 per cent of inmates falling into that category. [67] However, poor conditions and woefully inadequate care for the sick and infirm were highlighted in several investigations undertaken by the *Lancet* and coordinated by the Association for the Improvement of London Workhouse Infirmaries. These bodies, together with campaigners such as Florence Nightingale and Louisa Twining, founder of the Workhouse Visiting Association, prompted the Poor Law

---

63 Caplan, 'The New Poor Law and the Struggle for Union Chargeability', p. 300. The Act to Provide for the Better Distribution of the Charge for the Relief of the Poor in Unions (Union [Poor Law] Chargeability Act) 28 & 29 Vict. c. 79 also had important implications for rural unions and the system of open and closed parishes. See Dennis Mills, 'The Poor Laws and the Distribution of Population c 1600–1860, with Special Reference to Lincolnshire', *Transactions of the Institute of British Geographers*, 26 (1959), p. 187.

64 Act to Make Provision for Distributing the Charge of Relief of Certain Classes of Poor Persons over the Whole of the Metropolis (Poor Relief [Metropolis] Act), 27 & 28 Vict. c. 116, and Act to Make the Metropolitan Houseless Poor Act Perpetual (Metropolitan Houseless Poor Act), 28 & 29 Vict. c. 34.

65 *The Times*, 31 December 1864.

66 Ibid., 1 January 1866.

67 Gwendoline Ayers, *England's First State Hospitals and the Metropolitan Asylums Board 1867–1930* (London, 1971), p. 18.

Commissioners to undertake their own enquiries which confirmed the generally deplorable state of treatment in most London workhouses.[68]

However, thoughts of reform were rapidly overtaken by events. In 1866–67 the collapse of the Thames shipbuilding industry and an outbreak of cholera in eastern districts threw thousands onto poor relief. Between 1865 and 1867 the numbers of paupers and cost of relief in London rose by nearly 50 per cent, with eastern districts witnessing the steepest rises.[69] Since the Houseless Poor Act was confined to support of casual paupers only, it did nothing to tackle the structural problem of the poor law in such places. Throughout eastern districts the volume of applications for relief made it impossible to implement either a workhouse or labour test, thereby laying guardians open to the criticism that it was the indiscriminate nature of poor relief that was responsible for encouraging pauperism and not vice versa. This, it was argued, coupled with the flood of charitable donations from the West End bourgeoisie, merely encouraged thriftlessness, facilitated the crafty pauper and demoralised the honest poor.[70] The Poor Law Board remarked that 'The class of ordinary labourers, many of them already half pauperized, and others only just removed above pauperism, soon learn the advantage of living in a district where the alms of the benevolent flow in to eke out the legal provision from the poor rates.'[71]

Without additional expenditure on larger workhouses and continued vigilance to reduce outdoor relief, the Poor Law Commissioners, together with the newly established Charity Organisation Society (COS), could see little prospect of stemming the tide of pauperism.[72] Indeed, both argued that a positive inducement to grant outdoor relief would exist as long as the lack of workhouse

---

[68] See PP 1866 LXI Report of Dr E. Smith on metropolitan workhouse infirmaries and sick wards; PP 1866 LXI Report of H. B. Farnall on infirmary wards of metropolitan workhouses; PP 1867 LXI Report of U. Corbett and W. O. Markham relative to metropolitan workhouses; Poor Law Board, Nineteenth Annual Report (1866–67), 17; 'Commission to Inquire into the State of Workhouse Hospitals', *Lancet*, (15 April, 3 June, 1, 15, 29 July, 12, 26 August, 9, 23 September, 4, 18, 25 November, 23 December 1865, 20, 27 January, 17 February, 3, 10 March, 15 April 1866); Ernest Hart, *An Account of the Condition of the Infirmaries of the London Workhouses*, (London, 1866). See also Driver, *Power and Pauperism*, pp. 69–70; Ruth Hodgkinson, *The Origins of the National Health Service: The Medical Services of the New Poor Law 1834–1871* (London, 1967), pp. 468–99.

[69] See Poor Law Board, Twentieth Annual Report (1867–68), pp. 28–30, 303, 320, 337, 354. For a discussion of the crisis more generally see Michael Rose, 'The Crisis of Poor Relief in England 1860–1890', in W. J. Momsen (ed.), *The Emergence of the Welfare State in Britain and Germany*, (London, 1981), pp. 50–70.

[70] For further discussion of this point see Gareth Stedman Jones, *Outcast London: A Study of the Relationships Between Classes in Victorian Society* (Oxford, 1971), pp. 241–61.

[71] Poor Law Board, Twentieth Annual Report (1867–68), p. 14.

[72] See Local Government Board, Third Annual Report (1873–74), pp. 140–41; see also Driver, *Power and Pauperism*, pp. 53–6, 59–66.

accommodation made it impossible to impose a strict labour test. This, of course, was totally anathema to the new poor law and the Charity Organisation Society alike. However, hard pressed ratepayers in eastern and riverside districts were incapable of supporting any additional expenditure let alone the cost of building new workhouses or enlarging existing ones. In Bethnal Green, for example, rates had risen from 2s 2½d in 1864 to 3s 10½d in 1868, and those in neighbouring Stepney from 2s 5½d to 3s 7d.[73] In these and other surrounding districts, the burden of support was threatening to drag ratepayers themselves towards the unwelcoming embrace of the workhouse. For many the view expressed by the Metropolitan Board of Works in 1865, and reiterated by the Poor Law Board, that 'So heavy is the charge of local taxation become in the less wealthy districts ... that direct taxation of the occupiers of property there had reached its utmost limits', was very close to the truth.[74]

Redistribution achieved: the Metropolitan Poor Act and the impact on poor law policy

The dilemma was how to achieve some form of equalisation without surrendering the principle that local expenditure should be tied to local rates. Union chargeability had to some extent spread the cost of relief across constituent parishes and was a step towards greater collective responsibility amongst ratepayers for the poor within their district. The Houseless Poor Act had also introduced an element of centralised expenditure but had done so in a limited way only in relation to the casual poor. It was clear from experiences in poor eastern and southern districts that the measure had only scratched the surface of the problem. The casual poor were significant in terms of numbers but less so in relation to expenditure. In 1866 the Metropolitan Board of Works contributed £9,268 to the 28 unions which had made provision for the casual poor, a sum that represented only about one per cent of the total poor law expenditure in London.[75] Of far greater importance was how to provide for those groups of paupers that accounted for the bulk of expenditure, notably the sick and indoor poor.[76] Indeed, by that time the dividing line between

---

73 Figures from PP 1867 LX Return from unions and parishes in the metropolitan district of the amount expended for relief to the poor, 1857–66, rateable value and rate in pound, p. 109; PP 1868–69 LIII, Return of rate in pound of rateable value expended for relief of the poor in unions of England and Wales, 1867–68, p. 36.

74 Poor Law Board, Nineteenth Annual Report (1866–67), p. 17.

75 *The Times*, 7 January 1867.

76 For further discussion of this topic see David R. Green, 'Medical Relief and the New Poor Law in London', in Ole P. Grell, Andrew Cunningham and Robert Jütte (eds), *Health Care and Poor Relief in 18th and 19th Century Northern Europe* (Aldershot, 2002), pp. 234–9. In addition see Ruth Hodgkinson, *The Origins of the National Health Service*, pp. 468–99.

the two had become increasingly blurred as the workhouse population consisted increasingly of the frail and the elderly.

It was to extend provision for those groups that the Metropolitan Poor Act was passed in 1867.[77] The bill's passage through Parliament was unremarkable: it was introduced in February by Gathorne Hardy, president of the Poor Law Board and received the royal assent in March. A few MPs dissented on points of detail, a handful on points of principle, but there was no serious opposition to its passage. The reforms had three main objectives. The first was to streamline and improve the administration of relief, specifically by abolishing the remaining local act parishes and bringing them under the direct control of the Poor Law Commissioners. 'It is of the utmost necessity', Gathorne Hardy argued 'that any Board, and above all the Poor Law Board, should have eyes and ears multiplied; so multiplied that day by day and hour by hour it may see and hear what is going on in the workhouses of this metropolis.'[78] In removing the power of local act parishes to obstruct centralised inspection, it was hoped that the Poor Law Board could exercise much closer control over the provision of relief. This desire was further strengthened by allowing the Commissioners to nominate local guardians, though these nominees could never be in the majority. This addressed concerns about lax administration, especially in eastern districts that had experienced middle-class flight. There, boards of guardians controlled by local tradesmen, publicans and shopkeepers were thought to have favoured outdoor relief as a way of ensuring custom at the expense of the ratepayers.[79] Bringing all the local act parishes under the watchful eye of the Poor Law Board and the ability to nominate guardians addressed both these sets of concerns.

However, a more intractable issue was how to reduce overcrowding in London workhouses without which it would have been difficult if not impossible to enforce stricter discipline. According to Uvedale Corbett, the poor law inspector for London,

> … one of the great wants of the Metropolis is the establishment of new or the appropriation of existing Workhouses for the able-bodied classes of groups of Unions, in each of which one sex only should be received, a far more complete system of classification maintained than has hitherto been attempted, at least in Metropolitan Workhouses, and strict discipline enforced under proper regulations and superintendence.[80]

---

77 Act for the Establishment in the Metropolis of Asylums for the Sick, Insane, and other Classes of Poor, and of Dispensaries; and for the Distribution over the Metropolis of Portions of the Charge for Poor Relief; and for Other Purposes relating to the Poor Relief in the Metropolis (Metropolitan Poor Act), 30 & 31 Vict. c. 6.

78 *Hansard Parliamentary Debates*, 21 February 1867, p. 773.

79 See *The Times*, 7 May 1857. See also E. W. Holland, 'The Poor Laws and the Metropolitan Poor Law Administration', *Contemporary Review*, 8 (1868): 511–13.

80 Poor Law Board, Twentieth Annual Report (1867–68), p. 126.

Without this extra provision, he argued, guardians had little choice but to offer outdoor relief with the inevitable result that 'crafty' paupers would take advantage of the lack of investigation to get extra help. Meanwhile, the honest poor would themselves become demoralised and seek charitable handouts or poor relief rather than rely on their own efforts. However, in the context of perceived or real overcrowding in London workhouses during the 1860s, restricting outdoor relief to the deserving poor and forcing them instead to enter the workhouse was difficult to justify. But once provision had improved in both quantity and quality, such objections no longer held and the workhouse could then be used as a true test for destitution.

The second objective was therefore to create extra space in workhouses to accommodate different categories of paupers and in doing so to allow the enforcement of stricter indoor policies. To achieve this, and to address criticisms about inadequate medical care, new provision was to be made for sick paupers in specially constructed metropolitan asylums which in anything other than name were poor law hospitals. This in turn freed space in existing workhouses that would then enable officials to separate different categories of pauper and enforce stricter discipline. In this way the workhouse could then be used to perform its intended function as a place of deterrence for the able-bodied poor.

The Metropolitan Poor Act made possible the construction of new workhouse infirmaries and separate poor law hospitals.[81] By 1877 only six unions still treated the sick within mixed workhouses, the remainder having already designed or constructed separate infirmaries, and by 1881 these new facilities contained space for some 10,000 sick poor.[82] More significantly, it allowed for the construction of separate asylums for the treatment of infectious diseases, primarily smallpox and fever. The city was divided into separate asylum districts and by 1877 five new hospitals had been built at Fulham, Hampstead and Homerton to the north and Stockwell and Deptford in the south. The main emphasis in the treatment of infectious disease, particularly smallpox, had already swung away from vaccination towards isolation and therefore the new hospitals were built in peripheral locations, leaving workhouse infirmaries and sick wards in more central areas to deal with the chronically sick poor.

A new body called the Metropolitan Asylums Board was established to manage the poor law asylums. Fears that placing relief expenditure under the Board would remove local control and thereby become a bottomless pit strongly

---

81 See Poor Law Board, Twenty First Annual Report (1868–69), pp. 15–18; Hodgkinson, *Origins of the National Health Service*, p. 505. National expenditure on sick wards was disproportionately concentrated in London from the 1860s. See Driver, *Power and Pauperism*, pp. 88–90.

82 Charles Trevelyan, *Metropolitan Medical Relief* (London, 1879), p.105; Frederic Mouat, 'On Hospitals – Their Management, Construction and Arrangements', *Lancet*, (16 July 1881), p. 80.

influenced the nature of reform and ensured that members were drawn largely from poor law unions with only a minority from the Poor Law Board and its successor, the Local Government Board. These checks and balances in turn limited the extent to which centralised control over finance could supersede the wishes of local ratepayers.[83]

Whilst the Metropolitan Poor Act marked a decisive shift in terms of medical provision for the sick poor, separation of such relief from the stigma of pauperism was not achieved immediately. Indeed, the very fact that the new institutions were designated 'asylums' rather than 'hospitals' emphasised that receipt of medical relief under the poor law still constituted pauperism. This was in keeping with the prevailing ideology of the COS which opposed any attempts to extend the operation of the poor laws or to remove the stigma of pauperism from the receipt of relief.[84] Supporters opposed any attempts to sever the link between medical relief and the deterrent aspect of the poor law on the grounds that free medical aid to those who could afford it was the route to dependence, 'for which', noted Sir Charles Trevelyan, a prominent member of the COS, 'our London population is unhappily distinguished beyond the rest of their countrymen'.[85] It was only in 1883 that the Diseases Prevention (Metropolis) Act removed civil disabilities from patients admitted to Metropolitan Asylum Board hospitals, thereby finally ridding receipt of medical relief in such institutions from the stigma of pauperism.[86]

The last and perhaps most significant aspect of the legislation was to establish a mechanism by which to redistribute rateable income from wealthy to poorer unions in order to allow the construction of new workhouses, infirmaries and poor law asylums and to support certain types of relief. To do this the Poor Law Commissioners were given powers to assess the contributions of each union based on their rateable value and to redistribute funds for expenditure on categories of paupers permitted under the Act. Contributions to the common fund were levied on a 1d rate based on rateable value rather than expenditure and as such reflected differences in the relative wealth of districts. However, the fact that income from the common fund could only be used for certain

---

83 Pauline Ashbridge, 'Paying for the Poor: A Middle Class Metropolitan Movement for Rate Equalisation 1857–1867', *London Journal*, 22 (1997): 118.

84 For a discussion of the role of the Charity Organisation Society in London see Jones, *Outcast London*, pp. 256–80. See also Robert Humphreys, *Sin, Organized Charity and the Poor Law in Victorian England* (London, 1995). The Charity Organisation Society also opposed on similar grounds the provision of free poor law dispensaries under the terms of the Metropolitan Poor Act. By 1877 there were at least 57 operating in London. See Trevelyan, *Metropolitan Medical Relief*, pp. 3–5, 16.

85 Ibid., p. 3.

86 Act to Make Better Provision as Regards the Metropolis for the Isolation and Treatment of Persons Suffering from Cholera and other Infectious Diseases; and for Other Purposes (Diseases Prevention [Metropolis] Act), 46 & 47 Vict. c. 35.

categories of expenditure limited the extent to which redistribution could take place. Initially, the cost of maintaining lunatics, pauper children and the casual poor, in addition to the salaries of poor law officials and various forms of medical expenditure, were transferred to the Metropolitan Common Poor Fund (MCPF). In 1870, however, an additional subsidy equivalent to 5d per day was provided for the cost of each adult indoor pauper. By contrast, outdoor relief remained without subsidy, on the grounds that guardians who chose to provide that kind of relief should not expect ratepayers outside their own locality to foot the bill. In this way, and in keeping with the Local Government Board's crusade against outdoor relief in the 1870s, the Poor Law Commissioners sought to rein in what they considered to be extravagant expenditure arising from lax administration.

The net result of the MCPF was an immediate transfer of funds from wealthy districts to poorer eastern and riverside unions which in turn allowed districts to construct new workhouses or expand existing ones. As Figure 7.4 shows, in the first ten years of operation, the four districts that received most from the MCPF were Shoreditch, Whitechapel, St George in the East and Bethnal Green. Over the same period some 25 per cent of poor relief expenditure in St George in the East and 33 per cent in Bethnal Green came from the MCPF. By contrast, wealthier districts were net contributors, the largest of which, as befitted their financial status, were the City of London and St George Hanover Square. Between 1870 and 1890 contributions from these two districts alone amounted to nearly £2 million and accounted for nearly five per cent of the total expenditure on poor relief in the city as a whole. This flow of money significantly reduced the rate burden in poorer districts. Figure 7.5 shows that in Bethnal Green and St George in the East, for example, had it not been for the contributions of the MCPF, rates would have been between 1s and 1s 6d higher in order to cover expenditure. By contrast, in richer areas, such as the City of London and St George Hanover Square, rates would have fallen had it not been for the need to contribute to the MCPF. Over and above the new building that occurred as a result of the Act, its overall effect was therefore to reduce disparities in rates between poor law unions across the city.

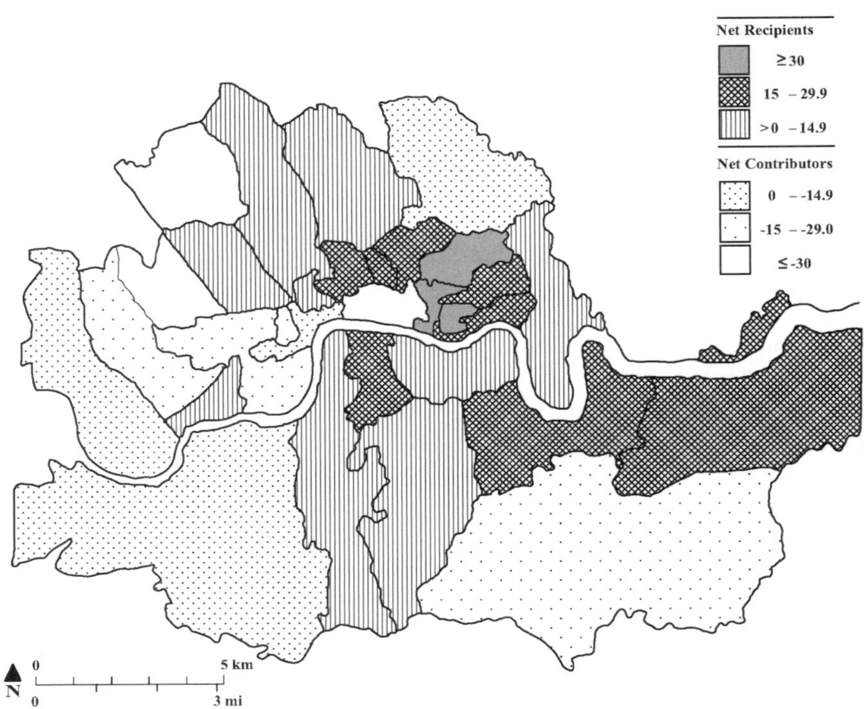

Figure 7.4 Metropolitan Common Poor Fund receipts and contributions 1868–1879 (% total relief)

Note: The percentage refers to the relative amounts contributed to or received from the Metropolitan Common Poor Fund as a percentage of the total expenditure on poor relief in each district.

Source: Poor Law Board, Twenty-third Annual Report 1869–70, Local Government Board, Annual Reports, 1871–91.

Bethnal Green
d in £
90
80
70
60
50
40
30
20
10
0
1870 1871 1872 1873 1874 1875 1876 1877 1878 1879 1880 1881 1882 1883 1884 1885 1886 1887 1888 1889 1890
With MCPF
Without MCPF

St George in the East
d in £
90
80
70
60
50
40
30
20
10
0
1870 1871 1872 1873 1874 1875 1876 1877 1878 1879 1880 1881 1882 1883 1884 1885 1886 1887 1888 1889 1890
With MCPF
Without MCPF

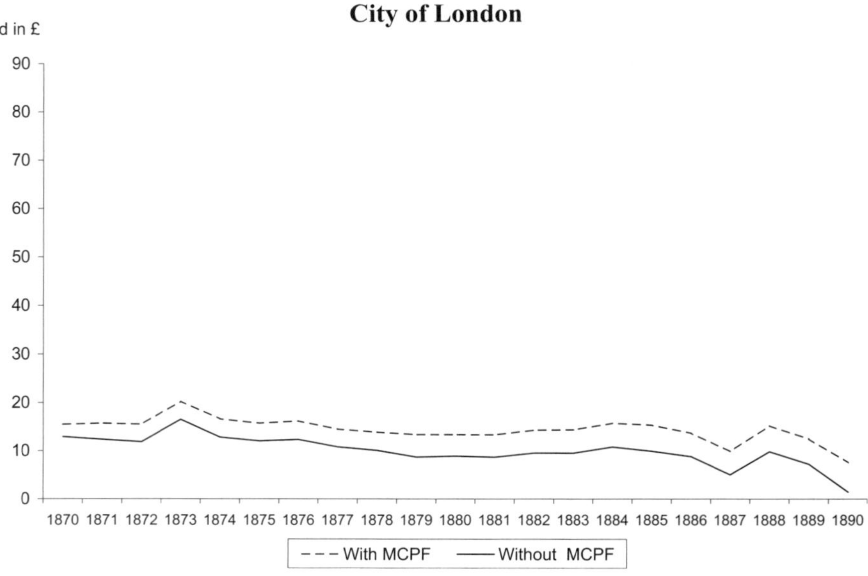

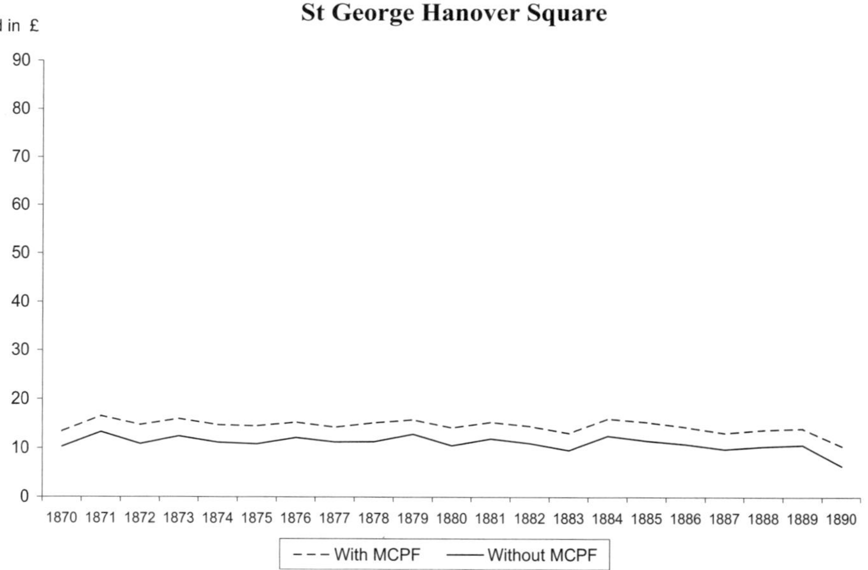

Figure 7.5 Poor Rates in the £ in Bethnal Green, St George in the East, City of London and St George Hanover Square 1870–1890

Source: Poor Law Board, Twenty-third Annual Report 1869–70, Local Government Board, Annual Reports, 1871–91.

The extent of rate equalisation over the city as a whole can be gauged by considering how rates would have differed with and without the MCPF and the coefficient of variation shown in Figure 7.6 is an attempt to assess that impact.[87] This figure is based on the amount of rates that would have had to be raised in each district to pay for poor relief with and without contributions to the MCPF. The higher the coefficient of variation, the greater the disparity in rates between districts. Without contributions from the MCPF rates in poor districts would have had to have risen considerably to pay for relief, whilst in wealthier districts they would have fallen. This situation would have resulted in much wider disparities between districts as measured by the upper line in the graph. However, as the lower line demonstrates, contributions to the MCPF evened out these differences and therefore disparities in rating levels between districts were reduced.

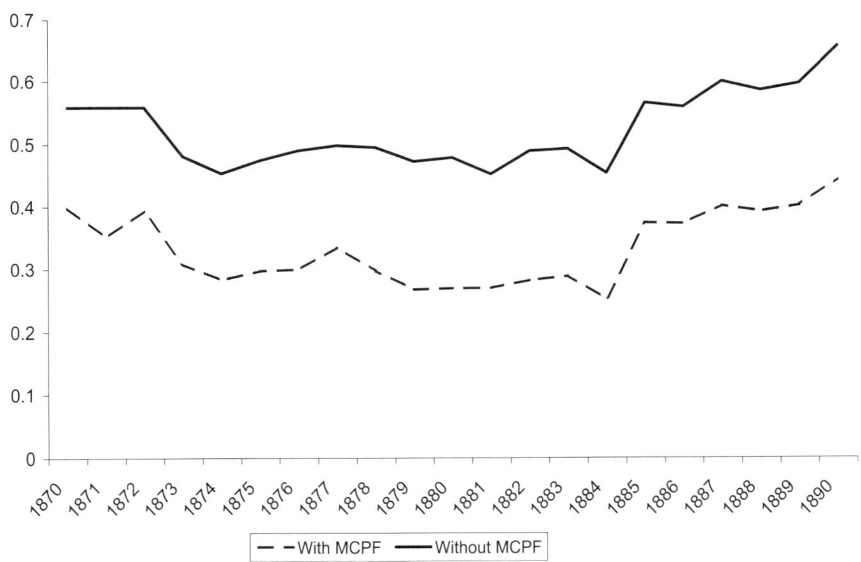

Figure 7.6 Poor Rates, coefficient of variation 1870–1890

Source: Poor Law Board, Twenty-third Annual Report, 1869–70, Local Government Board, Annual Reports, 1871–91.

87 The coefficient of variation is the standard deviation divided by the mean ($V=\sigma/x$) and is a measure of dispersion. The higher the figure, the greater the dispersion around the mean. For each district the amount of money needed to pay for poor relief without contributions from the MCPF was assessed. Then, taking into account the rateable value of property in each district, the rate in the £ needed to obtain this amount was calculated. The mean rate and standard deviation for each year was then established and the coefficient of variation calculated accordingly. The lower line measures the coefficient of variation taking into account contributions from the MCPF. Figures on the rate in the £ exist separately.

These changing financial arrangements allowed poorer districts to expand the institutional provision for different categories of paupers paid for by a metropolitan rate. In so doing, they were able to impose much stricter conditions on the receipt of relief, forcing paupers to enter the workhouse rather than be offered outdoor assistance. Indeed, the instructions issued by George Goschen, President of the Poor Law Board, in 1869 to impose strict conditions under which outdoor relief should be provided, would have been difficult to achieve had new building not taken place.[88] In expanding the number of places within workhouses and in allowing them to function as a test of destitution, the reforms had a dramatic impact on pauperism. Figure 7.7 shows that from 1871 onwards, as the crusade against outrelief gained momentum, the number of outdoor paupers fell and by the end of the decade had been surpassed by the indoor poor. East London unions, which in the absence of rating reform had no capacity to expand provision and which were the main beneficiaries of the changes, embraced this policy with greatest enthusiasm.[89] But outdoor pauperism fell throughout the city and by the 1890s London paupers were more than twice as likely as those elsewhere to be relieved in workhouses.[90] In that respect, similarities existed with the pattern of provision that had existed earlier in the century.

---

88 The crusade against outdoor relief is discussed in Elizabeth T. Hurren, *Protesting About Pauperism: Poverty, Politics and Poor Relief in Late-Victorian England, 1870–1900* (Woodbridge, 2007) pp. 23–4, 45–52; Mackinnon, 'English Poor Law Policy' and Rose, 'The Crisis of Poor Relief'.

89 See Pat Ryan, 'Politics and Relief: East London Unions in the Late Nineteenth and Early Twentieth Centuries', in Michael Rose (ed.), *The Poor and the City: The English Poor Law in its Urban Context* (Leicester, 1985), pp. 133–72.

90 In 1891–92, 83 per cent of London paupers were relieved in workhouses compared to 34 per cent in the rest of England. See George Boyer and Timothy P. Schmidle, 'Poverty Amongst the Elderly in Victorian England', *Economic History Review*, 61 (2008): 14.

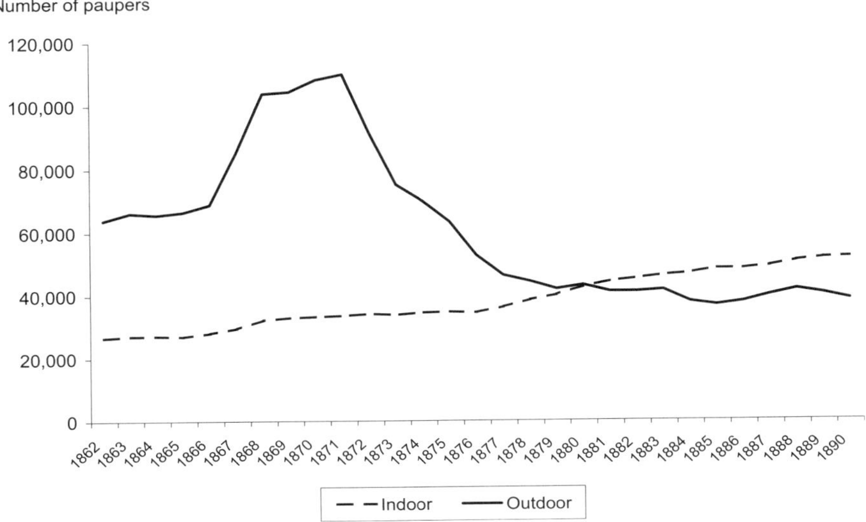

Figure 7.7 Average number of indoor and outdoor paupers relieved in London (excluding vagrants and lunatics) 1862–1890

Source: Local Government Board, Twenty Fifth Annual Report 1895–96, table 1–4, p. 416.

Conclusion

The crisis of relief in the 1860s heralded a major shift in poor law policy at both national and local levels.[91] At a national level, the dissolution of the Poor Law Board in 1871 and its incorporation into a much more powerful department of state, the Local Government Board, placed responsibility for poor relief on a new and politically more secure footing. Across the country as a whole this was accompanied by the restriction of outdoor relief, a process which was made financially possible by expanding the area of union chargeability and politically acceptable because of improved economic conditions that reduced the overall need for such relief.

In London it was the Metropolitan Poor Act which had the most profound impact on poor law policy. It helped to finance a wave of workhouse and hospital construction that took place from the 1870s onwards. It witnessed the incorporation of all remaining local act parishes under the Poor Law Amendment Act and the creation of an entirely new framework with which to redistribute the cost of relief

91 See Rose, 'The Crisis of Poor Relief in England 1860–1890', and Hurren, *Protesting About Pauperism*, passim.

across the metropolis as a whole. Spreading the cost of relief also encouraged ratepayers throughout the city to take a keener interest in poor law policy. Not least, the impact of these reforms was felt through ratepayers' pockets. Redistribution of the burden of relief also took note of the fact that the city as a whole was the appropriate scale for funding the poor law. Tentative steps had been taken in various ways – by the formation of district schools in the 1840s, the halting introduction of union chargeability and the operation of the Houseless Poor Act of 1865 – but it was not until the Metropolitan Poor Act in 1867 that the administrative machinery was finally put into place to achieve this end. Looking across the threshold of the 1870s was therefore to peer into a different administrative landscape in which collective metropolitan ratepayer responsibility became an accepted part of poor law policy. In this process of change London led the way and in that respect, as well as in others, it deserves to be called the pauper capital.

Appendix

London census registration districts

London did not appear as a separate division in the census prior to 1841. Until that date, information was provided for individual metropolitan parishes in the separate county totals for Kent, Middlesex and Surrey. In 1841 vital statistics were provided for metropolitan districts separately and in 1851 London became a separate census division in its own right. The 36 registration districts that comprised the London division in that year included those listed below which are shown on the accompanying map. This set of districts is that which is used to denote London throughout this book. For comparative purposes in Chapter 6, the separate registration districts have been amalgamated into seven broad groups.

West: Chelsea, Kensington, St George Hanover Square, St James Westminster, St John and St Margaret, St Martin in the Fields.
North: Hackney, Hampstead, Islington, St Marylebone, St Pancras.
Central: Clerkenwell, Holborn, St Giles, St Luke's, Strand.
City: City of London, East London, West London.
East: Bethnal Green, Poplar, Shoreditch, Stepney, St George in the East, Whitechapel.
Inner South: Bermondsey, Newington, Rotherhithe, St George Southwark, St Olave Southwark, St Saviour Southwark.
Outer South: Camberwell, Greenwich, Lambeth, Lewisham, Wandsworth.

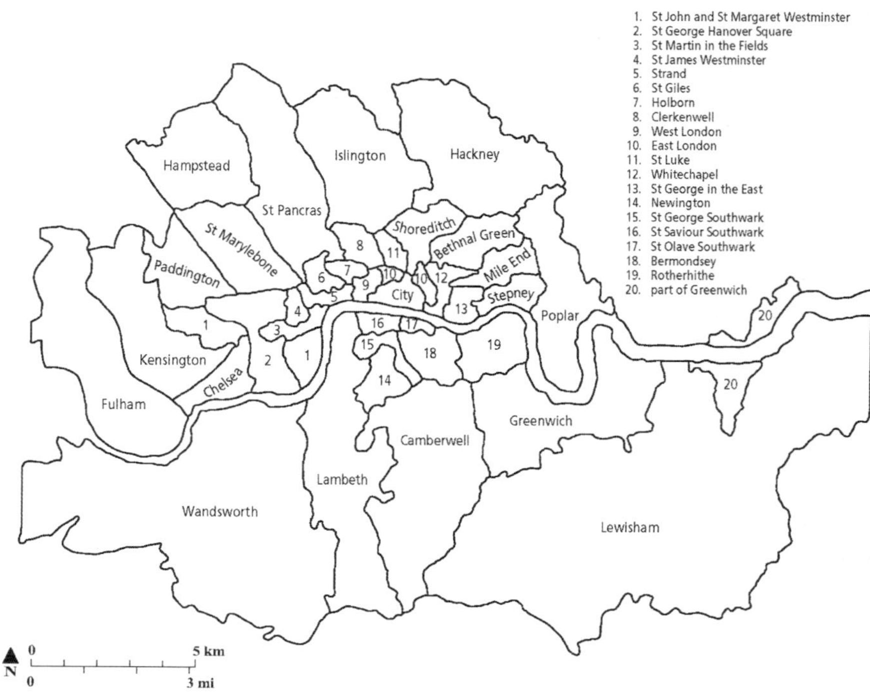

Figure 1 London Census Registration Districts

Bibliography

Manuscript Sources

Acts of Parliament

Act for Amending the Laws Relating to the Settlement, Employment, and Relief of the Poor (Knatchbull's Act), 9 Geo. I c. 7.

Act for the Amendment and Better Administration of the Laws Relating to the Poor in England and Wales (Poor Law Amendment Act), 4 & 5 Will. IV c. 76.

Act for the Better Protection of Parish Poor Children (Hanway's Act), 7 Geo. III c. 39.

Act for the Better Regulation of Vestries and for the Appointment of Auditors of Accounts in Certain Parishes of England and Wales (Vestries Act), 1 & 2 Will. IV c. 60.

Act for the Better Relief and Employment of the Poor (Gilbert's Act), 22 Geo. III c. 83.

Act for the Establishment in the Metropolis of Asylums for the Sick, Insane, and other Classes of Poor, and of Dispensaries; and for the Distribution over the Metropolis of Portions of the Charge for Poor Relief; and for Other Purposes relating to the Poor Relief in the Metropolis (Metropolitan Poor Act), 30 & 31 Vict. c. 6.

Act for the Further Amendment of the Laws Relating to the Poor in England and Wales (Poor Law Amendment Act), 7 & 8 Vict. c. 101.

Act for the Keeping Regular, Uniform and Annual Registers of all Parish Poor Infants under a certain Age, Within the Bills of Mortality, 2 Geo. III c. 22.

Act for the More Effectually Preventing Seditious Meetings and Assemblies (Seditious Meetings Act), 38 Geo. III c. 8.

Act for the Regulation of Parish Vestries (Parish Vestries Act), 58 Geo. III c. 69.

Act to Amend the Law for the Relief of the Poor (Select Vestry Act), 59 Geo. III c. 12.

Act to Amend the Laws Regarding the Removal of the Poor and the Contribution of Parishes to the Common Fund in Unions (Poor Removal Act), 24 & 25 Vict. c. 55.

Act to Amend the Laws Relating to the Removal of the Poor (Poor Removal Act), 9 & 10 Vict. c. 66.

Act to Amend the Laws Relating to the Removal of the Poor, until the First Day of October One thousand eight hundred and forty-eight (Poor Removal Act), 10 & 11 Vict. c. 110.

Act to Authorize the Issue of Exchequer Bills, and the Advance of Money out of the Consolidated Fund, to a Limited Amount, for the Carrying on of Public Works and Fisheries in the United Kingdom, and Employment of the Poor in Great Britain, in Manner Therein Mentioned (Poor Employment Act), 58 Geo. III c. 34.

Act to Continue until the Thirty-first Day of July One thousand eight hundred and forty-seven, and to the End of the then next Session of Parliament, the Poor Law Commission; and for the further Amendment of the Laws relating to the Poor in England (Poor Law Continuation Act), 5 & 6 Vict. c. 57.

Act to Make Better Provision as Regards the Metropolis for the Isolation and Treatment of Persons Suffering from Cholera and other Infectious Diseases; and for Other Purposes (Diseases Prevention [Metropolis] Act), 46 & 47 Vict. c. 35.

Act to Make Provision for Distributing the Charge of Relief of Certain Classes of Poor Persons over the Whole of the Metropolis (Poor Relief [Metropolis] Act), 27 & 28 Vict. c. 116.

Act to Make the Metropolitan Houseless Poor Act Perpetual (Metropolitan Houseless Poor Act), 28 & 29 Vict. c. 34.

Act to Provide for the Better Distribution of the Charge for the Relief of the Poor in Unions (Union [Poor Law] Chargeability Act), 28 & 29 Vict. c. 79.

Act to Regulate the Binding of Parish Apprentices (Parish Apprentices Act) 56 Geo. III c. 139.

Parliamentary Papers: House of Commons

1803–04 XIII Abstract of the answers and returns made pursuant to Act 43 Geo. 3, relative to the expense and maintenance of the poor in England.

1807 II Select committee on the state of criminal and pauper lunatics in England and Wales.

1814–15 III Select committee on the state of mendicity in the metropolis.

1816 V Select committee on the state of mendicity in the metropolis.

1817 VI Select committee to consider the poor laws.

1818 V Select committee to consider the poor laws.

1818 XIX Abstract of the answers and returns made pursuant to an act intituled 'An act for procuring returns relative to the expense and maintenance of the poor in England'.

1821 IV Select committee on existing laws relating to vagrants.

1828 IV Select committee on that part of the poor laws relating to the employment or relief of able bodied persons from the poor rate.

1830 IV Select committee appointed to inquire into the general operation and effect of the laws and usages under which select and other vestries are constituted.

1830 XXX Report from the Metropolitan Commissioners in Lunacy to the Secretary of State for the Home Department, 1829.

1830–31 XI An account of the money expended for the maintenance and relief of the poor ... for the five years ending 25th March 1825, 1826, 1827, 1828 and 1829.

1830–31 XIV Return of the number of public and private asylums and houses licensed for the reception of lunatics in each county in England and Wales.

1833 XVI Select committee on the removal of Irish vagrants to Ireland.

1834 XXVII Royal commission on the administration and practical operation of the poor laws, report.

1834 XXVIII Royal commission on the administration and practical operation of the poor laws, Appendix A, assistant commissioners' reports.

1834 XXIX Royal commission on the administration and practical operation of the poor laws, Appendix A, assistant commissioners' reports.

1834 XXXV Royal commission on the administration and practical operation of the poor laws, answers to town queries.

1834 XXXVI Royal commission on the administration and practical operation of the poor laws, answers to town queries.

1835 XLVII An account of the money expended for the maintenance and relief of the poor ... for the five years ending 25th March 1830, 1831, 1832, 1833 and 1834.

1837–38 XV Select committee on metropolis police offices.

1839 XLIV A return of the amount expended for the relief of the poor in each county of England and Wales during the year ended 25th March.

1841 Session 2 VI Metropolitan Commissioners in Lunacy, Annual Reports, 1835–41, to the Lord Chancellor.

1843 XLV Return of the number, names, and ages of all persons committed to any prison in England and Wales for any offence in a union workhouse.

1844 IX Select committee on medical poor relief.

1844 X Select committee on poor relief (Gilbert Unions).

1844 XXVI Metropolitan Commissioners in Lunacy, report to the Lord Chancellor.

1846 VII Select committee on establishment of district asylums for houseless poor in the metropolis.

1847 XI Select committee to inquire into the operation of the law of settlement, and Poor Removal Act.

1847 XLIX Workhouse schools: copies of extracts of all reports made by the assistant commissioners on the subject of workhouse schools since the 1st day of January 1846.

1847–48 XXXII Commissioners in Lunacy: further report to the Lord Chancellor, 1847.

1847–48 LIII Reports and communications on vagrancy.

1851 XXVI Report of George Coode to the Poor Law Board, on the law of settlement and removal of the poor.

1852–53 XXVIII Return of the number of houses rated to the house tax.

1852–53 LXXXIV Number of inmates of workhouses who were committed to prison during the year 1852 for offences committed while they were inmates.

1852–53 LXXXIV Returns showing the total number of persons who have become chargeable on any parishes and unions in England and Wales under the operation of the Poor Removal Act of 1846 and of the subsequent acts relating to the enactment for the past three years.

1854 XII Select committee to inquire into the mode in which medical relief is now administered in the different unions in England and Wales.

1854 XVII Select committee on poor removal.

1854 LV Poor Law (orders of removal). Returns showing the number of orders of removal from parishes, signed by justices, and executed in England and Wales, during the year ending 25 March 1853.

1854 LV Poor removal. Return showing the number of orders of removal from parishes, signed by justices and executed in England and Wales, during the year ending 25th day of March 1854.

1857–58 XLV Reports by Her Majesty's Inspectors of Schools on workhouse schools, 1857–58.

1857–58 Part I XLIX Grounds of settlement for persons removed from London in the year ending 25 day of March 1857.

1857–58 Part I XLIX Return showing the number of orders of removal from parishes signed by judges and executed in England and Wales during the year ending 25 day of March 1857.

1857–58 Part I LXIX Return of district schools established under orders of Poor Law Board, relating to cost, number of paid officers and expenditure, 1856–57.

1857–58 Part 1 LXIX Return of the average number of inmates in district union schools in England and Wales.

1859 Session 2 XIV Commissioners in Lunacy: thirteenth annual report to the Lord Chancellor, Appendix E, abstract of annual returns of pauper lunatics and idiots.

1859 Session 2 VII Select committee on the irremovable poor.

1860 XVII Select committee on the irremovable poor.

1861 IX Select committee to inquire into the laws and administration of relief of the poor under orders, rules and regulations of the Poor Law Commissioners and Poor Law Board.

1862 X Select committee to inquire into the laws and administration of relief of the poor under orders, rules and regulations of the Poor Law Commissioners and the Poor Law Board, third report.

1864 LII Return showing the number of orders for the removal of paupers executed and the number of persons removed during the years ended 31 day of December 1861 and the 31 day of December 1863.

1865 XLVIII Orders of removal. Return showing the number of orders of removal from parishes, signed by justices and executed in England and Wales, during the year ending the 25th day of March 1863.

1866 XXXIII Eighth report of the Medical Officer to the Privy Council.
1866 LXI Report by Dr Edward Smith, Poor Law Inspector and Medical Officer to the Poor Law Board, on the metropolitan workhouse infirmaries and sick wards.
1866 LXI Statement showing as respects workhouses authorised by orders of the Poor Law Board to be built in the metropolitan district.
1867 LX Return from unions and parishes in the metropolitan district of the amount expended for relief to the poor, 1857–66.
1867–68 LX Orders of Removal. Return showing the number of orders of removal from unions and parishes, signed by justices and executed in England and Wales, during the year ending 25th March 1868.
1868–69 LIII Return of rate in pound of rateable value expended for relief of the poor in unions of England and Wales, 1867–68.
1870 XXXIV Commissioners in Lunacy, twenty-fourth annual report to the Lord Chancellor.
1875 LXII Return of the number of persons (inmates and casuals) committed to prison from each union workhouse (England and Wales) for the half year ending on 25 day of March 1874.

Parliamentary Papers: House of Lords

Abstract of returns made pursuant to an act passed in the 16th year of the reign of his majesty King George the Third by the overseers of the poor within the several parishes, townships and places within England and Wales, 1776.

The National Archives

Home Office: Various Commissions: Records and Correspondence

HO/73/51–52 Home Office: Various Commissions: Records and Correspondence, Letters and Papers.
HO/73/51/38, ff. 280–83, Copy of reply from Poor Law Commissioners for Lord John Russell to resolutions passed by inhabitants of St Nicholas Deptford, maintaining that the union with St Paul Deptford, Greenwich and Woolwich stands, 17 November 1836.
HO 73/52/24, ff. 174–75, Letter from clerk to the guardians of Greenwich union to Poor Law Commission explaining problems with parishes of Woolwich and St Paul Deptford; concerns about case pending in King's Bench to declare union invalid, 13 May 1837.

Records created or inherited by the Ministry of Housing and Local Government, and of successor and related bodies, Poor Law Commission and successors

HLG 26/1 Legal Department and successors: Orders, Central London, South Metropolitan and North Surrey School Districts.

HLG 26/3 Legal Department and successors: Orders, Kensington, Lincolnshire and Nottinghamshire, West London, Finsbury, Forest Gate, Walsall and West Bromwich, Kensington and Chelsea, Brentwood, Central London, South Metropolitan, and North Surrey, Farnham and Hartley Wintney, S.E. Shropshire, Reading and Wokingham School Districts.

Records of the Poor Law Commissioners

MH1 Poor Law Commission, Minute Books, 1834–42.

MH3 Appendices to minutes of the Poor Law Commission.

MH10 Instructions to Assistant Poor Law Commissioners.

MH12 Local Government Board and predecessors: Correspondence with Poor Law Unions and Other Local Authorities.

MH12/5091–5097 Greenwich Board of Guardians, 1834–52.

MH12/6845–6851 Bethnal Green Board of Guardians, 1847–64.

MH12/7103–7107 St George in the East Board of Guardians, 1846–69.

MH12/7127–7130 St George Hanover Square Overseers of the Poor, 1834–69.

MH12/7286–7288 Holborn Board of Guardians, 1838–48.

MH12/7460–7462 City of London Board of Guardians, 1840–65.

MH12/7798–7800 Stepney Board of Guardians, 1834–40.

MH12/7834–7836 Strand Board of Guardians, 1834–42.

MH12/7915–7920 Whitechapel Board of Guardians, 1843–56.

MH12/12300–12312 St George the Martyr Southwark Overseers of the Poor, 1834–52.

MH17/32 Poor Law Commission and successors: Correspondence with Asylum Districts and Boards, Metropolitan Asylum District, 1845–61.

MH32 Local Government Board and predecessors: Assistant Poor Law Commissioners and Inspectors, Correspondence.

MH32/24 Henry Farnall, 1857–71.

MH32/36–37 Richard Hall, 1843–55.

MH32/49–50 James Kay, 1837–39.

MH32/56–57 Charles Mott, 1834–38.

Poor Law Commission

Annual Reports

Poor Law Commission, Annual Reports, 1834–47.
Poor Law Board, Annual Reports, 1848–70.
Local Government Board, Annual Reports, 1871–95.

Official Circulars

Official circular of public documents and information, 1840–51.

British Museum, Additional Manuscripts

Pelham Papers

Additional Manuscript MS 33111, Martin, Matthew, *Report on Mendicity in London* (1803).

Local Archives

London Metropolitan Archives

Bethnal Green

Board of Guardians, Minutes, 1836–68.
Notices of orders of removal from sundry parishes to Bethnal Green, 1843–48.

Greenwich

Vestry, Minutes, 1824–34.

Holborn

Board of Guardians, Minutes, 1836–45.

St George in the East

Board of Guardians, Minutes, 1836–68.

St George Southwark

Board of Guardians, Removals from St George Southwark to various parishes 8 August 1843 to 18 June 1846.

St Giles in the Fields and St George's Bloomsbury

Directors of the Poor, Settlement and Examinations, 1832–62.

St Leonard Shoreditch

Vestry, Draft Minutes, 1833–37.
Trustees of the Poor, Minutes, 1835–45.
Board of Guardians, Minutes, 1840–51.

St Marylebone

Directors of the Poor, Minutes, 1817–40.

West London

Board of Guardians, Minutes, 1839–64.

Corporation of London Record Office: Guildhall Manuscripts Collection

MS 19236/1 Overseers of the Poor of the parish of St Dionis Backchurch, papers relating to the removal of George and Elizabeth Durrant.

City of Westminster Archives Centre

St George Hanover Square

Vestry, Minutes 1827–38

St James Westminster

Vestry, Minutes, 1830–35.
List of Vestrymen, 1830.
List of Vestrymen, 1835.

St John Westminster

Vestry, Minutes, 1828–36.

St Margaret and St John Westminster

Directors of the Poor, Minutes, 1830–38.

St Marylebone

Vestry, Minutes, 1831–34.
A List of Vestrymen and Auditors of the Parish, 1829.
A List of Vestrymen and Auditors of the Parish, 1835.

Camden Local History Centre Archives

St Giles in the Fields and St George's Bloomsbury

Directors of the Poor, Minutes, 1830–68.
Annual abstract account of the receipts and expenditure for the relief of the poor in the year ending 1830.
Annual abstract account of the receipts and expenditure for the relief of the poor in the year ending 1834.
An abstract of the expenditure of the parishes in the years from 1828 to 1835 (1835).
[St Giles Vestry], Refutation of Charges against the Select Vestry Made in Several Printed Papers Dated 30 April, 26 May, 23 June, 15 December… etc. (London, 1829).

St Pancras

Vestry, Minutes, 1831–60.

Southwark Local Studies Centre

St George the Martyr Southwark

Vestry, Minutes, 1834–56.
Anderson, C., *An Account of the Alterations, Reductions, Exposures etc. Effected by the United Parishioners Society of St George the Martyr Southwark* (London, 1833).

[Anon], *Broadside, United Parishioners of St George the Martyr Southwark, meeting to be held on 31 January 1831* (London, 1831).

[Anon] *Rules and Regulations of the Society called the United Parishioners of St George the Martyr Southwark, established 13 January 1831* (London, 1831).

[Anon], *To the Worthy Inhabitants of the Parish of St George the Martyr, Southwark* (London, 1831).

Periodicals

Architectural Magazine
East London Observer
Hansard Parliamentary Debates
Illustrated London News
London Dispatch
Morning Chronicle
New Vestryman
Reynolds Newspaper
The Builder
The Times
Trades Newspaper and Mechanics Weekly Journal
True Sun
Weekly News
Workhouse Papers

Trade Directories

Boyles Court and Country Guide, 1830
Robsons London Directory, 1835

Special Collections, Senate House Library, University of London

Association for Promoting the Relief of Destitution in the Metropolis, Annual Reports, 1844–70.

Poor Man's Guardian Society, First Annual Report, 1846.

Society for the Suppression of Mendicity, Second Annual Report, 1819.

Primary Sources

['A Churchman'], *A General Statement of the Case of the Parishioners against the Select Vestry of St Mary-le-bone Parish* (London: G. Ribeau, 1828).

[A Metropolitan Poor Law Officer], *Remarks on the Laws* of *Settlement and Removal* (London: James Truscott, 1854).

[Anon], *An Account of the Work-houses in Great Britain in the Year MDCCXXXII* (London: W. Brown, 3rd edition, 1786).

[Anon], *Copy of Correspondence between the Committee of Parishioners of the Parish of St Marylebone Appointed at a Public Meeting to Investigate the Affairs of the Parish and Particularly to Watch the New Parochial Bill Brought into Parliament by the Select Vestry* (London: G. Ribeau, 1827).

[Anon] *Hints and Cautions for the Information of the Churchwardens and Overseers of the Poor of the Parishes of St Giles in the Fields and St George's Bloomsbury in the County of Middlesex* (London: no publisher, 1781, reprinted 1797).

[Anon], *The Settlement and Removal of the Poor Considered* (London: John Ollivier, 1847).

[Anon], *Workhouses and Women's Work* (London: Longmans, 1858).

Aschrott, Paul F., *The English Poor Law System: Past and Present* (London: Knight, 1888, reprinted in facsimile by Elibron Classics, 2006).

Baxter, W. R., *The Book of the Bastilles, or the History of the Working of the New Poor Law* (London: John Stephen, 1841).

Becher, John Thomas, *The Antipauper System: Exemplifying the Positive and Practical Good the Frugal, Beneficial, and Lawful Administration of the Poor Laws* (London: Simpkin and Marshall, 1828).

Bentham, Jeremy, *Management of the Poor or a Plan Containing the Principle and Construction of an Establishment in which Persons of Any Description are to be Kept Under Inspection* (Dublin: James Moor, 1796).

Bosanquest, Samuel, *The Rights of the Poor and Christian Almsgiving Vindicated* (London: James Burns, 1841).

Bosworth, James, *The Practical Means of Reducing the Poor's Rate, Encouraging Virtue, and Increasing the Comforts of the Aged, Afflicted, and Deserving Poor: As well as, of Repressing Able-bodied Pauperism by a Proper Application of the Existing Laws Respecting Select Vestries and Incorporated Houses of Industry* (London: Simpkin and Marshall, 1824).

Brooke, James, *The Democrats of Marylebone* (London: Cleaver, 1839).

Brown, John, *A Memoir of Robert Blincoe, an Orphan Boy; Sent ... to Endure the Horrors of a Cotton-mill* (Manchester: J. Doherty, 1832, reprinted Firle: Caliban, 1977).

Browne, R. P., 'Greenwich Union Poorhouse', *Quarterly Papers in Architecture*, 1 (1843): 1–7.

Burn, Richard, *The Justice of the Peace, and Parish Officer* (London: Strahan, 1800).

Capper, Charles, *The Port and Trade of London: Historical, Statistical, Local and General* (London: Smith, Elder & Co, 1862).

Carpenter, Mary, *Reformatory Schools for the Children of the Perishing and Dangerous Classes and for Juvenile Offenders* (London: Gilpin, 1851).

——, 'On Educational Help from Government for the Destitute and Neglected Children of Great Britain', *Journal of the Statistical Society*, 24 (1861): 22–9.

Chadwick, Edwin 'Extracts from the Information Received by His Majesty's Commissioners as to the Administration and Operation of the Poor Laws', *Edinburgh Review*, 63 (1836): 487–537.

Clarkson, W. M., *An Inquiry in to the Cause of the Increase of Pauperism and the Poor Rates* (published by the author, 1816).

Colquhoun, Patrick [A Magistrate], *An Account of a Meat and Soup Charity Established in the Metropolis in the year 1797* (London: Fry, 1797).

——, *A Treatise on the Police of the Metropolis* (London: Fry, 1797).

——, *The State of Indigence and the Situation of the Casual Poor in the Metropolis* (London: H. Baldwin, 1799).

——, *A Treatise on the Police of the Metropolis* (London: Mawman, 1806, 7th edition).

Day, John, *A Few Practical Observations on the New Poor Law Showing the Demoralizing and Enslaving Effects of this Anti-Christian Enactment* (London: Redford, 1838).

Dobie, Rowland, *A History of the United Parishes of St Giles in the Fields and St George Bloomsbury* (London: printed for the author, 1829).

Dod, Charles, *Electoral Facts 1832–1853, Impartially Stated, Constituting a Complete Political Gazetteer* (1853, reprinted Brighton: Harvester, 1972).

Eden, Frederick M., *The State of the Poor, or an History of the Labouring Classes in England*, 3 vols (London: Davis, 1797).

Evans, D. M., *The City, or the Physiology of London Business* (London: Baily Brothers, 1845).

Fletcher, Joseph, 'The Metropolis: Its Boundaries, Extent and Divisions for Local Government', *Journal of the Statistical Society*, 7 (1844): 103–43.

——, 'Statistical Account of the Constitution and Operation of the Police Courts of the Metropolis', *Journal of the Statistical Society*, 9 (1846): 289–309.

Gavin, Hector, *Sanitary Ramblings: Being Sketches and Illustrations of Bethnal Green*, (London, 1848).

Gilbert, William, *On the Present System of Rating for the Relief of the Poor in the Metropolis* (London: Association for Promoting the Equalization of the Poor Rate on an Equal Assessment over the Metropolitan District, 1857a).

——, *Address* (London: Association for Promoting the Equalization of the Poor Rate on an Equal Assessment over the Metropolitan District, 1857b).

——, *Poor Law Reform – Proceedings of the Metropolitan and County Association for the Equalization of the Poor Rate*, (London: Judd and Glass, 1860).

Glen, William C., *The General Orders of the Poor Law Commissioners, the Poor Law Board, and the Local Government Board Relating to the Poor Law* (London: Knight, 1898).

Grant, James, *The Great Metropolis* (London: Saunders and Otley, 1837).

Hallam, Henry and Slaney, R. A., 'Report to the Council of the Statistical Society of London from a Committee of its Fellows Appointed to Make an Investigation into the State of the Poorer Classes in St George's in the East', *Journal of the Statistical Society*, 11 (1848): 193–249.

Hart, Ernest, *An Account of the Condition of the Infirmaries of the London Workhouses* (London: Chapman and Hall, 1866).

Head, Edmund, 'Seventh and Eighth Reports from the Select Committee on Settlement and Poor Removal', *Edinburgh Review*, vol. 87 no. 176 (1848): 451–72.

Hollingshead, John, *Ragged London in 1861* (London: Smith, Elder, 1861, reprinted London: Dent, 1986).

Holland, E. W., 'The Poor Laws and the Metropolitan Poor Law Administration', *Contemporary Review*, 8 (1868): 502–13.

Hutchinson, G. L., *A Proposed Plan for the Equalization of the Poor Rates Throughout the United Kingdom* (London: Hansard, 1846).

——, *The Equalization of the Poor's Rate of the United Kingdom of Great Britain and Ireland* (London: Robert Hardwicke, 1858).

Kay, James Phillip, 'On the Establishment of County or District Schools for the Training of Pauper Children Maintained in Union Workhouses, Part 1', *Journal of the Statistical Society*, 1 (1838): 14–27.

Knight, Frederic W., *The Parochial System versus Centralization. Statistics of 'Close and Open Parishes'* (London: Shaw and Sons, 1854).

Leslie, John, *Remarks on the Present State of the Poor Law Question with Illustrations of the Advantages Arising for the Poor by Means of the Workhouse System of Relief* (London: Ridgeway, 1834).

Lewis, Samuel, *The History and Topography of St Mary Islington* (London: J. H. Jackson, 1842).

Lumley, W. G., 'On the Present State of the Administration of the Relief to the Poor in the Metropolis', *Journal of the Statistical Society*, 21 (1858): 169–95.

MacGill, George, *The London Poor and the Inequality of the Rates Raised for Their Relief*, (London: Rymer, 1858).

Mahon, James N., *The Poor Laws as They Were and as They Are, or Recent Alterations in the Poor Laws by the Statute 4 & 5 William IV Cap 76* (London: Thomas Hurst, 1835).

Marshall John, *A Digest of All the Accounts Relating to the Population, Production, Revenues, Financial Operations, Manufactures, Shipping, Colonies, Commerce &c &c of the United Kingdom of Great Britain and Ireland*, (London: Haddon, 1833).

Miller, Samuel, *Pauper Police: Letters Addressed, through 'The Times', to the Churchwardens, Overseers and Parishioners of the Several Parishes in the City of London* (London: Wilson, 1831).

Morley, Henry, 'The Quiet Poor', *Household Words*, 9 (1854): 201–6.

Mouat, Frederic, 'On the Education and Training of the Children of the Poor', *Journal of the Statistical Society*, 43 (1880): 183–250.

——, 'On Hospitals – Their Management, Construction and Arrangements', *Lancet*, (16 July, 1881): 78–82.

Nicholls, George, *A History of the English Poor Law*, 3 vols (London: King, 1898).

['One of the non-select'], *Considerations on Select Vestries Shewing from the Oppression and Corrupt Practices Now Prevailing in the Different Parishes* (London: Effingham Wilson, 1828).

Parkinson, J. C., 'On a Uniform Poor Rate for London', *Fortnightly Review*, 4 (1866): 184–92.

Pashley, Robert, *Pauperism and the Poor Laws* (London: Longman, Brown, Green and Longman, 1852).

Pemberton, Thomas, *An Attempt to Estimate the Increase of the Number of Poor During the Interval of 1785 and 1803* (London: John Murray, 1811).

Pettigrew, Thomas, *The Pauper Farming System: A Letter to the Rt Hon Lord John Russell on the Condition of the Pauper Children of St James Westminster* (London: Rodd, 1836).

Price Williams, R., 'The Population of London, 1801–1881', *Journal of the Statistical Society*, 48 (1885): 349–432.

Pugin, Augustus W., *Contrasts: or, a Parallel Between the Noble Edifices of the Middle Ages, and Corresponding Buildings of the Present Day; Shewing the Present Decay of Taste* (London: Charles Dolman, Second edition 1841).

Purdy, Frederick, 'The Statistics of the English Poor Rate Before and Since the Passing of the Poor Law Amendment Act', *Journal of the Statistical Society*, 23 (1860): 286–329.

Rose, George, *Observations on the Poor Laws and the Management of the Poor in Great Britain Arising from a Consideration of the Returns Now Before Parliament* (London: Hatchard, 1805).

Sclater, William, *A Letter to the Poor Law Commissioners of England and Wales on the Working of the New System* (Basingstoke: Cottle, 1836).

Senior, Nassau, 'Annual Reports of the Poor Law Commissioners for the Years 1835, 1836, 1837, 1838, 1839, 1840 and 1841', *Edinburgh Review*, 149 (1841): 1–44.

Shaen, Samuel, *Workhouse Management and Workhouse Justice: A Further Letter to the President of the Poor Law Board* (London: Williams and Norgate, 1869).

Stonestreet, George, *Domestic Union; or London as it should be!! Containing Observations on the Present State of the Municipality of London* (London: Walter, 1800).

[Strand Union], *The Strand Union Pauper Children at Edmonton* (London: Painter, 1852).

Sykes, W. H., 'Statistics of the Metropolitan Commission in Lunacy', *Journal of the Statistical Society*, 3 (1840): 143–60.

Symons, Jellinger C., *Tactics for the Times as Regards the Condition and Treatment of the Dangerous Classes* (London: Ollivier, 1849).

Thwaites, Thomas, *The Poor Laws Unmasked Being a General Exposition of our Workhouse Institutions with Especial Reference to the Law of Settlement and Removal of the Poor* (London: Thomas Day, 1859).
Toulmin Smith, Joshua, *A Letter to the Metropolitan Sanatory Commissioners* (London: Sweet, 1848).
——, *Government by Commission: Illegal and Pernicious* (London: Sweet, 1849).
——, *Local Self Government and Centralisation* (London: Chapman, 1851).
——, *The Metropolis and its Municipal Administration* (London: Saunders, 1852).
——, *The People and The Parish* (London: Stevens and Norton, 1853).
——, *Local Self Government Unmystified* (London: Stanford, 1857).
Townsend, Joseph, *Dissertation on the Poor Laws by a Well-Wisher to Mankind* (published by the author, 1786).
Trevelyan, Charles, *Metropolitan Medical Relief* (London: Longman, Green and Co, 1879).
Walker, Thomas, *Suggestions for a Constitutional and Efficient Reform of Parochial Government* (London: published by the author, 1834).
Warwick, Robert E., *Observations on the Laws of Settlements, Poor Removals and the Equalization of the Poor Rates*, (London: Tirebuck, 1855).
Weld, C. R., 'On the Condition of the Working Classes in the Inner Ward of St George's Parish, Hanover Square', *Journal of the Statistical Society*, 6 (1843): 17–23.
Weston, Charles, *Remarks on the Poor Laws and on the State of the Poor* (London: Payne, Mackinlay, 1802).

Secondary

Andrew, Donna, *Philanthropy and Police: London Charity in the Eighteenth Century* (New Jersey: Princeton University Press, 1989).
Apfel, William and Dunkley, Peter, 'English Rural Society and the New Poor Law: Bedfordshire 1834–1863', *Social History*, 10 (1985): 37–68.
Ashbee, C. R. (ed.), *Survey of London, Old St Pancras and Kentish Town*, vol. 19 (London: London County Council, 1938).
Ashbridge, Pauline, 'Paying for the Poor: A Middle Class Metropolitan Movement for Rate Equalisation 1857–1867', *London Journal*, 22 (1997): 107–22.
Ashforth, David, 'The Urban Poor Law', in Derek Fraser (ed.), *The New Poor Law in the Nineteenth Century* (London: Macmillan, 1976), pp. 128–48.
Aspinall, A. and Smith, E. A. (eds), *English Historical Documents: Volume 11, 1783–1832* (London: Eyre and Spottiswoode, 1959).
Ayers, Gwendoline, *England's First State Hospitals and the Metropolitan Asylums Board 1867–1930* (London: Wellcome Institute, 1971).

Bailey, Peter, '"Will the Real Bill Banks Please Stand Up?" Towards a Role Analysis of mid-Victorian Working-Class Respectability', *Journal of Social History*, 12 (1979): 336–53.

Bartlett, Peter, *The Poor Law of Lunacy: The Administration of Pauper Lunatics in Mid-nineteenth Century England* (Leicester: Leicester University Press, 1999).

Belchem, John, 'Republicanism, Popular Constitutionalism and the Radical Platform in Early Nineteenth-Century England', *Social History*, 6 (1981): 1–32.

——, *Orator Hunt: Henry Hunt and English Working-class Radicalism* (Oxford: Clarendon Press, 1985).

Besley, Timothy, Coate, Stephen and Guinnane, Timothy W., 'Incentives, Information and Welfare: England's New Poor Law and the Workhouse Test', in William Sundstrom, Timothy W. Guinnane and Warren C. Whatley (eds), *History Matters: Essays on Economic Growth, Technology and Demographic Change* (Stanford: Stanford University Press, 2003), pp. 245–70.

Blaug, Mark, 'The Myth of the Old Poor Law and the Making of the New', *Journal of Economic History*, 23 (1963): 167–72.

——, 'The Poor Law Report Re-examined', *Journal of Economic History*, 24 (1964): 229–45.

Booth, Charles, *The Aged Poor in England and Wales* (London: Macmillan, 1894).

——, *Life and Labour of the People in London, First Series, Poverty*, vol. 2 (London: Macmillan, 1902).

Boyer, George, 'The Old Poor Law and the Agricultural Labour Market in Southern England: An Empirical Analysis', *Journal of Economic History*, 46 (1986): 113–35.

——, 'The Poor Law, Migration and Economic Growth', *Journal of Economic History*, 46 (1986): 419–30.

——, *An Economic History of the English Poor Law 1750–1850* (Cambridge: Cambridge University Press, 1990).

——, 'The Evolution of Unemployment Relief in Great Britain', *Journal of Interdisciplinary History*, 34 (2004): 393–433.

—— and Schmidle, Timothy P., 'Poverty Amongst the Elderly in Victorian England', *Economic History Review*, 61 (2008): 1–30.

Broad, John, 'Parish Economies of Welfare, 1650–1834', *Historical Journal*, 42 (1999): 985–1006.

Brodie, Marc, *The Politics of the Poor: The East End of London 1885–1914* (Oxford: Clarendon, 2004).

Brundage, Anthony, *The Making of the New Poor Law: The Politics of Inquiry, Enactment and Implementation 1832–39* (London: Hutchinson, 1978).

——, *England's 'Prussian Minister': Edwin Chadwick and the Politics of Government Growth 1832–1854* (London: Penn State University Press, 1988).

——, *The English Poor Laws 1799–1930* (Houndmills: Palgrave, 2002).
Caplan, Maurice, 'The New Poor Law and the Struggle for Union Chargeability', *International Review of Social History*, 23 (1978): 267–300.
Chinn, Carl, *Poverty Amidst Prosperity: The Urban Poor in England, 1834–1914* (Manchester: Manchester University Press, 1995).
Clark, Gregory and Page, Marianne, 'Is There a Profit in Reforming the Poor? The English Poor Law 1830–42', unpublished paper, (Department of Economics, University of California, Davis, 2000).
Claus, Peter, 'Languages of Citizenship in the City of London, 1848–1867', *London Journal*, 24 (1999): 23–37.
Coats, A. W., 'Economic Thought and Poor Law Policy in the Eighteenth Century', *Economic History Review*, 13 (1960): 39–51.
Cody, Lisa Forman, 'The Politics of Illegitimacy in an Age of Reform: Women, Reproduction, and Political Economy in England's New Poor Law of 1834', *Journal of Women's History*, 11 (2000): 131–56.
Compton, Frank, *Workhouse Children* (Thrupp: Allan Sutton, 1997).
Cowherd, Raymond, *Political Economists and the English Poor Laws* (Athens: Ohio University Press, 1977).
Craig, F. W. S., *British Parliamentary Election Results 1832–1885* (London: Macmillan, 1977).
Crowther, Margaret, *The Workhouse System 1834–1929: The History of an English Social Institution* (London: Methuen, 1981).
Daunton, Martin (ed.), *Charity, Self Interest and Welfare in the English Past*, (London: University College London Press, 1996).
Davis, Jennifer, 'A Poor Man's System of Justice: The London Police Courts in the Second Half of the Nineteenth Century', *Historical Journal*, 27 (1984): 309–35.
Dean, Mitchell, *The Constitution of Poverty: Towards a Genealogy of Liberal Governance* (London: Routledge, 1991).
——, 'A Genealogy of the Government of Poverty', *Economy and Society*, 21 (1992): 215–51.
Deane, Phyllis and Cole, W. A., *British Economic Growth 1688–1959* (Cambridge: Cambridge University Press, 1969).
Digby, Anne, 'The Labour Market and the Continuity of Social Policy after 1834: The Case of the Eastern Counties', *Economic History Review*, 28 (1975): 69–83.
——, 'The Rural Poor Law', in Derek Fraser (ed.), *The New Poor Law in the Nineteenth Century* (London: Macmillan, 1976), pp. 149–70.
——, *Pauper Palaces: The Economy and Poor Law of Nineteenth-Century Norfolk* (London: Routledge and Kegan Paul, 1978).
Driver, Felix, *Power and Pauperism: The Workhouse System 1834–1884* (Cambridge: Cambridge University Press, 1993).
Dunkley, Peter, 'The "Hungry Forties" and the New Poor Law: A Case Study', *Historical Journal*, 17 (1974): 329–46.

——, 'Whigs and Paupers: The Reform of the English Poor Laws 1830–1834', *Journal of British Studies*, 20 (1981): 124–49.

——, *The Crisis of the Old Poor Law in England 1795–1834* (London: Garland, 1982).

Eastwood, David, *Governing Rural England: Tradition and Transformation in Local Government 1780–1840* (Oxford: Clarendon, 1994).

——, 'Men, Morals and the Machinery of Social Legislation 1790–1840', *Parliamentary History*, 13 (1994): 190–205.

Edsall, Nicholas, *The Anti-Poor Law Movement 1834–44*, (Manchester: Manchester University Press, 1971).

Englander, David, *Poverty and Poor Law Reform in Nineteenth-Century Britain 1834–1914* (Harlow: Addison, Wesley, Longman, 1998).

Epstein, James, 'The Constitutional Idiom: Radical Reasoning, Rhetoric and Action in Early Nineteenth Century England', *Journal of Social History*, 23 (1990): 553–74.

——, *Radical Expression: Political Language, Ritual and Symbol in England, 1790–1850* (Oxford: Oxford University Press, 1994).

Feinstein, Charles H., 'Pessimism Perpetuated: Real Wages and the Standard of Living in Britain During and After the Industrial Revolution', *Journal of Economic History*, 58 (1998): 625–58.

Feldman, David, 'Migrants, Immigrants and Welfare from the old Poor Law to the Welfare State', *Transactions of the Royal Historical Society*, 13 (2003): 79–104.

Fideler, Paul, *Social Welfare in Pre-Industrial England* (Houndmills: Palgrave, 2006).

Flinn, Michael, 'The Poor Employment Act of 1817', *Economic History Review*, 14 (1961): 82–92.

Flint, Kate (ed.), *The Victorian Novelist* (London: Croom Helm, 1987).

Foster, John, *Class Struggle and the Industrial Revolution: Early Capitalism in Three English Towns* (London: Routledge, 1977).

Foucault, Michel, *Discipline and Punish: The Birth of the Prison* (Harmondsworth: Penguin, 1977).

Fraser, Derek, 'The Poor Law as a Political Institution', in Derek Fraser (ed.), *The New Poor Law in the Nineteenth Century* (London: Macmillan, 1976), pp. 111–27.

——, *Urban Politics in Victorian England* (Leicester: Leicester University Press, 1976).

—— (ed.), *The New Poor Law in the Nineteenth Century*, (London, 1976).

Gatrell, Victor, *The City of Laughter: Sex and Satire in Eighteenth-Century London* (London: Atlantic, 2006).

George, M. Dorothy, *London Life in the Eighteenth Century* (Harmondsworth: Penguin, 1966).

Gestrich, Andreas, King, Steven and Raphael, Lutz (eds), *Being Poor In Modern Europe: Historical Perspectives 1800–1940* (Bern: Peter Lang, 2006).

Giffen, Robert, *Statistics* (London: Macmillan, 1913).

Goose, Nigel, 'Poverty, Old Age and Gender in Nineteenth Century England: The Case of Hertfordshire', *Continuity and Change*, 20 (2005): 351–84.

Gouda, Frances, *Poverty and Political Culture: The Rhetoric of Social Welfare in the Netherlands and France, 1815–1854* (Lanham: Rowman and Littlefield, 1995).

Green, Bryan S., *Knowing the Poor: A Case Study in Textual Reality Construction* (London: Routledge and Kegan Paul, 1983).

Green, David R., 'A Map for Mayhew's London: The Geography of Poverty in the mid-Nineteenth Century', *London Journal*, 11 (1986): 115–26.

——, *From Artisans to Paupers: Economic Change and Poverty in London 1790–1870* (Aldershot: Scolar, 1995).

——, 'Medical Relief and the New Poor Law in London', in Ole P. Grell, Andrew Cunningham and Robert Jütte (eds), *Health Care and Poor Relief in 18th and 19th Century Northern Europe* (Aldershot: Ashgate, 2002), pp. 220–45.

——, 'Pauper Protests: Power and Resistance in Early Nineteenth-Century London Workhouses', *Social History*, 31 (2006): 137–59.

—— and Parton, Alan, 'Slums and Slum Life in Victorian England: London and Birmingham at Mid-Century', in Martin Gaskell (ed.), *Slums* (Leicester: Leicester University Press, 1990), pp. 17–91.

Greenleaf, W. H., 'Toulmin Smith and the British Political Tradition', *Public Administration*, 53 (1975): 25–44.

Halévy, Elie, *The Growth of Philosophic Radicalism* (London: Faber and Faber, 1928).

Hallas, C. S., 'Poverty and Pragmatism in the Northern Uplands of England: The North Yorkshire Pennines c. 1770–1900', *Social History*, 25 (2000): 67–84.

Hanley, Margaret, 'Being Poor in Nineteenth-Century Lancashire', in Andreas Gestrich, Steven King and Lutz Raphael (eds), *Being Poor In Modern Europe: Historical Perspectives 1800–1940* (Bern: Peter Lang, 2006), pp. 69–89.

Harling, Philip, 'The Power of Persuasion: Central Authority, Local Bureaucracy and the New Poor Law', *English Historical Review*, 108 (1992): 30–53.

Harris, Bernard, *The Origins of the British Welfare State: Social Welfare in England and Wales, 1800–1945* (Houndmills: Palgrave, 2004).

Hennock, Peter, *The Origin of the Welfare State in England and Germany, 1850–1914: Social Policies Compared* (Cambridge: Cambridge University Press, 2007).

Henriques, Ursula, 'Bastardy and the New Poor Law', *Past and Present*, 37 (1967): 103–29.

Higginbotham, Peter, *The Workhouse*. [Online]. Available at: http://www.workhouses.org.uk/ [accessed: 2 October 2008].

Himmelfarb, Gertrude, *The Idea of Poverty: England in the Early Industrial Age* (London: Faber and Faber, 1984).

Hindle, Steve, 'Power, Poor Relief, and Social Relations in Holland Fen, c. 1600–1800', *Historical Journal*, 41 (1998): 67–96.

Hirst, David, 2004. 'Mott, Charles (*bap.* 1788, *d.* 1851)', *Oxford Dictionary of National Biography.* [Online]. Available at: http://www.oxforddnb.com/view/article/42189 [accessed: 18 September 2008].

——, '"A Ticklish Sort of Affair": Charles Mott, Haydock Lodge and the Economics of Asylumdom', *History of Psychiatry*, 16 (2005): 311–32.

Hitchcock, Tim, *Down and Out in Eighteenth-Century London* (London: Hambledon, 2007).

——, King, Peter and Sharpe, Pamela (eds), *Chronicling Poverty – The Voices and Strategies of the English Poor 1640–1840* (Houndmills: Palgrave Macmillan, 1997).

Hobsbawm, Eric, 'Labour in the Great City', *New Left Review*, 166 (1987): 39–51.

Hodgkinson, Ruth, *The Origins of the National Health Service: The Medical Services of the New Poor Law 1834–1871* (London: Wellcome Institute, 1967).

Hone, J. Ann, *For the Cause of Truth: Radicalism in London 1796–1821* (Oxford: Clarendon Press, 1982).

Horrell, Sara, Humphries, Jane and Vorth, Hans-Joachim, 'Destined for Deprivation: Human Capital Formation and Intergenerational Poverty in Nineteenth-Century England', *Explorations in Economic History*, 38 (2001): 339–65.

Horsbaugh, Michael, '"No Sufficient Security": The Reaction of the Poor Law Authorities to Boarding Out', *Journal of Social History*, 12 (1983): 51–73.

Howells, Gary, '"For I was Tired of England, Sir": English Pauper Emigrant Strategies 1834–60', *Social History*, 23 (1998): 181–94.

Humphreys, Robert, *Sin, Organized Charity and the Poor Law in Victorian England* (London: St Martin's, 1995).

Hurren, Elizabeth T., *Protesting About Pauperism: Poverty, Politics and Poor Relief in Late-Victorian England, 1870–1900* (Woodbridge: Boydell, 2007).

—— and King, Steven, '"Begging for Burial": Form, Function and Conflict in Nineteenth-Century Pauper Burial', *Social History*, 30 (2005): 321–41.

Huzel, James, 'Malthus, the Poor Law and Population in Early Nineteenth-Century England', *Economic History Review*, 22 (1969): 430–52.

Innes, Joanna, 'The "Mixed Economy of Welfare" in Early Modern England: Assessments of the Options from Hale to Malthus (c. 1683–1803)', in Martin Daunton (ed.), *Charity, Self Interest and Welfare in the English Past* (London: UCL Press, 1996). pp. 139–80.

James, Henry, *London Stories and Other Writings*, (Padstow: Tabb House, 1989).

Jones, Gareth Stedman, *Outcast London: A Study of the Relationships Between Classes in Victorian Society* (Oxford: Clarendon, 1971).

——, *An End to Poverty?* (London: Profile, 2004).

Joyce, Patrick, *Visions of the People. Industrial England and the Question of Class, 1848–1914* (Cambridge: Cambridge University Press, 1994).

Keith-Lucas, Bryan, *The English Local Government Franchise* (Oxford: Blackwell, 1952).

——, *The Unreformed Local Government System* (London: Croom Helm, 1980).

Kidd, Alan J., *State, Society and the Poor in Nineteenth-Century England* (Houndmills: Macmillan, 1999).

——, 'Civil Society or the State? Recent Approaches to the History of Voluntary Welfare', *Journal of Historical Sociology*, 15 (2002): 328–42.

King, Steven, 'Reconstructing Lives: The Poor, the Poor Law and Welfare in Calverley 1650–1820', *Social History*, 22 (1997), 318–38.

——, 'Poor Relief and English Economic Development Reappraised', *Economic History Review*, 50 (1997): 360–68.

——, *Poverty and Welfare in England 1700–1850: A Regional Perspective* (Manchester: Manchester University Press, 2000).

——, '"It is Impossible for Our Vestry to Judge His Case into Perfection From Here": Managing the Distance Dimensions of Poor Relief, 1800–40', *Rural History*, 16 (2005): 161–89.

—— and Tomkins, Alannah (eds), *The Poor in England 1700–1850: An Economy of Makeshifts* (Manchester: Manchester University Press, 2003).

Knott, John, *Popular Opposition to the 1834 Poor Law* (London: Croom Helm, 1986).

Landau, Norma, 'The Laws of Settlement and the Surveillance of Immigration in Eighteenth-Century Kent', *Continuity and Change*, 3 (1988): 391–420.

——, 'The Regulation of Immigration, Economic Structures and Definitions of the Poor in Eighteenth-Century England', *Historical Journal*, 33 (1990): 541–72.

——, 'The Eighteenth Century Context of the Law of Settlement', *Continuity and Change*, 6 (1991): 417–39.

Lees, Lynn, 'The Survival of the Unfit: Welfare Policies and Family Maintenance in Nineteenth-Century London', in Peter Mandler (ed), *The Uses of Charity* (Philadelphia: University of Pennsylvania, 1990), pp. 68–91.

——, *The Solidarities of Strangers: The English Poor Laws and the People, 1700–1948* (Cambridge: Cambridge University Press, 1998).

Levene, Alysa, 'Children, Childhood and the Workhouse: St Marylebone, 1769–1781', *London Journal*, 33 (2008): 41–59.

Lindert, Peter, 'Poor Relief Before the Welfare State: Britain Versus the Continent, 1780–1880', *European Review of Economic History*, 2 (1998): 101–40.

——, *Growing Public: Social Spending and Economic Growth since the Eighteenth Century* (Cambridge: Cambridge University Press, 2004).

McCord, Norman, *British History 1815–1906* (Oxford: Oxford University Press, 1991).

MacKay, Lynn, 'A Culture of Poverty? The St Martin in the Fields Workhouse 1817', *Journal of Interdisciplinary History*, 26 (1995): 209–31.

MacKinnon, Mary, 'English Poor Law Policy and the Crusade Against Outdoor Relief', *Journal of Economic History*, 47 (1987): 603–25.

——, 'The Use and Misuse of Poor Law Statistics, 1857 to 1912', *Historical Methods*, 21 (1988): 5–19.

Mandler, Peter, 'The Making of the New Poor Law *Redivivus*', *Past and Present*, 117 (1987): 131–57.

——, 'Tories and Paupers: Christian Political Economy and the Making of the New Poor Law', *Historical Journal*, 33 (1990): 81–103.

—— (ed.), *The Uses of Charity* (Philadelphia: University of Pennsylvania, 1990).

Marriott, John and Masaie Matsumura (eds), *The Metropolitan Poor: Semi-Factual Accounts* (London: Pickering and Chatto, 1999).

Martin, E. W., 'From Parish to Union: Poor Law Administration 1601–1865', in E. W. Martin (ed.) *Comparative Development in Social Welfare* (London: George Allen and Unwin, 1972), pp. 25–56.

Mills, Dennis, 'The Poor Laws and the Distribution of Population c. 1600–1860, with Special Reference to Lincolnshire', *Transactions of the Institute of British Geographers*, 26 (1959): 185–95.

Mitchell, B. R. and Deane, Phyllis, *Abstract of British Historical Statistics* (Cambridge: Cambridge University Press, 1962).

Morgan, Gwenda and Rushton, Peter, 'The Magistrate, the Community and the Maintenance of an Orderly Society in Eighteenth-Century England', *Historical Research*, 76 (2003): 54–77.

Morrison, Kathryn, 'The New Poor Law Workhouses of George Gilbert Scott and William Bonython Moffatt, *Architectural History*, 4 (1997): 184–203.

——, *The Workhouse: A Study of Poor-Law Buildings in England* (Swindon: Royal Commission on the Historical Monuments of England, 1999).

Murphy, Elaine, 'Mad Farming in the Metropolis, Part 2: The Administration of the Old Poor Law of Insanity in the City and East London 1800–1834', *History of Psychiatry*, 12 (2001): 405–30.

——, 'The Metropolitan Poor Farms, 1722–1834', *London Journal*, 27 (2002): 1–18.

——, 'The Lunacy Commissioners and the East London Guardians, 1845–1867', *Medical History*, 46 (2002): 495–524.

——, 'The New Poor Law Guardians and the Administration of Insanity in East London, 1834–44', *Bulletin of the History of Medicine*, 77 (2003): 45–74.

Neate, Alan, *St Marylebone Workhouse*, (London: St Marylebone Society, 2003).

Owen, David, *The Government of Victorian London 1855–1889: The Metropolitan Board of Works, the Vestries and the City Corporation* (London: Belknap, 1982).

Philo, Chris, 'Journey to Asylum: A Medical–Geographical Idea in Historical Context', *Journal of Historical Geography*, 21 (1995): 148–68.

Polanyi, Karl, *The Great Transformation* (Boston: Beacon Press, 1957).

Pollard, Sidney, 'The Decline of Shipbuilding on the Thames', *Economic History Review*, 3 (1950): 72–89.

Poynter, J. R., *Society and Pauperism: English Ideas on Poor Relief 1795–1834* (London: Routledge & Kegan Paul, 1969).

Prest, John, *Liberty and Locality: Parliament, Permissive Legislation, and Ratepayers' Democracies in the Nineteenth Century* (Oxford: Clarendon, 1990).

Prothero, Iorwerth, *Artisans and Politics in Early Nineteenth-Century London: John Gast and His Times* (London: Methuen, 1981).

Roberts, Andrew, 1990. *England's Poor Law Commissioners and the Trade in Pauper Lunacy 1834–1847*. [Online]. Available at: http://www.mdx.ac.uk/www/study/mott.htm [accessed: 18 September 2008].

——, *The Lunacy Commission: A Study of its Origin, Emergence and Character*. [Online]. Available at: http://www.mdx.ac.uk/www/study/01.htm [accessed: 18 September 2009].

Roberts, M. J., 'Public and Private in Early Nineteenth-Century London: The Vagrant Act of 1822 and its Enforcement', *Social History*, 13 (1988): 273–94.

——, 'Reshaping the Gift Relationship: The London Mendicity Society and the Suppression of Begging in England', *International Review of Social History*, 36 (1991): 201–31.

Rogers, Nicholas, 'Policing the Poor in Eighteenth-Century London: The Vagrancy Laws and their Administration', *Histoire Sociale-Social History*, 24 (1991): 127–41.

Rose, Michael, 'The Anti-Poor Law Movement in the North of England', *Northern History*, 1 (1966): 70–91.

——, 'The Allowance System under the New Poor Law', *Economic History Review*, 19 (1966): 607–20.

——, 'The Anti-Poor Law Agitation', in John. T. Ward (ed.), *Popular Movements 1830–1851* (London: Macmillan, 1970), pp. 78–84.

——, 'Settlement, Removal and the New Poor Law', in Derek Fraser (ed.), *The New Poor Law in the Nineteenth Century* (London: Macmillan, 1976), pp. 25–44.

——, 'The Crisis of Poor Relief in England 1860–1890', in W. J. Momsen (ed.), *The Emergence of the Welfare State in Britain and Germany*, (London: Croom Helm, 1981), pp. 50–70.

—— (ed.), *The Poor and the City: The English Poor Law in its Urban Context, 1834–1914* (Leicester: Leicester University Press, 1985).

Rowe, David (ed.), *London Radicalism 1830–1843: A Selection from the Papers of Francis Place* (London: London Record Society, 1970).

Ryan, Pat, 'Politics and Relief: East London Unions in the Late Nineteenth and Early Twentieth Centuries', in Michael Rose (ed.), *The Poor and the City: The English Poor Law in its Urban Context* (Leicester: Leicester University Press, 1985), pp. 133–72.

Schwarz, Leonard, 'Social Class and Social Geography: The Middle Classes in London at the end of the Eighteenth Century', *Social History*, 7 (1982): 167–85.

Scull, Andrew, *Museums of Madness: The Social Organisation of Insanity in Nineteenth-century England* (Harmondsworth: Penguin 1979).

Searby, Paul, 'The Relief of the Poor in Coventry 1830–1863', *Historical Journal*, 20 (1977): 345–61.

Shannon, H. A., 'Migration and the Growth of London, 1841–91: A Statistical Note', *Economic History Review*, 5 (1935): 79–86.

Sharpe, Pamela, '"The Bowels of Compassion": A Labouring Family and the Law c. 1790–1834', in Tim Hitchcock, Peter King and Pamela Sharpe (eds), *Chronicling Poverty – The Voices and Strategies of the English Poor 1640–1840* (Houndmills: Palgrave Macmillan, 1997), pp. 87–108.

Sheppard, Francis H. W., *Local Government in St Marylebone 1688–1835* (London: Athlone Press, 1958).

——, *London: The Infernal Wen 1808–1870* (London: Secker and Warburg, 1971).

—— (ed.), *Survey of London, The Parish of St James Westminster Part II North of Piccadilly*, vol. 32 (London: Athlone Press, 1963).

—— (ed.), *Survey of London, Poplar, Blackwall and the Isle of Dogs*, vol. 43 (London: Athlone Press, 1994).

——, Belcher, Victor and Cottrell, Philip, 'The Middlesex and Yorkshire Deeds Registries and the Study of Building Fluctuations', *London Journal*, 5 (1979): 176–216.

Sherman, Sandra, *Imagining Poverty: Quantification and the Decline of Paternalism* (Columbus: Ohio State University Press, 2001).

Slack, Paul, *The English Poor Law 1531–1782* (London: Macmillan, 1990).

Smith, Gregory, '"The Poor in Blindness": Letters from Mildenhall, Wiltshire 1835–36', in Tim Hitchcock, Peter King and Pamela Sharpe (eds), *Chronicling Poverty – The Voices and Strategies of the English Poor 1640–1840* (Houndmills: Palgrave Macmillan,1997), pp. 211–38.

Snell, Keith, *Annals of the Labouring Poor: Social Change and Agrarian England 1660–1900* (Cambridge: Cambridge University Press, 1985).

——, 'Pauper Settlement and Poor Relief', *Continuity and Change*, 6 (1991): 375–415.

——, and Millar, J., 'Lone Parent Families and the Welfare State: Past and Present', *Continuity and Change*, 2 (1987): 387–422.

Sokoll, Thomas, 'The Pauper Household Small and Simple? The Evidence from Listings of Inhabitants and Pauper Lists of Early Modern England Reassessed', *Ethnologia Europaea*, 17 (1987): 25–42.

——, 'Negotiating a Living: Essex Pauper Letters from London 1800–1834', *International Review of Social History*, 45 (2000): 19–46.

——, *Essex Pauper Letters 1731–1837* (Oxford: Oxford University Press, 2001).

——, 'Writing for Relief: Rhetoric in English Pauper Letters', in Andreas Gestrich, Steven King and Lutz Raphael (eds), *Being Poor In Modern Europe: Historical Perspectives 1800–1940* (Bern: Peter Lang, 2006), pp. 91–112.

Solar, Peter, 'Poor Relief and English Economic Development Before the Industrial Revolution', *Economic History Review*, 48 (1995): 1–22.

Stevenson, John, *Popular Disturbances in England 1700–1832* (Harlow: Longmans, 1992).

Summerson, John, *Georgian London* (London: Pleides, 1945).

Sweet, Rosemary, 'Freemen and Independence in English Borough Politics c. 1770–1830', *Past and Present*, 161 (1998): 84–115.

Tanner, Andrea, 'The Casual Poor and the City of London Poor Law Union, 1837–1869', *Historical Journal*, 42 (1999): 183–206.

Taylor, James, 'The Unreformed Workhouse 1776–1834', in E. A. Martin (ed.), *Comparative Development in Social Welfare* (London: George Allen and Unwin, 1972), pp. 57–84.

——, 'The Impact of Pauper Settlement 1691–1834', *Past and Present*, 73 (1976): 42–73.

——, *Poverty, Migration and Settlement in the Industrial Revolution* (Palo Alto: Society for the Promotion of Science and Scholarship, 1989).

——, 'A Different Kind of Speenhamland: Nonresident Relief in the Industrial Revolution', *Journal of British Studies*, 30 (1991): 183–208.

——, 'Voices in the Crowd: The Kirkby Lonsdale Letters, 1809–1836', in Tim Hitchcock, Peter King and Pamela Sharpe (eds), *Chronicling Poverty – The Voices and Strategies of the English Poor 1640–1840* (Houndmills: Palgrave Macmillan, 1997), pp. 109–26.

Taylor, Miles, *The Decline of British Radicalism 1847–1860* (Oxford: Clarendon, 1995).

Thane, Pat, *Old Age in English History: Past Experiences, Present Issues* (Oxford: Oxford University Press, 2000).

—— (ed.), *The Foundations of the Welfare State* (London: Longman, 1996).

Thompson, Edward P., *The Making of the English Working Class* (Harmondsworth: Penguin, 1968).

Treble, John, *Urban Poverty in Britain* (London: Batsford, 1979).

van Leeuwen, Marco, 'Surviving With a Little Help: The Importance of Charity to the Poor of Amsterdam 1800–50 in a Comparative Perspective', *Social History*, 18 (1993): 319–38.

——, 'Logic of Charity: Poor Relief in Preindustrial Europe', *Journal of Interdisciplinary History*, 24 (1994): 589–613.

——, *The Logic of Charity: Amsterdam 1800–1850* (Houndmills: Macmillan, 2000).

Vernon, James, *Politics and the People: A Study in English Political Culture c. 1815–1867* (Cambridge: Cambridge University Press, 1993).

—— (ed.), *Re-reading the Constitution: New Narratives in the Political History of England's Long Nineteenth Century* (Cambridge: Cambridge University Press, 1996).

Webb, Sidney and Webb, Beatrice, *English Local Government: English Poor Law History, Part 2 :The Last Hundred Years* (London: Longmans, Green and Company, 1929).

Williams, Karel, *From Pauperism to Poverty* (London: Routledge & Kegan Paul, 1981).

Williams, Samantha, 'Poor Relief, Labourers' Households and Living Standards in Rural England, c. 1770–1834: A Bedfordshire Case Study', *Economic History Review*, 58 (2005): 485–519.

Wohl, Anthony, *The Eternal Slum: Housing and Social Policy in Victorian London* (London: Edward Arnold, 1977).

Young, E., 'Paupers, Property and Place: A Geographical Analysis of the English, Irish and Scottish Poor Laws in the mid-19th Century', *Environment and Planning D*, 12 (1994): 325–40.

Unpublished Theses

Dickens, Anna, 'Architects and the Union Workhouses of the New Poor Law', unpublished Ph.D. thesis, Brighton Polytechnic, 1982.

Hitchcock, Timothy, 'The English Workhouse: A Study in Institutional Poor Relief in Selected Counties 1696–1750', unpublished Ph.D. thesis, University of Oxford, 1985.

Tanner, Andrea, 'The City of London Poor Law Union 1837–1869', unpublished Ph.D. thesis, University of London, 1995.

Index

Note: Figures are noted in bold type